THE COMPLETE GUITAR ENCYCLOPEDIA

First published by Parragon in 2012

Parragon
Chartist House
15-17 Trim Street
Bath, BA1 1HA, U.K.

www.parragon.com

Designed, produced, and packaged by
Stonecastle Graphics Limited

Designed by Sue Pressley and Paul Turner
Text by Nick Freeth
Edited by Philip de Ste. Croix
Photos courtesy of *Guitar & Bass* unless otherwise stated

ISBN 978-1-4454-9313-8

Printed in China

THE COMPLETE GUITAR ENCYCLOPEDIA

HISTORY · LEARN TO PLAY LIKE A PRO · GUITARIST PROFILES · TAKING CARE OF YOUR GUITAR

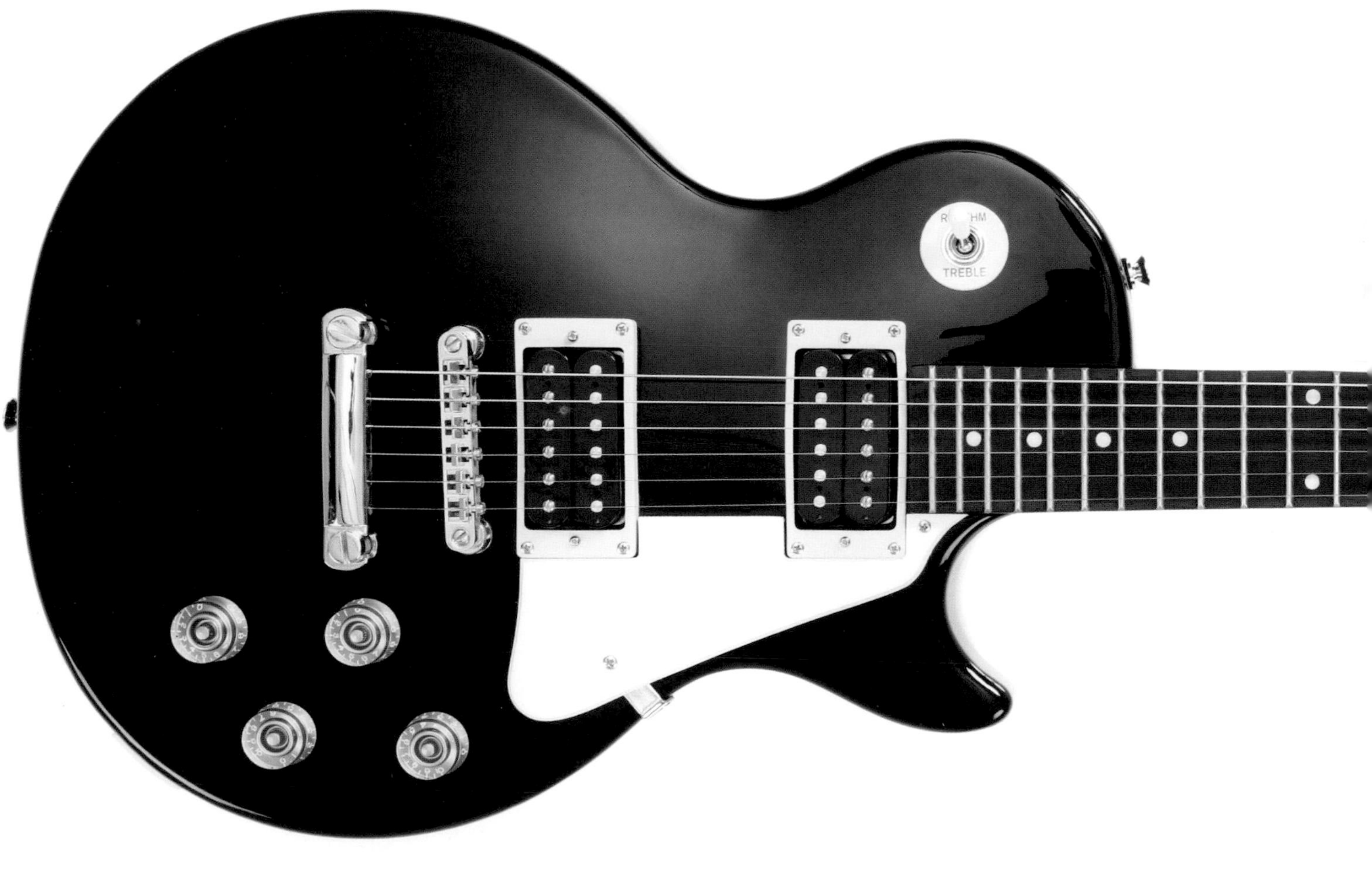

Parragon

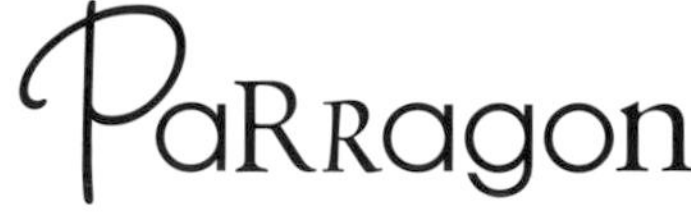

Bath • New York • Singapore • Hong Kong • Cologne • Delhi
Melbourne • Amsterdam • Johannesburg • Shenzhen

Contents

Introduction 6

History of the Guitar 10

The guitar and its evolution 12
Martin and the flat-top 14
Gibson and the archtop 16
The electric guitar arrives 18
The postwar scene 20
Fender forges ahead 22
Gibson pioneer 24
Troubled times 26
Fender and Gibson: recent history 28
Past, present, and future 30

The Greatest Guitars Ever 32

Fender Telecaster 34
Fender Stratocaster 36
Masterclass: **'Aging' a Fender Stratocaster** 38
Fender Precision Bass 42
Fender Jazz Bass 44
Fender Jazzmaster and Jaguar 45
Gibson Acoustics 46
Gibson ES-175 47
Gibson hollow-bodies 48
Gibson ES-335 50
Gibson Les Paul 52
Gibson SG 56
Gretsch 58
Masterclass: **Choosing 'that special guitar'** 62
Höfner Violin Bass 64
Martin 65
PRS 68
Rickenbacker 70
Rickenbacker basses 72
'Superstrats' 74
Takamine 76
Taylor 77
Masterclass: **Setting up a cheap acoustic** 78

Guitar Heroes 80

Duane Allman 82
Jeff Beck 84
Matt Bellamy 86
Ritchie Blackmore 88
Joe Bonamassa 90
Roy Buchanan 92
Eric Clapton 94
Kurt Cobain 96
Ry Cooder 98
Duane Eddy 100
The Edge 102
John Frusciante 104
Billy Gibbons 106
Masterclass: **Choosing your amp** 108
David Gilmour 110
Peter Green 112
Dave Grohl 114
Kirk Hammett 116
George Harrison 118
Jimi Hendrix 120
Steve Howe 122
John Paul Jones 124
Mark Knopfler 126
Paul Kossoff 128
Lemmy 130
Tony Levin 132

Phil Lynott 134
Yngwie Malmsteen 136
Johnny Marr 138
Masterclass: **Pedal plug-up perfection** 140
Brian May 142
John McLaughlin 144
Gary Moore 146
Scotty Moore 148
Tom Morello 150
Jimmy Page 152
John Petrucci 154
Bonnie Raitt 156
Randy Rhoads 158
Keith Richards 160
Carlos Santana 162
Masterclass: **Cleaning your guitar** 164
Joe Satriani 166
Slash 168
Pete Townshend 170
Derek Trucks 172
Steve Vai 174
Eddie Van Halen 176
Stevie Ray Vaughan 178
Jack White 180
Angus Young 182
Neil Young 184
Frank Zappa 186
Masterclass: **Upgrade your electric** 188

Learn to Play Like... 190
Duane Allman 192
Jeff Beck 194
Chuck Berry 196
Ritchie Blackmore 198
Joe Bonamassa 200
Eric Clapton 202
Ry Cooder 204
Duane Eddy 206
Noel Gallagher 208
David Gilmour 210
Kirk Hammett 212
Masterclass: **Setting up whammy bars** 214
John Paul Jones 218
Mark King 220
Mark Knopfler 222
Paul Kossoff 224
Lemmy 226
Brian May 228
Randy Rhoads 230
Masterclass: **Build your own pedalboard** 232
Slash 234
Sting 236
Pete Townshend 238
Stevie Ray Vaughan 240
Jack White 242
Neil Young 244
Masterclass: **Having the right tools** 246
'Unplugged' Rockers 248

Index 250

Above: *The Fender Telecaster is undoubtedly one of the greatest electric guitars ever produced and has been played by many of the world's most accomplished guitarists.*

Introduction

My intention in writing this new encyclopedia devoted to the guitar was to pack as much information into its 256 pages as possible and to illustrate it with an eye-catching selection of color photographs of individual instruments and the world's top rock guitarists. That's a "big ask" for just one author, but fortunately I had help at hand. I was able to draw on the knowledge of the expert contributors to the U.K.'s *Guitar & Bass* magazine, from whose recent articles and reviews some of what appears has been adapted. But much of the content is new, and my hope is that through this act of synthesis we have created something that is both interesting and enjoyable at first reading, but also comprehensive enough to merit a permanent place on your reference bookshelf.

The book starts, appropriately enough, with a section that outlines the genesis of the modern, steel-strung guitar, and the history of how it developed throughout the twentieth century. The instrument's evolution from its classical European roots took place principally in the United States, and Chapter One examines the key stages of this process, and the impact of the major American companies whose acoustics and electrics have been so innovative, and so widely used.

Chapter Two takes a closer look at the guitars that rocked the world. Here, along with a selection of seminal acoustics, will be found a fantastic gallery of color photographs of the most iconic and desirable electric guitars to have appeared since they first set the music world alight in the 1950s. Alongside text that explains the guitar's evolution and development, detailed photographs of landmark instruments and significant variants allow guitar fans to enjoy the beauty of these unique creations in superb close-up detail.

In Chapter Three the focus shifts to "Guitar Heroes." It includes illustrated biographies of the greatest rock guitarists of all time, plus information about their instruments. The list of musicians included is awesome—from Duane Allman to Frank Zappa, the gods of rock's pantheon will be found here. A musical rundown of each artist's career, together with details of their favorite gear—including the guitars, amps, and effects that have been closest to their hearts. Punchy quotations, action photographs and fascinating facts complete the picture.

Chapter Four ("Learn to Play Like…") then lifts the lid on the technical secrets of leading players and explains how you can mimic their signature techniques. Exercises based on characteristic riffs—presented in both staff notation and tablature (tab)—pinpoint exactly how readers can play in the style of their rock idols. These music-focused pages delve into the nitty-gritty of individual playing styles, analyzing players' distinctive fingering and the way they create a personal soundscape.

And there's more! Throughout the book you'll find a series of special masterclass features designed to help you get the best out of your own musical equipment. Some of them cover the basics (choosing the right guitar and amp, keeping them in optimum condition, connecting up and using effects pedals), while others explore more ambitious topics—the finer points of guitar set-up, and even an account of how a *Guitar & Bass* columnist created his own "aged" and customized Fender Stratocaster. Enjoy the book! It's designed to deepen your love of this extraordinarily versatile instrument, and the wonderful music it has inspired.

Nick Freeth

Right: *A solid-bodied electric in full flight. The introduction of pickups (this model is fitted with gold-covered humbuckers) enabled guitars to take a frontline role in bands, and was an essential factor in the development of the modern popular music scene.*

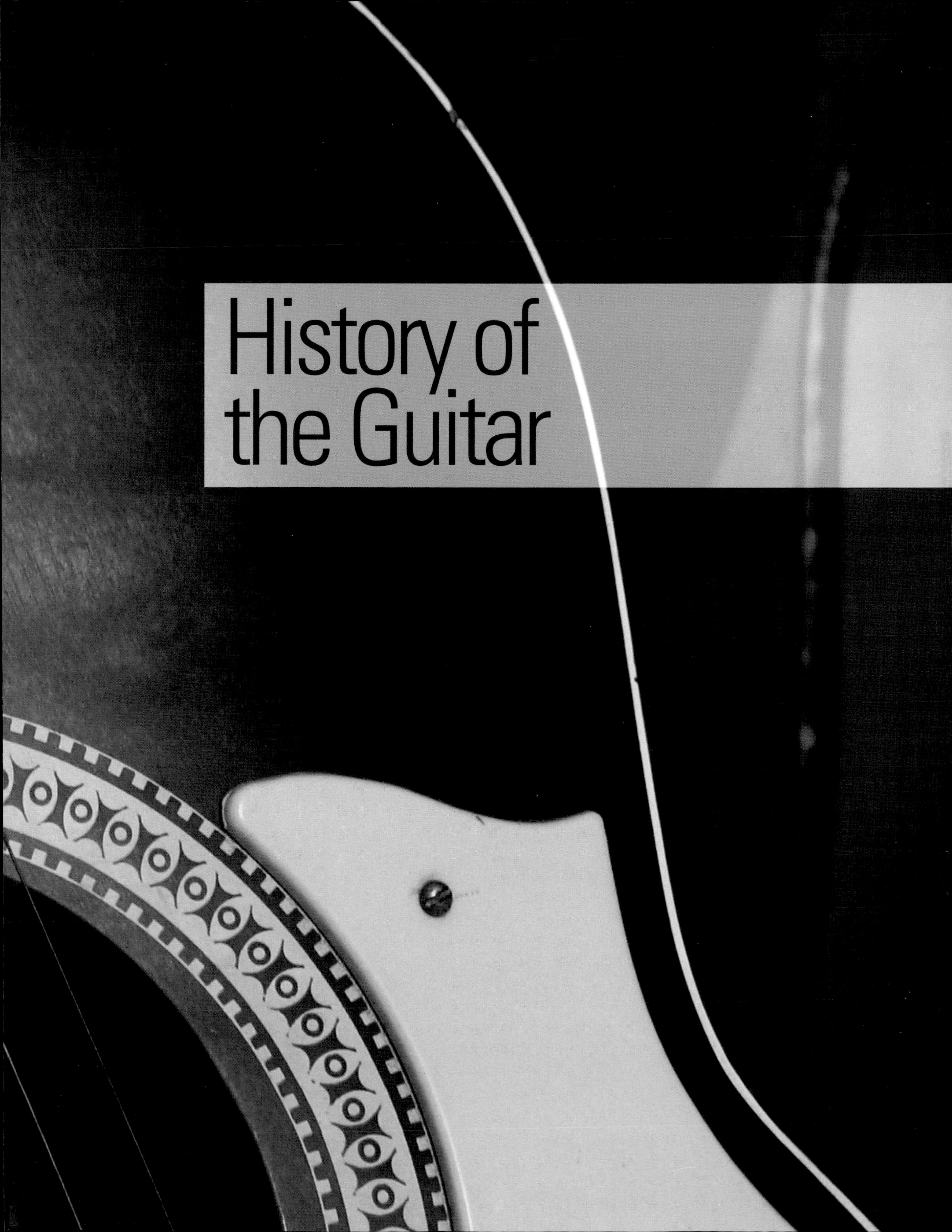

History of the Guitar

The guitar and its evolution

The guitar, more than any other instrument, is loved for both its sound and its appearance, and for the mood of intimate expressiveness it conjures up as it nestles in a player's arms. The reasons behind its seductive appeal (and an explanation for the bizarre phenomenon of "air guitar") lie in the realm of psychology…but the instrument also has simple, practical attractions for its fans, whatever their level of ability.

It's flattering to beginners, who can quickly produce a pleasing sound from it; budding trumpeters or violinists will take far longer to create something even passably tuneful. It's versatile, portable, and ideal for providing "music wherever you go." It's ideal for simple, strummed accompaniments, but can also be a platform for elaborate soloing. Thousands can be spent on a fine or vintage model, but cheap guitars are readily available. And modern guitarists enjoy a significant advantage over their musical predecessors. Two separate, but linked, developments—the adoption of steel strings and, subsequently, electric amplification—have given us instruments that can hold their own in the loudest band, and in the largest auditorium.

The European classical guitar dates back to the sixteenth century. It evolved principally in Spain and France, had gut strings, and was traditionally struck with the nails (or sometimes the fingertips) of a performer's picking hand. Other fretted instruments were strung with wire and picked with plectrums, but classical players, though aware that equipping their guitars with steel strings and using flat-picks would generate a more cutting, powerful tone, tended to be disparaging about the disadvantages of doing this. One late nineteenth-century guitar tutor railed about the "cranks [who] choose steel strings, which are an abomination." Nevertheless, the demand for extra volume, especially in the United States, led several early twentieth-century manufacturers to begin offering instruments with either gut or steel strings (though steel's greater tension required stronger construction, and different internal bracing), and to start making guitars specifically designed for steel stringing. Among these companies were two of the most famous ones: Martin and Gibson.

Left: *Portrait of Elizabeth, Lady Wallscourt by Sir Thomas Lawrence, 1825. By the nineteenth century, guitar playing was popular in English drawing rooms, and small, sometimes finely decorated instruments were in considerable demand.*

Opposite: *Classical guitars retain their appeal, and the one on the far right has a cutaway—more usually found on steel-strung models. Classical-style instruments are also popular with some Latin and folk players.*

Below: *The guitarist in this painting ("The Minstrel" by Friedrich von Keller) would struggle to be heard if the tavern was much busier!*

Gutted...

The classical guitar tradition, with its roots in European, and especially Spanish, music, continues to thrive—but classical and flamenco players no longer use gut strings. Nylon was invented by the American chemical company DuPont in 1935, and was first used to make guitar strings by a New York-based luthier, Albert Augustine, in the 1940s. Nylon strings were adopted by the great classical guitarist Andrés Segovia (1893–1987), and other players soon followed his example.

Martin and the flat-top

Christian Fredrick Martin (1796–1873) was a German-born instrument maker who established the firm that still bears his name in New York in 1833, and moved it to Nazareth, Pennsylvania, in 1839. During his first few years in the United States, Martin produced models with elaborate finishes, like those of his Austrian mentor, Johann Stauffer. Later nineteenth-century Martin instruments were less fancy, but with their gut strings, flat tops, and round sound-holes, they still resembled European classical guitars. However, by 1900 Martins were being offered, to special order, with steel strings. Initially, according to company historian Mike Longworth, such models "were few and far between."

The demand for steel came from ensemble players, who couldn't make themselves heard clearly without it and, increasingly, from enthusiasts for Hawaiian music. Popular fascination with the islands' culture, already growing in the 1900s, received a boost when the 1915 Panama-Pacific International Exposition was held in San Francisco. Sales of Martin's Hawaiian guitars (played on the lap, and strung with steel) surged. This encouraged regular guitarists, who held their instruments "Spanish-style" in their arms, to recognize the benefits of steel strings for themselves. By the mid-1920s, most Martins (to quote Mike Longworth again) "were being braced for gut or light steel." Within a few more years, steel-strung flat-tops had become the norm at the firm, and were developing separately from gut-strung "classical" models.

Martin wasn't alone in its adoption of steel strings, but it did pioneer another key aspect of flat-top guitar design. Its instruments, like their

Below: *Americans' interest in Hawaiian music boosted sales of ukuleles and guitars—though in our picture, which dates from about 1885, the guitarist is still playing "Spanish-style."*

Above: *Martin's 000 size formed the basis for the new Orchestra Model, and post-OM 000s were given necks with 14 frets clear of their bodies.*

European ancestors, originally had only 12 frets clear of their bodies, restricting access to the highest part of the fingerboard. Banjo necks—and those fitted to other types of guitar, such as the archtops discussed on the next two pages—gave players more scope for high treble work. In 1929, a well-known banjoist, Perry Bechtel (1902–82), asked Martin to make him a modified version of its 000-size flat-top guitar with 14 frets to its body. The altered design was named the "Orchestra Model" (OM). The reconfigured neck, as well as the pickguard also boasted by the OM, went on to be widely adopted not only on other Martins, but by the firm's rivals.

Right: *Eric Clapton plays his signature Martin 000-28EC at a concert in Antwerp's Sportpaleis, Belgium, May 2010.*

Below: *Part of the Martin guitar factory in Nazareth, Pennsylvania, in 2009. The company has been based in the town since 1839.*

Other early U.S. guitar makers

Lyon & Healy, Chicago

Founded in 1864 as a music store. By about 1890 it was selling 100,000 instruments of various kinds every year. These included its own Washburn guitars, named after one of the firm's creators, George Washburn Lyon.

Vega, Boston

Set up in the 1880s by the Nelson brothers (Carl and Julius), Vega produced a wide range of guitars, including small-bodied ladies' models. Also well known for its banjos, the firm was purchased by Martin in the 1970s.

Harmony, Chicago

Founded by Wilhelm Schultz (originally from Hamburg) in 1892. Initially a small-scale producer of guitars, mandolins, and ukuleles, it grew rapidly, was acquired by Sears, Roebuck in 1916, and went on to become a high-volume supplier of inexpensive instruments, most notably ukuleles and guitars.

Gibson and the archtop

The Gibson Mandolin-Guitar Manufacturing Company was set up in 1902. It took its name from instrument designer Orville Gibson (1856–1918), who was an adviser and consultant to the firm, but never a partner in it. "Orville-style" instruments are collectors' items, but the company achieved its greatest early successes with designs created after his departure from its Kalamazoo, Michigan, headquarters in 1909. The man behind these models was Lloyd Loar (1886–1943), a musician with great engineering skills who was in overall charge of the firm's fretted instrument output between 1919 and 1924. His guitars had steel strings, carved, arched tops, necks with 14 frets clear of the body, and f-holes. The first of them was the L-5, launched in 1922, and it was quickly adopted by jazzman Eddie Lang, as well as other leading players of the day, including Alvino Rey and country music star Maybelle Carter.

Left: *Orville Gibson gave his name to the Gibson guitar company, though he held no managerial position there. He had American and English parents, and was born in New York state.*

The L-5 was a groundbreaking design. All subsequent Gibson archtops owe a debt to it, and it inspired similar models by Stromberg, Epiphone, and other U.S. makers during the 1920s and 1930s. There was fierce rivalry between these firms, and constant attempts to "go one better" than the competition, chiefly by producing ever-wider bodies, and thereby boosting tonal power. The first L-5s were 16 in (40.6 cm) wide, but were later "advanced" to 17 in (43.2 cm). The Gibson Super 400, introduced in 1934, had an 18-in (45.7-cm) body; Epiphone (based in New York City) launched its 18.5-in (47-cm) Emperor in 1936,

Above: *Originally an acoustic without a cutaway, the L-5 has appeared in many different versions over the years. This L-5CES model first appeared in 1951: it has a spruce top, maple back and sides, and two single-coil pickups.*

Right: *Philipp Stauber playing a handsome blond-finish electric Gibson L-5 with humbucking pickups at a concert in Munich's Jazzclub Unterfahrt.*

Below: *Epiphone's Emperor acoustic archtop was introduced in 1936. The recent Emperor Regent in our photo tips its hat to the classic design.*

The Advanced L-5

"It was difficult for us to improve on the L-5—its traditional quality and beauty have made it so near perfect that for years, although it has been the most imitated guitar in the world, it was impossible for others to copy [its] real personality. The new Advanced L-5 has more volume—more cutting power for orchestral playing—the tone is richer—[and] its new design, decorations and finish make it a real thing of beauty."

Gibson publicity for the "Advanced" L-5 archtop, 1934

Bottom: *The real thing! These beautiful early Gibson Super 400s belong to vintage guitar lover Bernd Wannenwetsch, and were photographed by* Guitar & Bass *in 2005.*

while Stromberg of Boston's 1937 Master 400 measured a full 19 in (48.3 cm) across its lower bout—not a guitar for short-armed players!

Cutaway bodies, providing improved access to the higher frets, were to be another major selling point. Once again, these were a Gibson innovation, appearing on the L-5 and Super 400 in 1939. The company named the cutaway versions of its guitars "Premiere" models, and proudly trumpeted in an advertisement that "the signals are [now] set for 'Go' all the way up the fingerboard—from the first fret to the last." Cutaways, like larger bodies, were soon adopted by the competition, but by now, a more fundamental change—the introduction of electric instruments—was sweeping through the entire guitar market.

The electric guitar arrives

Guitars can be made louder by increasing the size of their bodies. This is what Gibson and its rivals did in the 1930s. Their sound can also be boosted with built-in metal resonator cones: this method was perfected (and patented in 1927) by John Dopyera, a craftsman based in Los Angeles. But once electronic amplifiers and loudspeakers had been developed, the best way of providing extra volume involved the use of an electro-magnetic pickup. The field it creates around a guitar's steel strings is disturbed when the strings vibrate after being struck. This produces an electrical current that can be fed from the pickup to an amplifier. Then the amplifier sends it to a loudspeaker that converts the amplified signal back into sound. Both the pickup and the loudspeaker are "transducers"—devices that change one form of energy into another—and steel strings are essential to the process, as gut has no magnetic properties.

The first mass-produced electric guitar, a Hawaiian model with a solid body, was introduced in 1932 by the Los Angeles-based "Ro-Pat-In Corporation" (the strange syllables may possibly stand for "Electro-Patent-

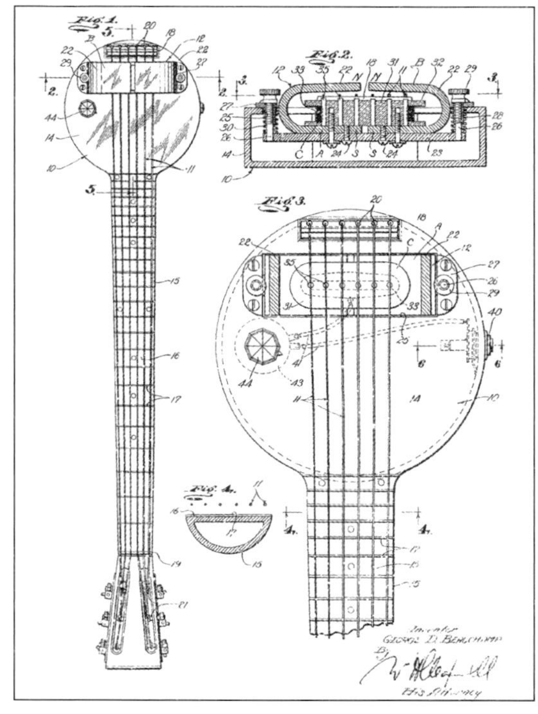

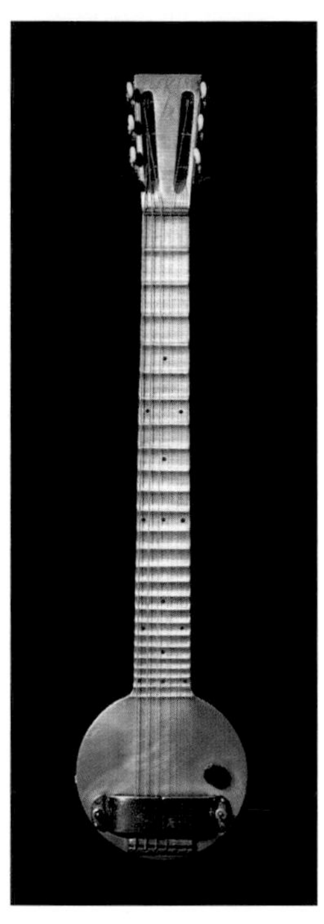

Above and above right: *Ro-Pat-In's "Frying Pan" Hawaiian guitar was the first mass-produced electric.*

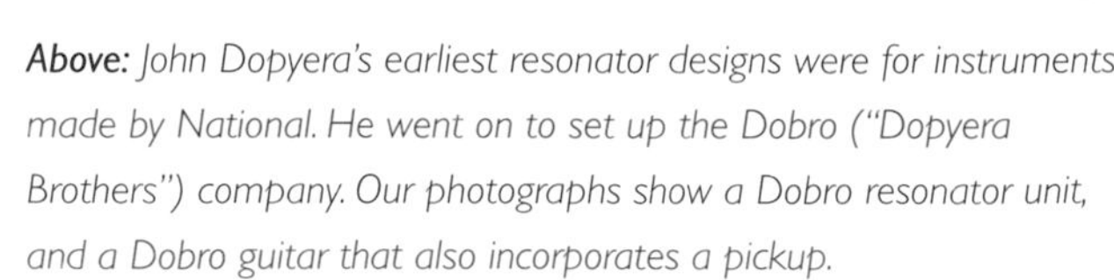

Above: *John Dopyera's earliest resonator designs were for instruments made by National. He went on to set up the Dobro ("Dopyera Brothers") company. Our photographs show a Dobro resonator unit, and a Dobro guitar that also incorporates a pickup.*

Instruments"). The firm's backers included Adolph Rickenbacker (1886–1976), who was to give his name to a famous postwar electric guitar firm. Gibson waited until 1935 to launch an electric Hawaiian instrument. Its first "Spanish-style" electric, the hugely influential ES-150, appeared the following year. It was a hollow-body archtop with a pickup installed near the end of its fingerboard: customers unfamiliar with electrics were reassured by Gibson ads that they could "hold it, tune it and play it just as [they] would any guitar…but strike the strings lightly and you have a tone than can be amplified to any volume you desire."

The ES-150 was adopted by several prominent players—and most famously by jazzman Charlie Christian (1916–42), who used it (and its later cousin, the ES-250) on his classic recordings with the Benny Goodman group between 1939 and 1941. His powerful, saxlike soloing (which would have been impossible on an acoustic) opened a new chapter in the history of jazz guitar, and the pickup fitted to the ES-150 and 250, though designed by Gibson engineer Walter Fuller, is still widely known as the "Charlie Christian" model.

Above: *Charlie Christian, photographed in about 1940 with a Gibson ES-250. The 250 was larger and more elegant than the ES-150, but had the same pickup.*

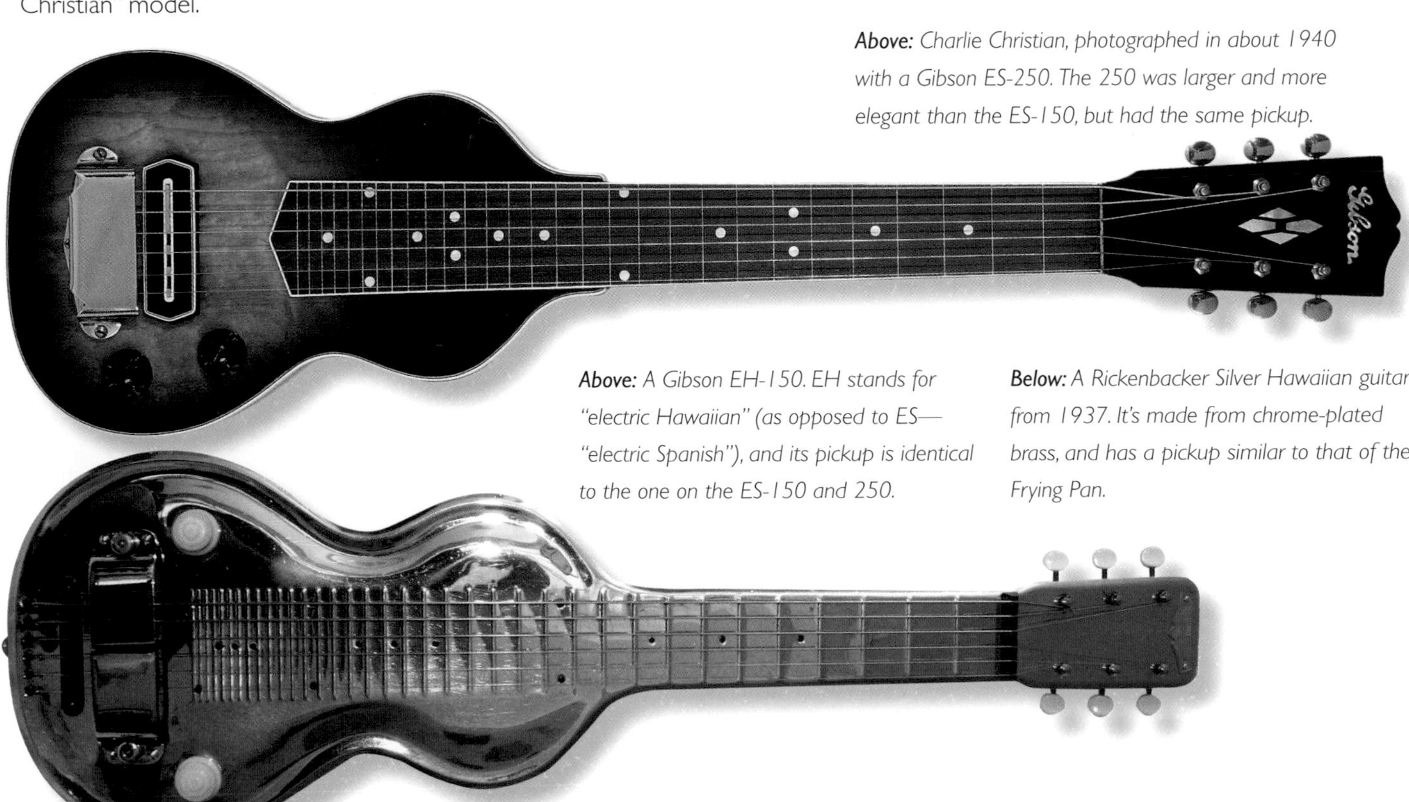

Above: *A Gibson EH-150. EH stands for "electric Hawaiian" (as opposed to ES—"electric Spanish"), and its pickup is identical to the one on the ES-150 and 250.*

Below: *A Rickenbacker Silver Hawaiian guitar from 1937. It's made from chrome-plated brass, and has a pickup similar to that of the Frying Pan.*

The postwar scene

During World War II, production of guitars and other non-essential products was severely restricted, and major U.S. manufacturers, including Gibson, took on defense-related work. Full-scale instrument making gradually resumed after VJ Day, but shakeups in the industry had begun well before then. Gibson was purchased by Chicago Musical Instruments in 1944: this deal provided the company with a much-needed injection of cash, and enabled it to respond to an important shift in the postwar market—the growing demand for electric guitars. To speed up production and reduce costs, the specifications and construction of some of these instruments were changed. Models such as the ES-150 had their arched tops pressed (rather than carved) into shape; and their bodies began to be made from cheaper, laminated woods, which also have the advantage of being resistant to the acoustic feedback that afflicts hollow-body electrics when they're played at high volume.

Above: *Guitarist and technical innovator Les Paul with two examples of the classic Gibson design he helped to develop, and which carries his name.*

Gibson's competitors underwent upheavals of their own after 1945. Epiphone changed hands in 1953, and in the same year Adolph Rickenbacker, the financial backer for Ro-Pat-In and its successor Electro in southern California, sold out to a local distributor, F. C. Hall, who went on to establish Rickenbacker as an internationally famous guitar brand. Indeed, some of the industry's boldest postwar developments emerged from California. They centered around a group of talented, innovative technicians and musicians who included machinist and inventor Paul Bigsby (1899–1968). Bigsby lived in Downey, a few miles southeast of Los Angeles, and is the man widely credited with making the first viable Spanish-style, solid-body electric guitar. His instrument, completed in 1948, was commissioned by country music star Merle Travis. It would certainly have aroused the interest of Bigsby's acquaintances Les Paul (the guitarist soon to give his name to a classic Gibson solid), Ted McCarty (who was appointed Gibson's General Manager in 1948 and became its President two years later), and Leo Fender. Leo had been making guitars himself since 1943, and had set up the Fender Electric Instrument Company in 1946. The similarities between his own soon-to-be-famous electrics and the Travis-Bigsby instrument remain a matter for speculation and controversy.

Right: *A 1947 Gibson L-7—this prewar acoustic design was discontinued in the 1950s.*

Below: *An autographed photo of Merle Travis (1917–83), an influential guitarist as well as a singer/songwriter (his most enduringly famous song is "Sixteen Tons") and movie star. He's holding the electric made for him by Paul Bigsby.*

Right: *Gibson's factory in Kalamazoo, Michigan. It produced guitars in the town, some 140 miles west of Detroit, until 1984.*

A meeting of minds...and bodies

"When Ted McCarty took over Gibson in 1948, they were only making hollow-bodies. He'd heard that there was something going on in southern California with solid-bodies and he flew down there to check it out, and that's when he met Paul Bigsby."
Paul Bigsby's biographer, Andy Babiuk, interviewed in *Guitar & Bass*, October 2009

Above: *A full-body photograph of the 1948 Bigsby "Merle Travis" solid body. It has a bird's-eye maple body, and its pickup surround, pickguard, tailpiece, and armrest are walnut.*

Fender forges ahead

Leo Fender (1909–91) was born in Anaheim, California. He had a practical knowledge of electronics, running a radio repair and public address hire firm in Fullerton (the town a few miles north of Anaheim that became his home), and was a capable craftsman, but he had no musical skills. For these, he initially relied on his friend "Doc" Kauffman, a multi-instrumentalist and inventor, with whom he began manufacturing electric Hawaiian guitars (also known as lap steels) in 1945. They called their company "K&F." The risks associated with expanding the business worried Kauffman, and the partnership ended in 1946. Leo immediately formed the Fender Electric Instrument Company.

He continued making lap steels, but was soon developing a Spanish-style, solid-bodied electric that bore some resemblance to the Travis-Bigsby instrument mentioned earlier: both had similar headstocks and single cutaways. However, there were also numerous differences, and Fender's guitar (introduced in 1950, and named the Broadcaster, then the Telecaster) was conceived for mass production, while Bigsby's was custom-built in limited numbers.

Left: *Leo Fender at work, with one of his Music Man amps behind him; he's wearing magnifying goggles. Visitors often commented on the noise from his workshop; while making adjustments to his instruments, he would strike their heavily amplified open strings.*

Looking forward

"Anybody can copy yesterday—at G&L we're producing for tomorrow!" A characteristically forward-looking slogan from an 1980 ad for Leo Fender's last company, G&L

Above: *The Tele's simple, functional design has endeared it to generations of musicians, and it remains one of the most popular and immediately recognizable electric guitars in the world.*

Left and above: *A 1952-style Fender Telecaster; its bridge pickup assembly was intended to be covered by a metal plate, but most players discarded this (or used it as an ashtray!).*

Though not a musician, Leo prided himself on basing the features of his guitars and amplifiers on the requirements of his customers, with whom he enjoyed close contact on their frequent visits to his Fullerton factory. However, such direct discussions became impossible to maintain as the business grew. After selling it to CBS (Columbia Broadcasting System) for $13,000,000 in 1965, he involved himself in two smaller guitar-making companies: Music Man (between 1972 and 1980), and G&L ("George and Leo," set up with ex-Fender employee George Fullerton) from 1980. The latter firm is based in Fullerton—Fender itself had left the town in 1985—and Leo used his workshop there right up to the day before he died. His notes and drawings were preserved as he left them, and Johnny McLaren, who subsequently became G&L's Plant Manager, told the author in 1999 that "every time we've had [production] problems here I can go back to Leo's filing cabinet and get the exact numbers. Everything's there—it's picture perfect."

Some Notable Fender Players

Buddy Guy American blues guitarist and singer, Guy (pictured) is well known for playing the Stratocaster throughout his long career. Fender has issued several different Buddy Guy Signature Stratocaster models since the early 1990s.

Eric Johnson Grammy-award-winning guitarist from Austin, Texas, Johnson is a long-time Stratocaster user. He has participated in developing an Eric Johnson Signature Stratocaster model with Fender.

Alex Lifeson The guitarist for Rush since 1968, first recorded with a black Stratocaster on Rush's 1977 album *A Farewell to Kings*. He's subsequently favored Strats equipped with Floyd Rose vibratos.

John Mayer Grammy-award-winning singer/songwriter. Mayer has made use of Stratocasters throughout his career, and a Fender Artist Series Stratocaster carrying his name has been produced in both standard and limited edition form.

Jim Root Guitarist for Slipknot and Stone Sour. His choice of guitars includes Fender Telecasters, Stratocasters, and a Custom Shop Jazzmaster.

Gibson pioneer

Ted (Theodore) McCarty was born in 1910. He worked for the Wurlitzer theater organ company before becoming General Manager of Gibson in 1948; he was appointed its Vice-President a year later, and was made President of the firm in 1950. He was a designer of several guitar-related components (notably the Gibson "Tune-O-Matic" bridge, for which he was awarded a patent in 1956) and was an experienced executive, but was not a musician.

His principal concern in the early 1950s was to boost Gibson's output of electric guitars. Through meeting Paul Bigsby, he knew that solid-body models were being developed in California, and was anxious to ensure that his company could compete with these. He did so by signing up guitarist and inventor Les Paul, and collaborating with him on the famous solid electric, bearing Les Paul's name, that was launched in 1952. McCarty continued to introduce exciting, innovative concepts throughout his 16 years in charge at Gibson. Some—like the semi-solid ES-335 that debuted in 1958—were immediately successful. Others, such as the Firebirds, whose body shapes were created by automobile designer Ray Dietrich, and the earlier, equally unconventional "modernistics"

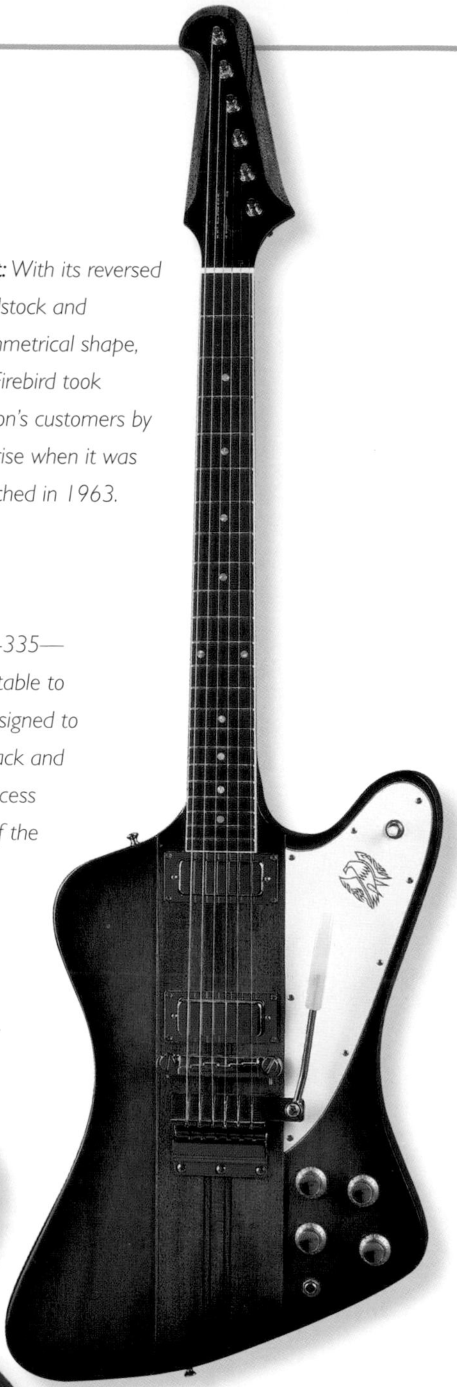

Right: *With its reversed headstock and asymmetrical shape, the Firebird took Gibson's customers by surprise when it was launched in 1963.*

Left: *The ES-335—slim, comfortable to play, and designed to resist feedback and give easy access to the top of the fingerboard.*

Left: *McCarty's ingenious Tune-O-Matic bridge allows each string to be separately adjusted for optimal intonation. He was granted a patent for the design in 1956.*

Right: *The Flying V, introduced in 1958, was ahead of its time: Ted McCarty must have been delighted by its appeal to later generations of rock players!*

Bigsby vibrato

"Guitar players either love or loathe the Bigsby vibrato. While it doesn't offer divebomb performance, it has a smooth, fluid action...and with very few moving parts—a single spring held in by string pressure and a roller bar/string anchor, plus a tension bar on most models, there's little to go wrong. It's the perfect tool for classic rock'n'roll, country, and rockabilly."

Guitar & Bass, October 2009

Above: *Paul Bigsby developed his famous vibrato unit in the 1940s after repairing a faulty vibrato on one of Merle Travis's guitars. Some manufacturers, including Gibson, factory-fit "Bigsbys" to instruments like this 335.*

(including the Flying V), were slower to catch on, but are now highly regarded by players and collectors. McCarty also managed Gibson's former rival, Epiphone, after it was acquired in 1957, and later relocated to Kalamazoo, by Chicago Musical Instruments (Gibson's owners).

In 1966, McCarty stepped down from the Gibson presidency, and bought his old friend Paul Bigsby's business, two years before Paul's death. Bigsby vibrato units had been available as an option on some Gibson guitars since the early 1950s, and McCarty remained at the helm of Bigsby Accessories until 1999, when he sold the firm to the Gretsch guitar company. In 1986, he began acting as a consultant and mentor to luthier Paul Reed Smith. Smith greatly admired the instruments McCarty had pioneered at Gibson, and issued the first PRS McCarty guitar in 1994; there have subsequently been several others.

Ted McCarty died in 2001, aged 91.

Troubled times

When interviewed in the 1990s, Ted McCarty recalled that Gibson was booming at the time of his departure in 1966. However, changes—and difficulties—were on the horizon. In December 1969, South American-based brewing company ECL acquired Chicago Musical Instruments, Gibson's parent since 1944. Norlin Industries officially took charge of the guitar maker in 1974: its name was created by combining those of Norton Stevens, President of ECL, and Maurice Berlin of CMI. Under the new regime, costs were cut and quality control suffered. There were parallel problems at Fender during its period under CBS ownership, which saw the departure of several senior management figures who'd been associated with the firm since before Leo Fender left.

The U.S. guitar industry's struggles in the 1970s and 1980s were the flip side of the successes enjoyed by Far Eastern manufacturers. While Gibson, Fender, and others were in decline, Japanese companies had improved the quality of their output, and were eager to supply affordable instruments—often based very closely on classic 1950s and 1960s American designs—to customers in the West. In 1976, Tokai (located in the coastal city of Hamamatsu southwest of Tokyo) launched a Les Paul replica, complete with a Gibson-styled "Tokai" headstock logo. It even carried the words "Les Paul Reborn" in the same script as Gibson's "Les Paul Model." The following year saw the arrival of the Tokai Springy Sound, modeled on a 1957 Fender Stratocaster, and featuring logos in identical lettering to Fender's. By the early 1980s, Tokai and other Japanese producers were exporting worldwide, and the American firms whose guitars had inspired these "copies" were considering legal action.

The more blatant copyright infringements were eventually seen off, and U.S. makers began to find more mutually beneficial ways of co-existing with Far Eastern companies. Gibson was already having Epiphones made in Japan, while Tokai, by far the most prominent of the so-called "lawsuit" guitar makers, had started supplying acoustic guitar parts to Martin in Pennsylvania as early as 1972. These links grew even stronger in the 1980s.

Below: *A Tokai Silver Star and Springy Sound, both dating from the early 1980s. American makers weren't flattered by such close imitations of their classic designs.*

Attention to detail

"Tokai guitars were seriously good. At a time when Fender was being driven by the cost and bottom-line imperatives of being part of the CBS conglomerate, Tokai was taking its time, working with the likes of Joe Walsh and Billy Gibbons to examine original models, dismantling, measuring, and taking hundreds of photographs. In fact, they did exactly what the big boys now celebrate in the press for their current reissues: they paid attention to detail."
Guitar & Bass, July 2008

Above: *Logo and lettering on the headstock of this Silver Star are unmistakably similar to Fender's.*

Left: *Tokai ST55 Goldstar Sound, 1984–5. Tokais may not be as vintage-accurate as the best of the new reissues, but they are still great guitars.*

Above: *"Made in Japan by rock and roll fanatics" (Tokai slogan).*

Above: *The 55 sticker on the neck of this Tokai originally indicated its price in thousands of yen.*

Fender and Gibson: recent history

CBS invested heavily in Fender and, in 1966, built the firm a new factory at Fullerton, California, close to the site where Leo Fender had started out back in the 1940s. By the 1980s, however, more money and a brisk change in strategy were required to halt the decline caused by cheap imported guitars. CBS responded by hiring three American businessmen who'd worked for Yamaha—Bill Schultz, John C. McLaren, and Dan Smith. It accepted their recommendation that Fender should set up a Japanese division, and use it to produce lower-price instruments of its own. These began to appear in 1982, and most (though not all) carried the Squier brand name on their headstocks.

Schultz (who died in 2006) was the central figure in a management-led takeover of Fender from CBS in 1985. The Fullerton premises weren't included in the deal, and the company's U.S. guitar production ceased until a new factory at Corona, some 25 miles to the east, was opened the following year. During this period, Fender's Japanese operation remained active, and provided the firm with vital revenue. In 1987, the now-famous Fender Custom Shop was established in Corona, and 11 years later even more manufacturing capacity was introduced at the site, which has been described as the world's most expensive and automated guitar-making facility. Its 177,000 sq ft (16,445 sq m) of space gives ample scope for future growth. Fender's HQ is now in Scottsdale, Arizona: it also makes instruments in Mexico, China, and Korea, and retains its Japanese subsidiary.

Once again, Gibson's recent history has mirrored some aspects of its rival's. In 1974, it opened a new headquarters in Nashville, Tennessee, abandoning its old home in Kalamazoo ten years later, in a move that was widely criticized at the time. In 1986, Gibson was sold to a management partnership, and Henry Juszkiewicz (once a neighbor of Chet Atkins in Nashville) has been its Chairman and CEO ever since. The company retains its base in "Music City," but makes its acoustic guitars in Bozeman, Montana. It has recently diversified into professional audio, in partnership with the Japanese Onkyo company.

Above: *Henry Juszkiewicz, Gibson's Chairman and CEO. An alumnus of Harvard Business School, he has been charge at the firm since 1986.*

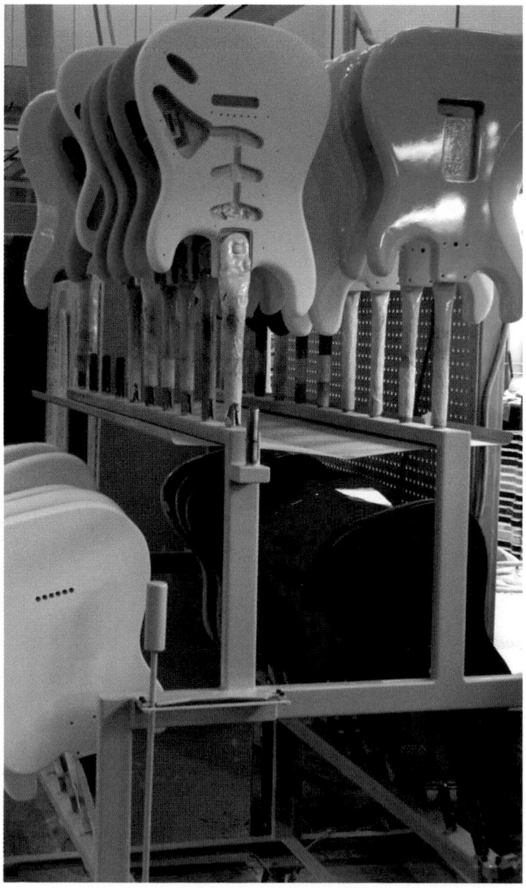

Left: *Producing Stratocasters at Fender's factory in Corona, California. These sprayed bodies are waiting for their necks and pickups.*

Right: *A Squier Satin Trans Fat Strat HH—the last two letters indicate that it's fitted with two humbucking pickups.*

Above: *The Squier Fat Strat alongside another recent model produced outside the United States—the Master Series Chambered Tele.*

Above: *Almost ready...racks of assembled Strats at Corona, about to be finished and inspected.*

Some Notable Gibson Players

Emmylou Harris uses various SJ-200 flat-tops, as well as a Dove—and the Gibson L-200 (described by the company as "smaller and thinner" than the SJ-200) that carries her name appeared in 2002.

Justin Hayward (The Moody Blues) has used an ES-335 for his entire career.

Ted Nugent (pictured) is closely associated with early 1960s Byrdland models in black, sunburst, and natural, and Gibson has developed a Byrdland model named for him. More occasionally, he's been seen with Les Pauls—like this "Stars-and-Stripes" model.

Rich Robinson (The Black Crowes) uses several different Gibson models—among them a 1968 Les Paul Goldtop, a 1964 ES-335, a Custom Shop Flametop Les Paul, vintage SGs and double-cut Les Paul Specials, and a Dove.

Rudolf Schenker (Scorpions) has a collection of over 70 Flying V models dating from 1958 to 2001. They include rare and vintage examples, along with several Custom Shop limited editions—among them a doubleneck Flying V.

Past, present, and future

Whatever type of music they are playing—rock, blues, jazz, metal, a blend of these or other elements, or something entirely new—most guitarists look to harness an inner sense of rebelliousness and iconoclasm. Yet one area where they tend to be traditionally minded, even conservative, is in their reverence for classic guitar designs, whether actual vintage instruments or more recently produced versions of Les Pauls, Strats, and other favorites. Musicians who are "born to be wild" will speak of guitars designed over half a century ago with almost religious fervor; and certain combinations of veteran ax and amp are frequently described as "the holy grail," "made in heaven," or simply "awesome"!

Above: *Some classic models indelibly associated with The Beatles: a Höfner bass, Gretsch and Rickenbacker guitars, and a Vox AC30 amp.*

There are good reasons for such enthusiasm. Many of the guitars in this book are masterpieces of functional, elegant design. Some radiate stylishness, or simply make us sound better than we deserve. When *Guitar* (as it then was) asked guitar guru George Gruhn about the specific appeal of vintage instruments in 2004, he suggested that they were, in some ways, "the ultimate piece of art because you can appreciate them on so many levels. Firstly, you can look at a guitar in the way you look at a painting or a sculpture: the woods, the carving, the inlays… Secondly, you can touch them; they're responsive, they feel almost alive. Thirdly, you can play them and listen to them. The unique thing is that if ten different musicians pick up a great guitar, they'll be inspired in ten different ways."

Left: *George Gruhn, one of the world's foremost experts on vintage guitars. Nashville-based Gruhn Guitars was established in 1970, and has become a Mecca for fretted instrument collectors.*

But did the era of great guitars die with "pre-CBS" Fenders and McCarty-period Gibsons? This is a controversial subject, but most commentators agree that new instruments measure up well to their predecessors—though, of course, they lack their history and, in the case of acoustics, may take time to develop the wonderful tone of a seasoned, vintage Martin. The use of precise, computer-controlled tools now makes it possible to mass-produce guitars to the highest standards of quality and consistency. Perhaps "the Golden Age of Guitar Making" is really the present day. As you read about "the instruments that rocked the world" in the next chapter, remember that the best may be still to come!

Fabulous and new

Guitar writer and musician Paul Day is skeptical about the perceived value and quality of vintage instruments. When asked by *Guitar* in January 2004 whether an old guitar was "better" than a new one, he replied: "Well, with acoustic guitars, yes, sometimes—they mature with age and get better when they're played. Solid-body electrics, on the other hand, don't get better with age...If you're lucky they stay the same, but most of the time they get worse...Modern guitars are fabulous: look at Paul Reed Smith, Music Man, Brian Moore. What's wrong with a shiny new guitar that you can put your own marks and playing wear on? That's what the original blues guys did!"

Above: *Maton Guitars in Box Hill, Melbourne, Australia. The company's Anthony Knowles told* Guitar & Bass *in 2007 that "There's no magic secret to making a great guitar—it's about quality components and refined processes."*

Right: *Rocking out with the tools of their trade—classic designs like these seem unlikely ever to lose their appeal.*

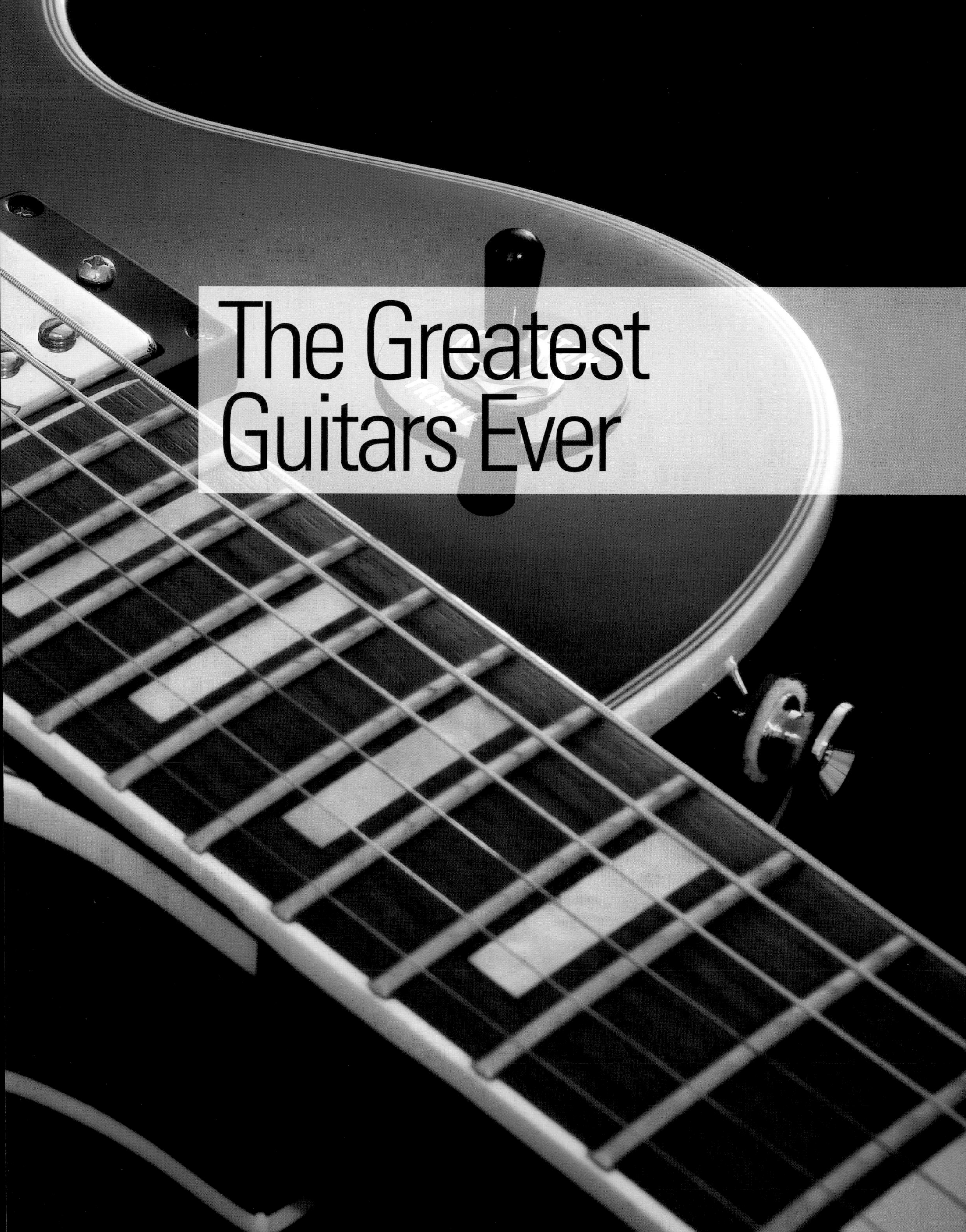

The Greatest Guitars Ever

Fender Telecaster

The Fender Broadcaster, launched in 1950 and quickly renamed the Telecaster after a trademark dispute, wasn't the first solid-bodied electric: Adolph Rickenbacker's company had introduced metal and bakelite guitars in the 1930s. But it was the first commercially marketed, twin-pickup, wood-bodied "Spanish-style" solid. (At the time, the term "Spanish" was used to differentiate regular, "in-the-arms" instruments from Hawaiian guitars, which are placed horizontally on the lap.) And it differed radically from the work of more traditional manufacturers, such as Gibson, because it was specifically conceived for mass production, and designed to be constructed cheaply and efficiently.

The first Telecasters had maple necks, and bodies built of ash—woods selected as much for their availability and low cost as their tone quality—and the instrument's simple, practical electronics reflected Leo Fender's background as an amplification engineer. Both pickups were shielded to protect them from hum: the neck unit with a metal cover, the bridge transducer with a metal baseplate, and a cover plate that was frequently detached. Their timbre, especially the bridge pickup's distinctive growl, won immediate favor with players. The less powerful front pickup has come in for some criticism over the years, but can also deliver impressive results.

1951 "Black Guard" Fender Telecaster

1973 Fender Tele Deluxe

The Tele's signal routing

The Telecaster's controls (two knobs and a switch) are mounted on a steel plate for ease of installation. The upper knob adjusts the guitar's volume; originally, the lower one acted as a pickup "blender" when the three-way switch was in the bridge position; centering the switch selected the neck unit on its own, while the upper setting routed the neck pickup's signal through a preset treble roll-off. In 1953, the blender became a regular tone control, but the "muddy" neck circuit remained until 1967, when the electronics were reconfigured in their current form, making it possible to select either or both pickups.

Lack of complexity, and the extensive "road-testing" and subsequent improvements that Leo Fender's prototypes underwent during the Tele's development, lie at the heart of its enduring attraction; and although there have been changes to the materials from which it's made, as well as modified versions such as the Telecaster Thinline, with three hollowed-out body cavities and a single, token f-hole, its makers have generally fared best by leaving their original design more or less alone. It's one of the very few electrics that has been used successfully in every genre of music: and if you have any doubts about how good it can sound, listen to Roy Buchanan, Steve Cropper of Booker T. & The M.G.'s, and Jimmy Page's solo from Led Zeppelin's "Stairway To Heaven."

Fender Style

Early Telecasters like our 1951 model (*opposite above*) had black pickguards made from bakelite; white ones, as fitted to the 1968 sunburst-finish Tele in the center photo, started to appear in 1954. Later variants of the original Tele design include the Deluxe (*opposite below*), introduced in 1973, and boasting two humbucking pickups designed by Seth Lover (the former Gibson engineer recruited by Fender in 1967) in place of the single-coil transducers favored by Leo Fender himself. The Deluxe also has individual volume and tone controls, and a larger, Stratocaster-style headstock.

1968 Fender Telecaster

"Guitars don't go out of date or become obsolete. They're not computers. There's nothing wrong with a '52 Tele or a '59 Les Paul—they've got all the bells and whistles of the new ones, and they'll last for 300 years with proper care."

Vintage guitar expert George Gruhn

Fender Stratocaster

Established guitar makers had initially mocked the Fender Telecaster—but its success led to the introduction of several rival electric solid-bodies, and Leo Fender's team were eager to retain their competitive edge with an exciting new instrument. Work on the Stratocaster (whose name, with its echoes of the Boeing Stratocruiser airliner, was the brainchild of Fender sales chief Don Randall) was under way by late 1953, and the guitar went into production the following year. It was the first solid-bodied electric to boast three pickups (one adviser had suggested fitting four!), and among its most innovative features was a combined bridge, tailpiece, and vibrato unit that could generate dramatic single-string pitch-bends and shimmering chordal effects.

The Strat's "comfort contoured" double-cutaway body was a response to those who had criticized the Telecaster's sharper edges. Its front was chamfered away to ease pressure on players' forearms, and there was a complementary contour on the rear to avoid digging into their ribs…or to make a little room for an ample belly! Its three control knobs (overall volume, plus tone controls for the neck and center pickups—the bridge unit had none) and selector switch were all within finger reach, and even the jack socket was a work of art: a nattily angled, recessed affair, whose design is generally credited to Fender employee George Fullerton.

The earliest Strats had a brown sunburst finish, combined with yellow after the first few months' production to create a striking two-tone effect. Three-tone sunburst (with red) had been introduced by 1958, and a year later the guitar's formerly all-maple neck was given a darker, Brazilian rosewood fingerboard. Custom-colored bodies were also available: by 1963, the options included Candy Apple Red Metallic, Daphne Blue, Foam Green, and Olympic White, all created with DuPont acrylic and nitro-cellulose paints developed for automobiles.

1965 Fender Stratocaster

Strat Fans

The Stratocaster caught the mood of the rock'n'roll revolution: Buddy Holly and Ike Turner were early users, and it's been the choice of subsequent stars like Jimi Hendrix, Stevie Ray Vaughan, and Eric Clapton. Its popularity has sometimes fluctuated, especially during the mid-1960s, when The Beatles prompted their contemporaries to choose Gretsches and Rickenbackers, but it is arguably the most influential, and certainly the most imitated, electric guitar of all time. Its enduring importance was demonstrated by the remarkable gathering of famous players—such as Pink Floyd's David Gilmour, Ronnie Wood from The Rolling Stones, Hank Marvin, and Gary Moore—who appeared at London's Wembley Stadium on September 24, 2004 as *The Strat Pack* to salute its fiftieth birthday.

"Aging" a Fender Stratocaster

Guitars with "distressed" finishes are very popular, and sometimes very expensive. Here we look at how *Guitar & Bass* expert Huw Price went about creating a homemade replica of the famously battered, sweat-soaked Fender Stratocaster owned (and played for decades) by Irish bluesman Rory Gallagher (1948–95). Huw's "donor guitar" was a secondhand Squier Affinity Strat…but unless you're really confident about your abilities, we suggest you admire his impressive results, without attempting to imitate them.

His first major task—after removing the pickups and other hardware from his Squier Strat, whose "innumerable dents made it look like it had a bad dose of acne"—was to strip off its polyester finish. He did so out of doors, with "a heat gun, a scraper, and lots of patience." There were numerous hazards: if the gun got too close, it would singe the wood; and a breathing mask and eye protection were essential, as red hot pieces of plastic were flying everywhere. Afterward, the body was sanded down to get the surface as smooth and evenly colored as possible.

1 The Squier Affinity Stratocaster before work started. Its previous owner had already tried "distressing" it.

The authentic appearance

Rory Gallagher's guitar dates from 1961, and the "sunburst" finishes on Stratocasters from this period were produced with a mix of red, amber, and black nitrocellulose lacquer. Huw had to combine these colors to create an authentic look, and also wanted to copy the original's heavily worn appearance, with its patches of surviving paintwork, the shapes of which were marked out on the body of his Squier using "life-size" printouts from images of Gallagher's Strat. After some intensive spraying sessions involving skillful use of masking tape, the lacquer on Huw's instrument was allowed to dry overnight, and a few layers of clear satin were added the following day.

The process of "aging" the Strat began when carbon—in the form of soot from Huw's recently swept chimney—was applied by hand, and gently worked across the grain of its body. Once the whole surface was covered, he dusted off the excess, melted a mixture of black shoe polish and Liberon Georgian Mahogany furniture polish in a double boiler, and brushed it on. Applying liquid wax to bare wood in this way ensures maximum penetration of the timber by the wax. Next, more polish was added straight from the can using superfine wire wool, and after a few layers had been built up, the polish was left to dry off before being buffed up with a clean cotton cloth. After twenty minutes, the wood looked forty years older.

2 With the electronics and other parts removed, the guitar body is ready for stripping.

Top Guitar Tip

The finish on Rory Gallagher's guitar was largely destroyed by his highly acidic sweat—a by-product of his unusual blood type. Modern, polyester-based finishes would have been unaffected by this: to quote Huw Price's words, polyester even "laughs in the face of paint stripper!"

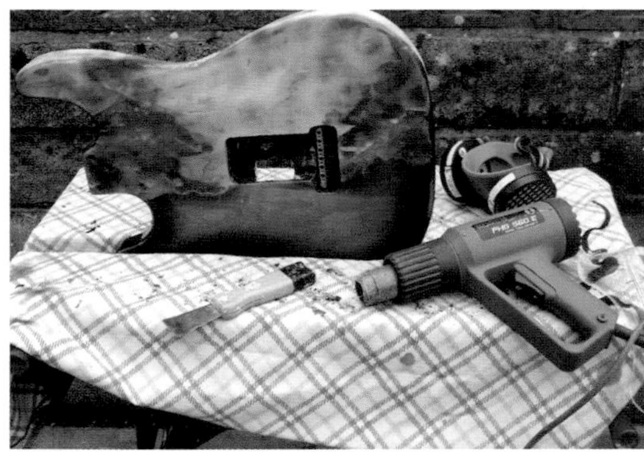

3 The polyester finish is still visible on the lower part of the body, but won't be there much longer…

4 The darker areas closely replicate the surviving paint patches on Rory Gallagher's guitar.

***Below:** The completed replica, with its "aged" components and early 1960s-style pickups, bears a remarkable resemblance to Rory Gallagher's original.*

5 Further spraying has given the Strat's body the right overall color.

6 After stripping, the back of the instrument was also sanded down and sprayed.

"Ageing" a Fender Stratocaster

An earlier owner had already cut down the large headstock on the Squier Affinity Strat to something approaching pre-1965 proportions, but its neck and fingerboard needed other modifications (such as replacement dot markers), as well as some simulated wear. Suitable machine heads (Sperzels) were fitted, plus a substitute bridge plate and saddles, and the new metalwork was given a rusty look by means of an electrolytic process involving a bath of saline solution and a 9-volt battery. A pickguard with the kind of green tinge that old plastic Fender parts tend to take on was purchased from Germany, and for extra authenticity, a "crack" was sawn near its upper neck pickup screw (see main photograph). A few other cracks were added with a craft knife, and some naphtha-based dark woodgrain filler was rubbed into them and the screw holes. Finally, the all-important pickups—supplied by Spencer Mumford at Shed Pickups—were added. They replicate the irregular stagger height of Rory's Alnico V polepieces, and were wound to vintage specifications with Formvar magnet wire.

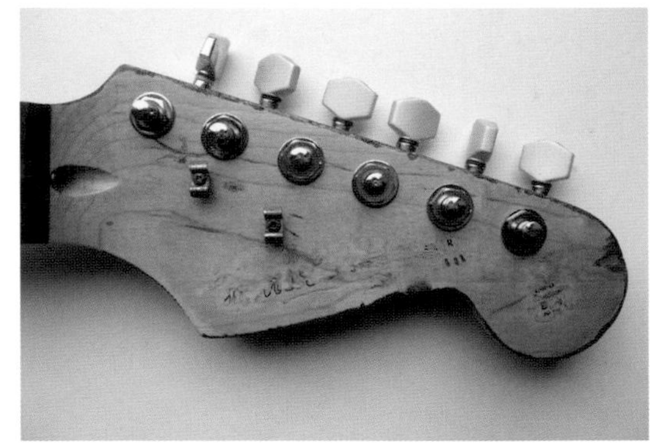

7 *The headstock looks authentically worn, and is also the right size. New Sperzel machine heads have been installed.*

Top Guitar Tip

This Gallagher-style replica cost approximately $300 to make—though this figure doesn't take into account the purchase of the donor guitar or the many hours of work. A Fender Custom Shop version of Rory's instrument was introduced in 2007 and priced at $4,126 in the 2008 catalog.

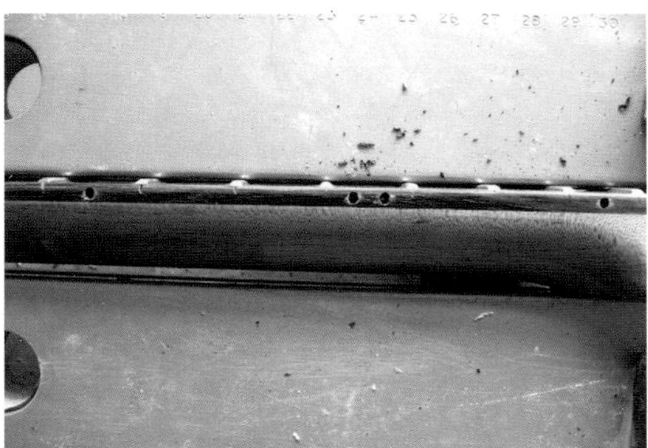

8 *Holes have been drilled on the side of the neck as part of the process of replacing the plastic dot markers.*

9 *One plastic dot was left at the 12th fret, corresponding to an odd, whitish marker on Gallagher's guitar.*

Below: *The green-tinged pickguard, sourced from Germany, with a 1960s-style set of pickup covers and control knobs from Fatboy Guitars. A few scratches were added and highlighted with grain filler.*

The Verdict

Huw Price comments that his project, which resulted in a realistic copy of a very famous instrument, "was a lot of fun…[and] the guitar has a lot more "pick up and play" appeal than it did before. In particular, those Shed pickups have made it sound way better than we ever expected."

Fender Precision Bass

The double bass is a fine orchestral instrument, and often indispensable for jazz. However, it's also bulky, cumbersome, and hard to hear in noisy environments—and it can be played painfully out of tune by performers who struggle with its unfretted neck. During the 1930s, Rickenbacker and others produced compact upright electric basses, and Regal made an acoustic, stand-up "bassoguitar" with frets…but it was Leo Fender who saw the need for a louder, more portable bass that offered precise note pitching. He invented the first-ever electric bass guitar, appropriately named the Precision.

60th Anniversary Fender Precision Bass

The so-called "P-Bass" was launched in late 1951, but officially unveiled at the U.S.A.'s NAMM (National Association of Music Merchants) trade show in July 1952. Its ash body, maple neck, and slimline headstock bore obvious resemblances to the Telecaster's, but it was the first Fender model to feature a double cutaway. It had a 34-in (86-cm) scale length—some 8 in (20.3 cm) shorter than that of a typical double bass—and its one-piece, four-pole pickup and bridge had chromed covers. The bridge cover contained a rubber mute, and a wooden finger rest was fitted near the strings.

The recommended Fender amplifier for the Precision was the Bassman combo, which appeared in 1952 and originally incorporated a single 15-in (38-cm) loudspeaker that couldn't handle the instrument's powerful low notes adequately. Subsequent versions had four 10-in (25-cm) speakers, and a "piggyback" design with a separate speaker cabinet and 12-in (30-cm) drivers was eventually adopted. The Precision, too, has undergone some changes: in 1957, it was given a split-coil pickup, and its "skinny" headstock was enlarged to resemble the Stratocaster's; two years later, rosewood fingerboards were introduced, and more recent models have had alder bodies.

***Above:** Jeremy Davis, bass guitar player for Paramore, plays a P-Bass.*

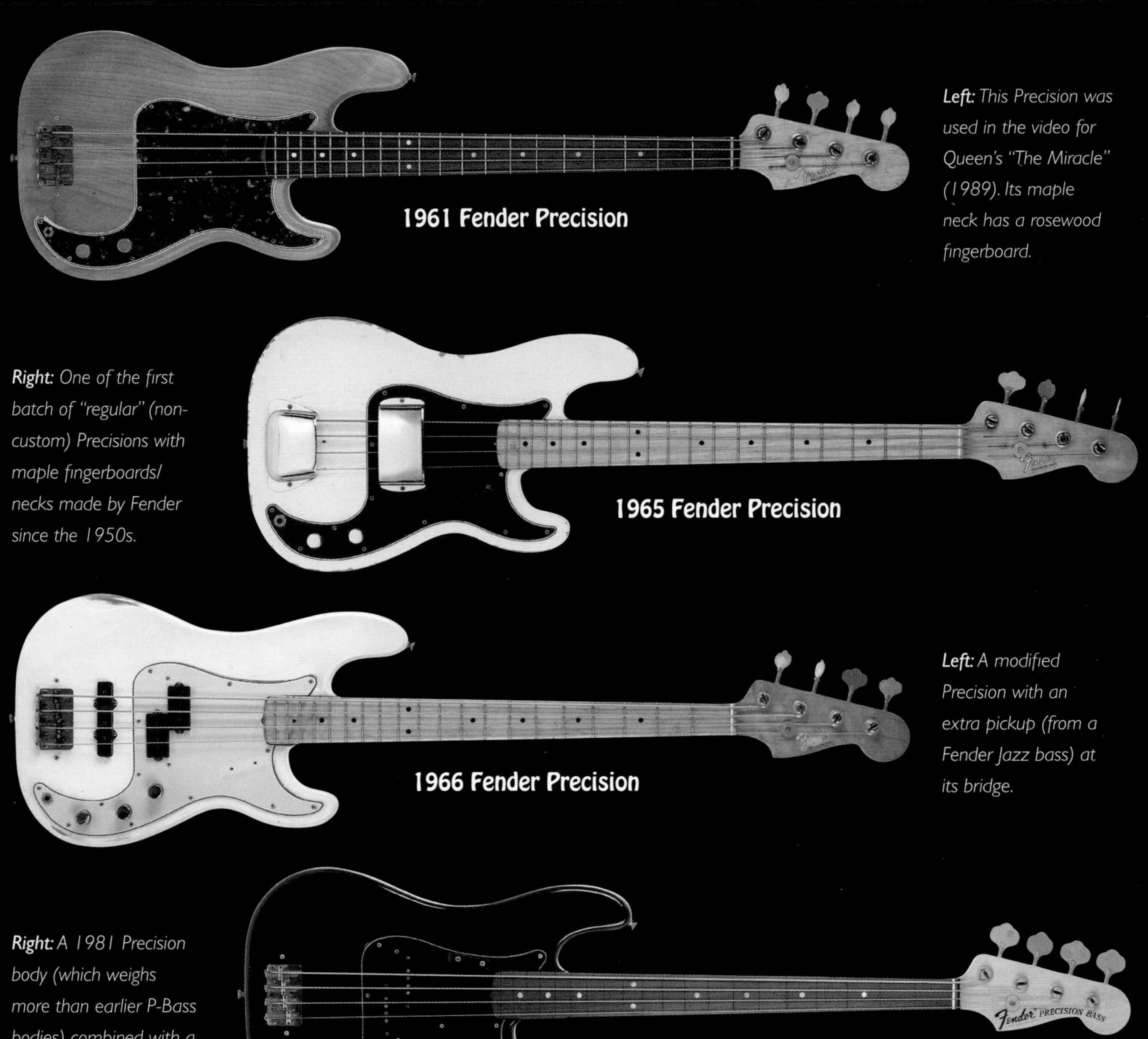

***Left:** This Precision was used in the video for Queen's "The Miracle" (1989). Its maple neck has a rosewood fingerboard.*

***Right:** One of the first batch of "regular" (non-custom) Precisions with maple fingerboards/necks made by Fender since the 1950s.*

***Left:** A modified Precision with an extra pickup (from a Fender Jazz bass) at its bridge.*

***Right:** A 1981 Precision body (which weighs more than earlier P-Bass bodies) combined with a 1973 neck.*

The ubiquitous Precision

The "P-Bass" defined a new genre—many users quickly found themselves being called "Fender bass" players—and helped propel a musical revolution. Its versatility is demonstrated by the diverse number of musicians who've made it their own: among its early adopters were jazzmen such as Roy Johnson and "Monk" Montgomery (both sidemen with vibes player Lionel Hampton), and it has gone on to be associated with everyone from Donald "Duck" Dunn (Booker T. & The M.G.'s), The Who's John Entwistle and Motown session man James Jamerson, to Glen Matlock from the Sex Pistols. It's hard to imagine today's popular music scene without it, and more than half a century after its creation, its glory days show no sign of fading.

Fender Jazz Bass

The Fender Jazz Bass debuted in 1960. In the nine years since the introduction of the Fender Precision, electric bass guitars had become familiar to musicians and audiences, and companies such as Rickenbacker, Gibson, Danelectro, and (in Europe) Höfner were all producing their own. Leo Fender responded to the competition with a new model that had offset waists ("contribut[ing] greatly to playing ease and comfort," to quote the firm's publicity), twin pickups (the P-Bass had just one), and a narrower neck for more agile fingering. The Precision measured $1\frac{3}{4}$ in (4.4 cm) at its nut, but the Jazz's fingerboard was just $1\frac{7}{16}$ in (3.65 cm) wide at the same point. Its controls were also unusual: originally, each pickup's volume and tone "pots" were mounted in tandem on a single shaft, though this arrangement was replaced by a more conventional, three-knob configuration in 1962.

The new bass's cool, streamlined look was complemented by a forceful "upfront" sound that has delighted rock, funk, and reggae artists as much as jazzmen (though most of them discarded the instrument's string mutes, intended to imitate a double bass's *pizzicato* tone).

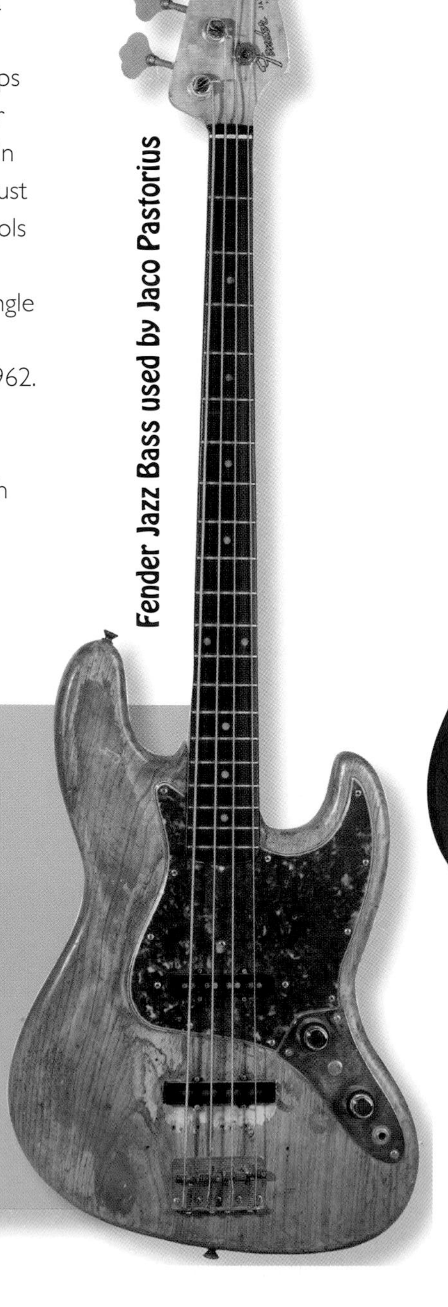

Fender Jazz Bass used by Jaco Pastorius

1963 Fender Jazz Bass

J-Bass players

Over the years, high-profile "J-Bassists" have included Larry Graham (Sly and the Family Stone), Aston "Family Man" Barrett (Bob Marley and the Wailers) and Berry Oakley (Allman Brothers), while the instrument's most celebrated user from the world of jazz is the late Jaco Pastorius (Weather Report). During his all-too-short career, Jaco played two J-Basses: a 1960 model borrowed from a friend (right), and his 1962-vintage "Bass of Doom," from which he famously removed the frets.

Fender Jazzmaster and Jaguar

1965 Sunburst Jazzmaster—left-handed

2012 Johnny Marr Signature Jaguar

Both these guitars were "top of the range" Fender models, costing substantially more than a Telecaster or Strat. As its name suggests, the Jazzmaster, introduced in 1958, was aimed at jazz guitarists, and it offered a number of "firsts" for Fender: a vibrato system with a "lock-off" mechanism to prevent tuning problems if a string should break; a patented offset-waist body (later adopted for the Jazz Bass as well); and ingenious pickup controls that enabled instant switching between user-preset rhythm and lead circuits. These proved too complicated for some musicians, and there were also snags with the pickups themselves, whose lack of shielding made them prone to electrical interference. Though it looked and sounded striking, with a richer, warmer tone than the Tele, the new instrument never caught on with the jazzmen for whom it was intended. Its most high-profile 1960s user was Bob Bogle of The Ventures ("Walk Don't Run," "Perfidia"), and it later became closely associated with New Wave artists, especially Tom Verlaine of Television and Elvis Costello.

The Jaguar

Like the Jazzmaster, the Jaguar, dating from 1962, was an offset-waist, multi-control guitar with a separate bridge and vibrato. Its metal-shielded pickups were less affected by buzz and hum than its predecessor's, and it also featured a spring-loaded string mute, a 24-in (61-cm) scale—1½ in (3.8 cm) shorter than other Fenders—for speed and comfort, and 22 frets instead of Fender's standard 21. It enjoyed an initial burst of popularity, thanks in part to its adoption by Carl Wilson of The Beach Boys, but has really come into its own more recently, finding favor with P. J. Harvey, Kurt Cobain, Dinosaur Jr.'s J Mascis, and John Frusciante of the Red Hot Chili Peppers. In 2012, Fender collaborated with Johnny Marr, famous for his work with The Smiths, to produce a Marr Signature Model Jaguar.

> "*When we built the Stratocaster we thought that was the world's greatest guitar. Then we said, let's make something even better—so we built the Jazzmaster.*"
>
> Fender's Freddie Tavares

Gibson acoustics

While Martin, Larson, and other firms were pioneering flat-top, steel-strung acoustic guitars, Gibson was more focused on its archtop instruments. It produced no flat-tops bearing its own logo until 1926, when it launched two 13½-in (34.3-cm) wide models, the L-1 and L-0. The 14¾-in (37.5-cm) L-00 appeared in 1932, and the example in our photo dates from four years later. An inexpensive guitar, it was initially available only in black: the sunburst finish seen here was introduced in 1933. The L-00 and its cousins were fine fingerstyle instruments that proved highly popular with blues and country musicians—but their reputation has often been overshadowed by that of Gibson's larger, louder, and costlier Jumbos.

These measured 16 in (40.6 cm) or more across their lower bouts, and were introduced in 1934 as competition to Martin's 15⅝-in (39.7-cm) Dreadnoughts, which had debuted in 1931. Jumbos were destined to became a formidable force in the flat-top marketplace, and none was more influential or desirable than the "Super Jumbo 200" (or SJ-200), launched in 1937–38. It looked as good as it sounded, with rich decorations, a distinctive "mustache" bridge, and a 16⅞-in (42.9-cm) body that was soon increased to a full 17-in (43.2-cm) width.

1936 Gibson L-00

1957 Gibson SJ-200

Flat-top Favorites

Developed in partnership with "singing cowboy" and film actor Ray Whitley (1901–79), composer of such prewar classics as "Back In The Saddle Again," The SJ-200 found favor with a galaxy of subsequent stars, from Elvis Presley, the Everly Brothers, and Rick Nelson to Pete Townshend, Gram Parsons, and Emmylou Harris…the cover of whose 1985 album *The Ballad of Sally Rose* featured a custom-finished pink SJ-200.

> "A Gibson flat-top can match the thunder of a storm and the roar of the wind. Or be as gentle and serene as a ripple in a springlike pond."
>
> *1972 Gibson advertisement*

1954 Gibson ES-295

Electrified archtops

As demand for electric guitars grew after World War II, Gibson produced updated versions of its classic 1920s and 1930s archtops, now fitted with pickups. These "deluxe" instruments continued to be made from solid (not laminated) woods, and their tops were hand-carved, not pressed into shape. An electric L-5 appeared in 1951, carrying the suffix CES ("cutaway electric Spanish"). It retained many of Lloyd Loar's characteristic features, but boasted two Alnico V transducers: these were Gibson's top-of-the-range units until the introduction of the humbucker in 1957. The L-5CES was favored by Elvis Presley's sideman Scotty Moore, and was also the choice of many top jazzmen, like its immediate contemporary, the Super 400CES.

Solid-wood electric hollow-bodies have undeniable aesthetic qualities, but they are more prone to feedback than those made from laminates; and while essential for a good acoustic sound, premium woods contribute little to the tone of a guitar whose top has already been deadened by heavy magnetic pickups. This is undoubtedly why Gibson chose to give its ES-5—boasting no fewer than three P-90s a laminated body. It debuted in 1949, and was described in the firm's publicity as "the supreme electronic version of the famed L-5" and "the instrument of a thousand voices." Humbler Gibson archtops were invariably made of laminated lumber, too.

Alexis Korner's ES-295

For one influential British player, Alexis Korner (1928–84), the gold-finished ES-295, with its deep plywood body, offered (in the words of Alexis' son, Damian) an ideal compromise: "the feel of an acoustic but the sound of an electric…when he laid down some riffs, he could really let rip on it."

Gibson ES-335

Any list of the greatest-ever electrics is inevitably subjective, but many players and collectors would place the Gibson ES-335 in their top three or four. The model has been described as a compromise without any drawbacks: one that succeeds in appealing to archtop-loving traditionalists while offering slimline looks, unrivaled sonic versatility and easy fingerboard access—as well as freedom from the feedback that can blight heavily amplified hollow-bodied guitars.

The 335 appeared in 1958, and its design and launch were spearheaded by Gibson's President, Ted McCarty. Viewed from the front, it resembles a fairly standard archtop electric, albeit a double-cutaway one with a 22-fret neck and a 19th-fret body join. However, it is only 1¾ in (4.4 cm) deep—the Gibson L-5CES and ES-295 on our preceding pages both measure a much bulkier 3⅛ in (7.9 cm)—and its internal construction has another unexpected feature, invisible from the outside. The guitar's center section is a 4-in (10.2-cm) wide maple block that provides solid-body-style sustain and greatly reduces feedback problems, while the hollow "wings" on either side supply some of the woody warmth of a more conventional electric-acoustic.

Its pickups, developed by engineer Seth Lover, are "humbuckers" whose twin coils are connected in series but out of phase with each other—resulting (as Lover himself put it) in "a pickup that bucks [rejects] hum," and also delivers a higher output with a distinctively rich, powerful tone. In 1957, the year of these transducers' introduction, Gibson had described them as "the ultimate for recording, broadcasting, or whenever truly fine performance is required." The 335's standard tailpiece was a "stop" or "stud" metal block, though a Bigsby vibrato was also available. A slimline electric bass, the EB-2, made its debut at the same time as the new "semi-solid."

The 335's users

Among the first star players to adopt the ES-335 were B. B. King, who subsequently switched to a variant model, the ES-355, Chuck Berry, and Roy Orbison. Englishman Alvin Lee of Ten Years After gave an unforgettable performance (immortalized on record and film) at the 1969 Woodstock music festival with his cherry-finished, heavily stickered 335, nicknamed "Big Red" and boasting three pickups. Eric Clapton famously used one with Cream. The 335 has attracted a host of other leading musicians, from Larry Carlton and Rush's Alex Lifeson to Eric Johnson, Dave Grohl, and Britpop pioneer Bernard Butler.

Above: *B.B. King with one of his Gibson ES-355 guitars—all named "Lucille."*

1963 Gibson ES-335

***Below:** When the 12-string craze took off in the 1960s, Gibson started offering a 12-string version of the 335. This one, according to its owner, gives "sustain to die for!"*

***Above:** A modern ES-335 with a blond finish like a classic older model. After 1960, the main color for 335s was cherry red.*

***Right:** A "limited run" 2006 ES-335 with a Bigsby vibrato, gold-plated hardware, and diamond cut-outs instead of f-holes.*

> Every one of these models—each with the Gibson "wonder-thin silhouette"—really does have that certain "feel" to it.
>
> *Gibson ad for the ES-335 and its thin-line cousins, 1958*

Gibson Les Paul

Les Paul (1915–2009) was a skilled inventor as well as a fine guitarist. As early as 1929, he had made a crude guitar amplifier out of a phonograph needle and a radio; and in 1940, he built "The Log"—a chunk of wood with pickups, a guitar neck and strings attached, to which he added the sides of a regular archtop instrument to produce an unwieldy, but feedback-free, electric semi-solid. (Later, more elegant models like the Gibson ES-335 use the same basic principle: *see* previous pages.)

In the early 1950s, Les Paul, then enjoying million-selling chart success with his wife, Mary Ford, was signed up to an endorsement deal by Gibson. The company was developing a solid-body electric to compete with the Fender Telecaster, and it came to be named the "Les Paul Model," although the degree of Les's contribution to its design is a matter of some debate. The first Gibson Les Paul appeared in 1952: it had a single cutaway, a gold-painted, carved maple top, two P-90 pickups, and a trapeze bridge/tailpiece. The trapeze unit proved unsatisfactory, and was quickly replaced by a one-piece wraparound fixture with two stud mounts; by 1955, a separate, adjustable "Tune-O-Matic" bridge had been added, and the stud-mounted metal block had become a string anchor.

> *It is the finest, most beautiful guitar there is.*
>
> Les Paul (*above*), speaking about the Gibson electric that carries his name

Les Paul + humbuckers = classic

In 1957, Seth Lover's new humbucking pickups were fitted in place of the single-coil P-90s, while a year later, the gold top was discontinued in favor of a sunburst finish, and the guitar was renamed the "Les Paul Standard." This incarnation of the instrument is regarded as an all-time classic, especially when paired, by Eric Clapton and countless others, with a British-made Marshall combo or stack—a combination described by former Gibson editorial director Walter Carter as "the perfect marriage of power guitar with power amplifier." However, the gold-topped, P-90-equipped Les Paul has also had passionate devotees, including bluesmen Freddie King and Hubert Sumlin, and rock'n'roll legend Carl Perkins.

The third member of this prime trio of Les Paul greats is the Custom: a deluxe model, introduced in 1954, that initially had two P-90 pickups like its cousin. Four years later Gibson gave it three humbuckers, altering its control switching to allow players to select the neck unit (for rhythm), center and bridge pickups together, or bridge pickup (for soloing). It's frequently nicknamed the "Black Beauty" (due to its striking finish) and the "Fretless Wonder," thanks to its ultra-low frets and string action.

1954 Gibson Les Paul model

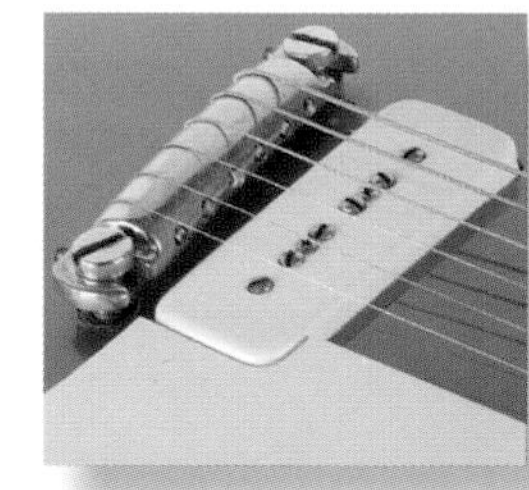

Above: *"A poem in gold and cream"...this Les Paul has a "stud" bar (designed by Ted McCarty) that serves as a bridge and tailpiece.*

1966 Gibson *Les Paul* Standard

1959 Gibson
Les Paul Standard

1960 Gibson Les Paul Custom

The Gibson Les Paul Junior—an unashamedly low-budget version of the much more expensive Standard and Custom—first appeared in 1954. It was the same size as its upmarket relatives, and its body and neck, like theirs, were made of Honduras mahogany, though Juniors had a flat top instead of an arched maple "crown." Just one pickup, a P-90, was fitted, there were simple dot position markers (rather than pearl inlays) along the unbound rosewood fingerboard, and at first the guitar was finished in Gibson's traditional two-colour brown-to-yellow sunburst.

At the time of its launch, the company's bosses could not have predicted the Junior's subsequent popularity with rock musicians. Its simplicity, low price and hot, raw sound appealed to late 1960s'/early 1970s' bands like Mountain and Mott The Hoople. A little later, it went on to become a favorite with punk and New Wave players such as Mick Jones of The Clash and Johnny Thunders (New York Dolls); and among its current devotees are Billie Joe Armstrong of Green Day, and New Zealander Keith Urban.

The Les Paul Special was introduced a year after the Junior. It cost a little more, and had two pickups, as well as a "limed" or so-called "TV" finish that may have been created to look better on the black-and-white televisions of the period, though there are several other theories about its origin. "Limed" Juniors were available, too: in this form, they were listed in the Gibson catalog as "Les Paul TVs."

Above: *Billie Joe Armstrong of Green Day with a "TV" Junior.*

1959 Gibson *Les Paul Junior*

1959 Double-cutaway Gibson Les Paul Junior

Early double-cutaway Gibson Les Paul Special

A change of shape

In 1958, the Junior's and TV's classic single-cutaway Les Paul shape was abandoned in favor of a double cutaway that the firm's publicity described as "ultra-modernistic in appearance and practical in performance." Among its advantages was improved access to the highest reaches of the guitars' fingerboards. The Special was given the same body outline (plus an optional cherry finish) in 1959, when Les Paul's name was removed from it and from the TV. Both models were now to be called "SG" (Solid Guitar), but they retained their 1958-style bodies until 1961—the year in which the sharp-horned cutaways associated with regular Gibson SGs were brought in (*see* photographs here and on the next two pages). The Junior also acquired an SG-type outline in 1961, but this already confusing progression is further complicated by the fact that despite its new shape, its name did not change from Les Paul Junior to SG Junior until 1963.

"Limed" finish Les Paul Special

Les Paul Specials like this one first appeared in 1955, and boasted two P-90 pickups. They're widely regarded as less effective than the single-pickup Juniors; expert Phil Harris, writing in *Guitar & Bass*, suggests that "maybe two P-90s on a mahogany body is just a bad combination." Within four years, the Special was to acquire a double cutaway body.

Gibson SG

After peaking in 1959, sales of Gibson Les Pauls fell the following year. The company was keen to usher in the new decade with a restyled electric guitar that could challenge the Fender Stratocaster. The body design on which it pinned its hopes was described by the firm's publicists as "ultra-thin, hand-contoured, [with a] double cutaway," and versions of the Les Paul Standard, Custom, and Junior in the new shape appeared in 1961. Single-cutaway Les Pauls were to stay out of production for the next seven years.

For a while, the Standard, Custom, and Junior retained the "Les Paul" name, even though the man himself was less than enthusiastic about the radical changes his instruments had undergone: he later commented to guitar expert Tom Wheeler that "a guy could kill himself on those sharp [cutaway] horns."

The situation altered in 1963, when Les's endorsement deal with Gibson ended; at the time he was in the throes of his divorce from Mary Ford, and was unwilling to sign a new one. Without a contract, Gibson could no longer call its guitars "Les Pauls," and it renamed them "SGs" (for "Solid Guitars"). The appellation had been in use since 1959 on the former Les Paul TV and Special.

SGs never eclipsed the original Les Pauls (whose eventual return to the Gibson catalog speaks for itself), but they are impressive, influential instruments with a character all their own. Despite the reintroduction of the single-cutaway models they were intended to replace, they've survived and flourished in their own right—and have been adopted by a host of leading musicians.

Five Top Gibson SG Users

FRANK ZAPPA

Composer, iconoclast, and leader of the Mothers of Invention, Zappa often used an SG to produce his inimitable guitar lines, playing through a Marshall stack or sometimes even a tiny Pignose amp.

PETE TOWNSHEND

From 1968 to 1971 (a classic period for The Who, taking in *Tommy*, *Live At Leeds,* and the Woodstock and Isle of Wight festivals), Townshend could frequently be seen and heard with an SG Special.

ERIC CLAPTON

Eric bought his first SG (a secondhand 1964 model) in 1967, and used it until the demise of Cream in November 1968.

TONY IOMMI

Black Sabbath's early crushing guitar sounds were created with a left-handed SG routed through a customized Dallas treble booster and a Laney amp. Though Iommi's allegiance lay for a long time with his John Birch solid-body, he's currently back in the Gibson SG saddle, playing a suitably all-black instrument.

ANGUS YOUNG

"I liked SGs 'cos they were light," admits AC/DC's perennial schoolboy. "Fenders were too heavy and they didn't have the balls."

Above: *Angus Young.*

1961 Gibson Les Paul/SG Custom

Recently reissued Gibson SG Standard

Gretsch

The Gretsch company was a family business, established in New York in 1883. It made its first guitars in the 1930s, and its prewar archtops were strong rivals to those of both Gibson and Epiphone. When Gretsch's Synchromatic models appeared in 1939, the company, then run by the founder's son, Fred Gretsch Sr., began to assemble a musically diverse group of endorsees that eventually came to include folksinger Burl Ives, "Tennessee Plowboy" Eddy Arnold and two leading jazzmen, Hank Garland (later poached by Gibson) and Mundell Lowe.

Fred Sr.'s son, Fred Gretsch Jr., became the firm's boss in 1948; working alongside him was Jimmie Webster, the skilled musician, salesman, and inventor who was responsible for signing up rising country music star Chet Atkins (1924–2001) as a Gretsch design consultant. The Nashville-based guitarist was understandably keen to develop his own "signature" instruments, and while Fred Jr. was initially uncertain about "pay[ing] a hillbilly guitar player to use his name on our guitars," his skepticism must have been swept away when the first fruit of the Gretsch/Atkins collaboration, the 6120 Hollow Body, debuted in 1955. Though the new model had some teething troubles—Atkins didn't care for its "Western" fingerboard inlays (which were subsequently removed) or the over-bassy pickups (remedied by the introduction of Filter'Tron transducers in 1958)—it became a classic, and has been used by many other leading players, from Eddie Cochran and Duane Eddy, to Pete Townshend and Brian Setzer.

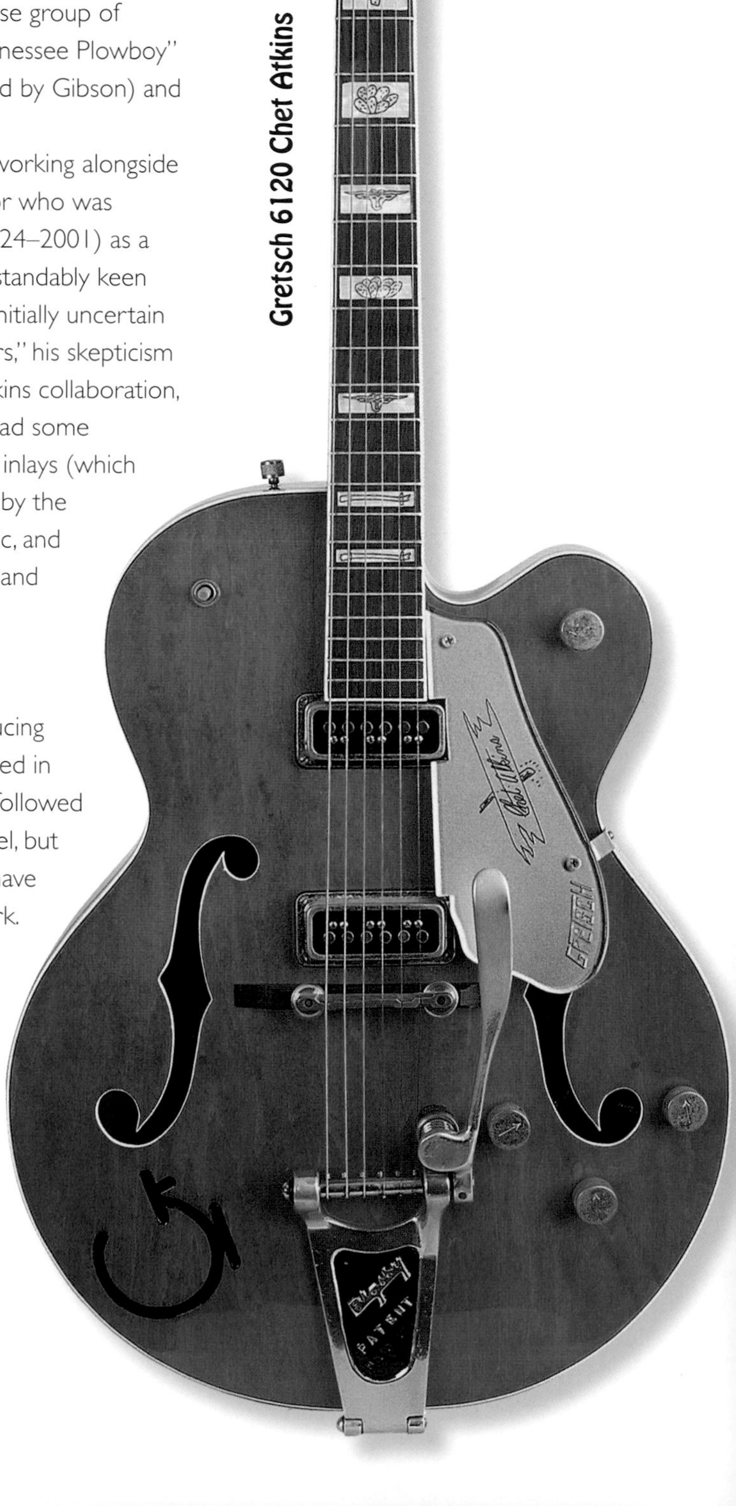

Gretsch 6120 Chet Atkins

More Gretsches

Gretsch quickly capitalized on its commercial opportunity by producing other guitars carrying Chet Atkins's name. A Solid Body was launched in 1955, and the Country Gentleman and Tennessean hollow-bodies followed three years later. The single-pickup Tennessean was a cheaper model, but the Gentleman, which cost more than the original 6120, is said to have been Atkins's personal favorite, and his regular choice for stage work.

Other major names associated with Gretsches include George Harrison and Neil Young, though Young has a signature guitar. The company's most controversial endorsement deal was surely that with the "manufactured" mid-1960s pop group The Monkees (or their agents). Two members of the quartet (Mike Nesmith and Peter Tork) actually used Gretsch instruments, but the "Monkees Rock'n'Roll" guitar, dating from 1967, doesn't reflect their preferences: a two-pickup semi-acoustic, it is finished in the brightest of all possible reds, and carries the group's name on its pickguard and truss rod cover.

Far left: A 1961 Chet Atkins Country Gentleman with Filter'Tron pickups.

Center: Chet Atkins' own Super Chet, with modified and added controls.

Left: A 1967 Monkees Rock'n'Roll. The group's TV series ended in 1968, and this guitar was discontinued the following year.

> *I was thrilled to have my name on a guitar like Les Paul had his name on the Gibson. At the time I was full of ambition and I wanted to be known all over the world as a great guitarist, and that was one brick in the edifice that would help that happen.*
>
> Chet Atkins, speaking in 1995

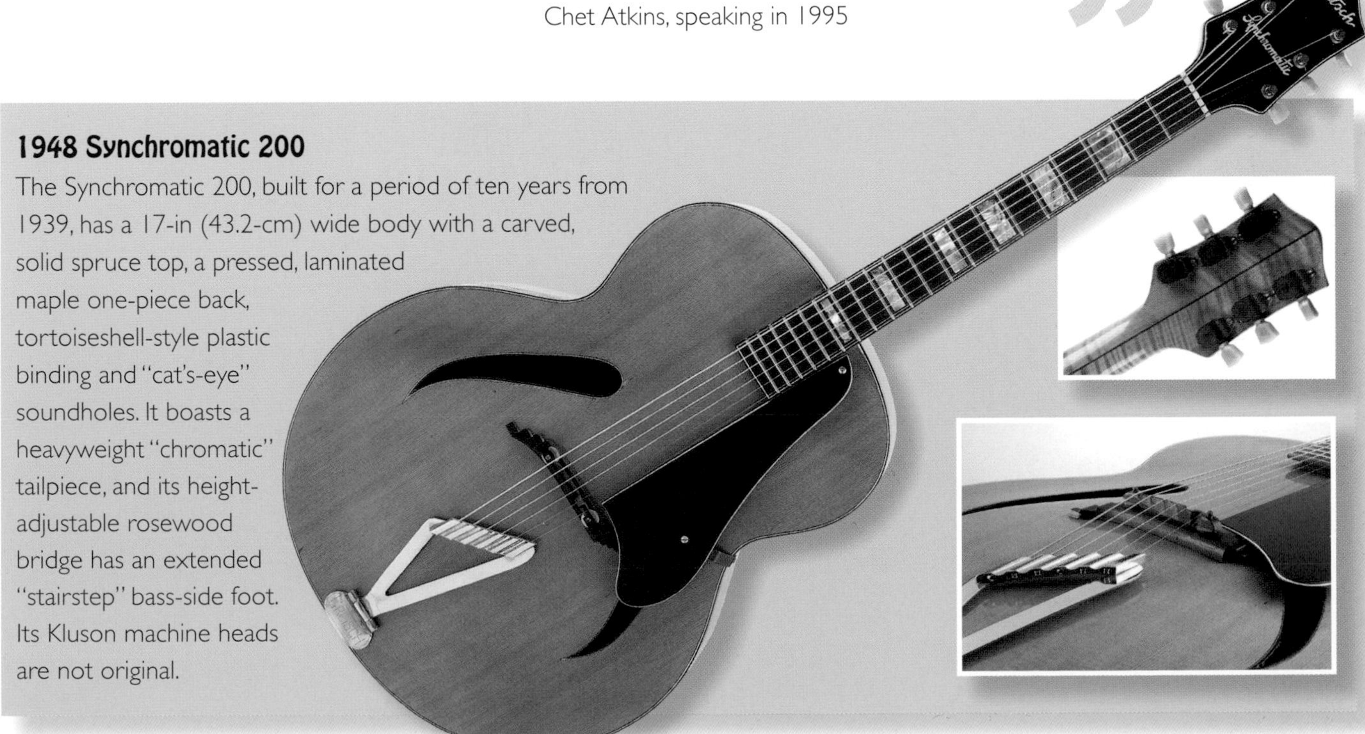

1948 Synchromatic 200

The Synchromatic 200, built for a period of ten years from 1939, has a 17-in (43.2-cm) wide body with a carved, solid spruce top, a pressed, laminated maple one-piece back, tortoiseshell-style plastic binding and "cat's-eye" soundholes. It boasts a heavyweight "chromatic" tailpiece, and its height-adjustable rosewood bridge has an extended "stairstep" bass-side foot. Its Kluson machine heads are not original.

The White Falcon 17-in (43.2-cm) hollow-body was certainly Gretsch's most ostentatious guitar. It started out as a trade-show display model, put together in 1954 under Jimmie Webster's supervision, but its sparkle finish and gold-plated parts attracted so much attention that it went into production (with the catalog number 6136) a year later. It was, in fact, a Webster "signature" instrument in all but name: Jimmie invariably used one for demonstrations, and added his own photograph to the White Falcon page in most of the company's catalogs. Initially, the Falcon was given two single-coil DeArmond pickups, but in 1958 these were replaced by Gretsch's own Filter'Tron humbuckers, designed by Scotty Moore's amp guru, Ray Butts.

Over the years, the White Falcon has also been fitted with a succession of bizarre, subsequently abandoned gadgets: the "Project-O-Sonic" faux-stereo system; a complex four-switch array providing, in theory, no less than 54 tonal presets; and a "Floating Sound Unit" which, according to the company's promotional literature, would "give your sound richer, fuller life" and improve its sustain. Neil Young is one of the few famous players who still uses a stereo White Falcon, and in its numerous forms and reissues the guitar retains a substantial following. Billy Duffy of The Cult is another enthusiastic user—though his model is a mono one!

1970 Gretsch White Falcon

Closedown

In 1967, Fred Gretsch Jr. sold his firm to the Baldwin Music Company, and after a troubled decade that saw poor sales, a downturn in quality, and a devastating factory fire, Gretsch closed down in 1980. In 1985, however, Fred Jr.'s nephew, Fred Gretsch III, bought back the family business. Since its relaunch, Gretsch has been manufacturing an impressive range of guitars in the Far East and the United States. Among them are instruments endorsed by Brian Setzer, Keith Scott, Stephen Stills of Crosby, Stills, Nash & Young, and AC/DC's Malcolm Young. The firm has also resumed production of its Chet Atkins guitars. These had been discontinued when Chet ended his association with Gretsch in 1979; for a while, his signature instruments were made by Gibson. In 2008, Gretsch celebrated the 125th anniversary of its foundation.

Above: *Neil Young playing a Gretsch White Falcon.*

> *There's always been a good market for Gretsches. The people that love them really do go bananas for them.*
>
> *Guitar & Bass* magazine columnist Phil Harris

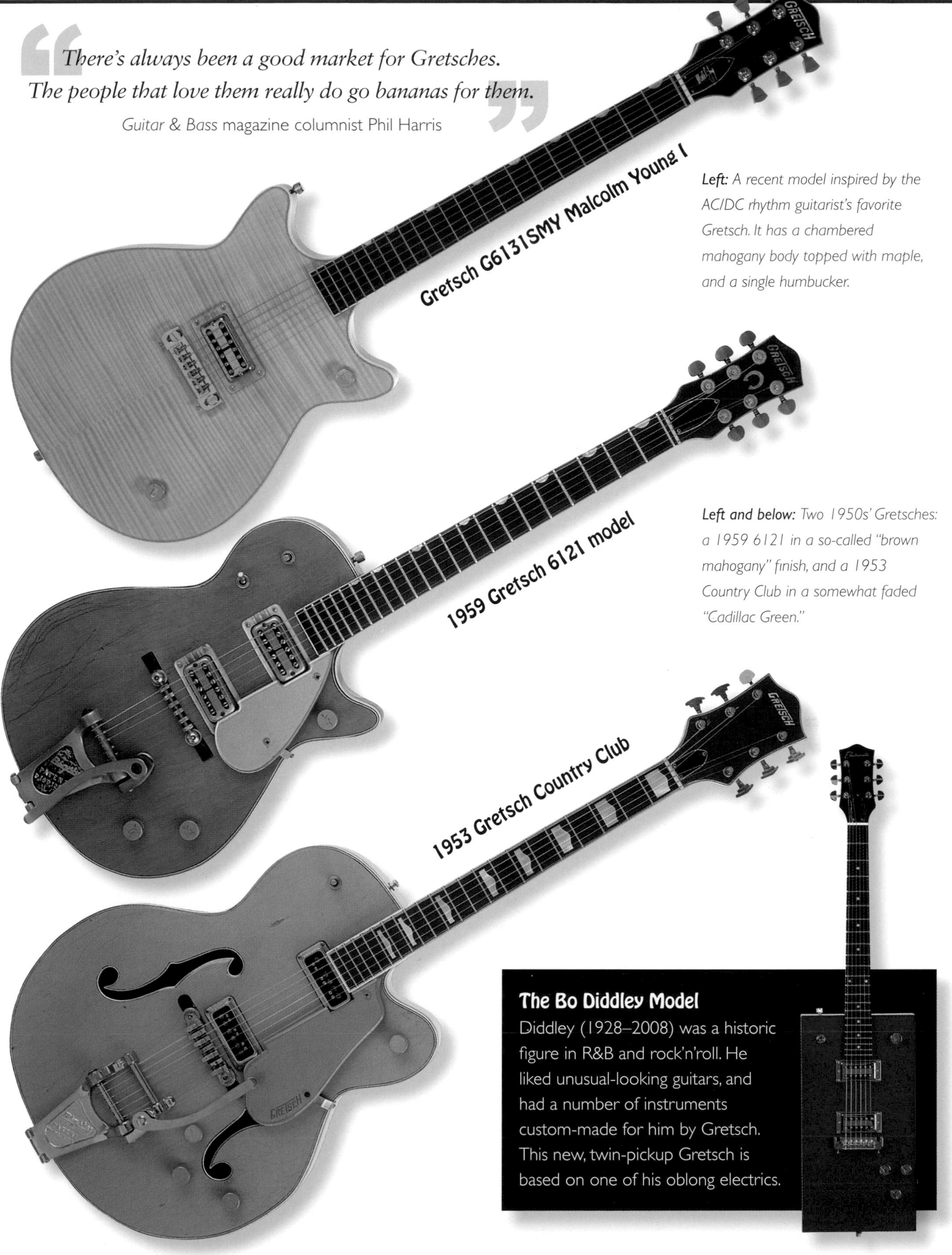

Left: *A recent model inspired by the AC/DC rhythm guitarist's favorite Gretsch. It has a chambered mahogany body topped with maple, and a single humbucker.*

Left and below: *Two 1950s' Gretsches: a 1959 6121 in a so-called "brown mahogany" finish, and a 1953 Country Club in a somewhat faded "Cadillac Green."*

The Bo Diddley Model

Diddley (1928–2008) was a historic figure in R&B and rock'n'roll. He liked unusual-looking guitars, and had a number of instruments custom-made for him by Gretsch. This new, twin-pickup Gretsch is based on one of his oblong electrics.

Choosing "that special guitar"

When selecting a guitar, what should you look out for? No one can tell you exactly what to buy, but there are some useful guidelines to bear in mind when shopping for an instrument. Naturally, the condition of any guitar you consider is important. Cosmetic blemishes may be only skin deep, but wear and damage that affect playability are much more significant. The very first thing to check for is the near-incurable "twisted neck." Place the lower bout of the guitar on the floor, and look straight down the top of the fingerboard from its nut end. If there's excessive twisting, reject the instrument straight away. Don't confuse twisting with neck relief: most guitars' necks should curve very slightly along their length, and if you fret a string simultaneously at the 1st and 14th fret there should be a small gap between the string and the 7th fret.

These days any new guitar should have perfectly serviceable frets, but if buying secondhand, watch out for areas (often around commonly played chords) where the tops of the frets might be worn flat, causing string buzzing and rattling. Rectifying this may involve a fret stone and dress, or even a refret, and both can be expensive.

A guitar's action—the height of the strings above the fretboard—can usually be adjusted to your preference. Some musicians like it low and easy-playing; others want it set higher, producing a fuller tone, and making string bending and vibrato more controllable. Also, consider string gauges, and change them if necessary.

Assessing the guitar's qualities

When assessing an electric guitar, check that its weight and balance suit you. Try playing it unplugged: does it sound dull and dead, or clear and responsive? Does it have much low end, or is it a bit thin and bright? Can you feel the body of the guitar vibrating when you play it? The instrument should retain those qualities when amplified, providing the potential for great tone. Without them, even the finest pickups aren't likely to transform it into a winner.

When plugging in, don't be afraid to tell the shop what kind of amp you'd prefer to use, and if you're really serious, arrange to take in your own. At this point, assessing a guitar becomes instinctive. If you find yourself constantly fiddling with your amp controls, something's not quite right. On the other hand, if you can't put the instrument down and are eager to keep playing for hours—even beyond the shop's closing time—that guitar is probably "the one."

1 Check for twisting by looking down a guitar's neck. Make sure you've got plenty of space first.

2 A sideways look at the fingerboard allows you to inspect the action and check for protruding fret ends.

3 Take your potential purchase for a lengthy musical "test drive," using an amp like your own.

Right and bottom: *A well-stocked guitar shop is full of tempting instruments like the Fenders and Rickenbacker shown here. Finding the right one can be daunting.*

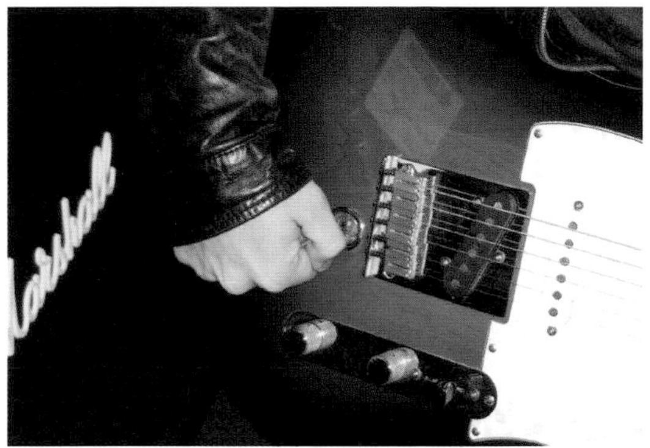

4 Don't be tempted by widgets you don't need—like this B-string bender, designed for country players.

Höfner Violin Bass

Since its inception in Schönbach, Germany, in 1887, Höfner has become one of Europe's leading instrument manufacturers. Its guitars first appeared in 1925, and archtop Höfners haunted European jazz, skiffle, and beat clubs during the 1950s and 1960s, thanks in part to their affordability. At the time, Fenders, Gibsons, and other top American brands were hard to come by in Britain and Europe, or simply too expensive for youngsters there.

Today, Höfner is probably best known as the "Beatle bass company." The reasons for this date back to April 1961, when the young Paul McCartney purchased a Höfner 500/1 bass in Hamburg, where he and the other Beatles had a nightclub residency. McCartney was attracted to the 500/1 not only by its competitive price, but by its symmetrical body—its appearance wasn't affected when he played the bass left-handed. It was also lighter than other models, due to its hollow construction, and its short scale made it easy to play.

The rest—as they say—is history. The "violin bass" was a familiar sight and sound throughout The Beatles' early years, although the instrument Paul bought in Hamburg was subsequently stolen, and has never been recovered. He later became associated with Rickenbackers, but continues to use a Höfner to this day. The 500/1 and its siblings and replicas have also been the choice of musicians from other musical genres: reggae star Robbie Shakespeare plays one, as does Dale Davis (best known for his work with Amy Winehouse), while Chris Wood (of organ trio Medeski, Martin, & Wood) has demonstrated just how jazzy this unassuming little instrument can be.

1964 Höfner 500/1

Below: *Paul McCartney plays a Höfner Violin Bass at a concert in 2010.*

Martin

Christian Frederick Martin I (1796–1873) was born in Germany, and served an apprenticeship in Vienna with an eminent Austrian guitar maker, Johann Stauffer. Martin emigrated to the United States in 1833, opened a music store in New York City and sold his own guitars there. Six years later, he established a workshop in Nazareth, Pennsylvania, where C. F. Martin & Company has been based ever since. Always a family business, the firm is currently run by Chris Martin IV, the founder's great-great-great-grandson.

Martin has played a key role in the evolution of flat-top, steel-strung guitars. The internal X-bracing that contributes so much to their sound was adopted by C. F. Martin I, though his own instruments all had gut strings. The company began to introduce steel ones, as well as wider guitar bodies, in the early twentieth century, as part of its quest for extra volume. In 1929 came another innovation: the OM (Orchestra Model) guitar, with a slightly narrower neck and 14 (rather than 12) frets clear of the body. And in 1931 Martin launched its largest, most influential, and most extensively copied flat-top: the Dreadnought. Named after a British battleship, it was, in fact, derived from a design previously produced by Martin for the Oliver Ditson music store.

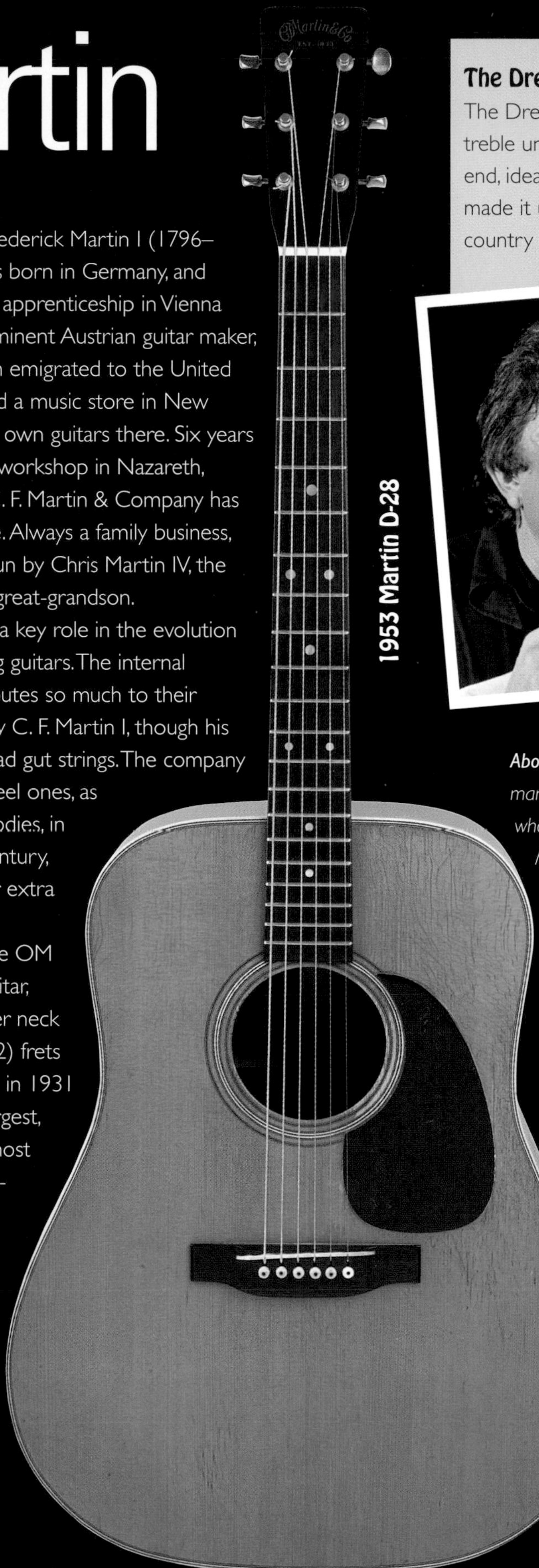

1953 Martin D-28

The Dreadnought

The Dreadnought's tonal traits—a clean, powerful treble underpinned by an extremely strong bottom end, ideal for flat-picked rhythm and bass lines—have made it universally popular. Its users have included country and bluegrass players (Johnny Cash, Tony Rice) rock stars such as Neil Young and Jimmy Page, and bluesmen like Skip James and Brownie McGhee.

Above: Johnny Cash is among many famous performers who have favored the Martin Dreadnought.

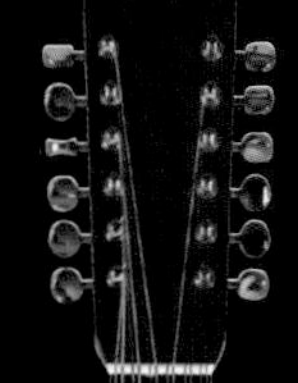

1973 Martin D12-28

Martin names most of its guitars using a system that dates back to the company's early years, though it's undergone some subsequent modifications. First come letters or a number designating an instrument's **body type**: D stands for Dreadnought ($15\frac{5}{8}$ in/39.7 cm wide), OM for "Orchestra Model," and 000 for "Auditorium" (both 15 in/38.1 cm wide), 00 for "Grand Concert" ($14\frac{1}{8}$ in/35.9 cm or $14\frac{5}{16}$ in/36.4 cm wide), and so on. After a hyphen comes a number that represents a particular model's **style**; each Martin "style" is a specific combination of woods, inlays, bindings, and finish. In comparison to the bewildering names and abbreviations favored by other manufacturers, Martin's method of classification is consistent, and provides immediate information about particular instruments.

Our photos show two Dreadnoughts: the D-45 (below) and the D-41 (opposite above). Like all Style 45 guitars, whatever their body type, the D-45 (purchased by *Guitar & Bass* columnist Phil Harris from Roddy Frame of Aztec Camera) has abalone fret markers and abalone inlays in the center ring of its rosette, on the edges of its body, and around the sides of the fingerboard that overlap its spruce top; its back and sides are rosewood. The early 1970s Style 41—formerly the property of British bluesman Alexis Korner—is made of similar woods, but is a little less fancy, lacking the abalone inlay around the top of its fingerboard.

> *"Martin's strong point has always been its traditional methods and old-style craftsmanship. It kept them as the highest-quality proponent of the steel-string guitar through all those years."*
>
> Player and guitar maker Eric Schoenberg

1989 Martin D-45

Martin electroacoustics

Like all long-established acoustic guitar makers, Martin has had to move with the times. While it continues to produce the classic flat-top models on which its reputation rests, its current catalog also contains an extensive portfolio of electroacoustics equipped with high-quality pickup systems. Perhaps the only downside to this development is that it has spoilt the company's once-simple naming system. Both the electro models featured here are identified by a confusing string of letters and numbers, though it's still possible to see that they are Style 16 instruments with cutaways.

The 00C-16DBRE is a 00 (Grand Concert) model incorporating a Fishman Ellipse Matrix blender system, the output from whose gooseneck microphone (attached under the soundhole) can be combined with the signal from a piezo transducer mounted in the guitar's bridge saddle. The JC-16RE is something comparatively new for Martin: a 16-in (40.6-cm) wide Jumbo flat-top, rather than one in the Dreadnought shape that's always been its "trademark" large-body design. Built into it is the Fishman Aura system—a sophisticated, programmable preamplifier linked to the guitar's undersaddle pickup, and providing digitally processed "sound images" generated from a variety of stage and studio microphones.

Acoustic bass guitars are another fairly recent Martin product line—although it had made electric basses as part of its short-lived "CFM" range of solid-body models in the late 1970s and early 1980s. The one shown in our photograph dates from 1989.

Alexis Korner's Martin D-41

Martin 00C-16DBRE Electroacoustic

Martin JC-16RE Aura Electroacoustic

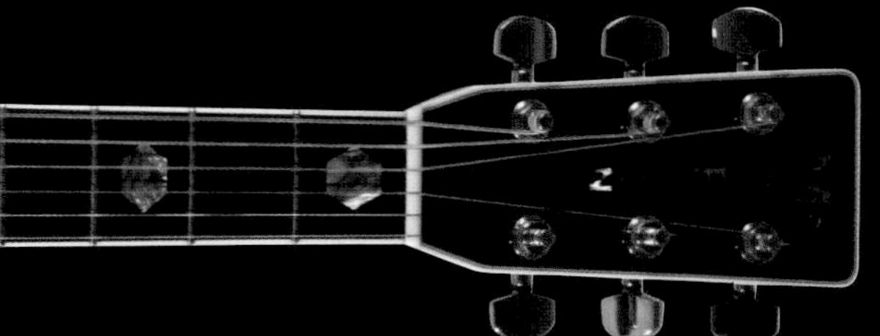

1989 Martin B40e

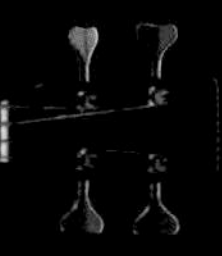

PRS

PRS are the initials of Paul Reed Smith, whose company, based in Stevensville, Maryland, is currently the United States third-biggest guitar producer, behind Fender and Gibson. Smith was born in nearby Bowie in 1956, and set up PRS in 1985, having already supplied custom-built guitars for major names such as Ted Nugent, Peter Frampton, and the man who would become his most prominent endorsee, Carlos Santana. PRS is best known for double-cutaway designs, but in 2000 it launched its Singlecut, with a body outline that has some similarities to the Gibson Les Paul's. Gibson went on to sue for trademark infringement, and following a court ruling in 2004, PRS had to stop making the Singlecut. A year later, however, the firm won an appeal against the earlier legal decision, and was able to resume production of its guitar. The Singlecut shown here is a Standard, with a mahogany neck and body, a carved maple top and two PRS 7 humbucking pickups.

The PRS Mira

The Mira is in a more typical PRS shape. The model appeared in 2007, and our photo shows a Maple Top version dating from a year later. Beneath its maple "crown," the body, like the Singlecut's, is mahogany. There's unrestricted access to the highest reaches of its 24-fret fingerboard, whose elegant "bird" inlays are a characteristic PRS feature. The "stoptail" bridge has carved grooves providing optimum intonation for the light-gauge strings used by most rock players, and the humbucking pickups are equipped with a coil tap.

PRS Singlecut Standard

2008 PRS Mira Maple Top

Both these guitars are fairly expensive, and it was apparently Carlos Santana himself who suggested that PRS should provide some more affordable instruments. The firm now produces cost-effective models with its Korean-made SE range of electrics. Our SE Torero is a twin humbucker-loaded double cutaway in a 24-fret version produced exclusively for the U.K.; models sold elsewhere have 22 frets. The maple-veneered top on its mahogany body is flat, which helps keep costs down, while the ebony fingerboard has no position markers. But a Floyd Rose locking vibrato is fitted, build quality is high, and the SE Torero's playability and versatility have won it warm praise.

Our last PRS, an Electric Bass, is one of the company's upmarket American-built basses. Its body is carved from a single piece of alder, and has a two-piece flame maple top; there are two humbucking pickups, plus an active onboard preamp.

PRS SE Torero

PRS Electric Bass

PRS Nick Cantanese

The "Evil Twin"

The "Nick Catanese" SE, like the Torero, is manufactured in Korea. It's a signature model made for the guitarist known as Zakk Wylde's "evil twin" in the American heavy metal band Black Label Society—and Catanese's "ET" logo is emblazoned on its black lacquered body. The instrument boasts active EMG humbucking pickups in striking red surrounds; similarly colored bindings adorn the fretboard, headstock and top edge of the body.

Rickenbacker

Adolph Rickenbacker's Los Angeles-based company, first known as "Ro-Pat-In," then "Electro," pioneered electric guitar production in the 1930s (see Chapter One). In 1953, Adolph, then in his late sixties, sold the business to F. C. Hall, whose Radio-Tel firm had been Fender's original distributors. Early the following year, Hall hired German-born luthier Roger Rossmeisl, previously at Gibson, to come up with new guitar designs. Rossmeisl worked at Rickenbacker until 1962. The first models he created for his new employer were the solid-body Combos, but in 1958 his hollow-body Capris made their debut. These stylish guitars would form the basis for much of Rickenbacker's subsequent success, although the "Capri" name itself was soon dropped, and the instruments became known as the "300 series."

Rickenbacker and The Beatles

An important factor in the 300s' popularity was F. C. Hall's far-sighted gifts of them to The Beatles, made when the group visited New York City in February 1964 to appear on the Ed Sullivan TV show. John Lennon had, in fact, been using a Model 325 since 1960, but it was now a little road-weary. Hall presented him with a free replacement, and George Harrison ended up with an even greater prize: one of the company's experimental 360-style 12-string electrics. Both young stars were eager to use their new instruments, and Harrison's opening chord on "A Hard Day's Night" (recorded that April) introduced millions of listeners to the distinctive, jangling sound of a Rickenbacker 12-string.

A rush for the guitars followed. The British weekly music paper *Melody Maker* called electric 12-strings "the beat boys' secret weapon," and among the young players who subsequently fell in love with them was Roger McGuinn of The Byrds. His 360/12 can be heard on classic songs such as "Turn, Turn, Turn," "Eight Miles High," and "Mr. Tambourine Man," and he signed the scratchplate of the more recent Rickenbacker 12-string in our photo (right), which was made in the early 1990s.

> *The Rickenbacker 12-string sound is a sound on its own.*
>
> George Harrison, The Beatles

Rickenbacker 360/12 signed by Roger McGuinn

Below: A recent 360/12 in a "mapleglo" finish, with Hi-Gain single-coil pickups, and mono and stereo ("Rick-O-Sound") outputs.

Right: Rickenbackers with f-holes instead of the more usual "slashes" were produced for export to Europe; this one was marketed by Rose Morris in London.

Below: Guitar & Bass *called this "thin full body" deluxe model "as wide as the ocean, and twice as glamorous."*

More Rickys

Six-string Rickenbacker 300s, have attracted a long list of eminent musicians, from The Who's Pete Townshend to Peter Buck of R.E.M., Susanna Hoffs (The Bangles), and Johnny Marr (The Smiths), while many of the company's post-Rossmeisl models are also strikingly distinctive. The competitively priced 200 series, launched in 1984, was created (as the firm's publicity put it) "to satisfy even the most demanding musicians, with low cost being only a secondary design factor." The 250 "El Dorado" seen here dates from the 1990s.

Rickenbacker basses

Rickenbacker's first bass guitar was the 4000 model, designed by Roger Rossmeisl and launched in 1957. Unlike the 1951 Fender Precision bass, which had a bolted-on neck, the 4000 was a "neck-through-body" design, in which the extended neck section forms the central core of the instrument, optimizing strength and sustain. The horns of its cutaways were in a "cresting wave" shape matched by the outline of its headstock, and it was fitted with a horseshoe pickup of the type that Rickenbacker had used since the 1930s.

The through-neck construction found on the 4000 was also adopted for two twin-pickup models—the 4001—introduced in 1961 and its plainer cousin, the 4001S. These added a conventional neck pickup to the "horseshoe" bridge unit (which was replaced by a more up-to-date transducer after 1964), and the 4001 sported a bound body and neck, plus deluxe triangular-shape fingerboard markers in place of the 4000's dots. The 4001S had dot markers and was unbound.

Once again, The Beatles (this time, specifically Paul McCartney) played an essential role in promoting these new Rickenbackers. During the group's visit to the Unite States in summer 1965, McCartney was presented with a left-handed 4001S, which he used on the studio recording sessions for the *Rubber Soul* album the following year. From that point on, he would alternate between the 4001S and his iconic Höfner violin bass, though by the time the sessions for *Sgt. Pepper* began (late 1966), the 4001S had become his main studio instrument.

1971 Rickenbacker 4001

In the limelight

Rickenbacker basses have subsequently been the choice of many other leading rock musicians: Chris Squire of Yes, John Entwistle (The Who), Geddy Lee from Rush, and, of course, Lemmy (Motörhead) are among their most prominent users. Lemmy, who played a 4000 during his time with Hawkwind, and has a 4001 bearing the stenciled slogan "Born To Lose, Out To Lunch," now favors the more recent 4003 and 4004 models. In 2001, Rickenbacker honored him with a limited edition 4004LK signature bass, boasting three pickups, gold hardware, and an elaborately carved body. The company has also been keen to promote its earlier instruments, especially those with now-historic associations. Its vintage reissue program, begun in 1984, has included two McCartney-style 4001s, while its current range offers bassists the best of both old and new, as well as fretless, five-string, and even eight-string models.

Above: *Lemmy playing his "Born to Lose, Out to Lunch" Rickenbacker.*

1966 Rickenbacker 4001S

1965 Rickenbacker 4005 Semi-acoustic

1976 Rickenbacker 4001 D63

Rickenbacker 4003S/8 8-stringer

1990s' Rickenbacker Paul McCartney model

> *"It's the shape. I'm a very cosmetic kind of bloke. If it doesn't look good, then I won't play it. I used to get Rickenbackers and then I'd have to change the pickups on them, but you don't have to do that now…they sound good as they are."*
>
> Lemmy explains why he likes Rickenbacker basses

"Superstrats"

The first players of Leo Fender's Stratocaster tended to use its vibrato only for comparatively gentle pitch bending. Though Jimi Hendrix and others went on to take things much further, there were physical limitations to the capabilities of Fender's original design, and by the late 1970s ,virtuoso rock players were seeking improved guitar hardware—not just vibratos, but also hotter pickups and faster necks—that would allow them to reach new heights of technical mastery and deliver their musical goods more effectively.

Two of the prime movers in this revolution were machinist Floyd Rose and ace guitarist Eddie Van Halen. Rose patented his now-famous "Locking Tremolo" in 1979: it clamps the strings at both the nut and the bridge, allows their pitches to be raised *and* lowered by its "whammy bar" (Fender's system and others permitted only lowering), and keeps the guitar in tune even when a player employs "divebombing" or other extreme techniques. Van Halen was the first high-profile adopter of the Floyd Rose system; he fitted it to a stripped-down Stratocaster-like instrument, known as the "Frankenstrat," that he had already put together using body and neck components purchased from a Californian guitar builder, Wayne Charvel.

Right: *The Eddie Van Halen Wolfgang model on the left features a quilted maple top and two humbuckers. The slim-bodied Washburn in the middle is equipped with a Floyd Rose trem, while the Ibanez on the right has an Edge Pro double-locking trem.*

What makes a Superstrat?

The Floyd Rose trem or a derivative, plus a mutated Stratocaster-style body equipped with very powerful pickups—often humbuckers, rather than the single-coil transducers favored by Fender—became the essential ingredients of what's come to be termed the Superstrat. Companies such as Kramer, which initially had an exclusive licensing deal with Floyd Rose, and was endorsed by Van Halen for several years, and Jackson, which acquired Wayne Charvel's business in 1978, were at the forefront of its development. The Jackson Soloist—perhaps the archetypal Superstrat—appeared in 1984, and more recently, other firms, including Washburn and Peavey, have produced similarly hot-rodded solids.

Above: *Def Leppard guitarist Phil Collen plays a Jackson Superstrat.*

Left and right: *Both the Jackson Soloists on this page are "neck through body" designs with alder bodies and Seymour Duncan pickups. The SL2HT on the left has a Floyd Rose tremolo.*

Takamine

The liner notes for Ry Cooder's 1979 album *Bop Till You Drop* credit "Mass K. Hirade, Takamine Guitars." Hirade had joined the Japanese company—named after Mount Takamine in central Japan—11 years earlier, and had made the custom electroacoustic flat-top, incorporating a bridge transducer and preamp, that Cooder had featured on the album. The same year saw the launch of Takamine's first "production" acoustic-electric model, the PT-007S, and its instruments quickly gained a following among guitarists seeking to use amplified acoustics on stage without a microphone. Early adopters included Cooder's friend and colleague David Lindley, Glenn Frey of The Eagles, Jerry Garcia of the Grateful Dead and Bruce Springsteen. Today, Takamines are the choice of a substantial percentage of acoustic-electric players around the world.

Above: *Ry Cooder.*

21st-century developments

The firm has retained its innovative edge. It was the first manufacturer to install a digital preamp in a guitar, and, in 2004, it pioneered the CoolTube unit—powered by an onboard dual-triode valve whose output can be "dialed in" to provide extra sonic warmth and volume. In 2005 it was invited to produce a commemorative guitar (appropriately named the GOO80TH) to mark the 80th anniversary of the Grand Ole Opry in Nashville, Tennessee, and it celebrated its own half-century of lutherie in 2012. Takamine currently makes its high-end guitars in Japan, but also has factories in China, Taiwan, and Korea.

Takamine *EF360SBG Bluegrass Dreadnought Electro*

Takamine *EAN 10C*

Takamine *EGMINI-BK Travel*

> "Think acoustic.
> Live electric.
> Play Takamine."
>
> *Takamine ad slogan*

Taylor

Luthier Bob Taylor cofounded the company bearing his name in 1974. It's always been based in Southern California, and its current headquarters are at El Cajon, a few miles east of San Diego. From small beginnings, Taylor has developed into a major producer of fine guitars, and it now makes several hundred a day. Such impressive production figures are possible thanks to its use of Computer Numeric Control (CNC) systems that combine automation, speed, and a high degree of precision. Taylor has a lengthy list of famous customers: its guitars are played by Dave Matthews, Prince, Zac Brown, John Rzeznik, Leo Kottke, and many other major names.

The firm is best known for its flat-tops, ranging from top-of-the-line Presentation and 900 series instruments to cheaper models—like the 200 and 100 series—that have laminated backs and sides (but solid spruce tops), and are built at a plant just across the Mexican border. More recently, Taylor has introduced some electrics, the most innovative of which is the thinline, cutaway-body T5 "hybrid" electroacoustic shown here. It's fitted with three transducers, though only one—the narrow, lipstick-like humbucker near the bridge—is visible externally. There's a second humbucker buried under the upper end of the fingerboard, and a "body sensor" mounted a few inches behind the bridge. They are selected and combined via a five-way switch, and can deliver everything from delicate, acoustic-like timbres to full-on electric sounds. To make the most of the instrument's versatility, Taylor recommends that players route its signals through two separate amp se-ups.

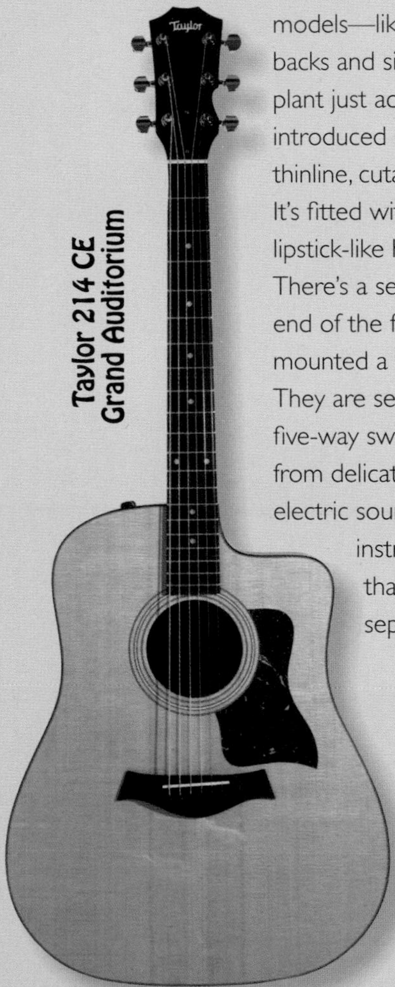

Taylor 214 CE Grand Auditorium

Taylor T5 Standard

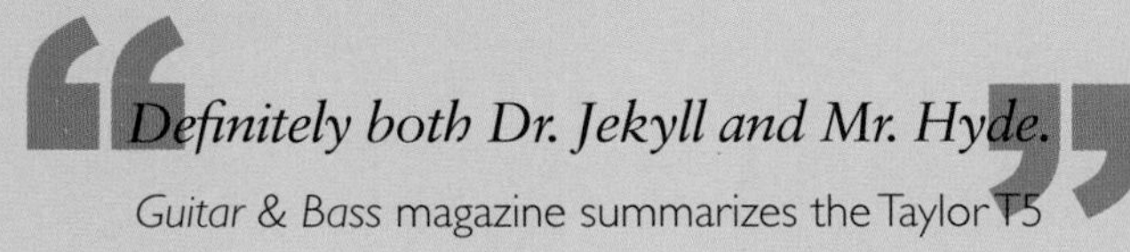

Definitely both Dr. Jekyll and Mr. Hyde.

Guitar & Bass magazine summarizes the Taylor T5

Setting up a cheap acoustic

Even budget-priced acoustics can have their playability and sound improved with a "setup." This involves some careful adjustments and a few new parts. Here we show how a guitar technician would undertake such a task. As you'll see, the process requires considerable skill and some specialized tools, and this feature is only intended to give you an idea of what's involved; you shouldn't attempt the job for yourself unless you really know what you're doing.

The guitar in our photographs has a plastic nut and bridge saddle, neither of which transmit vibrations as well as bone. Also, its neck requires a tweak, its frets need leveling and re-profiling, and it would benefit from having its plastic bridge pins replaced with ebony ones, which will produce a better overall sound. The original, glued-in nut is removed by placing a block of wood behind it, and tapping the block gently with a hammer. Once the nut's been taken out, the neck is straightened by adjusting the guitar's truss rod and checking the results with a straightedge. Next, an oilstone is used to level the frets, which are then profiled with files and glasspaper, and polished using 0000-grade steel wool and lemon oil.

A new blank (uncut) nut made from bone is put in position, and filed or ground into shape. A replacement saddle is also inserted, and ebony bridge pins are substituted for the original plastic ones. Holes for these are cut with a tool called a "reamer;" the holes need to be tapered, so that the pins fit tightly into them.

Fitting the strings

All the preceding tasks are carried out with no strings on the guitar, but now it's time to wind them on, cut slots for them in the new nut, and make fine adjustments to ensure that the action (the distance between the strings and the tops of the frets) is set to the player's preference. The top and bottom E strings are fitted first, and tightened sufficiently to keep them taut while slots are made to accommodate them, using special nut files. Once the outer strings are in position, the rest are added, and grooves are cut for these as well.

When the action's been optimized, strings, nut, and saddle are removed, and everything is polished and cleaned again before being reassembled. This time, though, a dab of glue is placed under the nut to hold it in place. Finally, once the guitar is tuned to pitch, the truss rod is given a final adjustment to leave a slight hollow in the face of the fretboard.

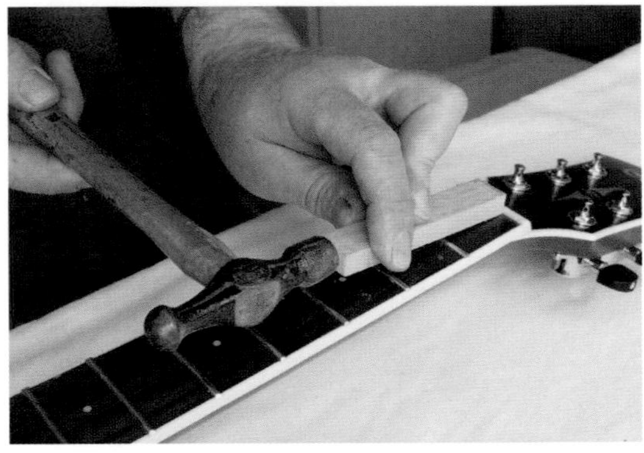

1 Removing the nut is done very cautiously, with the unstrung guitar laid down on a covered surface.

2 The oilstone—which must itself be completely flat—is a type of whetstone used to level the frets.

3 A needle file is applied to the fret ends, which are being rounded. This is delicate work!

Top Guitar Tip

Acoustics constructed entirely of laminated wood won't sound very much better, even after a setup. The instrument's top plays a key part in transmitting sound from its strings, and ideally this should be made of solid wood. It doesn't matter so much if the back and sides are laminated.

Below: *A modest flat-top like this one can be improved considerably by a setup—though it will never quite match the sound and feel of a more expensive model.*

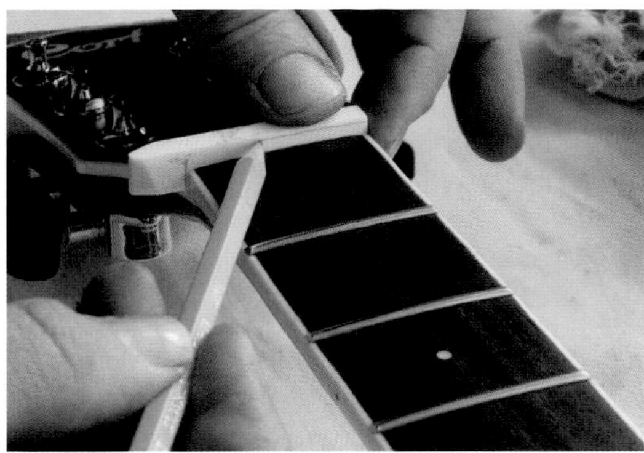

4 Initially, the top of the nut is set about 1/8 in (3 mm) higher than the fretboard, but it's lowered later.

5 A reamer making the tapered holes for the new bridge pins. The saddle's already in position.

6 The slots on the nut have been carefully adjusted to give the perfect final string height.

Guitar Heroes

GUITAR HERO

Duane Allman

Duane Allman's ghost stalks the history of electric slide guitar with an eerie resonance. Born in Nashville, Tennessee, in 1946, he and his family moved to Jacksonville, Florida, 11 years later. Duane and his younger brother Gregg, who later appeared with him in The Allman Brothers Band, became obsessed with music at an early age, and Duane was strongly influenced by hearing Jesse Ed Davis's slide guitar work on Taj Mahal's "Statesboro Blues" (recorded on the *Taj Mahal* album, released in 1968).

Duane Allman developed a revolutionary style, informed by Jimi Hendrix but underscored by post-bop jazz saxophonist John Coltrane, and his soaring leads alongside guitarist Dickey Betts propelled The Allman Brothers Band, formed in 1969, into the premier division. He also undertook regular session work at Alabama's legendary Muscle Shoals studio, where he appeared on tracks by (among others) Aretha Franklin, Clarence Carter, and Wilson Pickett. Allman's guitar work on Pickett's version of "Hey Jude" (1968) greatly impressed Eric Clapton, and in August 1970, he invited Allman to visit Criteria Studios in Miami, where Clapton's band Derek and the Dominos were recording what became the *Layla and Other Assorted Love Songs* album. At their first meeting the two guitar giants apparently jammed nonstop for over 15 hours. Allman refused an invitation to join the Dominos, but his distinctive playing is featured extensively on the double LP—most famously on its title track.

The Dominos' album appeared in 1970, and with the release of Allman Brothers' own live double *At Fillmore East* the following year, Duane Allman looked to be set for global stardom. However, tragedy was to intervene, and before the depth of his musicianship had been fully appreciated, he died, aged just 24, on October 29, 1971, after his Harley-Davidson motorcycle collided with a truck in Macon, Georgia.

Above: *Duane Allman often played a 1961-62 cherry-finish Gibson Les Paul SG Standard—a gift from fellow band member Dickey Betts.*

> *The naturalness of a spur-of-the-moment type of thing is what I consider the valuablest asset of our band.*
>
> Duane Allman

Below: *Duane takes a break during a studio session in about 1970, with his Les Paul still strapped on.*

Favorite Gear

Duane Allman used a Gibson SG and a Gibson Les Paul, played through 50-W Marshalls and 4 x 12-in (30-cm) cabinets with no effects. His slide was made from a glass Coricidin (cold and flu medicine) bottle, whose sound he preferred to that of a metal slide; many later players have copied his choice.

Major Albums

1969

The Allman Brothers Band

The group's debut album, with Duane and Dickey Betts on guitar, Duane's brother Gregg on vocals and organ, Berry Oakley on bass, and two drummers: Butch Trucks and Jai Johanny Johanson. Includes the classic "Whipping Post."

1970

Idlewild South

The Allmans' second LP, which sold better than its predecessor, and features standout tracks such as "In Memory of Elizabeth Reed."

1970

Derek and the Dominos: Layla and Other Assorted Love Songs

Duane's arrival at the sessions for this album by Eric Clapton and his band provided both inspiration and focus for the project, and his contribution to "Layla" itself was especially important. Clapton subsequently recalled that "It was only after Duane arrived and I'd said 'Would you mind playing on the album?' that we sat down and composed the lines and things."

1971

At Fillmore East

Recorded live at the famous New York venue. Showcases the band's powerful, extended improvisations; "Mountain Jam" clocks in at 33 minutes plus, and makes full use of Duane Allman's and Dickey Betts's" twin guitars for harmony and counterpoint.

1972

Duane Allman—An Anthology

This posthumous compilation contains a valuable cross section of Allman's work, including tracks from his Muscle Shoals sessions.

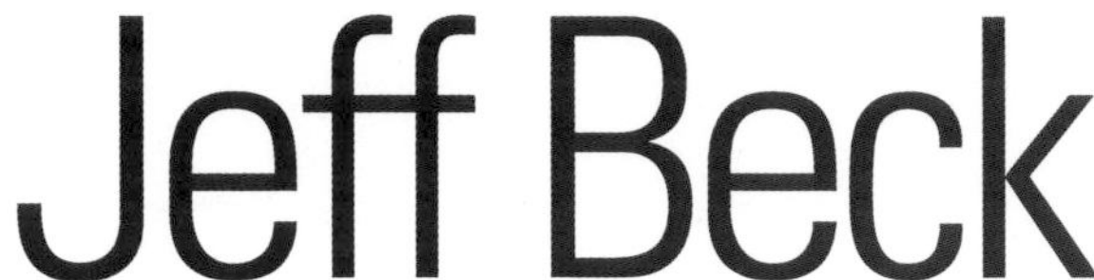

Jeff Beck

Jeff Beck was born in the southeastern English county of Surrey in 1944. From an early age, he was influenced by rock'n'roll, jazz, and blues, and he also recalls hearing Les Paul and Mary Ford's ingeniously overdubbed "How High The Moon" (1951) on the radio as a boy: "I remember sitting up and listening to it at night and my mum said, 'Don't get too excited, it's all done with tricks!' And from the minute she told me not to take it seriously…I took it seriously!"

Though his musical career began in 1963 with an obscure London group, The Tridents, it was when he replaced Eric Clapton in The Yardbirds in 1965 that Beck first registered on the rock radar. He made just one LP with the band, but was soon pushing the boundaries (and the decibel levels) of popular music with his unique soloing style. He, Rod Stewart, and Ronnie Wood went on to form The Jeff Beck Group, which took Cream's blues-inspired riffing one crucial stage further, and created a template that was subsequently copied by countless heavy metal groups.

His next major venture was the "power trio" Beck Bogert Appice (1972–74), and he then embraced jazz-fusion on a pair of platinum-selling instrumental albums, *Blow By Blow* (1975) and *Wired* (1976). Both were produced by Sir George Martin, famous for his work with The Beatles and one of Beck's heroes: "He was a career-maker for me. Delightful in every way…He brought out the best in me…[and] I wish I'd done more with him."

There have sometimes been lengthy gaps between Jeff Beck's albums, but *Emotion & Commotion* (2010), his first for seven years, is one of his finest and most eclectic, and won two Grammy awards in 2010. At the Grammy ceremony in Los Angeles, Beck performed music made famous by Les Paul, who had died the previous year. He's paid further tribute to his early idol with a live album, *Rock'n'Roll Party (Honoring Les Paul)*, released in 2011.

Left: *A recent replica of the heavily modified, "oxblood" finish 1954 Gibson Les Paul used by Beck in the 1970s.*

Below and opposite: *Beck in action on stage. Below, he is using his thumb to pick out a riff on a surf green Fender Stratocaster.*

Favorite Gear

Jeff Beck's main guitar is a Fender Stratocaster. In the 1980s, he switched from using a pick to playing fingerstyle: "I kept dropping [the pick at gigs]…and in the end I just carried on with my thumb and fingers. One night I realized I'd done half an hour without it. The whole audience was waiting for me to pick it up, and I thought, 'Sod 'em!'" He uses Marshall and Fender amps, and tends to avoid effects.

> *It just proves if you keep going you just might get there.*
>
> Jeff Beck

Major Albums

1966

Yardbirds (released in the United States and elsewhere as *Over Under Sideways Down*), Beck's only LP with the band: it contains feedback-drenched highlights like "Lost Woman," "The Nazz Are Blue," and the eponymous "Jeff's Boogie."

1968

The Jeff Beck Group: Truth

This album's sometimes described as having "invented heavy metal": to record Beck's guitar, the engineer locked his amp in a cupboard and placed a mic outside the door! Also features Rod Stewart, Ronnie Wood (on bass, not guitar), and drummer Micky Waller.

1975

Blow By Blow

1976

Wired

For many, these jazz-influenced instrumental LPs are pure, undiluted genius. Keyboard player Jan Hammer, famous for his work with John McLaughlin's Mahavishnu Orchestra, guests on *Wired*.

2010

Emotion & Commotion

Scarily wide-ranging, from the orchestral Led Zeppisms of "Hammerhead" to a whammied take on "Somewhere Over The Rainbow" and a fabulously bluesy "I Put A Spell On You."

Matt Bellamy

Matt Bellamy of Muse was born in Cambridge, England in 1978. His father, George, was active on the British music scene in the 1960s and 1970s, and is best known for playing rhythm guitar on the Tornados' classic instrumental hit "Telstar" (1962), produced by Joe Meek. Matt spent most of his childhood and teenage years in the coastal town of Teignmouth, south Devon, where the band that eventually became Muse came together in 1994.

Bellamy is Muse's guitarist, pianist, singer, and principal songwriter; its other two members are drummer Dominic Howard and bassist Chris Wolstenholme. The group spent the mid-1990s gigging until Dennis Smith, owner of the famous Sawmills recording studio (located on the River Fowey in Cornwall, some 65 miles/105 km west of Teignmouth) launched its recording career with a couple of EPs on his own label, and set up the Taste Media production company to look after the band. Taste released Muse's first three albums (starting with *Showbiz* in 1999), and steering clear of large record companies in their early years gave Bellamy and his colleagues the freedom they needed to develop. Muse eventually established the Helium 3 label (a subdivision of Warner Brothers) for *Black Holes and Revelations* (2006), which reached No.1 in the U.K. and No.9 in the United States. The band has enjoyed massive subsequent success with its unique brand of eclectic, often histrionic rock. Bellamy's lyrics display an obsession with shadowy politics, conspiracy theories, and apocalyptic events, while his guitar work is dizzyingly pyrotechnic, and his skillful use of effects can make Muse sound more like a ten-piece than a trio.

Below: *Muse's Matt Bellamy has been called "the 21st century's first real guitar hero." His Hugh Manson guitars feature touch sensitive MIDI control screens that can adjust effects and operate stage lighting.*

Favorite Gear

Matt's equipment is almost all customized or modified. Devon-based luthier Hugh Manson builds many of his guitars, which are combined with effects such as ZVex's Fuzz Factory and Vexter Wah Probe, and the MXR Phase 90. His other axes include an Ibanez Destroyer, a Gibson Les Paul DC Lite, a limited edition Fender Aloha Stratocaster with an aluminum body, a Parker Fly for whammy work, a Gibson SG-X, a Peavey EVH Wolfgang, and a Yamaha Pacifica. He's a bit of a pedal junkie, but lately he's refined his pedalboard by adding a MIDI controller. Favorite devices include the Line 6 Echo Pro that he used extensively on Muse's *Absolution* album (2003). Amp-wise, he can choose from a Diezel VH4 MIDI-controlled head, a Marshall JCM 2000 DSL 100 with 4 x 12-in (30-cm) cabs, a Fender Hotrod DeVille 410, a Soldano Decatone, and a Matchless DC-30.

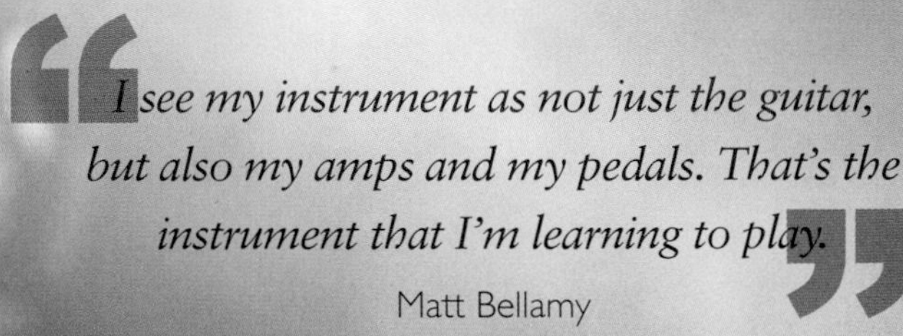

I see my instrument as not just the guitar, but also my amps and my pedals. That's the instrument that I'm learning to play.

Matt Bellamy

This page: *Matt Bellamy on tour with Muse in Hungary and Portugal in 2010. His double-neck instrument—known as the "Casinocaster"—is another Hugh Manson special, with a fretless upper fingerboard.*

Matt Bellamy in Other People's Words...

"To my generation Eric Clapton was someone who excelled at his instrument. I don't come across any musicians in the U.K. who can show it off in the same way, except Matt Bellamy from Muse."
Producer John Leckie

"For a three-piece Muse make such an incredible sound. We picked up a lot from them and I did get some tips from Matt Bellamy. For a guitar player he's got very small hands with very short fingers!"
Daniel Fisher formerly of The Cooper Temple Clause

Ritchie Blackmore

Ritchie Blackmore comes from England's West Country: born in 1945 in Weston-super-Mare, he was given his first guitar at the age of 11 by his father, who made him take classical lessons for a year. While Blackmore benefited from this formal teaching, jazz, rock'n'roll, skiffle, and the wizardry of Les Paul were more important teenage influences, and he credits session man Big Jim Sullivan (famous for his long association with Tom Jones) for helping him to develop his musical skills in the way he needed. In 1962, aged just 17, he had a brief stint in Screaming Lord Sutch's backing group; he went on to work for legendary pop producer Joe Meek, and, over the next few years, was involved in a range of other musical projects in Britain and Germany.

He joined what became Deep Purple in 1968. The group's first major hit was a cover version of Joe South's "Hush" (1968), but by 1970 it had moved away from its original, progressive/psychedelic style toward all-out rock. Though overwhelmingly successful, the band suffered from internal tensions and splits: Blackmore left in 1975 to form Rainbow, and Purple itself broke up in 1976. Rainbow, too, was a dominant force in British rock, but was dogged by personnel changes and musical differences; after its implosion in 1984, Blackmore agreed to rejoin a "classic" Deep Purple lineup, alongside keyboardist Jon Lord, singer Ian Gillan, bassist Roger Glover, and drummer Ian Paice. Gillan was replaced in 1989 by ex-Rainbow vocalist Joe Lynn Turner, but had returned to the band by 1992. However, continuing disagreements resulted in Blackmore's final departure from Purple in November 1993.

A relaunched Rainbow was active until 1997, but Blackmore then made a radical change in direction, forming Blackmore's Night with American singer Candice Night, whom he married in 2008. The group uses acoustic and electric instruments, is strongly influenced by Renaissance music, and favors small, intimate venues where (as Ritchie says) he can "connect with his audience rather than blow them away."

Favorite Gear

Blackmore used a Gibson ES-335 at the start of his career, but is most closely associated with the Fender Stratocaster. He customizes his Strats by scalloping their fretboards—taping up the frets, then using sandpaper. "I groove out the wood between the frets so they're concave. I can get a really good bend to the note this way." With Deep Purple and Rainbow, he mainly played through modified Marshall stacks. "I knew Jim Marshall personally, and he boosted them for me…[so they were] pushing out about 500 watts." For his acoustic work in Blackmore's Night, he favors Lakewood and Alvarez-Yairi flat-tops, amplified as little as possible.

Below: *Ritchie Blackmore performing with Blackmore's Night at Chicago's House of Blues on October 17, 2009. The set included old favorites like "Black Night," as well as more recent material.*

"That was just a riff I made up on the spur of the moment in Switzerland...It was a case of just keeping it incredibly simple. Pete Townshend told me "you've got to keep things simple and take the audience with you." That was very profound."

Ritchie Blackmore speaks about the genesis of his famous riff for "Smoke On The Water" (1972)

Major Albums

1970

Deep Purple in Rock

Showcases the band's "classic" lineup (Blackmore, Gillan, Lord, Glover, Paice), and—as suggested by the title—defines its musical direction. Standout tracks include the 10-minute, 18-second-long "Child In Time," on which Blackmore plays a Gibson ES-335 instead of a Strat.

1972

Deep Purple: *Machine Head*

Recorded in Montreux, Switzerland: "Smoke On The Water," a song about the fire in the Casino there during a Frank Zappa concert in 1971, features one of the best-known rock guitar riffs of all time.

1976

Rainbow: *Rising*

Perhaps this band's finest album. Ronnie James Dio is on vocals, and Blackmore's solo on "Stargazer" is a tour de force.

2001

Blackmore's Night: *Fires at Midnight*

A good introduction to Ritchie Blackmore's current musical direction.

Right: *Blackmore in the mid-1970s—playing live with Deep Purple on a*

Joe Bonamassa

Joe Bonamassa (born in New Hartford, upstate New York, in 1977) started playing guitar when he was four, and discovered the blues soon afterward. He undertook his first paid gig as an 11-year-old, and his talent quickly attracted the attention and praise of some of the genre's stars. He won endorsements from James Cotton, Albert Collins, and, most famously, B.B. King, with whom he undertook a 15-date tour while still at school.

His influences include not only American blues and rock, but also British artists such as Eric Clapton, Jeff Beck, Paul Kossoff of Free, and Gary Moore: "I grew up listening to English stuff... When I first got [to the U.K.] I expected every kid on the corner would have a Les Paul, a Bluesbreaker combo and play like Peter Green. But what I found was a whole bunch of guys with Strats and Super Reverbs trying to be Stevie Ray Vaughan... I got to [Stevie Ray] later. He's a fantastic guitar player and I liked the way he put it together, but by that time I'd kinda heard it before." Much as Bonamassa loves the blues, he's also aware of its melodic and harmonic limitations. "Inevitably, after 50 or 60 years of the electric guitar, all those guys that came before me... have played all the notes on the fretboard way before I played them. The only hope for new players is to combine various styles that wouldn't normally go together... maybe mix a little classical music with some blues or even put some bluegrass with rock. It's extremely hard when you're working within the blues framework to keep it fresh for yourself, let alone your audience."

Bonamassa's first solo album, *A New Day Yesterday*, was released in 2000, and his recordings and concerts have been highly acclaimed on both sides of the Atlantic. He's issued ten other solo CDs to date, and is also part of the supergroup Black Country Communion, with Glenn Hughes (ex-Deep Purple) on vocals and bass, keyboard player Derek Sherinian, and drummer Jason Bonham (son of Led Zeppelin's John Bonham).

Left: *The Gibson Joe Bonamassa Les Paul Studio model, launched in 2011.*

Below: *Bonamassa appearing at Budapest's Millenáris Theatrum in May 2009.*

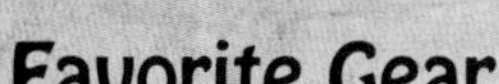

Favorite Gear

Bonamassa owns over 200 guitars. His favorite is his Joe Bonamassa signature Gibson Les Paul (serial number 001); other "regulars" include two Gibson Les Paul '59 reissues, a 1981 Gibson Flying V and three Gibson Firebirds. His amps are Marshalls and Van Weeldens, and for effects he uses a Jeorge Tripps Custom Crybaby Wah and Fuzz Face, a Lehle ABC switch, a Whirlwind phaser, an Ibanez Tube Screamer, and a Way Huge Pork Loin overdrive.

> *Whether you're conscious of it or not, your guitar playing is part, or all, of your personality…Everybody has their own sound instinctively inside them.*
>
> Joe Bonamassa

Major Albums

2000

A New Day Yesterday

The album demonstrates Bonamassa's lifelong allegiance to British rock by taking its title from a late 1960s Jethro Tull song; there are also covers of numbers by Rory Gallagher and Free. Guest musicians include Gregg Allman, Leslie West of Mountain, and Rick Derringer.

2004

Had To Cry Today

Whether playing at warp speed, or remodeling B.B. King's "Never Make Your Move Too Soon" Bonamassa manages to sound familiar, yet inventive, at the same time.

2006

You & Me

Any album that starts with a 1920s Charley Patton number ("High Water Everywhere," inspired by the devastating Mississippi flood of 1927) shows this man is serious! Blues for the new millennium.

Above: *This combined baritone- and regular-neck guitar was made for Joe by Ernie Ball in 2009. The baritone neck is the upper one.*

Right: *Joe says he needs a Les Paul "to be himself."*

Roy Buchanan

Roy Buchanan (1939–88) was born in Arkansas, but grew up in Bakersfield, California, where his earliest meaningful musical experiences were at religious meetings: "Gospel was how I got into black music," he later recalled. His first instrument was a pedal steel guitar, but in 1953 he bought the Fender Telecaster that proved to be his "ticket to ride." Two years later, he'd headed south to Los Angeles, and by 1958 was lead guitarist for Dale Hawkins, composer of the rockabilly classic "Susie-Q." In about 1961, he moved on to work for Dale's cousin Ronnie, another prominent rockabilly artist, whose backing group also featured Robbie Robertson (soon to be famous with The Band). Robertson benefited from Buchanan's tuition and advice, and describes him as "the most remarkable guitarist I had seen." Despite Buchanan's abilities, however, he remained in obscurity, and spent most of the 1960s in Washington, D.C., where, for a time, he took a hairdressing job to support his family. By the early 1970s, though, he was back in full-time musical action, and belatedly attracting attention from press and TV.

His first solo album, *Roy Buchanan*, was released in 1972, and *Second Album* a year later. They caught the ears of The Rolling Stones, who some years before, had allegedly sought to recruit him as Brian Jones's replacement before settling on Mick Taylor. Roy turned them down, just as he'd rebuff Bob Dylan and John Lennon over the years. "I didn't want to travel…I didn't know the material and I didn't figure I could do the job right," was how he explained his decision. He quit recording in the early 1980s, but was persuaded to return to the studio by Alligator Records, which issued *When A Guitar Plays The Blues* in 1985. It won a Grammy nomination for best blues album of the year, and follow-ups *Dancing On The Edge* and *Hot Wires* also sold well. However, his career—and his life—were derailed by tragedy after his youngest grandchild became a cot-death victim. Following a period of increasingly bizarre behavior, Buchanan was arrested for public intoxication in Fairfax, Virginia, in August 1988, and was later found hanged in his cell.

Left: *An early Telecaster similar to Roy Buchanan's. "I liked the tone...it sounded a lot like a steel guitar," he said later.*

Favorite Gear

"Nancy," Roy Buchanan's 1953 Fender Telecaster, is the guitar that remains most closely associated with him. Nancy had a massive neck and (according to pickup expert Don Mare) a partially shorted bridge pickup coil, giving her a uniquely shrill sound. He also had '54 and '55 Teles in his studio armory, and, toward the end of his career, collaborated with luthier Roger Fritz on a line of signature electrics. His acoustic workhorses were two Martins: a D-28 and a D-35.

Early on, Buchanan favored Fender amps (a 4 x 10-in/25-cm Super Reverb or a 2 x 10-in/25-cm Vibrolux), and later opted for a Roland JC120 Jazz Chorus, a 100-W Marshall with reverb, or a Peavey Classic 2 x 12-in (30-cm) combo.

> *Roy, if you don't play with feeling, don't play it.*
>
> A long-remembered piece of advice from Buchanan's first music teacher

***Left:** Buchanan on stage in The Netherlands, February 1985.* When A Guitar Plays The Blues, *his first album in four years, appeared that summer.*

Facts about Roy Buchanan

He never learned the names for most of the chords he used.

His first-ever guitar hero was jazz player Barney Kessel.

He once had a heart-shaped electric made for him out of solid granite.

He wore his guitar high, copying the style of Les Paul, and in his early days, would play with his back to the audience so no one could steal his licks.

Eric Clapton

Eric Clapton was born in the English county of Surrey in 1945. His early musical inspiration came from the blues, and, as he recalls, "I started my career playing an acoustic guitar in a pub by myself." However, it was his electric work with The Yardbirds (which he joined in 1963) and then John Mayall's Bluesbreakers that won him fervent admiration, and even worship: a piece of London graffiti from the period proclaimed "Clapton is God." Cream, the seminal "power trio" he formed in 1966 with bassist Jack Bruce and drummer Ginger Baker, split up after two years: Clapton then collaborated with Baker in the short-lived Blind Faith, before starting a musical association with American husband-and-wife Delaney and Bonnie Bramlett. Three members of Delaney & Bonnie and Friends were to join him in Derek and the Dominos, whose classic album *Layla and Other Assorted Love Songs* appeared in 1970.

Derek and the Dominos was Clapton's last "official" group and, at the time of its breakup, he was suffering from serious drug problems. An allstar live concert, designed to relaunch his career and organized by The Who's Pete Townshend, took place at London's Rainbow Theater in January 1973. It also marked Clapton's first appearance with "Blackie," the Fender Stratocaster that had supplanted Gibson Les Pauls and ES-335s as his favorite instrument. "Blackie" would enjoy 12 years in the spotlight; in 1985, it was replaced as Clapton's "live workhorse" by the signature model custom shop Strats he's used ever since.

From his classic covers of songs by J.J. Cale ("After Midnight," "Cocaine") and Bob Marley ("I Shot The Sheriff") to his collaborations with George Harrison, B.B. King, Bob Dylan, and other greats, and his multiple Grammy-winning *Unplugged* album (1992), Clapton's solo work has been so rich and varied that it's almost impossible to summarize. In 2004, he told *Guitar & Bass* that he considered himself "just…a musician who plays the blues," and was keen to emphasize his continuing dedication to performing and recording: "I'm not retiring yet. In a way, I've been retiring all my life…I mean, I quit The Yardbirds when I was 19, and I was pretty convinced it was the end then!…I guess one day I'll retire, but I don't know when."

Above left: *A recent "Blackie" replica. Clapton auctioned the original to raise funds for his Crossroads Center in 2004.*

Above: *Eric Clapton playing live at the Hard Rock Calling Festival on June 28, 2008 in London's Hyde Park.*

Favorite Gear

Eric Clapton rarely strays from Fender Stratocasters as his main stage electrics. As Lee Dickson, his longtime guitar tech, explains: "We basically take four out on the road: a slide one, a main one, an identical spare and a 'spare spare'." Dickson describes Clapton's amp selection as "ever-changing," though Fender Twins, Marshalls, and Music Mans have all been favorites over the years. His acoustics include vintage Martins (he used a 1939 000-42 on the *Unplugged* album), as well as National and Dobro resonators.

When you find the pocket with other musicians, when you hit something that doesn't have to necessarily go anywhere because it feels so right—and seeing how long you can keep that feeling—that's where the joy is.

Eric Clapton, 2005

Did You Know?

Clapton, who has had widely publicized past problems with drink and drugs, set up the Antigua-based Crossroads Center for the treatment of recovering substance abusers in 1998. He established the Crossroads Guitar Festival in 2004 to help fund the project.

Cream's *Wheels Of Fire* (1968) was the first-ever platinum-selling double album.

Eric Clapton has used a variety of unusual pseudonyms for his guest appearances on record: these have included Mr Crapdock, Eddie Clayton, King Cool, and Sir Cedric Clayton.

He made his first solo appearance at London's Royal Albert Hall in January 1987, and is the only person ever to have been allowed to smoke on stage there. He's now given up!

Clapton cannot read music.

Above: *On stage at the Crossroads Guitar Festival in Toyota Park, southwest Chicago, on June 26, 2010.*

Left: *Clapton and his band (drummer Steve Jordan is behind him) on June 1, 2006 at Ahoy, a sporting arena in Rotterdam, Holland, that regularly hosts large-scale rock concerts. Also appearing were Robert Cray and Derek Trucks.*

GUITAR HERO

Kurt Cobain

The career of Kurt Donald Cobain (1967–94) bears numerous, often unhappy, parallels with that of another short-lived rock star from a generation earlier: Jimi Hendrix. Both emerged from Seattle, in the American northwest; both were left-handed; both fronted three-piece bands; and both have left an enduring musical mark despite producing only a handful of albums.

Cobain grew up on the Pacific coast some 100 miles (160 km) west of Seattle, and formed Nirvana—sometimes described as the archetypical "grunge" group—with bassist Krist Novoselic in about 1986. Dave Grohl replaced Chad Channing as the band's drummer in 1990. Major success came a year later with the release of Nirvana's single "Smells Like Teen Spirit," a few days prior to the launch of the *Nevermind* album from which it was taken. Both were massive sellers, but Cobain struggled to cope with the effects of fame. Drug- and health-related problems held up work on new material, resulting in the release of a compilation CD, *Insecticide* (1992), as Nirvana's follow-up to *Nevermind*. A studio album, *In Utero*, appeared the following year, and proved to be another chart-topper; however, Cobain's personal difficulties had grown steadily worse, and on April 5, 1994, five months after Nirvana had recorded its now-celebrated *Unplugged in New York* session for MTV, he shot himself at his home in Seattle. His suicide note contained a line from Neil Young's "My My, Hey Hey": "It's better to burn out than to fade away."

When discussing his future plans at the start of the year, he had spoken of his many unfulfilled musical ambitions. "I have lots of ideas that have nothing to do with the mass conception of grunge that has been force-fed to the record-buying public for the last few years. Whether I will be able to do everything I want to do as a part of Nirvana remains to be seen."

Left: *The Jag-Stang combines aspects of Kurt Cobain's two favorite Fender guitars: the Jaguar and the Mustang. This one's finished in sonic blue.*

Right: *Kurt Cobain on stage with Nirvana at the U.K.'s Reading Festival in August 1991. The slogan on his black Strat was borrowed from Arizona punk rockers, The Feederz.*

Favorite Gear

Cobain's favorite guitars were Fender Jaguars and Mustangs, and he collaborated with Fender on the development of a new model combining aspects of both instruments, named (simply but appropriately) the Jag-Stang. His amp setup varied: on stage he'd often use a PA amp for a guitar head, "because I can never find an amp that's powerful enough, and because I don't want to have to deal with hauling ten Marshall heads. I'm lazy—I like to have it all in one package." His equipment also included a Mesa/Boogie preamp, Radio Shack speakers, an echo flanger, and a Roland distortion pedal.

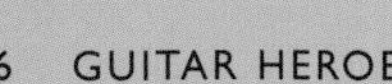

> *The Bay City Rollers after an assault by Black Sabbath.*
>
> Kurt Cobain's (tongue-in-cheek?) description of Nirvana's sound

Nirvana's Studio Albums

1989

Bleach

Recorded (for the independent Sub Pop label) before Dave Grohl joined the band; drums are played by Chad Channing and Dale Crover. Well received by the critics, but not initially a big seller, though it benefited from the band's subsequent success.

1991

Nevermind

Given the provisional title *Sheep*, this was Nirvana's "breakthrough" album, and its first for a major label, Geffen subsidiary DGC. It has sold more than 30 million copies worldwide, and contains four hit singles: "Smells Like Teen Spirit," "Come As You Are," "Lithium," and "In Bloom."

1993

In Utero

The band's final studio disc, with a much rougher-edged sound than its predecessor, and a generally darker mood: among the songs are "Heart-Shaped Box," "Dumb," and the ominously titled "Rape Me."

> *I can't play like [classical guitarist Andrés] Segovia...the flip side is that Segovia can't play like me.*
>
> Kurt Cobain

Ry Cooder

Ry Cooder has been described as "the unpaid curator of American roots music" and his fascination with genres such as blues and Tex-Mex, as well as his more recent collaborations with Cuban and Indian performers, have been a constant "ear-opener" for audiences and fellow musicians.

Best known as a slide guitarist—though he plays in many styles, and on other fretted instruments—Cooder was born in Los Angeles in 1947. He absorbed the blues not only from records, but through meeting and learning from musicians such as Josh White and Sleepy John Estes. His early career included stints in The Rising Sons (with Taj Mahal) and Captain Beefheart's Magic Band, and he quickly became a "first-call" L.A. session player; his deft slide work can be heard on LPs by (among many others) The Rolling Stones, Randy Newman, Van Morrison, and Little Feat.

His solo albums for Warner Bros., which came to feature a fairly regular team of collaborators—other top L.A. session men, gospel/R&B vocalist Bobby King, and accordionist Flaco Jimenez—covered fascinating, often neglected areas of popular music. Two of the finest are *Into The Purple Valley* (inspired by the Great Depression, and released in 1972), and *Bop Till You Drop* (1979). In the 1980s, Cooder was increasingly involved in movie soundtrack work, providing atmospheric scores for films such as *The Long Riders* (1980) and *Paris, Texas* (1984). 1987 saw the release of *Get Rhythm*, his final solo album for Warners, and over the following years, his musical focus was to widen. In the 1990s, he recorded with Indian *Mohan veena* virtuoso V. M. Bhatt (see Important Albums) and Malian guitarist Ali Farka Touré, and produced the platinum-selling *Buena Vista Social Club* album (1997). This classic album of Cuban music was recorded in Havana, and Cooder was fined $25,000 by the U.S. Government for participating in the project, which fell foul of its Trading With The Enemy Act.

Among Cooder's most recent work are his solo discs *Chávez Ravine* (2005) and *My Name is Buddy* (2007); both have contributions from his son, Joachim, who plays timbales and other percussion.

Favorite Gear

Cooder's electric guitars are rarely standard models. He combines bodies and pickups to create the distinctive sounds he requires (*Bop Till You Drop* featured a customized 1960s Stratocaster fitted with a pickup from an Oahu lap steel), and he has a penchant for Japanese-made instruments—like his electroacoustic Takamine, and his sometime bizarre-looking solids. Among his many acoustics are a Martin 00-28 and 000-18. Amps include a Magnatone, a Standel 25L, and a Gibson GA-20 (twinned with a 100-W Hiwatt Custom slave for live work), plus gizmos such as a Dan Armstrong Orange Squeezer and a Demeter Tremulator.

Left: *A recent Takamine electroacoustic—Ry Cooder was among the earliest major U.S. players to use Takamines, and his other Japanese guitars include electric models by Guyatone and Teisco.*

> *"I use a lot of tunings. I tune [my guitars] all different ways; chords, partial chords, sometimes unison. Sometimes it knocks itself over and bumps into another tuning."*
>
> Ry Cooder

Important Albums

1972

Into The Purple Valley

Features a memorable version of Woody Guthrie's "Vigilante Man," as well as a calypso to mark President Franklin D. Roosevelt's visit to Trinidad in 1936.

1979

Bop Till You Drop

Cooder's impeccable slide on tracks such as "I Think It's Going To Work Out Fine" and the sinister "The Very Thing That Makes You Rich…" sets a standard by which all pretenders to his throne are judged.

1984

Paris, Texas

Ry Cooder's soundtrack for Wim Wenders' movie includes bluesman Blind Willie Johnson's "Dark Was the Night, Cold Was The Ground." Cooder has spoken of Johnson's "completely unique" use of slide techniques, and his influence is strongly evident here. Cooder's own slide is made from the top of a sherry bottle. "I hate metal bottlenecks…they just don't sound right. You get a sharp edge but you lose the body of the sound."

1993

A Meeting By The River

A collaboration with V. M. Bhatt; his *Mohan veena* is a modified archtop fitted with 19 strings and played lap-style.

1994

Talking Timbuktu

On this Grammy winner, Cooder teams up with Malian star Ali Farka Touré (1939–2006), whose playing style has intriguing parallels with American blues.

Left: Ry Cooder performing in Milan, Italy, in 2009.

Duane Eddy

Duane Eddy is famous, above all, for his bassy guitar "twang"—a sound once likened by a record company executive to "somebody trying to stretch wire across the Grand Canyon!" His use of the lower strings for his distinctive riffs contrasts starkly with the higher-lying licks that were the order of the day before his emergence in the late 1950s, and his classic instrumentals are perennially popular.

Eddy was born in upstate New York in 1938, but moved to Arizona at the age of around 13. The music-loving teenager had already been playing guitar for several years, and spent much of his spare time at a local radio station in Phoenix. There, he made friends with Lee Hazlewood (1929–2007), a disc jockey who, as Eddy's record producer, was to take a major role in developing his echoey sound. Its key component was a 2,000-gallon water tank bought from a junk yard and installed in the studio: a loudspeaker connected to Eddy's amp was placed at one end of the tank, and a microphone at the other. As the guitarist recalls, "we blended [the signal] with a little tape echo, which was very popular in those days... Then Lee would take [the tapes] to get overdubbed at Gold Star in Hollywood, where they'd add a little bit of their chamber echo to our tank echo. I still like echo—it gives an atmosphere that's missing from a lot of records these days."

Duane Eddy's twangy guitar brought him a string of major American and European hits in the late 1950s and early 1960s (see panel). He went on to be a successful film actor and record producer, and in recent years his playing has graced records by The Art Of Noise, Cliff Richard, and other major names. His influence reaches even more widely—Lemmy, John Entwistle of The Who, The Pixies, Brian Setzer, and even The Cramps have all been admirers.

Right: *Gretsch unveiled this G6120DE Duane Eddy Signature guitar in 2011. It features DynaSonic single-coil pickups, a brass nut, an orange lacquer finish...and, of course, Duane's beloved Bigsby vibrato.*

Opposite: *Duane Eddy on stage at London's Royal Festival Hall—one of several shows he undertook in 2010 to mark the fiftieth anniversary of his first British tour.*

Favorite Gear

Duane Eddy is most closely associated with the red Gretsch 6120 (incorporating a Bigsby vibrato), that he purchased new in 1956, and used on his classic recordings. As he told *Guitar & Bass* in 2008, "The neck is so superior, it's the perfect shape. I just love it!...I did have a '52 or '53 [Gibson] Les Paul goldtop solidbody before that...I traded it in for the Gretsch." He has also used a signature model Gibson electric, as well as a Danelectro six-string bass. "The Dano is an octave lower than a regular guitar. With [some songs], I couldn't quite get the low sound that I like with a regular guitar, so I switch over to the Dano and it solves that problem." His amps have included a 100-W Magnatone with a spring echo and a 15-in (38-cm) JBL loudspeaker, and a Rivera.

> *[Music] doesn't change as much as people think—we're still playing three chords today; sometimes less! Any changes are superficial. Heavy metal is just rock'n'roll turned up to 11 instead of 6.*
>
> Duane Eddy, 2004

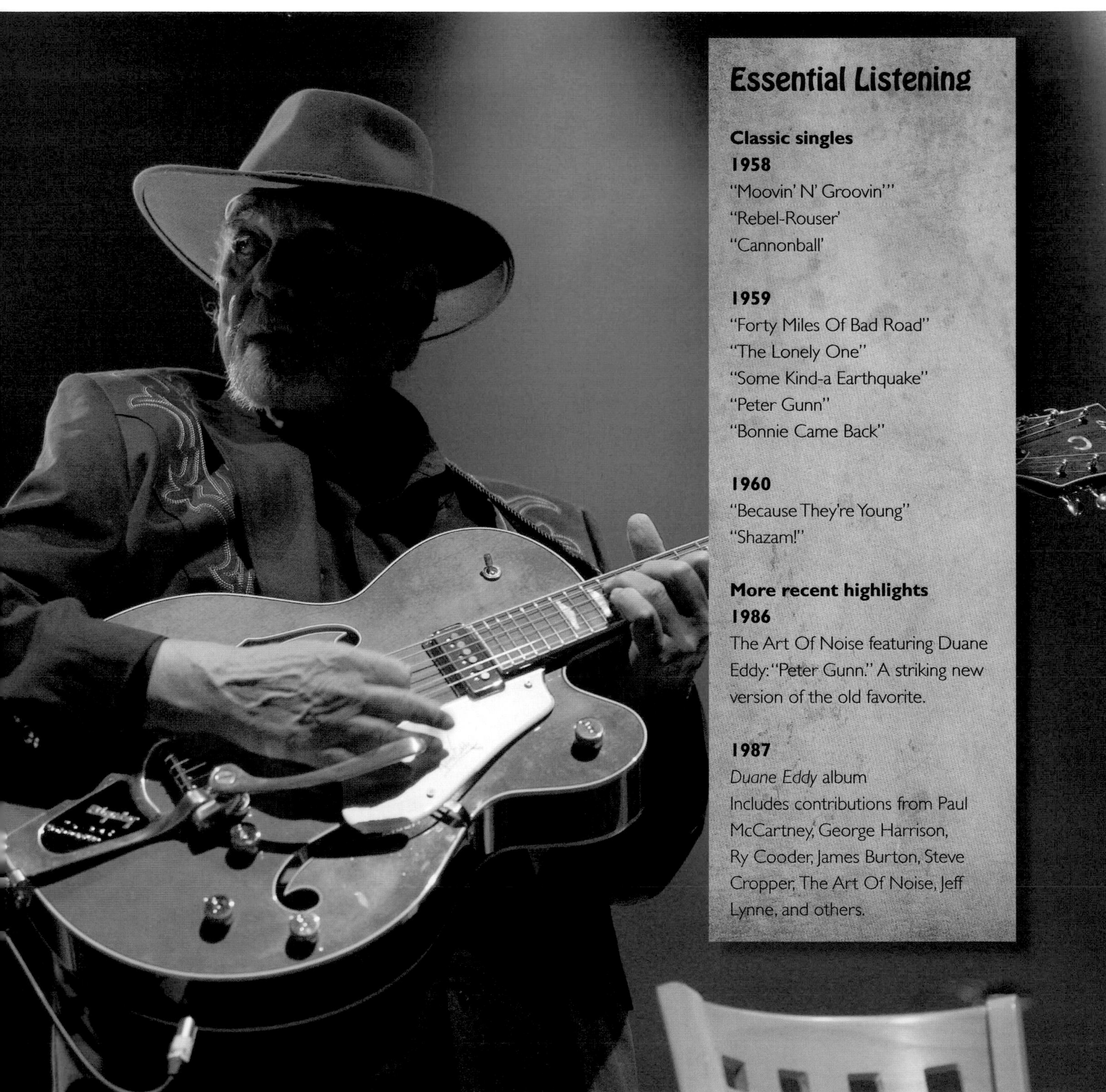

Essential Listening

Classic singles

1958

"Moovin' N' Groovin'"
"Rebel-Rouser'
"Cannonball'

1959

"Forty Miles Of Bad Road"
"The Lonely One"
"Some Kind-a Earthquake"
"Peter Gunn"
"Bonnie Came Back"

1960

"Because They're Young"
"Shazam!"

More recent highlights

1986

The Art Of Noise featuring Duane Eddy: "Peter Gunn." A striking new version of the old favorite.

1987

Duane Eddy album
Includes contributions from Paul McCartney, George Harrison, Ry Cooder, James Burton, Steve Cropper, The Art Of Noise, Jeff Lynne, and others.

GUITAR HERO

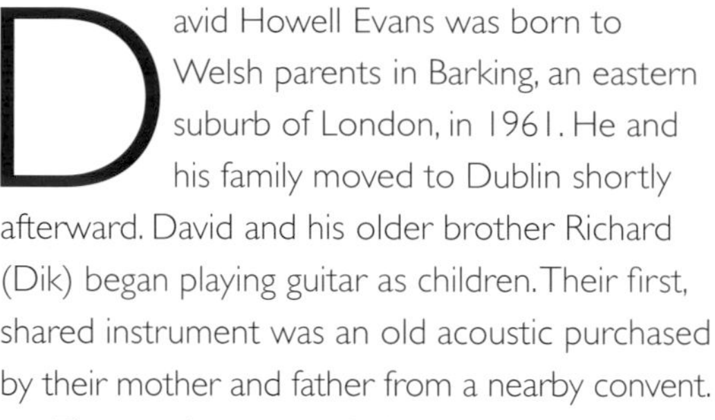

The Edge

Below: *A Gibson Explorer. The design was launched in 1958, but proved too radical for 1950s players.*

David Howell Evans was born to Welsh parents in Barking, an eastern suburb of London, in 1961. He and his family moved to Dublin shortly afterward. David and his older brother Richard (Dik) began playing guitar as children. Their first, shared instrument was an old acoustic purchased by their mother and father from a nearby convent.

The two boys attended Mount Temple Comprehensive School in Clontarf, on Dublin's Northside. There, in 1976, they responded to a note posted on a bulletin board by a fellow pupil, Larry Mullen Jr., seeking musicians for a band. The ad brought together five teenagers from Mount Temple: Mullen (a budding drummer), David and Dik Evans (on guitars), singer Paul Hewson, and bassist Adam Clayton. They started to perform as Feedback, and then as The Hype. Hewson was soon calling himself "Bono Vox" (or just "Bono"), while Dave Evans acquired a more enigmatic nickname: "The Edge." He remembers that "I didn't like much guitar playing when I was growing up…I just knew I didn't want to sound like anyone else." The young group flourished, and in 1978, after parting company with Dik Evans, chose a new name for itself: U2.

The quartet signed to Island Records in 1980, and although its first four albums sold well, it didn't enjoy global success until *The Unforgettable Fire* (1984), produced by Brian Eno and Daniel Lanois. A memorable appearance at Live Aid in 1985, followed by the release of *The Joshua Tree* (1987)—a Grammy winner, and U2's biggest seller to date—cemented the band's status, and its fortunes have since gone from strength to strength. It has now made 12 studio albums, and in 2010, it topped the Forbes.com website's list of high-earning musicians, with an income of $130m (nearly £85 million).

The Edge has been described as an "anti-guitar hero," and the ringing, richly textured electric sound he contributes to U2 owes much of its impact to delays and other signal processors. He explained to *Guitar & Bass* in 1995 that "I don't think about playing through an effect, I think about playing the whole thing," and added: "I have a deep-rooted sense that the most interesting territory is that which is beyond convention. In terms of creativity, instinct is always the thing, not intellect."

Above: *Bono and The Edge at Gillette Stadium, Foxborough, Massachusetts, September 2009. The venue has over 68,000 seats.*

Favorite Gear

The Edge's trademark guitar is his 1976 Gibson Explorer. He still uses it in the studio, though it's now been retired from live shows. His other instruments include Fender Stratocasters and Gibson Les Pauls, and he also has a 1962 Epiphone Casino (a twin-pickup, double cutaway thinline hollow-body), and a Gibson SJ-200 flat-top. His principal amp has always been his 1964 Vox AC30TB (TB stands for "top boost") combo, and among his numerous rack and pedal effects are digital delays by Korg, AMS (Advanced Music Systems), and TC Electronic.

> *Whenever I pick up a new instrument I try to find my own voice, find out what it can do.*
>
> The Edge

Below left: *The Edge performs at FedEx Field, Landover, Maryland on September 29, 2009, during U2's "360° Tour."*

Below: *Another gig from the "360° Tour," in Milan, Italy, July 8, 2009. The tour featured 110 performances worldwide.*

Did You Know?

In 2009, The Edge appeared, alongside Jack White and Led Zeppelin's Jimmy Page, in a documentary about the electric guitar, and the three stars' differing approaches to it. The film—named, appropriately, *It Might Get Loud*—was directed by Davis Guggenheim.

The Edge, a Welshman, is one of two U2 members who weren't born in Ireland; the other is the band's English bassist Adam Clayton.

In November 2005, The Edge, record producer Bob Ezrin, and Gibson CEO Henry Juszkiewicz set up the "Music Rising" charity to assist musicians whose instruments had been destroyed by the devastations of Hurricane Katrina. U2 supported the cause with a concert at New Orleans' Superdome in September 2006; the show also featured Green Day.

John Frusciante

John Frusciante was born in New York City in 1970. After his parents' marriage broke up, he and his mother moved west to Los Angeles. Obsessed by a wide range of music as a teenager, he developed a special fascination for a local band: the Red Hot Chili Peppers—studying and analyzing their songs, absorbing their distinctive blend of rock and funk, and becoming friendly with their guitar player Hillel Slovak. A few months after Slovak's death from a drug overdose in 1988, Frusciante was recruited as the group's guitarist, and a new drummer, Chad Smith, was also brought in alongside the two remaining founder members, bassist Flea and singer Anthony Kiedis.

The Chili Peppers' next two albums (*see* panel) were big sellers, but success took its toll on Frusciante, who suddenly quit the band during a Japanese tour in May 1992. *Guitar & Bass* later reported that he had even "attempt[ed] to break his arm so that he couldn't be talked out of his decision." Despite a serious drug problem, he had already begun work on a solo CD, *Niandra LaDes and Usually Just a T-Shirt*, which appeared in 1994. After recovering from illness and addiction, he rejoined the Chili Peppers four years later, and stayed until 2009. Throughout his long second stint with the band, he undertook numerous other projects, including solo albums, guest appearances on record with The Mars Volta, and, in 2004, sessions and gigs with Ataxia. That year, when speaking about his prolific output, he explained that "I write about 60 percent of the [Chili Peppers'] stuff, but it's as a guitar player, and that's it…I don't ever write the words for the band…So if a song comes to me and it's just an interesting guitar part, then I give it to [them]. If it comes to me and I'm singing and pulling out my notebook, then it's for me."

Frusciante's eventual departure from the Chili Peppers was an amicable one (his replacement, Josh Klinghoffer, had collaborated with him in Ataxia), and his guitar playing—sparser and more emotive than in his earlier years—is as widely admired as ever. A total of 30,000 listeners to BBC Radio 6 voted him "the greatest guitarist of the last 30 years" in 2010.

Above: *A 1961 Fender Stratocaster. "Pre-CBS" models like this are rated highly by John Frusciante and many other star players.*

Important Albums

Red Hot Chili Peppers albums featuring John Frusciante

1989
Mother's Milk
1991
Blood Sugar Sex Magik
1999
Californication
2002
By The Way
2006
Stadium Arcadium

Solo work

Frusciante has issued ten solo CDs; these include:

1994
Niandra LaDes and Usually Just a T-Shirt
2001
To Record Only Water for Ten Days
2004
Shadows Collide with People
2010
The Empyrean

> *The guitar players who I really get something out of are people like Sterling Morrison and Lou Reed with Velvet Underground, the guys in Fugazi, Matthew Ashman from Bow Wow Wow and Keith Levene from Public Image—people who used interesting chords and textures…It's extra important for me to understand why the person chose the notes they did, and to listen to it in relationship to the other instruments going on.*
>
> John Frusciante

Below: *John Frusciante in action during the Third Annual Hullabaloo (held to raise funds for the Silverlake Music Conservatory) at the Music Box, Henry Fonda Theater, Los Angeles, May 5, 2007.*

Favorite Gear

John Frusciante is a Fender devotee: "I love old Telecasters, Stratocasters and Jaguars—although when I first bought a Jaguar it was because I thought Tom Verlaine of Television played one, when in fact he was actually using a Jazzmaster. My first electric guitar was a Strat, though. I just love the way the Strat can be so many different instruments depending on who's playing it and the approach they take." Among his other favorites are Gibson SGs, a Gretsch White Falcon, and Martin acoustics. He uses Marshall amps, plus a wide range of effects pedals.

Billy Gibbons

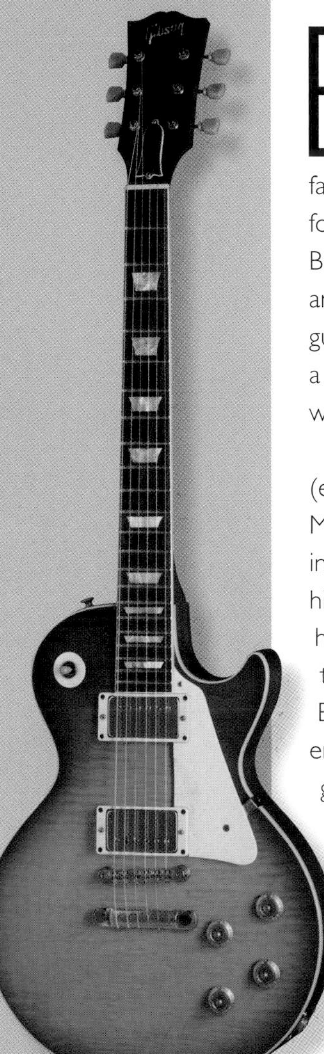

Billy F. Gibbons was born in Tanglewood, adjacent to the Uptown western suburb of Houston, Texas, in 1949. He shares his middle name, Frederick, with his father (1908–81), a pianist and bandleader who formerly provided live backing for silent movies. Billy's musical skills manifested themselves from an early age, and he acquired his first electric guitar, a Gibson Melody Maker (also the choice, a few years later, of Runaways' leader Joan Jett), when he was just 13.

Inspired by Elvis Presley, Jimmy Reed, and (especially) bluesman McKinley Morganfield, aka Muddy Waters, Billy Gibbons quickly became an integral part of his local music scene. In 1967, his group The Moving Sidewalks had a regional hit with his song "99th Floor"; a year later they were hired to support The Jimi Hendrix Experience for several U.S. tour dates, and Jimi endorsed Billy as an emerging talent. The young guitarist's musical future, though, lay not with the psychedelia of the Sidewalks, who split up in 1969, but in the bluesier, Tex-Mex-flavored style epitomized by ZZ Top. The all-Texan trio, also featuring Dusty Hill (bass) and Frank Beard (drums), made their concert debut in February 1970, and recorded their first LP the same year. The band's fame grew steadily throughout the decade (their first hit single, "La Grange," came from their 1973 album, *Tres Hombres*), but reached its zenith in the 1980s when their combination of musical potency and distinctive visual style made them favorites on MTV, which had launched in 1981. Their most successful album, currently certified as 10x platinum (having sold more than 10,000,000 in the United States) is *Eliminator*, released in 1983, and including classic numbers such as "Legs" and "Sharp Dressed Man." Subsequent records and sellout tours have kept them at the forefront of rock—an impressive achievement for an outfit that has remained together, with no personnel changes, for over 40 years.

Above left: *A Gibson replica of "Pearly Gates"—the guitar has a figured maple top, and Seymour Duncan pickups.*

Above: *Billy Gibbons in concert with ZZ Top on October 11, 2011 at the Pikes Peak Center in Colorado Springs, Colorado.*

Favorite Gear

Billy Gibbons' all-time favorite among his many guitars is his 1959 Les Paul Standard, nicknamed "Pearly Gates," and produced in a replica custom edition by Gibson in 2009; fifty of these highly priced models were signed by the guitarist himself. The often weird-looking instruments used by Gibbons and ZZ Top bassist Dusty Hill on stage—including guitars decorated with rhinestones and covered in sheepskin—are created by Matthew Klein of the Gibson Custom Shop. Billy Gibbons uses Marshall amplification.

> *Sounds like the blues are composed of feeling, finesse, and fear.*
>
> Billy Gibbons

Did You Know?

ZZ Top's fifteenth studio album—their first since 2003's *Mescalero*—is due for release in 2012; it will be produced by Rick Rubin, and released on his American Recordings label. Rubin, who also founded Def Jam, has worked with everyone from Johnny Cash to the Red Hot Chili Peppers.

Billy Gibbons was named 2012's Texas State Musician by the Texas Commission on the Arts. Every year, the Commission also appoints a Texas State Poet Laureate, and State Visual Artists in two-dimensional and three-dimensional categories.

Billy Gibbons uses a 5-peso Mexican coin as a guitar pick.

His main non-musical passion is collecting and customizing automobiles.

Left and below: *More photos from the Pikes Peak Center gig—with Billy Gibbons using a Telecaster! The show concluded with two encores: "La Grange" and "Tush."*

Choosing your amp

When choosing guitars, a degree of personal emotion is inevitable and perhaps even advisable, but where amps are concerned, a harder-nosed approach is best. Make a list of the features you require. Are you a one-sound, plug-and-play sort of guitarist, or do you need channel switching to go from clean to dirty? Do you already own some stompboxes, or are you seeking an amp with built-in effects? Would you prefer a combo, or a head and cabinet, and will you be able to transport the latter to and from your gigs?

The choice between tubes and solid-state circuitry has been vexing guitarists for decades. While transistorized amps have improved dramatically over the years, most of us would still opt for tubes, which not only sound great, but generally feel more playable and touch-sensitive—though in a straight watts-per-cost comparison solid-state amps will win. Speaking of power…when PA systems were primitive or non-existent, lots of it was essential to make yourself heard, but these days most venues have PAs, and most authorities have noise regulations, so unless you're appearing at massive outdoor festivals, a 100 W amp will be too loud to crank up for overdrive. If you primarily want clean sound, or rely on effects, 30 W–40 W pushing a pair of 12-in (30-cm) speakers should be plenty, even for medium-to-large venues. If you prefer tube-power overdrive and don't care for clean tones, 15 W–25 W might be sufficient. To obtain both options, a channel-switching amp with a master volume for the overdrive channel could be best. Lots of players are after a practice amp to use at home, and here, even a 4 W–5 W tube unit will still be too loud to turn up in most domestic environments.

How much will it cost me?

Around $100 should buy you 5–10 W of tube power, which (through an efficient speaker) can be adequate for smaller pub gigs—so long as you're not too concerned about playing clean. They're great for recording, too. Over $200 will get you into 15–20 W territory, and more money will buy you extra power and bigger cabinets. However, pricier amps tend not to feature digital effects, unless you're considering higher-end modeling amps like the one in our photograph. If you can afford over $1,000 you can start investigating top-of-the-line products from all the well-known manufacturers, as well as custom builders. And whatever your taste or budget, if you use your ears and your head (rather than your eyes and your heart) to choose an amp, then you won't go far wrong.

1 Modeling amps like this one offer a flightdeck of choices—including stompbox simulations.

2 The Princeton, a tube-powered Fender classic, delivers 15 W through a 10-in (25-cm) speaker.

3 Traynor, named after its co-founder Peter Traynor and set up in 1963, is a highly regarded Canadian amp maker.

Above: *Motörhead in concert, promoting their 2010 album* The Wörld Is Yours. *Lemmy (right) and guitarist Phil Campbell both favor multiple Marshall stacks for their amplification.*

Left: *Finding an amp that'll suit you and your guitar is essential. Combos (incorporating speakers) like the one here are comparatively easy to transport, even though they're fairly heavy.*

David Gilmour

David Gilmour was born in the English city of Cambridge in 1944. As a budding teenage musician, he got to know Syd Barrett (1946–2006), who later became a founder member of Pink Floyd. In an interview for *Guitar & Bass*, Gilmour recalled: "We were friends first, then we picked up guitars later on...We sat around learning Beatles songs, Rolling Stones songs, R&B, blues songs...He'd know something, I'd know something, and we'd just swap, as people do in back rooms everywhere." After leaving college in Cambridge, Syd Barrett moved to London, where Floyd was formed in 1965. However, by the end of 1967 his unstable mental state was having a damaging effect on the band, and David Gilmour (who'd launched his own musical career with the little-known Jokers Wild) was brought into Floyd—initially to assist Barrett on guitar and vocals, but then as his replacement. Gilmour's first recordings with the group appeared on its second album, *A Saucerful of Secrets* (1968).

Left: *Strats have always been available in black, but David Gilmour's started out with a sunburst finish.*

Above: *David Gilmour plays a fundraising gig for the Crisis charity at London's Union Chapel in 2009.*

His distinctive electric and acoustic guitar work soon made its mark, and some of his finest playing can be heard on Pink Floyd's *Meddle* (1971) and *Dark Side of the Moon* (1973)—currently one of the top ten all-time worldwide best-sellers. He released a solo album, *David Gilmour*, in 1978, a year before the launch of Floyd's epic, *The Wall*. Musical and personal tensions within the band led him to undertake numerous side projects over the next few years, including another solo record (*About Face*, 1984). He took artistic charge of Pink Floyd after bassist Roger Waters' departure in 1986, though the band was briefly reunited for the "Live 8" concert at London's Earl's Court on July 2, 2005. Pink Floyd's keyboard player, Richard Wright, died of cancer in 2008. Three years later, Gilmour and Floyd's drummer Nick Mason made a one-off guest appearance at London's O2 Arena as part of "The Wall Tour," organized by Waters.

David Gilmour's most recent albums are *On An Island* (2006) and *Live in Gdańsk* (2008), and in 2004 he starred, with other members of "The Strat Pack," at a Wembley Stadium show marking half a century of the Fender Stratocaster.

Favorite Gear

David Gilmour's first "serious" electric, a white Fender Telecaster, was a 21st birthday present from his parents. Before recording *A Saucerful Of Secrets* with Floyd, he acquired another Telecaster, which he used with a 50-W Selmer amp, a 4 x 12-in (30-cm) cab and a Binson Echorec delay. This second Tele was stolen, and replaced with a white '66 or '67 Fender Stratocaster—a gift from the other Floyds. The famous "Black Strat" that became Gilmour's main guitar was bought in New York in 1970. By now, he was using Hiwatt amps, and had amassed a large number of effects pedals: "I had a huge line of pedals sitting on stage with wires everywhere; batteries kept running out and everything kept breaking." The problem was solved in 1972, when all the pedals were built into a cabinet. Gilmour's favorite acoustics are his Martin D-18 and D-35, and he also has a Fender 1000 twin-neck pedal steel guitar, purchased from a pawnshop in Seattle in 1970.

*There are moments when you make a record, you come across notes or find a piece of music that comes out of the air, and you get it to sound really nice in the studio and you've done everything right, and you go and think: "That's so ******* brilliant!" And you'll say "thank you" to whatever higher being has guided it toward you.*

David Gilmour

Below: *The second leg of Gilmour's "On An Island" tour included this gig at Munich's Königsplatz on July 29, 2006.*

Did You Know?

When creating a solo in the studio, Gilmour likes to do five or six "takes" on separate channels of a multitrack recorder. "My usual procedure…is to make a chart, putting ticks and crosses on different bars as I listen [to the alternative versions]—two ticks if it's really good, one if it's good, and a cross if it's no-go. Then I follow the chart, whipping one fader up, then another, jumping from phrase to phrase and trying to make a really nice solo all the way through."

Attending Pink Floyd concerts can be a risky pastime. On July 15, 1989, the band played a historic gig in Venice, and the sheer volume of its sound was reported to have caused structural damage to Italy's canal city. At Philadelphia's JFK Stadium a few years earlier, Floyd was only just able to finish its set before a gigantic thunderstorm broke, and the concert was aborted. The eight-month tour promoting *The Division Bell* (1994) was a triumph, yet at Earl's Court, London, the entire project was put in jeopardy when a section of seating in a 1,200-seat stand failed, and eight people were taken to hospital. Fortunately, no one sustained serious injury.

Gilmour refused what was rumored to be a $150 million offer for the "re-formed" Pink Floyd to play in the U.S.A., commenting: "It's completely mad and we won't do it. The idea for "Live 8" [in 2005] was a one-off."

GUITAR HERO

Peter Green

Above: Peter Green with a Gibson Les Paul, photographed in London for Guitar & Bass in 2007. His interviewer Julian Piper described him as having "the air of a kindly, benevolent uncle."

Peter Green, an East Londoner, was born Peter Greenbaum in 1946. He learned the basics of guitar playing from his brother Len, but was more excited by hearing The Yardbirds, with Eric Clapton, at clubs around the capital as a young adult: "For me [their music] was a new high, a climactic thing that really seemed to be going somewhere." Legend has it that Green frequently sought playing tips from the slightly older, more experienced Clapton after Yardbirds' gigs.

Eric Clapton quit The Yardbirds to work with John Mayall's Bluesbreakers, but Peter Green was soon to step into his shoes in Mayall's band—first for a short period in 1965, then more permanently in 1966 after Clapton's departure to form Cream. At Green's audition, Mayall told him: "You're the best I've heard since Eric," and the guitarist made his impressive recording debut on the Bluesbreakers' LP *A Hard Road*, issued in 1967. That year, though, Green himself left Mayall to become a founder member of Fleetwood Mac. Alongside him in the new venture were drummer Mick Fleetwood, bassist Bob Brunning (quickly replaced by John McVie), and guitarist Jeremy Spencer. Both Fleetwood and McVie had also been Mayall sidemen. In 1968, a third guitarist, Danny Kirwan, was recruited—because, according to Green, Jeremy Spencer "couldn't play my tunes."

Peter Green composed some of Fleetwood Mac's most successful early material, including the hit singles "Black Magic Woman" (1968), and "Albatross," "Man Of The World," and "Oh Well" (all 1969)—but by 1970 his heavy use of LSD, and his antipathy to touring and commercial success, had made it impossible for him to continue with the band. He left Fleetwood Mac that May, and, after a long, often troubled period out of the limelight, did not fully re-emerge onto the music scene until 1997. He then enjoyed a new lease of musical life with his Splinter Group, whose first lineup featured leading rock drummer Cozy Powell. The band broke up in 2004, but Green has continued to perform—and to talk about his extraordinary, though erratic, career. When interviewed for *Guitar & Bass* in 2007, he was "feel[ing] good in [him]self," but unsure about his future plans. However, he's subsequently undertaken a series of gigs in Europe and Australia.

Above: *A modern Gibson replica of a 1959 Les Paul. The instrument owned by Peter Green and Gary Moore (see "Favorite Gear" left), though similar, has some distinctive patches of wear, and lacks a scratchplate.*

Favorite Gear

After using a Harmony Meteor semi-acoustic in his very early days, Peter Green acquired a sunburst 1959 Gibson Les Paul, and a 50-W Marshall amplifier with a single 4 x 12-in (30-cm) cabinet, when he was hired by John Mayall in 1966. The Les Paul can be heard on many of his classic recordings for Mayall and Fleetwood Mac, though in the latter group, his amp was often a Fender Bandmaster, with two Fender cabs. In 1972, he sold the Les Paul to Gary Moore, who featured it on his own classic single "Parisienne Walkways" (1979). Subsequently, Peter Green has used a variety of guitars. During his period with the Splinter Group, he favored a black semi-acoustic Gibson Howard Roberts and a selection of Fender Stratocasters.

> *I always thought I was like a metal worker who should have been doing woodwork. Life's like that. You might end up knowing things before you die, but don't bet on it.*

Peter Green on being told that B. B. King regarded him as one of the very finest bluesmen

Below: *More photos from the* Guitar & Bass *2007 shoot, which took place at a hotel near London's Tower Bridge.*

Selected Albums

With John Mayall's Bluesbreakers
1967
A Hard Road

With Fleetwood Mac
1968
Peter Green's Fleetwood Mac
Mr. Wonderful
1969
Then Play On
Fleetwood Mac In Chicago
None of the singles mentioned in the text originally appeared on the band's albums

The Best of Peter Green's Fleetwood Mac (2002) contains all the singles mentioned in the text.

Dave Grohl

While multi-instrumentalists are common in pop and rock, comparatively few players combine guitar and drums—or excel at both like Dave Grohl.

Grohl was born in Warren, Ohio, in 1969, but grew up some 300 miles (480 km) to the southeast in Springfield, Virginia, attending two high schools in nearby Alexandria. He started out on guitar, but took up drums as a teenager, and his professional career blossomed when, at the age of just 17, he became the drummer for prominent Washington, D.C. punk outfit, Scream. He stayed with the group until its split in 1990, and was then recruited by Kurt Cobain and Krist Novoselic of Nirvana, who'd been impressed by a live Scream show. Grohl's drums were an effective addition to Nirvana's already distinctive sound. He also cowrote "Smells Like Teen Spirit" and "Scentless Apprentice," and was the sole composer of "Marigold," released on the B-side of Nirvana's "Heart-Shaped Box" (1993).

Dave Grohl's songwriting was inevitably overshadowed by Cobain's, though *Pocketwatch* (a set of his songs issued on cassette in 1992 under the pseudonym "Late!") was further evidence of his capabilities. The first Foo Fighters album (the name derives from the term applied to UFOs by American pilots in the 1940s) was an even more significant achievement. Grohl recorded it just six months after Cobain's death, composing all its songs and supplying all its vocals and instrumental parts, with the exception of one guitar solo. The Foo Fighters band did not make its debut until after the record's completion. Despite many subsequent changes in its line up, the group has gone on to enjoy massive worldwide success, and has won 11 Grammy awards to date.

Dave Grohl focuses on singing, songwriting, and guitar playing in Foo Fighters, but supplies drums for Them Crooked Vultures (whose other members are guitarist Josh Homme of Queens of the Stone Age and bassist John Paul Jones of Led Zeppelin), and has been involved in a wide range of collaborations and side projects, involving everyone from Paul McCartney to Slash.

Foo Fighters Albums

1995
Foo Fighters
1997
The Color and the Shape
1999
There Is Nothing Left to Lose
2002
One by One
2005
In Your Honor
2007
Echoes, Silence, Patience & Grace
2011
Wasting Light

Favorite Gear

Dave Grohl is closely associated with the Gibson Trini Lopez Standard semi-solid, a version of the ES-335 with diamond-shaped soundholes and six tuners in line on its headstock. The regular 335 has conventional f-holes, and three tuners per side. Grohl collaborated with Gibson's Custom Shop on the DG-335 model, issued in 2007, incorporating these features and finished in Pelham Blue. He uses Fender and Mesa amplification, and a variety of effects pedals.

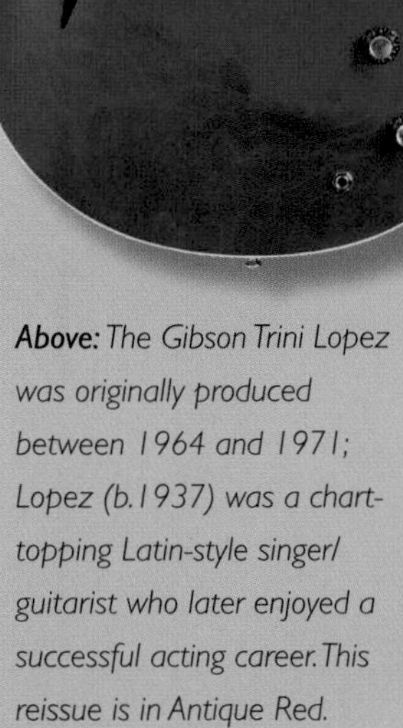

Above: *The Gibson Trini Lopez was originally produced between 1964 and 1971; Lopez (b.1937) was a chart-topping Latin-style singer/guitarist who later enjoyed a successful acting career. This reissue is in Antique Red.*

> "…shows that the human element of making music is what's most important… it's not about being perfect…it's not about what goes on in a compu"
>
> Dave Grohl accepting the Best Rock Performance award for "Walk" (from Foo Fighters' album *Wasting Light*) at the 2012 Grammys

Above and right: *Dave Grohl playing his Gibson DG-335, based on the Trini Lopez model shown opposite. It's in Pelham Blue.*

GUITAR HERO

Kirk Hammett

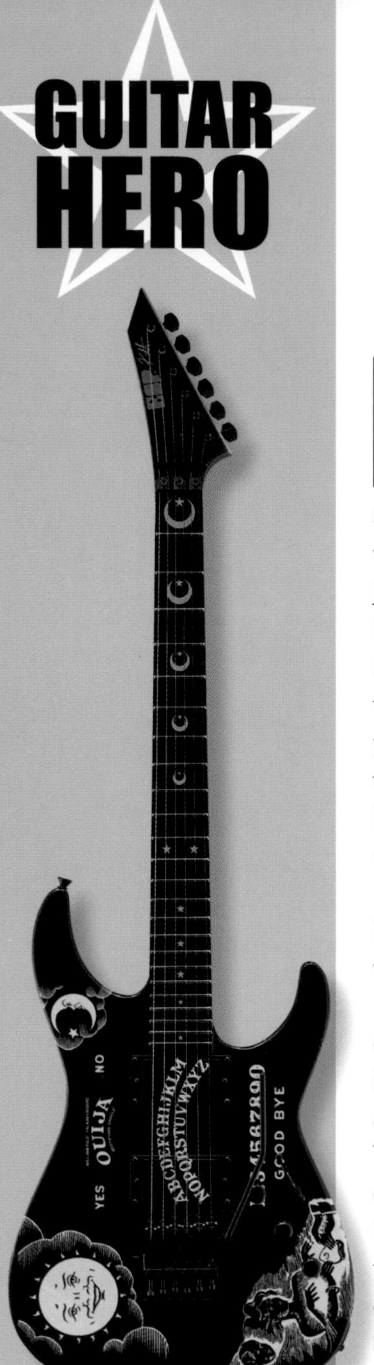

Kirk Hammett was born in 1962, and grew up in El Sobrante, on the eastern side of San Francisco Bay. In 1980, he became a founder member of Exodus, a local thrash metal band; around this time, he was also having guitar lessons from rock virtuoso Joe Satriani. Speaking to *Guitar & Bass* in 2010, Hammett recalled that "Joe taught me the importance of using exercises—and not only that, but also the importance of coming up with your own exercises that correlate with your own technique." The profound love for melody he inherited from Satriani has been a key element in much of his subsequent soloing.

Exodus frequently supported more famous bands at live gigs: one of these was Metallica, whose members recruited Hammett in spring 1983 to replace Dave Mustaine. Hammett moved east to New York to join his new colleagues, and his guitar work was quickly added to their debut album *Kill 'Em All*, released in July of that year. Time pressure obliged Hammett to base some of his *Kill 'Em All* guitar parts on Mustaine's, but his own strongly blues-influenced style—often featuring heavy use of wah-wah—is now an essential part of Metallica's sound. His skills have been boosted by intensive periods of practice and study (he's been quoted as saying that he plays for 361 out of 365 days of the year!). His personal musical tastes are wide; among his musical idols are Jeff Beck, Deep Purple, and jazz saxophonist John Coltrane. Metallica is currently rated the seventh biggest-selling band in U.S. history: its most commercially successful album to date is *Metallica* (aka *The Black Album*), released in 1991, and including classic Hammett riffs like the one for "Enter Sandman" (also a top-selling single). In 2009, Kirk and the rest of the band were inducted into America's Rock and Roll Hall of Fame, and a year later, they played a series of gigs across Europe as part of thrash metal's "Big 4"—alongside Anthrax, Slayer, and Megadeth.

Left and above: *The ESP KH-2 Kirk Hammett Ouija signature model guitar was first made available in 1999, but quickly discontinued. A limited edition reissue, with mirror inlays and an ebony fingerboard, was introduced ten years later.*

Favorite Gear

Kirk Hammett mostly uses "KH" signature guitars made by ESP; the company was founded in Japan, but has its headquarters in southern California. He also plays Gibson Les Pauls and Flying Vs, a Fender Stratocaster, and a variety of other electrics. He favors amplification by Mesa/Boogie for live work; his choice of studio amps includes models by Marshall, Matchless, Fender, and Vox. Among his favorite effects are Dunlop Crybaby wah-wahs, a Roland VG-8 "modeling" processor, an Ibanez Tube Screamer, and a Lovetone Meatball envelope follower.

Right: *Kirk Hammett with Metallica in Milovice, Czech Republic, July 19, 2009. The gig was part of the first-ever Sonisphere rock festival—a touring event that visited six European locations.*

Three Classic Metallica Albums

1988

...And Justice for All

Progressive and complex, each track an exercise in musical endurance—this record solidified the reputations of Kirk Hammett and fellow Metallica axman James Hetfield as metal's newest guitar heroes.

1991

Metallica ("The Black Album")

With a more streamlined approach, the group achieved a commercial and creative peak. Kirk shines on the sonic blast of "Enter Sandman."

2008

Death Magnetic

Metallica reinvigorated with new energy and maturity, and firing on all cylinders in a refined, classic setting courtesy of producer Rick Rubin.

George Harrison

George Harrison was born in Liverpool in 1943. His interest in music was stimulated by skiffle and rock'n'roll, and he acquired his first guitar as a teenager. One of his school friends was Paul McCartney, and by 1958 both boys had joined John Lennon's band, The Quarrymen. This group developed into The Beatles, whose members—including Pete Best on drums and, initially, bassist Stuart Sutcliffe—honed their performing skills during nightclub residencies in the German city of Hamburg. The band appeared at Liverpool's Cavern Club for the first time in February 1961. A few months later, Sutcliffe left (he died the following year), and McCartney switched from guitar to bass. The Beatles auditioned for Parlophone Records in London in summer 1962. The label's staff producer, George Martin, wasn't impressed by Best's drumming, and he was replaced by Ringo Starr shortly afterward.

Harrison's economical lead guitar work, and his ear for a good riff—"I Feel Fine" (1964) and "Day Tripper" (1965) are two striking examples—gave the band much of its individuality and charm. His songwriting took a little longer to develop, but he was to compose such Beatles' classics as "While My Guitar Gently Weeps" (1968), "Here Comes the Sun," and "Something" (both 1969). In the wake of the group's split, he issued his triple LP *All Things Must Pass* (1970). Coproduced by Phil Spector, it contained the hit single "My Sweet Lord" and featured such rock luminaries as drummers Ringo Starr, Ginger Baker, and Phil Collins, plus Eric Clapton on guitar.

Harrison's post-Beatles' career embraced not only music, but also humanitarian activities (notably the fund-raising "Concert for Bangladesh" at New York's Madison Square Garden in 1971); and in 1978, he launched HandMade Films, whose first production was *Monty Python's Life of Brian*. He enjoyed later success with his album *Cloud Nine* (1987), coproduced with Jeff Lynne from the Electric Light Orchestra, and including the chart-topping "Got My Mind Set On You." He was one of The Traveling Wilburys (the other Wilburys were Lynne, Bob Dylan, Tom Petty, and—until his death in 1988—Roy Orbison).

George Harrison died of cancer at his Hollywood home in 2001, aged 58.

***Right:** George was one of the most influential users of Rickenbacker 12-string guitars. The model in this photo is a 370/12.*

Favorite Gear

In his early Beatles' days, Harrison often used a Gibson J-160E electric jumbo, as well as Gretsch semi-acoustics, including a Country Gentleman. He was given a prototype Rickenbacker electric 12-string by the company in 1964, and this became an important and influential part of The Beatles sound. His amp for live Beatle's shows was a Vox AC30 combo. He favored a wide range of instruments and amplification in later years: in The Beatles' movie *Let It Be* (1970) he plays a specially made, rosewood-bodied Fender Telecaster, and on the cover of *Cloud Nine* (1987) he's pictured with a Gretsch 6128 Duo-Jet.

Above: *George Harrison in rehearsal for an appearance on "Toast of the Town," the CBS-TV show hosted by Ed Sullivan, New York, August 14, 1965. He's playing a Gretsch Tennessean.*

Right: *Here George is playing a Gibson ES-335; he sometimes used another double-cutaway Gibson, the ES-330.*

Harrison's Essential Post-Beatles' Albums

1970
All Things Must Pass (triple LP)
1971
The Concert For Bangladesh (live)
Also features Bob Dylan, Eric Clapton, Ravi Shankar, Ringo Starr, and other familiar names
1973
Living In The Material World
1974
Dark Horse
1987
Cloud Nine
1988
Traveling Wilburys Vol. 1
1990
Traveling Wilburys Vol. 3
(There is no Vol. 2!)

> "*We were the Spice Boys.*"
>
> George Harrison, speaking about The Beatles

Jimi Hendrix

Jimi Hendrix was born in Seattle in 1942. He began playing guitar in high school: a left-hander, he used restrung right-hand instruments, turning their bodies upside down. After a brief spell in the U.S. Army, he worked as a backing musician for artists such as Little Richard, Ike and Tina Turner, and the Isley Brothers, but established his own group, Jimmy James and the Blue Flames, in 1966. While appearing with them in New York, he attracted the attention of Englishman Chas Chandler (1938–96), ex-bassist with The Animals, who became his manager and took him to the U.K. Chandler recalled that during their initial discussions, Hendrix had asked whether he could introduce him to Eric Clapton in London: "I said when Eric heard him play he would be falling over himself to meet Jimi. That clinched it!"

In Britain, Chandler put together The Jimi Hendrix Experience, featuring bass player Noel Redding and drummer Mitch Mitchell. Its debut album, *Are You Experienced?* (1967), took audiences by storm—and within 12 months of his arrival, the previously unknown young American had succeeded in surpassing the ruling English triumvirate of Eric Clapton, Jeff Beck, and Pete Townshend as the world's most flamboyant and influential rock guitarist. Cream's bassist Jack Bruce commented: "I thought Eric was a great guitar player, but Jimi was a force of nature." It was thanks to another British star, Paul McCartney, that Hendrix won a place on the bill at California's Monterey Pop Festival in June 1967. There, he quite literally burned his name into his native country's psyche… by setting light to his guitar on stage!

The Experience recorded two more albums: *Axis: Bold as Love* (1967) and the increasingly adventurous *Electric Ladyland* (1968). They broke up in June 1969,

Right: *A Gibson replica of the "Psychedelic" Flying V Hendrix used for concerts in 1967–68.*

Favorite Gear

Hendrix is synonymous with "upside-down" Fender Stratocasters—right-hand models restrung and played left-handed. "The Stratocaster is the best all-round guitar for the stuff we're doing," he commented. His Strats were standard instruments; Jimi preferred rosewood necks, and, from mid-1967, he tended to tune his strings a semitone lower than normal to facilitate bending. His other guitars included a Gibson Flying V, a Les Paul, and a Hagstrom eight-string bass. In 1966, he acquired three Marshall 100-W amps, with four 4 x 12-in (30-cm) speaker cabs; he favored Marshalls until about mid-1969, when he began using Sunn amps. His effects included a Fuzz Face distortion unit, a Vox wah-wah pedal, a Uni-Vibe tremolo/vibrato, and a Roger Mayer Octavia octave doubler.

> *"Blues is easy to play, but hard to feel."*
> Jimi Hendrix

although two months later, Mitchell shared the stage with Hendrix during his Woodstock Festival set, with its epic, feedback-laden rendition of "The Star-Spangled Banner." March 1970 saw the launch of the live album *Band of Gypsys*, with Billy Cox on bass and drummer Buddy Miles. The band split up before its release, and Cox and Mitchell partnered Hendrix on his final gigs. He died in London, aged just 27, on September 18, 1970, as a result of an overdose of barbiturates.

Right: *Hendrix's hats (sometimes decorated with a feather) and colorful outfits all contributed to his vivid onstage image.*

Below: *Hendrix and the Experience ended their European tour at London's Royal Albert Hall in February 1969.*

Hendrix...in Other Musicians' Words

"With Jimi, I didn't have any envy. I never had any sense that I could ever come close."
Pete Townshend

"He hit me like an earthquake. I had to think long and hard about what I did next."
Jeff Beck

"Hendrix, intentionally, was not a huge influence on me because it was very hard to be a black guitar player and escape the ghost of Hendrix."
Tom Morello

"Jimi was a supernova of music. I measure all that I try to do with my guitar against what he accomplished in his short amount of time."
Joe Satriani

Steve Howe

Steve Howe is often considered the archetypical "progressive rock" guitarist, although his personal musical style is much broader, reflecting his interest in everything from the classics to jazz, blues, and country.

Born in north London in 1947, his early tastes were shaped not only by rock'n'roll but by recordings of top U.S. guitarists such as Les Paul, Jimmy Bryant, and Wes Montgomery. He began his career in The Syndicats, covering R&B songs—and, while working with them, bought the Gibson ES-175D electric he uses to this day. He went on to be part of pioneering British psychedelic rock band Tomorrow, and, in 1970, was invited to join vocalist Jon Anderson, bassist Chris Squire, organ and piano player Tony Kaye, and drummer Bill Bruford in Yes, replacing guitarist Peter Banks. Howe's arrival was the prelude to major success for the group: *The Yes Album* (its third LP, and the first to feature him) appeared in 1971 and went platinum. Yes became a household name among rock cognoscenti; and though there were several changes of lineup, Howe was to remain a member until 1981.

Yes's somewhat "symphonic" musical style has inspired more than a little mockery over the years, and Howe is admirably down-to-earth about it. "Yes was fundamentally a rock band—and we got very arty and proggy and orchestral," he told *Guitar* in 2003. "There was a lot of what I call "prannying around," and sometimes I do wonder if we lost too much." However, it's impossible to deny the popularity of the brand of "prog-rock" he helped to establish: Yes albums topped the charts on both sides of the Atlantic, its concerts sold out the biggest venues, and Steve went on to win subsequent acclaim with Asia (with whom he played from 1982 to 1984) and GTR.

He continues to enjoy a busy career as a soloist, and in his own groups Remedy (which has included his sons Virgil, a keyboard player, and Dylan, a drummer) and The Steve Howe Trio (with Dylan). There have also been numerous collaborations and reunions with former colleagues: reformed versions of Yes and Asia are currently active, and Howe has spent much of 2012 touring with them, and recording with Asia.

Left, above, and opposite below: *Steve Howe playing a Gibson ES-175D. Howe describes his 1964 model as "my thoroughbred guitar. I've dedicated myself to it and have become all-knowledgeable about it, its little quirks and tonal advantages."*

Favorite Gear

Howe's 1964 Gibson ES-175D is his most prized electric guitar; and among his favorite acoustics are a 1953 Martin 00-18 and a newer MC-28. Gibson issued a Custom Shop signature model Steve Howe ES-175 in 2002, while in 2008 Martin produced a Steve Howe Special Edition MC-38 flat-top, inspired by the MC-28. On recent tours the guitarist has used a Line 6 amplifier, one of the same company's Variax "modeling" guitars, Roland and Korg effects, and a range of other instruments and equipment.

The whole day of the concert is about preparation…I have a special hour on my own before the performance in which I consider all that's about to happen. I do that by combining meditation with a little gentle exercise…That moment when I get on stage has really got to work for me…I can't remember when I last got nervous about going on stage. I'm excited—I can't wait to go on stage and start the music—but that isn't nerves. That comes with experience.

Steve Howe, speaking about his preconcert routine

Important Albums

Yes: Four Platinum-Selling Classics

1971

The Yes Album

Fragile

1972

Close To the Edge

1973

Yessongs (live)

Steve Howe: Recent Projects

1999

Pulling Strings (solo—live)

2003

Steve Howe's Remedy: *Elements*

2010

Steve Howe Trio: *Travelling* (live)

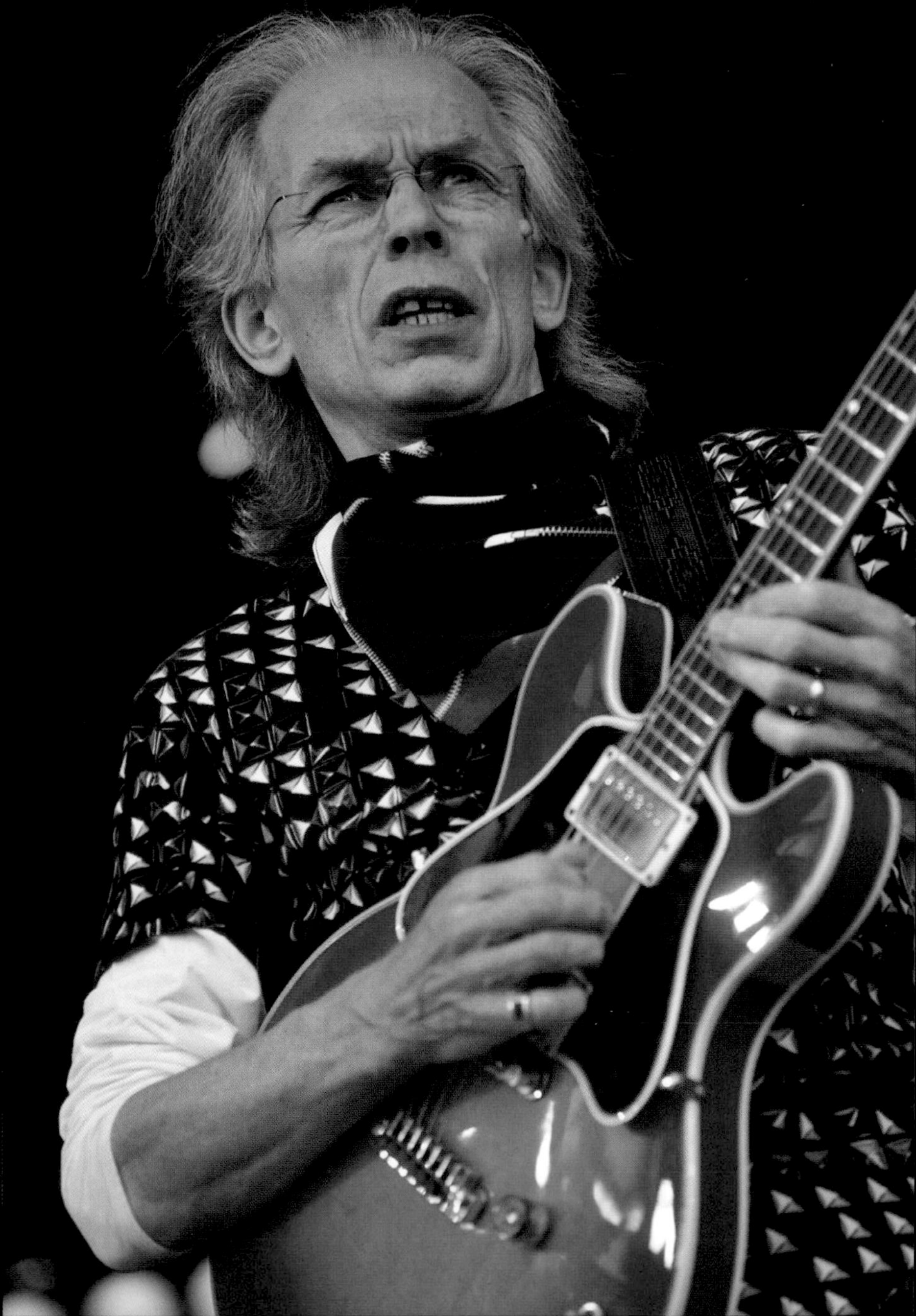

Right: *The double-cutaway guitar here is a Gibson ES-Artist, to which Steve Howe has added an extra scratchplate.*

John Paul Jones

John Paul Jones was born John Baldwin in 1946; he comes from Sidcup, in London's southeastern suburbs. He had little formal musical education: "I went to a fairly unmusical school and I had a few piano lessons which I hated. [However,] my father was a very good pianist...He was also an arranger and a musical director, so my training was watching and listening to him." As a teenager, he combined church organ playing with mastering the bass, and, by the late 1960s, had become a busy London-based session player and arranger. His commissions during this period included the orchestral string parts for The Rolling Stones' *Their Satanic Majesties Request* album in 1967.

The story of how, in 1968, John Paul Jones's friend and fellow session musician Jimmy Page assembled Led Zeppelin can be read on pages 152–3. Collectively, as Page put it, the quartet were "a group of musicians who could lay down some good things," and Jones's contributions were crucial. As a bassist, he can be heard at his very best on tracks like "The Lemon Song" (*LZ II*, 1969), and delivering the powerful main riff for "Black Dog" (*LZ IV*, 1971), while his other instrumental skills add an extra dimension to the band's sound: check out his mandolin and keyboard work, and the multitracked recorders on "Stairway To Heaven" (*LZ IV*).

Post-Zeppelin, Jones has produced artists as diverse as soul star Ben E. King, The Mission, and all-female American "old-time" group Uncle Earl. He also provided string arrangements for R.E.M.'s *Automatic For The People* (1992), and has made two well-received solo albums—*Zooma* (1999) and *The Thunderthief* (2001). His highest-profile recent project has been Them Crooked Vultures, alongside Dave Grohl and Josh Homme.

Above: *The Hugh Manson John Paul Jones signature bass.*

Favorite Gear

In the late 1960s, John Paul Jones used a 1963 Fender Jazz Bass. Later he favored a 1951 Fender Precision, a fretless Precision, and a Fender Bass V, as well as Alembics (this Californian company's other notable customers have included Mark King of Level 42, jazzman Stanley Clarke, and John Entwistle of The Who). Jones is now closely associated with Hugh Manson basses. His bass amps are SWR: "I've always liked transistor solid-state for larger bass rigs."

Did You Know?

When he was aged 17 in 1963, John Paul Jones auditioned successfully for two ex-Shadows, Tony Meehan and Jet Harris, who had just topped the British singles charts with "Diamonds," on which Jimmy Page played guitar. The following year Jones worked with The Tony Meehan Combo. Meehan (1943–2005) was full of praise for the young musician: "John Paul always displayed good taste and good ideas. He wasn't a run-of-the-mill player."

John Paul Jones's 1960s' session diary was full and remarkably varied. "You would do The Rolling Stones, The Everly Brothers, French rock'n'roll, easy listening, Engelbert [Humperdinck], Tom Jones—all in the same day—quite often."

Among Jones's more unusual post-Zeppelin credits is his work with avant-garde vocalist and performance artist Diamanda Galás. He produced her album *The Sporting Life* (1994), and was part of her touring band. He has also taught musical composition at Dartington College of Arts in the English West Country.

Below: *John Paul Jones in action with a Hugh Manson 8-string bass (main photo) and a mandolin.*

> *"Well, I'm a bass player for a start, so I suppose I didn't have that much to say musically until then!…It probably took me that long to get around to it because I kept saying "Yes!" to other people's projects."*
>
> John Paul Jones explains why he didn't release a solo album before 1999

Mark Knopfler

Mark Knopfler was born in Scotland in 1949. His father was Hungarian and his mother English. He grew up in Newcastle-upon-Tyne, northeastern England, where, as a teenager, he had two defining musical experiences: attending a Chuck Berry concert, and hearing bluesman B. B. King's *Live At The Regal* LP, recorded in Chicago. He'd already acquired his first electric guitar—a Höfner V2 that appealed to him because, as a Shadows' fan, he wanted a red solid-body shaped like a Fender Stratocaster. He moved on to a double-cutaway Gibson Les Paul Special, and subsequently to real Strats.

***Below:** Mark Knopfler with a vermilion red, Tele-shaped electric made for him by American luthier David Schecter.*

After a spell as a newspaper reporter, and an English degree from Leeds University, Mark Knopfler based himself in London, combining a teaching job and a busy musical schedule. Dire Straits—with Mark and his brother David on guitars, bassist John Illsley, and drummer Pick Withers—made a demo tape that caught the ear of DJ and popular music historian Charlie Gillett (1942–2010); a recording deal followed, and in 1978, the band's eponymous debut LP was released. It contained "Sultans Of Swing" (one of the songs on the demo), which made Knopfler's songwriting, laid-back singing, and distinctive fingerpicking familiar to millions.

International fame beckoned, though Dire Straits' lineup was to undergo some upheavals. David Knopfler departed in August 1980, prior to the completion of *Making Movies*, and only John Illsley and Mark Knopfler himself stayed with the band throughout its life. It gave memorable performances at Live Aid (July 1985) and the Nelson Mandela 70th birthday concert (June 1988), both at London's Wembley Stadium. It also won numerous BRIT and Grammy awards—and the first-ever video aired by MTV Europe in August 1987 was "Money For Nothing" from *Brothers In Arms*. However, even at the height of Dire Straits' success, Knopfler was taking on other projects: movie soundtracks (his first was for *Local Hero*, released in 1983); record production (including work on Bob Dylan's 1983 LP *Infidels*); a collaboration with another of his idols, guitarist Chet Atkins (*Neck and Neck*, 1990); and an album with The Notting Hillbillies (1990). Since Dire Straits' dissolution in 1995, Knopfler's musical activities have ranged even more widely and, to date, he's made six best-selling solo albums.

Favorite Gear

Mark Knopfler is best known as a user of Fender Stratocasters, and of instruments with similarities to them. "Sultans of Swing" was recorded on a Fiesta Red 1961 Strat, and Mark's impressive collection of electrics includes the so-called "Jurassic Strat" dating from 1954 (the model's first year of production). Since 1988, he's often been seen and heard with Pensa-Suhr electrics: Pensa-Suhr #001 was based on a sketch made by Knopfler on a napkin while he and luthier Rudy Pensa were lunching together in New York. He's used a wide range of amplification and effects over the years; among his current choices are amps and cabs made by Colorado-based Bob Reinhardt.

> *I like the way I play in my heart and wouldn't want to be anyone else, but I'm conscious that there's a whole world of playing out there that I don't do…I'll find something and make it my own either by adding my own style…or because I couldn't play it properly in the first place!*
>
> Mark Knopfler

Left: *Knopfler plays a Les Paul during a concert with Emmylou Harris at the Heineken Music Hall in Amsterdam, March 29, 2006. The device in his ear is a foldback monitor.*

Important Albums

With Dire Straits:
1978
Dire Straits
1979
Communiqué
1980
Making Movies
1982
Love Over Gold
1985
Brothers In Arms

With Chet Atkins:
1990
Neck and Neck

With The Notting Hillbillies:
1990
Missing…Presumed Having a Good Time

Some solo albums
1996
Golden Heart
2000
Sailing to Philadelphia
2009
Get Lucky

Paul Kossoff

Paul Kossoff was born in North London in 1950. As a teenager, he was a member of a club band, Black Cat Bones, which also included drummer Simon Kirke. The two young performers linked up with singer Paul Rodgers and bassist Andy Fraser to form Free, in spring 1968: the name was suggested by veteran British bluesman Alexis Korner, who also helped the quartet obtain a contract with Island Records.

Free released two LPs in 1969: its debut, *Tons of Sobs*, and the eponymous *Free*. That summer it supported Blind Faith on a U.S. tour, bringing Kossoff into close contact with Eric Clapton, one of his musical heroes. In 1970, the group appeared at the Isle of Wight Festival, and launched *Fire and Water*—featuring the classic hit single "All Right Now." However, Kossoff had mixed feelings about the song, describing it as "a part of us, but a frivolous part," and the band's bluesy roots, where his heart lay, were already diminishing in importance. Cream, Hendrix, and older greats, such as Albert Lee, had once been its role models, but it was the music of Robbie Robertson and The Band that informed *Highway*, the group's fourth LP in two years, also issued in 1970.

Highway sold disappointingly, and after internal disagreements, Free broke up in 1971. Kossoff was badly affected by the decision. After the split, as drummer Simon Kirke recalls, "Koss...sought refuge and solace in drugs, and they got the better of him." Kirke and Kossoff went on to record with Japanese bassist Tetsu Yamauchi and American keyboard player John "Rabbit" Bundrick, but the guitarist was often unwell during the sessions. In 1972, Free reunited in an attempt to remotivate him. His abilities shone through on that year's *Free At Last*, but he made only sporadic contributions to *Heartbreaker* (1973), the band's final album.

The rest of Kossoff's short life was marred by drug dependency and increasingly serious health scares, though he issued a solo LP, *Back Street Crawler*, in 1973, toured with Island stablemate John Martyn in 1975, and subsequently worked with his own band, also named Back Street Crawler. He died on a plane flight between California and New York on March 19, 1976, aged just 25.

Favorite Gear

Paul Kossoff is especially identified with Gibson Les Pauls—notably his 1959 Standard, which has been lovingly replicated by the company—and he also owned other Gibson and Fender electrics, as well as several flat-tops, though he was rarely seen with these. His amplification, nicknamed "The Enterprise," included two cabinets specially made for him by Marshall, each with eight 12-in (30-cm) speakers. They were powered by two Marshall amps. While his effects were minimal, he would occasionally use a phase shifter, a Leslie rotating speaker, and a wah-wah pedal.

Above: *A recent Gibson Paul Kossoff 1959-style Les Paul VOS: it has a figured maple top, a mahogany body, and two "Custom Bucker" pickups.*

> *I've sung with the greatest guitar players in the world since leaving Free, and I've never had the rapport I had with Koss.*
>
> Paul Rodgers, vocalist with Free, Bad Company and (currently), Queen

Classic Kossoff Tracks

"The Hunter" (from *Tons of Sobs*, 1969)
Has to be No.1 in any selection. This stage staple was a last-minute inclusion on Free's first album at the insistence of producer Guy Stevens. It retains nearly all the swagger of the live version, which can be heard on *Free Live!* (1971).

"Fire and Water" (from *Fire and Water*, 1970)
The outstanding title track from Free's best album. Koss leaves space for Paul Rodgers' vocal, before taking the spotlight with a faded-in, sustained howl that lasts for a full 15 seconds. His guitar break then builds relentlessly for just over a minute, taking the song to a new level before Rodgers rejoins the joyous proceedings.

Right: *Kossoff, with his 1959 Gibson Les Paul Standard, performing in Denmark in 1970. Behind him is the massive amplification setup known to fans and roadies as "The Enterprise."*

Lemmy

Ian Fraser Kilmister was born in Stoke-on-Trent, in the English county of Staffordshire, in 1945. Following the breakup of his parents' marriage, he spent much of his childhood with his mother and stepfather in Anglesey, north Wales. There he developed a taste for rock music, and acquired the nickname "Lemmy"...the origins of which are uncertain.

On leaving school and moving to Stockport, Greater Manchester, Lemmy enjoyed some success as guitarist with The Rockin' Vickers in the mid-1960s. After relocating to London, he took a job as a roadie for The Jimi Hendrix Experience, while continuing to play guitar himself. He only switched to bass when he joined Hawkwind in 1971. A year later he sang the lead vocal on the band's hit single "Silver Machine." In 1975, however, he spent five days in a Canadian jail on drug possession charges, and was fired.

He initially named his next band "Bastard," then "Motörhead"—slang for an amphetamine user. The addition of an umlaut to the second "o" may have been inspired by Hawkwind's liberal use of umlauts on one of its album sleeves. Motörhead made its reputation with three classic heavy rock albums—*Bomber* (1979), *Ace Of Spades* (1980), and the live *No Sleep 'Til Hammersmith* (1981). They all featured guitarist "Fast" Eddie Clarke and drummer Phil "Philthy Animal" Taylor. They've since moved on, but the current lineup—Lemmy, Phil Campbell (guitar), and Mikkey Dee (drums)—has remained solid, hardworking—and very loud!—since the mid-1990s. Motörhead's 20th album, *The Wörld Is Yours*, was released in 2010.

Lemmy, who now lives in Los Angeles, cites Paul McCartney and The Who's John Entwistle as his two main influences and, when interviewed by *Guitar & Bass* in 2004, was as down-to-earth (and droll) as ever when discussing his own distinctive approach to the bass. "I wouldn't say I was always improving, but I wouldn't say I was deteriorating either...I may have reached a plateau, I suppose. I'm always thinking of new bits to put in, but it's not really an improvement in playing; it's more of shifts in style sometimes."

***Above:** Lemmy delivering the goods as only he can—with Motörhead at the Velodrom in Brno, Czech Republic, in July 2009.*

***Opposite:** In all the photos here, Lemmy is playing his signature Rickenbacker bass, with its hand-carved walnut body.*

Favorite Gear

Lemmy has favored Rickenbacker basses for many years: his preferred models are his "signature" instrument, the Rickenbacker 4004LK, and the 4003. He amplifies them with a pair of Marshall stacks: each comprises a Marshall 1992 Super Bass 100 MkII amp, and 4 × 12-in (30-cm) and 4 × 15-in (38-cm) cabs. In 2008 Marshall issued an 1992LEM signature series amp in his honor. He doesn't use effects.

"if we moved in next door to you, your lawn would d"

Lemmy speaking about Motorhead's music

Lemmy...In His Own Words

"Actually Duane Eddy was one of my bass heroes. He played bass, really, he just played it on guitar."

"You feel like a bit of a t**t practicing bass on your own. It's not really one of those instruments, you know? I do play guitar on my own, though."

"[Switching to bass] was a happy accident! Because immediately I was a good bass player, but I was always a ****ing mediocre guitarist…"

"I'm a great believer in 'if it works, don't fix it.'"

GUITAR HERO

Tony Levin

Tony Levin was born in Boston, Massachusetts, in 1946. He's been playing bass since childhood, though he started out on a "stand-up" orchestral double bass, and used an Ampeg Baby Bass—an amplified upright instrument—before switching to bass guitar. Levin studied at the prestigious Eastman School of Music in Rochester, New York, and began his professional career as a New York City-based session musician.

Among his high-profile projects in the early 1970s were contributions to albums by Cher, Don McLean, Tim Hardin, and jazz organist Brother Jack McDuff. In 1975, he appeared on Paul Simon's *Still Crazy After All These Years*, for which his friend and fellow Eastman alumnus Steve Gadd supplied the drum parts. Around the same time, Levin worked with producer Bob Ezrin on Alice Cooper's *Welcome To My Nightmare*. It was thanks to Ezrin that the bassist began his continuing collaboration with Peter Gabriel, whose first solo LP (recorded in Toronto, produced by Ezrin, and featuring Levin on both tuba and bass) was released in 1977. Through Gabriel, Levin met two other Englishmen who've become his frequent musical associates: Robert Fripp and drummer Bill Bruford. Bruford and Levin have both been key members of Fripp's King Crimson.

Tony Levin pioneered the use of "Funk Fingers"—wooden sticks attached to a player's picking hand that strike the bass strings instead of a finger or plectrum. These can be heard on several Peter Gabriel and King Crimson songs, and on Yes's album *Union* (1991). He's also been a longtime champion of the Chapman Stick, a multistring electric instrument (invented by former jazz guitarist Emmett Chapman) on which both hands produce notes by means of a "two-handed tapping" technique. Recently, Levin featured the Stick with his own band Stick Men, whose album *Soup* came out in 2010.

Above: *Tony Levin and his Chapman Stick—he's probably the most prominent of all the musicians who use this versatile instrument.*

Right: *Levin playing a Chapman Stick during a show in the Canary Islands in July 2010—part of a tour by his Stick Men.*

Favorite Gear

This list of the equipment Tony Levin used for a Peter Gabriel tour in 2007 gives some idea of what his setup often comprises.

Basses: Music Man Stingray five-string 20th Anniversary and Anniversary four-string models; Stingray fretless five-string; Ned Steinberger Electric Upright.

Other instruments: Chapman Stick, Steinberger Cello, Nord Lead synthesizer keyboard.

Amp: Ampeg SVT-VR head with an 8 x 10-in (25-cm) cab.

Effects: Retrospec and Analog Man compROSSor compressors; modified Electro-Harmonix Big Muff fuzz; EBS Octabass; volume pedal; digital delay.

> *I like [being a bandleader and a sideman] equally. Once you're doing the show, it's the music, the band, the audience that make it fun. Fronting the band means setting up the gigs, interviews and publicity, arranging money and hotels, checking the sound, the running order…it makes me appreciate how utterly easy it is to just be the bass player!*
>
> Tony Levin

Right: *Levin combines chords and melodies on his Chapman Stick. Emmett Chapman developed it in the 1960s because he was seeking a fretted instrument that could provide the musical freedom enjoyed by pianists.*

Two Tony Levin Classics

"Sledgehammer" from Peter Gabriel's *So* (1986) and "50 Ways To Leave Your Lover" from Paul Simon's *Still Crazy After All These Years* (1975) are two of the most famous tracks to have been graced by Levin's playing. As he explains, the process of putting each one together was quite different.

"50 Ways…"

"Paul Simon takes some time in the studio with the band, getting close to what he wants from a track, but you always have the feeling that he'll know it as soon as he hears it—so once you've found the right groove, it's quickly done. Once [drummer] Steve Gadd added his unique rudimental groove to the piece, Paul opted to start with that, and we knew it was a done deal—all I had to do was stay out of the way and let it groove."

"Sledgehammer"

"[This] was done quite quickly, at the end of a long period of recording…[On the track,] I fell into playing fretless with a pick and an Octaver, with one or two compressors. Later I heard that they added still more compression in the mix, and boosted the bass to be a main feature of the song. That's part of the fun of being in at the early part of rhythm tracking—you never know whether, in the end, your part will be quietly in the background or thundering out in front."

Phil Lynott

Philip Parris Lynott was the illegitimate son of a Brazilian father and an Irish mother; he was born in West Bromwich, near Birmingham in the English West Midlands, in 1949. Growing up in Dublin, he made his early reputation as the singer with Skid Row, for whom Gary Moore played guitar. Lynott's stint with the band ended in 1969. He acquired his first bass guitar from Skid Row's Brendan "Brush" Shiels, and formed Thin Lizzy later that year with Brian Downey (drums), Eric Bell (guitar), and keyboardist Eric Wrixon (who soon departed). Lizzy enjoyed only limited success until they received a brutal "wake-up call" from Chas Chandler, manager of Slade, the chart-topping group whom the young Irishmen were supporting on tour. Chandler told them that they "looked like three ****in' statues" on stage, and ordered Lynott to wear colorful clothes that would exaggerate his movements.

Lynott went on to be one of the most charismatic and powerful frontmen in rock, and Thin Lizzy had its first taste of fame with a version of the folk song "Whiskey In The Jar" in 1973. Eric Bell left that December. He was briefly replaced by Gary Moore, but 1974 saw the arrival of Scotsman Brian Robertson and American Scott Gorham—creators of the band's trademark "twin lead guitar" style. *Jailbreak* (1976), featuring the single "The Boys Are Back In Town," brought Thin Lizzy massive acclaim and worldwide stardom. Two years later came the classic double LP *Live And Dangerous*, but also the final departure of Robertson (who'd already been in and out of the band). Lizzy's lineup was to undergo numerous other changes throughout the rest of its career. Lynott himself issued solo albums in 1980 and 1982. In 1983, he announced the breakup of Thin Lizzy, stating they'd become "predictable and directionless." He remained active as a solo artist, though Grand Slam, the new group he founded in 1984, achieved little, and soon split up. By now, years of drug abuse had undermined Lynott's health, and he died in 1986 of heart failure and pneumonia following septicemia, aged just 36.

Above left and opposite: *Phil Lynott performs live on stage with Thin Lizzy in London on July 29, 1978. A few weeks earlier, the band had released its highly successful double album,* Live And Dangerous.

Favorite Gear

Phil Lynott rang the changes with his basses before settling on the black Fender Precision with the mirror pickguard that became his trademark instrument in the mid-1970s. Earlier he'd favored a Dan Armstrong "see-through" Plexiglas bass, and a Rickenbacker. Other occasional choices included an Ibanez Roadster and a BC Rich Mockingbird. He started out using Marshall amplification, switched to Acoustic amps after being impressed with the tone Slade's Jim Lea obtained from them on tour, and subsequently opted for a Dynacord 100-W stack.

Philip had incredible energy, incredible determination—you couldn't put the guy down. He had this vision that he wanted to be rich and famous, and nothing was going to stop him. He was about 80 percent of the driving force to make the band a success.

Eric Bell, ex-Thin Lizzy guitarist, 2011

Phil Lynott...In Other People's Words

"Phil Lynott hit those strings harder than I've seen anybody hit bass guitar strings, and it's really what kept everybody in line…because even if you couldn't hear the drums, there was that steady groove all night long. Everybody knew where they were, just through Phil. That's how strong the guy played."
Scott Gorham

"[Phil was] tired and bored with being a macho heavy metal stud…[His record company] wanted "The Boys Are Back In Town Part 40," while Philip wanted to be a bluesy Jack Kerouac."
Jim Fitzpatrick, Thin Lizzy's album sleeve designer and Lynott's close friend

"He would love to have been remembered as a dashing romantic buccaneer type—a great guy with the chicks and a great guy with the blokes. A swaggering personality. And of course he'd like to be remembered for his songwriting, which he took extremely seriously."
Eric Bell

Yngwie Malmsteen

The ultra-high-speed playing style known as "shredding" owes much of its popularity to Sweden's Yngwie Malmsteen—the undisputed king of this genre for more than two decades, and an artist who draws inspiration from both rock music and classical virtuosi, such as violinist Niccolò Paganini (1782–1840). Yngwie was born in Stockholm in 1963. He claims that his passion for electric guitar was triggered when, as a seven-year-old, he watched coverage of Jimi Hendrix's death on TV. The other crucial factor in the young Swede's musical development was Deep Purple; in a 2005 interview with *Guitar & Bass*, he referred to the British band as "probably the biggest single rock influence on me, bar none."

Malmsteen came to the United States in 1982. His first high-profile project here was a contribution to Steeler's self-titled 1983 album. However, he soon moved on to membership of Alcatrazz, before striking out on his own with Rising Force. He used this name as the title of his 1984 debut solo album, and subsequently adopted it for his band. Early shows included gigs in what was then the Soviet Union, preserved on CD as *Trial By Fire: Live in Leningrad*. The group's longest-serving member is Swedish drummer Patrick Johansson, who's been with Yngwie since 2001; its most recent recruit, U.S. vocalist Tim "Ripper" Owens (ex-Judas Priest), made his debut with the band in 2008. Malmsteen's latest studio album, *Relentless*, came out in 2010.

The guitarist's other activities have included an appearance on the 2003 G3 tour alongside fellow virtuosi Joe Satriani and Steve Vai. He also composed and performed a classical-style *Concerto Suite for Electric Guitar and Orchestra*, which he first recorded in 1998, and later revived at a live concert in Japan (issued on DVD in 2002). He's described the experience of working with a conductor as "very similar to being in my band, [where] I am conducting what happens on stage all the time…But doing it [with an orchestra of] 96 people, that's something else…I have great respect for what those guys do."

Above left: *Yngwie Malmsteen playing the Sala Apolo in Barcelona in July 2008. Beside him is vocalist Tim "Ripper" Owens, recruited a few months earlier.*

Favorite Gear

Like Hendrix and Ritchie Blackmore of Deep Purple, Yngwie Malmsteen has always favored Fender Stratocasters and Marshall amplification. He scallops his guitars' fingerboards (as Blackmore does) to facilitate string bending, and also prefers staggered pickup pole-pieces, which "give me [a] certain violin-sounding tone that I really like." His Marshall amp is "a vintage Marshall Plexi head. It doesn't have a master volume or anything, so it all goes to 11. I use the same rig in the studio as on stage. All of this gets played through Marshall 4 x 12s. I don't use much in the way of effects, except for a stereo delay with a long [setting] so I can harmonize with myself."

The music is the easiest part. I just pick up the guitar and it's there. I never have to try. What does take work is the lyrics—I spend way longer searching for ideas for them than I do for the music.

Yngwie Malmsteen, speaking about songwriting, 2005

Below: *A dramatic moment from a U.K. gig at Carling Academy, Sheffield, during Malmsteen's summer 2008 tour.*

Yngwie Malmsteen... In His Own Words

"I'm like Pablo Picasso or Leonardo da Vinci and people like that—I'm the creator and I won't feel satisfied unless I have total control. I suppose that attitude is very unusual in rock'n'roll where, traditionally, it's one big party."

"If I hear something I want to be able to do it, and I'll do whatever it takes to be able to play it. I'm extremely stubborn."

Johnny Marr

Below: *Johnny Marr brandishes a Gibson—probably the 1968 ES-345 he's used with The Healers.*

John Maher was born, of Irish parents, in Ardwick, Greater Manchester, in 1963. As a teenager, he was active on the local music scene: one of his early bands also featured Andy Rourke (later to be The Smiths' bassist, but then still playing guitar). Maher had wider horizons than many of his punk-obsessed peers: his tastes embraced Motown classics, the American rock of The Byrds and Creedence Clearwater Revival, and—more surprisingly—the music of leading British folk guitarists Bert Jansch (a founder member of Pentangle) and Richard Thompson, whose career began in Fairport Convention. These and other influences all contributed to his own distinctive sound, which reached a wider public when he and Steven Patrick Morrissey launched The Smiths in 1982. Rourke and Mike Joyce were enlisted on bass and drums, and Maher altered his stage name to Johnny Marr in order to avoid any confusion with John Maher of The Buzzcocks.

The Smiths' singles and albums are widely regarded as classics: readers of *Rolling Stone* magazine voted *The Queen Is Dead* (1986) No.7 of its "10 Best Albums of the Eighties," while Johnny Marr came third in a 2010 BBC Radio 6 poll for "top guitarist from the last 30 years." However, the band split up in 1987, and when asked about a possible reunion in 1991, Marr was dismissive of the possibility: "Getting back with the Smiths isn't something I think about. You've got to be a bit Zen about it. We'd gone as far as we could go, and it was time for me to try something else."

Those "somethings" have included a remarkable range of projects, from collaborations with New Order's Bernard Sumner in Electronic, and more recent work with Modest Mouse and The Cribs, to countless session dates, among them a contribution to *Crimson Moon* (2000) by Bert Jansch. In 2000, Marr also launched The Healers, whose album *Boomslang* came out three years later; its drummer is Zac Starkey, Ringo Starr's son.

Favorite Gear

Johnny's most iconic guitars with The Smiths were his Rickenbacker 330, chosen for its "Byrdsian" jangle, and a 1959 cherry Gibson ES-355. His choice of amplifier was a Fender Twin Reverb—or more than one…the throbbing "chugga-chugga" of "How Soon Is Now" (1984, featured on the *Hatful of Hollow* compilation) was achieved by running his rhythm part through no less than four Fender Twins, with their tremolos set to different tempos. Boss pedals provide Marr's chorus, overdrive, and delay effects.

Opposite: *Johnny Marr on his home turf...appearing at the Night and Day Cafe, Manchester, U.K., in September 2011 with The Healers. He's playing a Fender Jaguar.*

> *I always thought that the greatest thing you can achieve as a musician is to be called an inspiration—aside from a big house in Sunningdale obviously…I believe that rock music, and pop music, is an art form and should be an art form, and it's all about inspiration. I'll continue to try to live up to it.*
>
> Johnny Marr, on receiving the Ivor Novello Inspiration Award in May 2010

Marr's Major Albums

With The Smiths

1984
The Smiths

1985
Meat Is Murder

1986
The Queen Is Dead

1987
Strangeways, Here We Come

With Electronic

1991
Electronic

1996
Raise the Pressure

1999
Twisted Tenderness

With Modest Mouse

2007
We Were Dead Before the Ship Even Sank

Pedal plug-up perfection

When chaining effects pedals together, the accepted wisdom for creating the best interaction and sound is as follows. Put tone filters and equalizers (EQs) first, boosters and overdrives second, modulation devices (such as phasers and choruses) third, and delays fourth. The idea is to filter or EQ the raw guitar before distorting and boosting it, distort and boost it before making it spin or wobble (thereby spinning or wobbling the fully driven sound), and finally echo or reverberate everything that's come before. A common variation is to swap around the middle pair of these four stages, as some modulation devices work best when inserted before overdrive or fuzz pedals. This is because they provide an element of filtering-type tone shifting, and sending an already distorted signal into their frequency-twisting mayhem can generate audible "hairballs" of toneless mush...while injecting an ethereal swirl into the overdrive or fuzz that follows it may work a certain special magic.

Of course, plenty of big-name artists don't abide by these rules: by experimentation they have come up with their own individual setup that suits what they want to say musically. Ultimately, you must go with what sounds good to you.

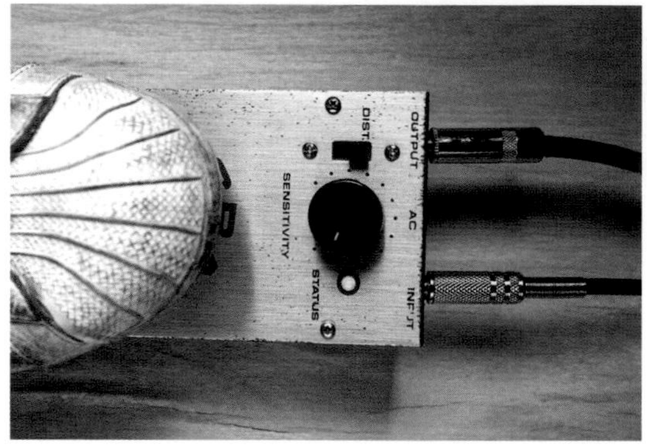

Above: *An effects pedal will modify your guitar's signal, and interact with other devices to create an overall sound that may be wonderful—or disappointing.*

Below: *Guitarist Mike Einziger of the band Incubus using an array of effects mounted in a customized pedalboard with its own power supply.*

Standard Pedal Order

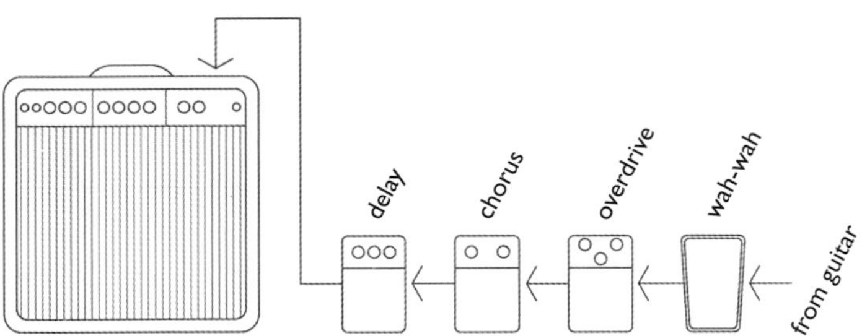

Try this classic order before you start going crazy: tone filter or EQ first, in this case a wah-wah (which sweeps across successive bands of frequencies and applies a boost to them as you move its pedal); followed by overdrive (distortion); then your modulation devices (such as choruses and phasers); and any delay device last.

Alternative Standard

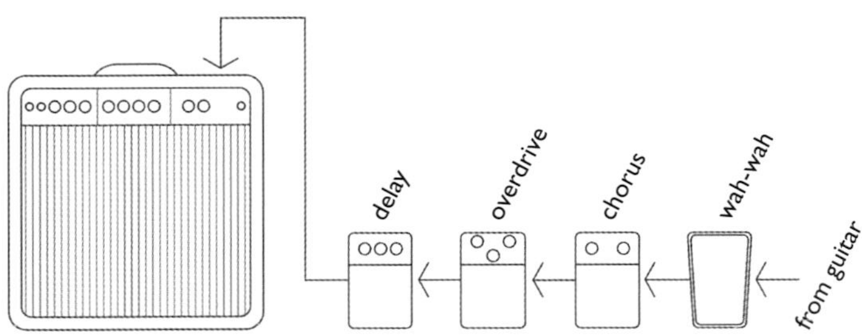

A common variation is to change round the boost/ overdrive and modulation effects. This can work really well with vintage-style modulators that include filtering, like the Uni-Vibe (made famous by Jimi Hendrix and David Gilmour). Such devices function best when inserted before overdrive or fuzz pedals.

Vintage Squash

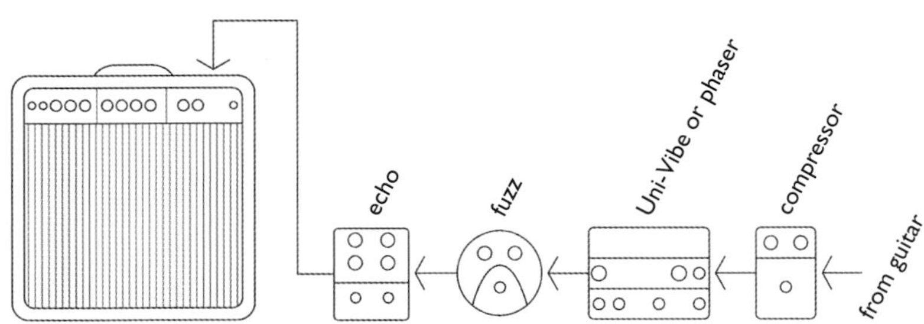

Here's a good solution for vintage-style rigs that include a compressor. Never place compressors at the end of an effects chain: their function is to reduce the dynamic range of the signals they're fed, and if positioned last, they will amplify all the built-up hiss.

Wah Heat

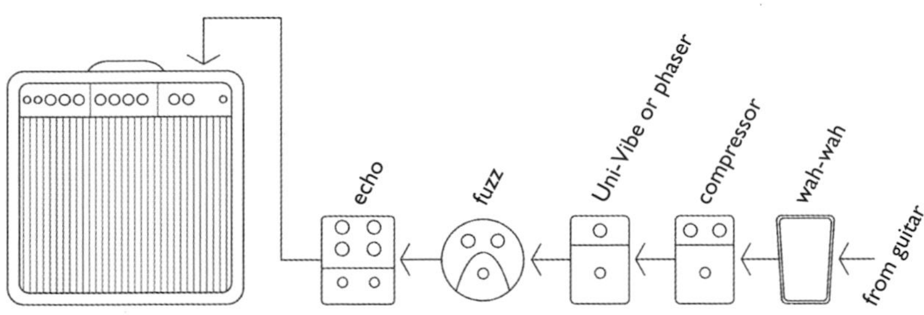

As above, but with a wah-wah. It's best to filter your tone before you get into boosting or overdriving, so stick your wah-wah in pole position, where it can have first bite at the signal from your guitar.

Brian May

Brian May was born in the London suburb of Hampton in 1947. He was academically gifted, obtaining a degree in mathematics and physics from Imperial College, London, but put aside his doctoral thesis on astrophysics in 1970 due to the demands of his burgeoning career in rock.

He'd been a musician from an early age, initially strumming chords on his father's banjolele, but soon progressing to the guitar. As a student, he was in a group called Smile; its drummer was Roger Taylor, and after Smile broke up, the two young men became part of Queen with vocalist Farrokh Bulsara (who renamed himself Freddy Mercury) and bassist John Deacon. The band's eponymous debut album appeared in 1973, but it was *Queen II*, a year later, that brought major chart success—both for the LP itself, and for the single taken from it, "Seven Seas of Rhye." The scene was now set for Queen's rise to megastardom, and *Sheer Heart Attack* (1974) contained one of the group's all-time classics, "Killer Queen." In a 1991 interview, with *Guitar*, Brian May spoke about how its main solo "starts off as a single guitar, then the other guitar parts come in not in harmony, but as bells, as we called it. I got that idea from listening to jazz bands such as the Temperance Seven, building up chords in arpeggios…Each part has its own melody but they also interact together."

Right: *Brian May performs at a concert in Hyde Park, London, on June 27, 2008 to celebrate the 90th birthday of Nelson Mandela (July 18) and to promote Mandela's "46664" charity.*

Brian May's instantly recognizable guitar work, sometimes subtly layered, sometimes full of drama and fireworks, proved to be a crucial factor in Queen's musical makeup, and is obvious on the band's 15 studio albums—the last of which, *Made In Heaven*, appeared in 1995. It was completed by May, Deacon, and Taylor following Freddie Mercury's death four years before. Since then, Brian has rarely been out of the spotlight. He gave an unforgettable rendition of "God Save The Queen" from the roof of Buckingham Palace as part of Queen Elizabeth II's Golden Jubilee celebrations in 2002, and has undertaken many other musical projects—from "Queen + Paul Rodgers" gigs to collaborations with Lady Gaga.

Favorite Gear

Brian May's homemade "Red Special" guitar has been his main instrument throughout his career. He's also famous for his devotion to Vox AC30 amplifiers. He bought his first ones secondhand in London's Wardour Street in 1967. "Later on, we bought them at quite a rate—some current ones but also some secondhand ones, because we figured the older ones had a particular sound to them. Really, though, it was just a question of suck it and see. If it sounds good, it is good. It's still true!" In his early days, he favored Echoplex tape-based delays, but now has digital ones made by MXR, as well as a treble booster designed by Queen bassist, John Deacon.

> *It was very scary. A million things could have happened outside my control—a broken string, temperature changes putting me out of tune—anything, in front of a million people, live, and I would have looked a complete idiot. But as soon as the roof bit was over, the rest was a doddle. I was beaming the whole time because it had worked!*

Brian May remembers the Golden Jubilee show at Buckingham Palace in 2002

The "Red Special"

"I was about 15 when I started building my guitar with my dad," May told *Guitar* in 1991. "It took a couple of years. We used all sorts of junk—the neck was from an old fireplace and an old oak table was the basis of the body. The rest of the body was blockwood and veneer, with the oak taking the strain. I bought [the] fretwire from…a guitar shop in Cambridge Circus, but it was very high fretwire so I made a little jig to cut it down, smooth it out and get the [fret] profiles right…—we went to great lengths!" May used mother-of-pearl buttons for position markers, and the tremolo system includes motorbike valve springs and a bike saddlebag support! The pickups were originally homemade, but later replaced by Burns Tri-sonics. The "Red Special" has been described as sounding "like a cross between a Les Paul and a Strat, but with a lot more range than either." May plays it with an old coin known as a sixpence.

This page: *More photos of Brian May (with his "Red Special") at the Nelson Mandela birthday concert at Hyde Park, London, in 2008.*

John McLaughlin

John McLaughlin is Britain's most internationally famous jazz guitarist, admired for his extraordinarily rapid, sensitive playing technique and for the remarkable range of his musical achievements. He was born in Doncaster, Yorkshire, in 1942. His mother was a classical violinist, and John himself learned violin and piano prior to focusing on the guitar. After making his mark on the 1960s' London jazz scene, he headed for New York, where he became a member of the jazz-rock fusion group Lifetime, led by drummer Tony Williams. He was also a sideman for trumpeter Miles Davis, on whose classic late 1960s'/early 1970s albums (notably *In A Silent Way* and *Bitches Brew*) McLaughlin was to figure prominently.

Right: *In 2004, John McLaughlin told* Guitar *that "the work I do, in music and in life, is to find my way."*

Opposite: *McLaughlin on stage at the 1998 Jazz à Vienne Festival in southeast France. The festival has been held every year since 1981.*

However, it was when the young Englishman assembled his own "dream team," the Mahavishnu Orchestra, that he took fusion to hitherto unscaled heights. The band, based in New York, featured musicians from several countries (including Czech keyboardist Jan Hammer, Panamanian-born drummer Billy Cobham, and French violinist Jean-Luc Ponty) in its various lineups, and won critical acclaim and commercial success for LPs such as *The Inner Mounting Flame* (1971). Prior to its split in 1976, he had already launched a new acoustic venture, Shakti. This drew, like Mahavishnu, on his fascination with Indian culture, and its name comes from a Sanskrit word for enablement or empowerment. McLaughlin's gone on to lead other bands, and has enjoyed fruitful collaborations with fellow guitarists like Paco De Lucía and Al Di Meola (with whom he recorded the live album *Friday Night In San Francisco* in 1981), as well as Carlos Santana. He's also paid tribute to his jazz influences on *Time Remembered* (1993)—featuring the music of pianist Bill Evans—and, more recently, with *To The One* (2010), inspired by saxophonist John Coltrane.

Now in his early seventies, John McLaughlin remains full of positive energy: he told *Guitar & Bass* in 2010 that "musically and artistically I feel good…especially with the players in [my band, the 4th Dimension] being so inspiring and so passionate about what they do. That's like the petrol in your motor, really. Without that passion, you don't amount to much."

Favorite Gear

According to John McLaughlin, much of his work with Miles Davis was done on "an old, beat-up Fender Mustang—a great little guitar, really good." In the Mahavishnu Orchestra he was often seen with a Gibson EDS-1275 double-neck (6-string and 12-string), and he's used several other Gibsons, including an ES-345, a Johnny Smith, and an SJ-200 acoustic. Among his specially commissioned guitars are four by former Gibson consulting luthier Abraham Wechter; he also has a Godin LGXT with a MIDI adaptor. His choice of amp and ancillary gear varies, and when playing live, he frequently plugs his guitar into a laptop via a Yamaha interface, taking the output from the computer to feed the PA and monitors.

> *I thank God every day not only for being a musician but a working musician with the possibility of recording, writing and basically doing what I want. Believe me, I know a lot of musicians who are not able to have that privilege. I try to do justice to it.*
>
> John McLaughlin, 2004

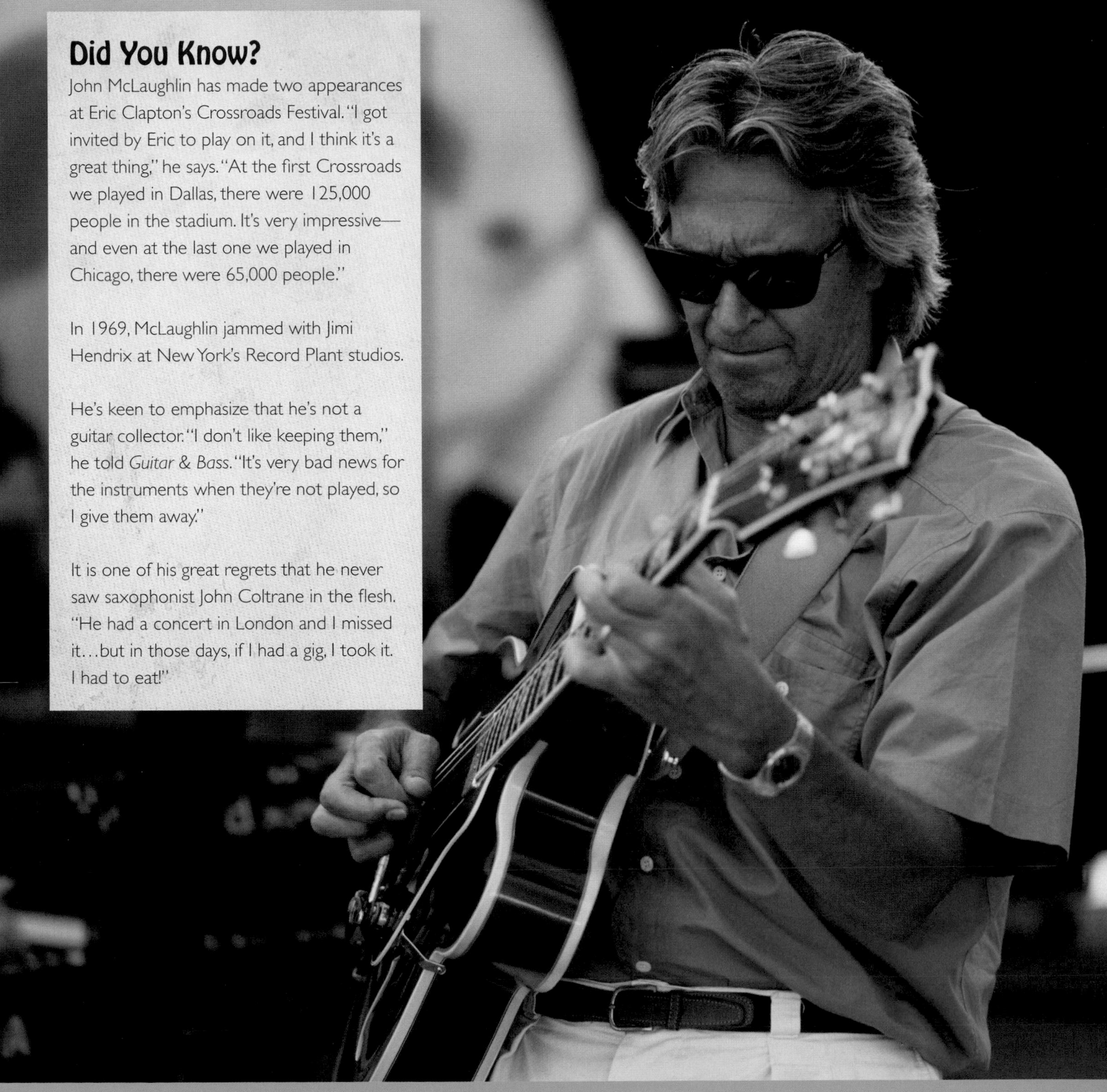

Did You Know?

John McLaughlin has made two appearances at Eric Clapton's Crossroads Festival. "I got invited by Eric to play on it, and I think it's a great thing," he says. "At the first Crossroads we played in Dallas, there were 125,000 people in the stadium. It's very impressive—and even at the last one we played in Chicago, there were 65,000 people."

In 1969, McLaughlin jammed with Jimi Hendrix at New York's Record Plant studios.

He's keen to emphasize that he's not a guitar collector. "I don't like keeping them," he told *Guitar & Bass*. "It's very bad news for the instruments when they're not played, so I give them away."

It is one of his great regrets that he never saw saxophonist John Coltrane in the flesh. "He had a concert in London and I missed it…but in those days, if I had a gig, I took it. I had to eat!"

Gary Moore

Gary Moore was born in Belfast, Northern Ireland, in 1952. His father was a concert promoter, and Gary made his stage debut at the age of six, singing with a showband at the city's Queen's Hall. As a teenager, he found fame with Skid Row, the hard-rocking Dubliners whose original singer was Phil Lynott. Gary was in the group from 1968 to 1971. Next he made a low-key debut album, *Grinding Stone* (1973), before working in Thin Lizzy with Lynott, and then in England with jazz-rockers Colosseum II. Gary greatly admired Colosseum's leader, drummer Jon Hiseman, describing him as "very good at putting me on the right path, teaching me about music and integrity."

Below: *Gary Moore in concert. "I come from the blues, I guess. Hey, that's just the way I play."*

Moore returned to Thin Lizzy in 1977—initially as a temporary replacement for Brian Robertson, then on a more permanent basis, until his unhappiness with the band's drug-fueled lifestyle, and disagreements with Phil Lynott, led to his departure in 1979, halfway through a U.S. tour. A few months earlier his "Parisienne Walkways," featuring vocals from Lynott, had reached the U.K. Top 10. Gary remained in Los Angeles to reinvent himself as a guitar hero with the band G-Force, but it was back in Britain, with his LP *Corridors of Power*, that his solo career really began to take shape. A series of rock albums followed—then, in 1990, the Irishman made a significant musical shift with the multimillion-selling *Still Got The Blues*.

The 1990s (which also included a stint in the supergroup BBM with former Cream members Ginger Baker and Jack Bruce) was to be Moore's blues decade, and though he relished his success, he was frustrated that public and critics seemed to resist his attempts to step outside the genre. His highly autobiographical *Dark Days In Paradise* (1997) and *A Different Beat* (1999), with its fashionable dance rhythms, both received a lukewarm reception, and record company pressure led to 2001's *Back To The Blues*—whose title speaks for itself. His selection of material at some 2010 festival appearances hinted that a return to straightforward rock might have been imminent. Gary Moore died of a heart attack, during a Spanish holiday, on February 6, 2011, aged 58.

Favorite Gear

Gary Moore's most famous guitar was the sunburst 1959 Gibson Les Paul he bought from Peter Green in 1972, used on "Parisienne Walkways" and many other recordings. Among his other favorites were four more Gibsons: his "Gary Moore" signature Les Paul, an ES-335, an SG, and an Explorer. His amps and cabs were Marshalls; he also had an Orange Rockerverb ("it's got that spooky sound I love..."), and his few effects included an Ibanez Tube Screamer.

"A guitar album like Joe Satriani or Steve Vai? I wouldn't know how. I'm from a different school. Theirs is a more intellectual process to music. I don't have that…I play from feel, from the gut. Everything I've ever done has been what I felt like doing at the time."

Gary Moore, 2004

Right and below: *Gary Moore playing a Gibson Firebird in a cherry finish; the model looks like a Firebird V, though it lacks a vibrato. Moore occasionally used Firebirds throughout his career.*

Did You Know?

Gary Moore played, with other members of Colosseum II, on *Variations*, Andrew Lloyd Webber's composition for cello and rock band. The piece was written in 1977 for Lloyd Webber's cellist brother, Julian, and part of it was used as the signature tune for London Weekend Television's *The South Bank Show* in the U.K.

Still Got The Blues includes guest appearances from blues greats Albert Collins and Albert King. Collins and B. B. King feature on Gary Moore's *After Hours* (1992), and Moore supported B. B. King on the elderly bluesman's farewell European tour in 2006.

Moore's album *Blues For Greeny* (1995) was his tribute to Peter Green of Fleetwood Mac, one of his major influences.

Scotty Moore

Scotty Moore, the last surviving member of Elvis Presley's original trio, was born in Gadsden, Tennessee, some 80 miles (130 km) northeast of Memphis, in 1931. After service in the U.S. Navy, he became well known as a guitarist on his local music scene, and was a regular at Memphis's Sun Studios, whose proprietor, Sam Phillips, hired him and string bassist Bill Black for a session with Elvis in 1954. The song they recorded was "That's All Right" by Arthur Crudup—the kind of "low-down" blues singer that Presley's deeply religious family would "scold him at home" for listening to. The three young men's version of "That's All Right" is widely regarded as the very first rock'n'roll record, and was a substantial regional hit.

Above: *Scotty Moore, aged 72, appearing in the U.K. in 2003. His Gibson Chet Atkins Country Gentleman carries his own signature on its scratchplate.*

That year Gladys Presley asked Scotty Moore to take her son under his wing, and Scotty served as Elvis's manager until 1955, when radio presenter and promoter Bob Neal was brought in to do the job; "Colonel" Tom Parker took over the reins in 1956. However, Moore's main role was as the singer's musical right-hand man, and his distinctive guitar sound ("one of my trademarks is that I have a very clear tone") and flexible "thumbpick-and-three-fingers" technique were to grace all Elvis's early records. Things changed when the star's career was interrupted by two years in the Army, followed by an increasing focus on movies. Scotty Moore took a post as studio manager for Sam Phillips, went on to open a recording facility of his own in Nashville, and performed with Elvis for the last time on an NBC-TV special in 1968.

After that show, Moore virtually stopped playing, and concentrated on audio engineering-related work for the next 24 years. Happily, his musical retirement ended in 1992 when he appeared with fellow rock'n'roll legend Carl Perkins at the Ellis Auditorium in Memphis. Subsequently, there have been several tours and records (notably 1997's *All The King's Men*, also featuring Elvis Presley's drummer D. J. Fontana and Rolling Stones Ronnie Wood and Keith Richards), as well as widespread recognition for Moore's special place in popular music history. In 2000, he was inducted into the Rock and Roll Hall of Fame.

Scotty On Elvis

According to Scotty Moore, Elvis Presley's guitar playing was basic but effective. "What few chords he knew he used very well. At first he sort of just wore the guitar around his neck to have something for his hands because he wasn't accustomed to being on stage, but after he started the dancing moves he didn't fool with the guitar much any more. He wasn't a bad piano player [either]. The Jordanaires [the quartet who provided vocal backing for Elvis] said [he] used to come in in the middle of the night and they'd play all night long—he'd play piano and they'd all sing gospel songs."

Favorite Gear

As Scotty Moore told *Guitar & Bass* in 2004, he played only four guitars—all Gibsons—during his time with Elvis Presley. "The first one was an ES-295, which was a new one that I bought in 1953. The next one I had was an L-5, which was one of my favorite guitars of all time. Then I played two Super 400s." More recently, he's been using a Gibson Chet Atkins Country Gentleman. The amp he's most closely associated with is the 25-W EchoSonic (incorporating a tape delay), custom-built for him by Ray Butts, the engineer who also developed Gretsch's Filter'Tron humbucking pickups. Scotty purchased the amp in 1955, and used it on every Elvis session from that year onward.

> *Oh, it's just like hugging a big fat woman! But don't she sing purty?*
>
> Carl Perkins (1932–98), of "Blue Suede Shoes" fame, trying out Scotty Moore's Gibson Super 400

***Below:** Scotty Moore in 1997, with another Gibson Chet Atkins Country Gentleman (this one has only red dot markers).*

Tom Morello

Tom Morello was born in New York in 1964, but grew up in Chicago. The paternal side of his family are Kenyans with a history of involvement in politics, and Morello himself, a Harvard graduate, creates music that engages with political issues in a way that harks back to singer-songwriter Woody Guthrie (1912–67)—composer of "This Land is Your Land" (performed by Morello when he appears as The Nightwatchman: *see* below), and "Deportees" (covered by him in 2010 in collaboration with Outernational).

After completing his degree, Morello moved to Los Angeles, where his musical skills received wider exposure when he joined Lock Up in 1988. They released their only album, *Something Bitchin' This Way Comes*, the following year, and broke up in 1990. He attained major success with Rage Against The Machine: its other members were rapper/vocalist Zack de la Rocha, whom Morello had first heard in action at a gig in L.A., bassist Tim Commerford, and drummer Brad Wilk. The band served up a potent brew of political rhetoric and a sound dominated by Morello's distinctive guitar work. He claims to have used the same effects setup, featuring a DigiTech Whammy plus a digital delay and wah-wah pedal, since the early days of RATM. The group achieved major success and massive sales with the three CDs they released between 1992 and 1999. De la Rocha's departure in 2000 led to their temporary disbandment, but RATM reunited seven years later, and continue to appear together.

In the aftermath of the breakup, Morello, Commerford, and Wilk formed Audioslave with vocalist Chris Cornell from Soundgarden. The band made three albums (their self-titled debut and 2005's *Out of Exile* were both platinum sellers) but folded shortly before RATM reformed in 2007. Morello's other major musical activity over the last decade has been his appearances with an acoustic guitar as The Nightwatchman, an identity he has described as "my political folk alter ego." Most recently, he's contributed to Bruce Springsteen's album, *Wrecking Ball* (2012).

Above left: *Tom Morello on stage in 2008 with his "Arm the Homeless" guitar, featuring a Stratocaster body, EMG pickups, and components from various other sources.*

Favorite Gear

In 2005, Morello told *Guitar & Bass* that his favorite electric guitars included his early 1980s Fender Telecaster, a customized Fender Stratocaster, a Gibson Les Paul Standard, and a gold Gibson Explorer. He amplifies them with Marshall 2205 50-W head, running into a Peavey 4 x 12-in (30-cm) cab, and his effects include a DigiTech WH-1 Whammy, a Boss delay, and a Dunlop Crybaby wah-wah. For his performances as The Nightwatchman, he accompanies his solo voice with an Ibanez Galvador acoustic, nylon-strung guitar.

> *"When I first picked up the guitar it wasn't for the traditional motives—money, girls…it was more like a virus, catching a cold, and it hasn't left my system yet."*
>
> Tom Morello, 1995

Below: Morello, playing a Gibson Les Paul, appearing with Audioslave at the Fillmore Auditorium, Denver, Colorado, in 2003.

Morello On Songwriting

In 2005, Tom Morello spoke to *Guitar & Bass* about how he creates songs, "I have an incredibly disciplined approach to it all," he explained. "As soon as one record is finished I get a cassette recorder and begin recording riffs and ideas for the next. I then catalog each idea and mark it, say, whether it's an A+ riff or a B. When it comes to writing for the next album I refer back to those lists…It's that obsessive-compulsive nature that got me where I am today."

Jimmy Page

Jimmy Page was born in 1944 in west London. His family later moved to Epsom in Surrey, where Jimmy took up guitar at the age of about 12. He built a reputation on the local music scene, and had become a top London session player by his early twenties. "Anyone needing a guitarist went to Big Jim Sullivan or myself," he later told *Guitar*. The work was well-paid and varied, but he found it uninspiring, and abandoned it to join The Yardbirds in 1966, playing bass with them at first. He went on to share guitar duties with Jeff Beck, and became the band's sole guitarist after Beck's departure.

The group broke up in 1968 with a series of Scandinavian tour dates already booked. For these shows Page created a quartet known as "The New Yardbirds," comprising himself, singer Robert Plant, bassist John Paul Jones, and drummer John Bonham. Their decision to rename themselves Led Zeppelin was inspired by a comment from The Who's drummer Keith Moon that another project featuring Page, Beck, and Moon would be as unlikely to take off as "a lead zeppelin."

Any doubts about Zeppelin's prospects quickly vanished. They were massively successful during the 1970s, and stories of their offstage antics are now part of rock mythology. However, they ultimately owe their fame to their formidable performing and composing skills—and particularly to Page's rich guitar style, a synthesis of rock, blues, folk ,and much more. They disbanded in 1980, following Bonham's death, but the rapturous reception they received at their London reunion in 2007 (when Bonham's son Jason played drums) demonstrates their enduring hold on their fans' loyalties. Jimmy Page's post-Zep career—especially his collaborations with Robert Plant—has also been artistically bold and rewarding. He, Jack White, and U2's The Edge appeared together in the electric guitar documentary *It Might Get Loud* in 2008. Jimmy Page was awarded the Order of the British Empire in 2005 for his charity work on behalf of Brazilian children.

***Below:** A Gibson "VOS" (vintage original specification) recreation of Jimmy Page's "Number Two" Gibson Les Paul, incorporating special pickups.*

Favorite Gear

Jimmy Page's first-choice electric guitar until 1969 was often a Fender Telecaster acquired from Jeff Beck; he played it on the first two Led Zeppelin albums (1969), and for the solo on "Stairway to Heaven" (*LZ IV*, 1971). He began using a Gibson Les Paul Standard in 1969, and the company has gone on to produce several special models based on his iconic "Number One" and "Number Two" instruments. Among his other Zeppelin-period electrics was a Gibson EDS-1275 double-neck. In later years he's been seen with a Gibson ES-350, a Jerry Jones (Danelectro-style) double-neck, and a PRS. His choice of amps has included gear by Marshall, Fender, Orange, Supro, and many others.

Among the acoustic guitars he's favored in the studio and on stage are a Gibson SJ-200 and Everly Brothers, a Martin D-18 and D-28, and the Harmony flat-top heard on the intro to "Stairway to Heaven," and now on display in the Rock and Roll Hall of Fame in Cleveland, Ohio.

> *"Ultimately, I wanted Zeppelin to be a marriage of blues, hard rock and acoustic music topped with heavy choruses—a combination that had never been done before."*
>
> Jimmy Page

Below left: *Page at the 24th Annual Rock and Roll Hall of Fame Induction Ceremony, Cleveland, Ohio, April 4, 2009. He inducted Jeff Beck into the Hall of Fame during the event.*

Jimmy Page's Inspiration

"I'm really just a fan of music. That's what I've always been. I accessed early rock'n'roll before I accessed the blues. It was just purely what was available to be heard in those days. And somehow I started listening to the speaker and this kind of arm came out and grabbed me in. I was sort of seduced to listen—and that was it from that point onward…I was listening to all of those early rock'n'roll artists, the ones that came out of Memphis…Little Richard, Presley, Jerry Lee Lewis. Presley was doing a lot of blues, but he was doing it his way, which is brilliant. That's the way that music keeps moving, it's a wonderful thing."

Below: *Page clutches a Gibson replica based on his 1970s' EDS-1275 double-neck.*

John Petrucci

John Petrucci is one of today's most outstanding and original rock guitarists. Born in New York State in 1967, he enrolled, aged 18, at the prestigious Berklee College of Music in Boston, Massachusetts, where he and two fellow students, drummer Mike Portnoy and bassist John Myung, formed Majesty. The band's early repertoire embraced songs by Iron Maiden and Rush, and its name apparently stemmed from Portnoy's description of Rush's "Bastille Day" as "majestic."

Rebranded as Dream Theater, the band released its debut CD, *When Dream and Day Unite*, in 1989, and Petrucci, Portnoy, and Myung remained at its core for 21 more years and nine further studio albums. The biggest-selling of these was 1992's *Images and Words* (one of its tracks, "Pull Me Under," features in the video game *Guitar Hero World Tour*). Portnoy announced his departure in September 2010; his final album with the group was 2009's *Black Clouds & Silver Linings*. He's been replaced by former Steve Vai sideman Mike Mangini, who features on Dream Theater's most recent CD, *A Dramatic Turn of Events* (2011).

John Petrucci's numerous side projects have included appearances on the first two Liquid Tension Experiment albums (1998 and 1999) with Portnoy and keyboardist Jordan Rudess (who subsequently joined Dream Theater), as well as a string of appearances, since 2001, on Joe Satriani's G3 guitar tour. When he spoke to *Guitar & Bass* in 2007, Petrucci explained the special appeal of a G3 show. "It's different, a night of instrumental guitar music. There's no keyboards, no vocals, and the guitar does all the work—all the melodies, all the songs. There's a lot more improvisation. We all get to jam at the end on Hendrix and stuff, and that's not something we generally get to do with Dream Theater! I always come back from G3 very inspired." Joe Satriani's influence can be heard on "Curve" from Petrucci's 2005 solo album *Suspended Animation* (2005)—the track he advises listeners to check out "if you really want to hear what I play like..."

Above left: *Petrucci on stage with Dream Theater in Denver, Colorado, June 14, 2010.*

Favorite Gear

Petrucci's signature guitars are made by Ernie Ball/Music Man. When asked how much a top-class instrument contributes to a musician's personal sound, he replied: "I've had discussions with guitar players, and it seems that everyone agrees that a lot of the sound and the tone and everything is in your hands, no matter what guitar you play. Two people playing the same instrument will sound completely different. But...I'm in the very fortunate position to have had a guitar made that's the perfect tool for me. It's unbelievably comfortable, and it does everything I want it to do. I have my comfort zone, so when I pick up anything else, it does feel kinda foreign at first." He uses Mesa/Boogie amplification, and his effects include units by TC Electronic, Eventide, and Boss.

I always want a solo to be an important part of the song, not just something for the sake of having a solo and playing some notes. You have to approach it with the enthusiasm you would any other part of the song, be as creative as you can, as original as you can. [It's an] important musical moment, just like any vocal part, and you have to treat it with that respect.

John Petrucci explains what he seeks from his guitar solos

Did You Know?

Petrucci is married to Rena Sands, guitarist in the all-female band Meanstreak.

He enjoys teaching other guitarists, in person and via books and DVDs. "I love sharing what I know. When I first started getting recognition, I was keen to do instructional videos and clinics. I'd taught guitar before—I went to Berklee, so I've studied music. I have the training and the experience…it's another fun part of it."

He's an avid Sega Saturn gamer, and wrote two tunes for *Digital Pinball: Necronomicon* (1996).

Above and left: *Another shot from the Denver gig at the Comfort Dental Amphitheater—part of "The Final Frontier" tour, on which Dream Theater appeared with Iron Maiden.*

Bonnie Raitt

Below: Bonnie playing one of her Fender Signature Stratocasters, with a "blueburst" finish, in 2009.

Bonnie Raitt was born in Burbank, California, in 1949: her father John was a Broadway musical star who appeared with Doris Day in the film version of *The Pajama Game* (1957), and her mother was a pianist and singer. Surrounded by music as a child, Bonnie was soon having piano lessons.

Opposite: Bonnie Raitt—the doyenne of American blues guitarists. Her 2012 album, Slipstream, was produced by Joe Henry—Madonna's brother-in-law!

Her parents bought her a Stella acoustic for Christmas, and she soon grew passionate about blues, and fascinated by the struggles and achievements of its black performers—some of whom (notably Mississippi Fred McDowell and John Lee Hooker) later became her close friends and musical associates. "They were thrilled that I was interested in what they did and we hit it off personality wise. There was mutual respect, playfulness, fun and then a more serious side, where I learned from them what it was like to be a victim of racism. These were wonderful, wonderful people and having them as part of my life has been a huge gift and a blessing."

Raitt's slide guitar playing and singing won wide acclaim, and her first, eponymously titled album appeared in 1971. Substantial success arrived six years later with *Sweet Forgiveness* (and the single from it, Del Shannon's "Runaway"), but it was subsequent records such as *Nick of Time* (1989) and *Luck of the Draw* (1991) that were her biggest sellers. She's also been in consistent demand as a guest musician, and has worked with a remarkable range of artists, including Ladysmith Black Mambazo, Jackson Browne, Elton John, and Aretha Franklin. Alongside her musical activities, Bonnie's pursued numerous political and charitable projects, and participated in fund-raising concerts for Farm Aid, Amnesty International, and many others. More recently, she launched the Bonnie Raitt Guitar Foundation together with Fender and the Boys & Girls Clubs of America, using profits from the sales of her Signature Model Stratocaster to pay for access to instruments and tuition for youngsters.

Bonnie Raitt's first album for seven years, *Slipstream*, was released in April 2012: among its tracks are songs by Bob Dylan, Loudon Wainwright III, and Gerry Rafferty.

Favorite Gear

Bonnie Raitt's favorite guitar is her brown Fender Stratocaster—a 1965 model she purchased for $120 in 1969. "It sounds the same as when I bought it and always does. I think it is a truly remarkable and unique instrument." She adds, however, "in terms of the sound I get, only I can get it to sound the way it does live. That must have something to do with my touch!" She uses a Bad Cat amplifier, with a Boss compressor pedal for slide work.

The whole recording industry was different back then. You were allowed to develop and grow…I was lucky that I got my foot in the door as a woman guitarist, as I wasn't an original singer-songwriter. The mix of songs I had was sufficiently unique that I got to have my own path. Today? It just wouldn't happen.

Bonnie Raitt on her early days with Warner Bros. Records

How Bonnie Met the Blues Greats

"It was when I was [a student] at Harvard. I had become a fan of country blues when I'd been given a copy of the *Blues At Newport 1963* album, which had John Lee Hooker, Brownie McGhee, Sonny Terry, Mississippi John Hurt, and Reverend Gary Davis on it. I was blown away and taught myself to play every song on the record. One day I was listening to the Harvard college radio station and Son House—the father of Delta blues—was talking on a program. Then a friend called me up and said that Dick Waterman, who managed and rediscovered Son, lived [nearby], and [asked] would I like to meet him? My life changed forever after that." Waterman took Bonnie Raitt under his wing, introduced her to the men who had become her heroes, and went on to be her booking agent.

Randy Rhoads

Randy Rhoads—one of the heavy metal greats—was born in Santa Monica, California, in 1956. The son of a music store owner, he started to learn guitar when he was six, and studied classical playing in his formative years. Among his rock influences were Leslie West of Mountain, Michael Schenker, Gary Moore, Eddie Van Halen, and jazz rocker Allan Holdsworth.

He began his career with Quiet Riot, and appeared on the band's first two albums (released, only in Japan, in 1977 and 1978) before joining Ozzy Osbourne's group. There, he quickly established his own style, based on an impressive array of blues-based pentatonic minor licks, a significant dash of classical influence, and a degree of control rarely found in rock guitarists at the time. However, he never lost his desire to keep learning, and even while touring with Ozzy would frequently seek out guitar teachers in the cities they visited to arrange lessons. Predictably, he'd often find himself turning the tables on his starstruck tutors, and showing them how to play like him!

Thanks to his technical prowess, Randy Rhoads was able to overdub fast-moving passages with remarkable precision on his recorded solos; lesser players often use electronics to obtain a similar, though less impressive effect. Speaking about "Crazy Train" on *Blizzard of Ozz* (1980), one of the two Osbourne studio albums to which Rhoads contributed, engineer/producer Max Norman recalls that its solo "was triple-tracked. If you listen to that song

Above: *Randy Rhoads recording Ozzy Osbourne's* Blizzard of Ozz *album at Ridge Farm Studio in West Sussex, England, in May 1980.*

Left: *The Gibson Randy Rhoads Les Paul Custom—the company's recent, limited edition recreation of Rhoads' famous 1974 instrument.*

Favorite Gear

Randy Rhoads' two main guitars were a 1974 cream Gibson Les Paul Custom, and a Flying V-style model made for him by California-based luthier Karl Sandoval. He also commissioned and collaborated on the design of the now-famous Jackson Rhoads V guitar. His amps were Marshalls, and their cabs were fitted with Altec 417-8H loudspeakers. Rhoads used four MXR pedals: a Distortion Plus, a Stereo Chorus, a flanger, and a ten-band graphic equalizer. His other devices included a Cry Baby wah-wah and a Roland RE-201 Space Echo.

real close, you'll hear there's one main guitar around the center…and there are two other guitars playing exactly the same thing, panned to the left and right, but back somewhat. And actually what happens is you don't hear them—you just hear it as one guitar."

Rhoads' second and final album with Ozzy Osbourne was *Diary of a Madman* (1981). By early 1982, the young guitarist was reportedly considering taking a break from rock in order to study classical guitar at university. He was killed on the morning of March 19 that year, when the light plane in which he was a passenger crashed in Florida, where Ozzy's band was due to perform, after attempting an aerobatic stunt. The pilot (Osbourne's tour bus driver) and another member of the band's entourage also died in the accident.

> *To this day I don't have a guitar idol. I have people who are my favorites.*
>
> Randy Rhoads

Did You Know?

To achieve his distinctive guitar sound on Ozzy Osbourne's *Diary of a Madman* (1981), Randy Rhoads often detuned his guitar by a semitone (so its open strings—top to bottom—were set to Eb, Bb, Gb, Db, Ab, Eb).

"Rhoadsfest" tribute concerts are held every December and March to commemorate the dates of Randy Rhoads' birth and death.

In a recent *Rolling Stone* poll of the "100 Greatest Guitarists of All Time," Rhoads was voted No.36; Jimi Hendrix was the winner.

Joel McIver's biography of Rhoads, *Crazy Train*, was published in 2011. It has a foreword by Zakk Wylde, and an afterword by Yngwie Malmsteen.

Right: *Rhoads on the U.K. leg of Ozzy Osbourne's "Blizzard of Ozz" tour, fall 1980. Rhoads' Les Paul was a gift from the other members of his previous band Quiet Riot.*

Keith Richards

Keith Richards was born in 1943 in Dartford, Kent, just to the southeast of London. His grandfather was a jazz saxophonist, but among Keith's formative musical experiences was listening to rock'n'roll at night on Radio Luxembourg. "They played 'Heartbreak Hotel' and 'Long Tall Sally'," he later recalled. "I knew from the minute I heard Elvis and Little Richard that that's what I wanted to do." His favorite guitarists were Presley's sideman Scotty Moore ("I could never work out how he played [the break on Elvis's 'I'm Left You're Right She's Gone'], and I still can't. It's such a wonderful thing…I almost don't want to know"), and Chuck Berry—who so excited him that he'd buy Berry's records before even hearing them.

Below: *Keith Richards attending the premiere of Martin Scorsese's Rolling Stones' documentary "Shine a Light" at the 58th Berlin Film Festival on February 7, 2008.*

Richards's fascination with rock'n'roll led him to delve deeper into American rhythm and blues—and when, as an art student in 1960, he had a chance meeting on a train with a former schoolfriend, Mick Jagger, they began discussing the R&B albums Jagger was clutching…and Richards was later invited to join Jagger's band, Little Boy Blue & The Blue Boys. This was the start of the Glimmer Twins' long and sometimes bumpy association. The Rollin' Stones (as they were originally known) came together in 1962, and Richards's dynamic, minimalist guitar style, which was to earn him the sobriquet "The Human Riff," has always been integral to their distinctive sound.

A new facet to his already distinctive playing began to emerge when (as he told *Guitar & Bass*) "in 1966 I was listening to my old blues records and realized they used different tunings." This led to his increasing adoption of slide and open G, about which he learned a lot from ace session man Ry Cooder (whose own slide guitar work can be heard on 1971's *Sticky Fingers*). Richards has said that exploring open tunings "rejuvenated my enthusiasm for playing guitar, because you'd put your fingers where you thought they'd go, and you'd get accidents happening."

Keith Richards's wild, hedonistic image has often obscured his remarkable musical accomplishments. As the late Jack Nitzsche (the American keyboard player and arranger who introduced the band to Ry Cooder) put it, "Without Keith's rhythm guitar, there'd be no Rolling Stones. What Keith does is play guitar without trying to be flash. It's all taste."

Favorite Gear

Keith Richards is an inveterate collector and, although some have been stolen, lost, or destroyed over the decades, he could still take no fewer than 80 instruments on the road for the Stones' 1997–8 *"Bridges To Babylon"* tour. His highest-profile electrics, however, are two Fender Telecasters—a 1953 model nicknamed "Micawber" (after the character in Charles Dickens's novel *David Copperfield*), and another Tele, known as "Malcolm" and dating from a year later. Both are tuned to open G, and have no sixth strings fitted. His favorite amps are also Fenders: he often uses a Twin on stage, and likes to record with a Champ.

"[P]laying safe is not what it's about. This music is all about beautiful ****-ups. And beautiful recoveri[es]."

Keith Richards

Keith Richards—In His Own Words

"I would rather be a living legend than a dead legend."

"There was really just one song ever written, and that was by Adam and Eve. We just do the variations."

"[The Rolling Stones is] a balancing act. But you can fall down and get up…I guess I got over my embarrassment of doing that in public long ago."

"I didn't say I was a 'rhythm' guitarist. Other people made my reputation for me."

Carlos Santana

Above: *"The most valuable possession is an open heart" (widely quoted words of Carlos Santana).*

Right and opposite top left: *Carlos Santana performs at the 20,000+ capacity Gorge Amphitheater in George, Washington, on September 2, 1995.*

Carlos Santana was born in Autlán de Navarro, southwest of the Mexican city of Guadalajara, in 1947; his father, José, was a mariachi violinist. Later, the family moved north to the border city of Tijuana, and then to Northern California, settling in San Francisco. Already a blues fan, Carlos absorbed—and became a part of—the Bay Area's rich cultural mix, and formed the first incarnation of the Santana Blues Band (later known simply by his own surname) there in 1966.

The group's heady fusion of rock, blues, and Latin idioms soon had a substantial following. A memorable appearance at the Woodstock festival in August 1969 brought it even wider recognition, and its debut album, recorded earlier that year, was a massive success. Among the standout tracks was "Evil Ways," which also became a hit single. Carlos's fiery, intense soloing style was subsequently showcased not only on his own group's records (which were best-sellers throughout the 1970s, despite frequent lineup changes), but on collaborations such as the *Carlos Santana & Buddy Miles! Live!* LP (1972), made with the former drummer for Jimi Hendrix's Band of Gypsys, and *Love Devotion Surrender* (1973) with John McLaughlin.

In the 1980s and 1990s, Carlos Santana undertook a wide and artistically fruitful range of projects—from *Havana Moon* (1983), on which he was joined not only by his father but also by both Booker T. Jones and The Fabulous Thunderbirds, to *Blues For Salvador* (1987), which brought him his first Grammy award. However, none of these enjoyed sales comparable to those he'd achieved previously…until he and his band issued *Supernatural* in 1997. Its star-studded list of guest contributors ranged from former Fugees Lauryn Hill and Wyclef Jean to Eric Clapton, and its multiplatinum status has made it the greatest commercial triumph of Santana's career. In the 21st century, he's been responsible for two other big-selling albums, *Shaman* (2002) and *All That I Am* (2005), and was himself a guest star on 2005's *Possibilities*, released by his old friend, jazz keyboardist Herbie Hancock.

Favorite Gear

In the mid-1970s, Carlos Santana began working with Yamaha to develop an electric guitar that would have the body mass, and the resultant rich tone, that he was seeking. The outcome of their collaboration was the Yamaha SG2000, and Santana continued to use Yamahas until the early 1980s. Since then, he's been closely associated with PRS instruments, and the company has issued a number of Santana models. He's also a longtime fan of Mesa/Boogie amplifiers, and is said to have coined the second half of their name when—after trying one out in 1969—he told Randall Smith, their designer, "Man, that little thing really boogies!"

> *My job in this life is to give people spiritual ecstasy through music. In my concerts people cry, laugh, dance. If they climaxed spiritually, I did my job. I did it decently and honestly.*
>
> Carlos Santana

Below: *Carlos Santana performing at a free concert presented by T-Mobile in Hero's Square, Budapest, Hungary, on June 28, 2008.*

Guitarists v Gunslingers

In a 2003 interview with *Guitar*, Carlos Santana revealed that when he meets fellow guitar greats such as Eric Clapton or John McLaughlin, they often swap tips and advice about equipment and technique. When *G&B* mused that only a guitarist of similarly exalted stature could get away with telling the likes of Clapton anything, Santana frowned and shook his head. "If you can't talk about tone, you're not a musician," he proclaimed. "You're just some kind of gunslinger. Most of the people with that mentality…they suck, anyway. They play a bunch of pyrotechnics, like a guy lifting weights to show his muscles…Not all [ultra-fast players]; I see the validity in [Eddie] Van Halen or Joe Satriani. You can hear [their] intelligence, but the others sound like gibberish. I'd rather listen to John Lee Hooker play one note."

Cleaning your guitar

Accumulated dirt on a guitar mainly comes from your skin and its oils and sweat. Whenever you play, the acidity in the secretions from your hands affects the strings, frets, and fingerboard. Simply wiping the strings down with a lint-free cloth at the end of a gig or practice session will prolong their life, but periodically you need to give the instrument a more thorough clean. Start by placing your guitar on a table covered in a soft towel, and support its neck with a dedicated caul or a rolled-up towel.

Protect the top of the guitar as shown in the photographs (use low-tack masking tape), then take off the strings and discard them. To remove heavy deposits of fingerboard gunk, try a not-too-damp cloth. Then use a piece of extra-fine 0000-grade steel wool to clean any tarnished frets, and finish by using the steel wool to rub the fingerboard (unless it's maple, the lacquered finish of which will be damaged by steel wool—see tip opposite), working in the direction of the grain. Mask off the fingerboard and polish the frets with metal polish; now remove the tape and apply a small drop of lemon oil to the board, allowing it to soak in before polishing to a lovely sheen. On an electric guitar, once all the steel-wool cleaning is done, carefully sweep away any residue and remove the tape covering the pickups.

Polished performance

A good hand-rubbing polish—which must be silicone-free—buffed with a lint-free cloth will remove built-up dirt from an electric guitar body with a modern gloss polyurethane finish. Treat acoustic guitars similarly, but if the finish is a "satin" one, skip the polishing, and just use a cloth with a hint of moisture to get rid of the muck, before wiping down with a dry cloth. Be especially cautious with vintage guitar finishes, and if you're uncertain about cleaning them, consult a specialist.

The nut plays a crucial role in anchoring the strings and transferring their tone to the guitar's body. If its slots are dirty and causing string snagging, clean them out with 320- and then 1200-grade sand-paper as shown here, before lubricating with pencil graphite.

Old-fashioned metal polish is fine for cleaning the chrome-plated steel or "gold"-plated hardware on most electric guitars. After using a stiff-bristled paintbrush to remove dust from the bridge and saddles, mask off the surrounding finish, and apply the polish before buffing. Once everything's clean, reward your guitar with a fresh set of strings.

1 When cleaning the fingerboard, shield an acoustic's body with low-tack masking tape to protect it.

2 On an electric, you should also mask off the pickups, as pieces of steel wool will be attracted to them.

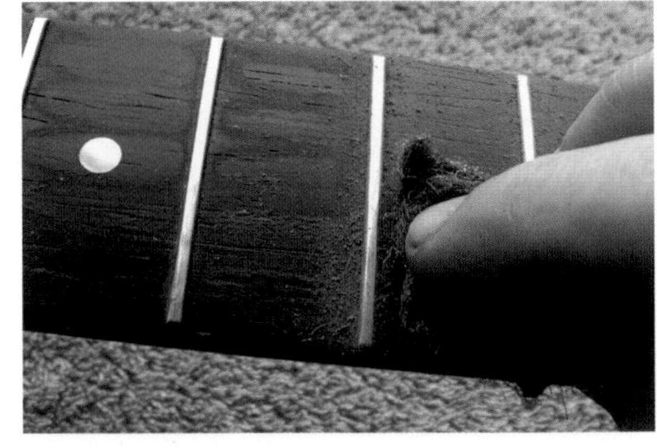

3 Take it very carefully when using 0000-grade steel wool on the frets and fingerboard.

Top Guitar Tip

Never use steel wool on a maple fingerboard, and cover the maple with masking tape if you're going to remove tarnishing from the frets with it. However, the easiest way to clean both the lacquered maple and the frets is with a good cleaner/polish.

Below *This Strat is immaculately clean. Simply wiping its strings and body down after playing will help to keep it in pristine condition for some time.*

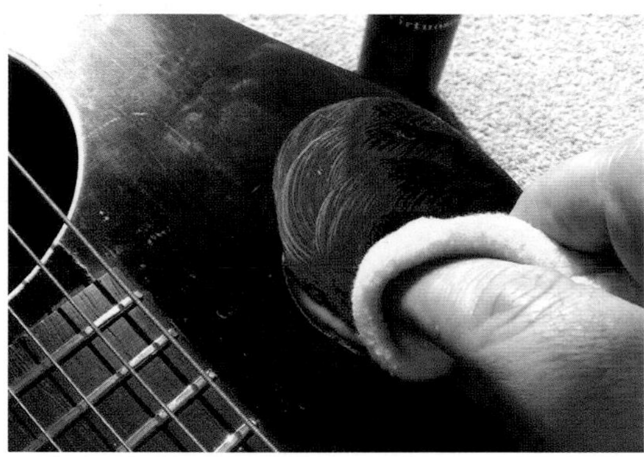

4 Work in small circles when applying silicone-free polish to a guitar body.

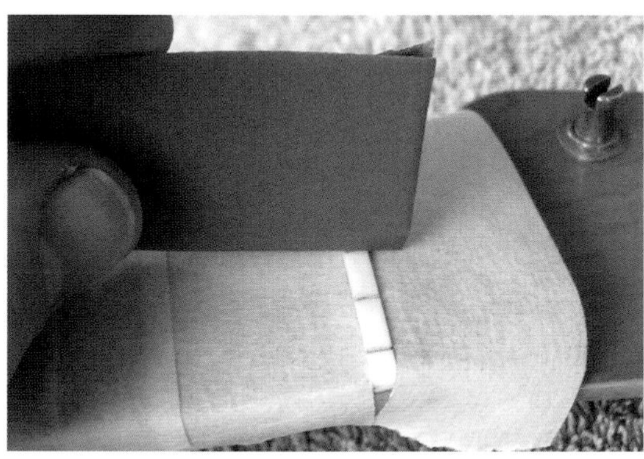

5 After masking off the neck, 320- and then 1200-grade paper can be used—very gently—to clean the nut slots.

6 Start with a brush when removing accumulated deposits of dirt and dust from the bridge.

GUITAR HERO

Joe Satriani

Joe Satriani was born in Westbury, some 25 miles (40 km) east of New York City, in 1956. Influenced by Jimi Hendrix, he took up the guitar aged about 14, and was skilled enough to start giving lessons to others barely two years later; among his early pupils was Steve Vai. In his late teens Satriani studied briefly with New York-based jazz guitarist Billy Bauer (1915–2005), and with Bauer's regular collaborator, pianist Lenny Tristano.

In 1978, Satriani moved to Berkeley, across the bay from San Francisco, where he taught several soon-to-be-stars, including Kirk Hammett of Metallica, at a local guitar studio. His own band, The Squares, struggled for recognition, but his self-confessedly bizarre instrumental recordings—released as a five-track, self-titled vinyl disc in 1984—led to a groundswell of critical acclaim, and a contract with Relativity Records, which issued his first full-length solo album, *Not of This Earth*, in 1986.

Satriani's major breakthrough came with the platinum-selling *Surfing with the Alien* (1987), and in 1988 his profile was raised even further when he worked as guitarist for Mick Jagger on tours of Japan and Australasia. Satch's subsequent solo records have all enjoyed substantial success; the most recent of them, released in 2010, is *Black Swans and Wormhole Wizards.*

His live work has included a stand-in stint with Deep Purple (following the departure of Richie Blackmore in November 1993), and he inaugurated the G3 concert tours in 1996, starring in their initial lineup alongside Eric Johnson and Steve Vai. A string of other top players has participated in later shows. Since 2008, he's been part of the rock "supergroup" Chickenfoot, with Sammy Hagar, Michael Anthony, and Chad Smith. The band released its first, eponymous album in 2009. The (rather perversely titled) follow-up, *Chickenfoot III*, came out in 2011 and in May 2012 the band embarked on its "Different Devil" U.S. tour.

Above: *Joe Satriani was a skilled guitarist by the time he was just 16 years old.*

Right and opposite: *Satriani in action: "What I do is rock'n'roll—you just hadn't heard anything quite like it before."*

Favorite Gear

Joe Satriani has a long-standing association with Ibanez, which produces the trailblazing JS series of instruments he endorses. When on tour, he uses a selection of new, easily replaceable Ibanez electrics, leaving his most treasured guitars safely at home. Ibanez has also developed a Satriani signature acoustic, the all-black JSA, which he's featured on tour with Chickenfoot. Two versions are currently available: both have cutaways, and are fitted with Fishman pickups and preamps. Satch's amps have included Peaveys, a Fender Bassman, a Soldano, and a Mesa/Boogie, but he is currently developing a signature amp with Marshall. Among the devices in his effects rig are a Fulltone DejáVibe and Ultimate Octave, Jim Dunlop wah-wah and Rotovibe units, and various other pedals by Boss and DigiTech.

> *"I just love playing live music with a band in front of an audience... You really open up your heart to the audience, and they are there projecting all of their energies toward you. [It's] a unique situation in a musician's life...the only place where that happens."*
>
> Joe Satriani

Satriani's Advice On Practicing

"When practicing I suggest you get yourself any set of exercises you can think of and play them. The key is to make sure you do them very slowly, with the idea that at the end of the day you've played any scale or exercise correctly more than you've played it incorrectly. To play something beyond your level for two hours everyday, where you might play it wrong most of the time—I don't think that's a really good thing to be doing. It's like you're creating an experience of making errors. The idea rather is to create an experience of not making errors, so you have to slow down so that your body learns what it's supposed to do, when it's doing it right."

GUITAR HERO

Slash

Opposite: Slash playing Sunway Surf Beach, Sunway Lagoon Theme Park, Kuala Lumpur, Malaysia, August 5, 2010 (left); posing for a Gibson publicity shot (right).

Saul Hudson—better known as Slash—was born in London in 1965, but moved to the United States (his African-American mother's birthplace; his father is British) aged 11. His childhood passion for BMX racing gave way to music after he acquired a guitar as a teenager. Already a Led Zeppelin and Rolling Stones fan, Slash became obsessed with playing, dropped out of high school and, in 1983, formed the short-lived Road Crew in Los Angeles with drummer Steven Adler and bassist Duff McKagan. Slash and Adler subsequently joined Hollywood Rose, which split the following year. Its lead singer, Axl Rose, was formerly part of L.A. Guns—several of whose members came together with Hollywood Rose personnel as Guns N' Roses in 1985.

After further changes, the "classic" G N' R lineup emerged: Rose, Slash, Adler, and guitarist Izzy Stradlin from Hollywood Rose, plus ex-Road Crew bassist McKagan. They recorded *Appetite for Destruction* (1987)—the U.S.A.'s largest-ever-selling debut album—and *G N' R Lies* (1988). Adler's drug dependency led to his sacking in 1990. Slash, too, had serious substance abuse problems, but underwent rehab, and remained with G N' R until 1996. However, a year earlier, disagreements with Rose had caused him to take time out and record the highly acclaimed *It's Five O'Clock Somewhere* with Slash's Snakepit.

Post-G N' R, Slash has devoted more time to session and guest appearances, working with Michael Jackson (who had already called on the guitarist's services for his 1991 album *Dangerous*), Alice Cooper and other major names. He reconstituted Slash's Snakepit for *Ain't Life Grand* (2000) and a world tour supporting AC/DC, and enjoyed significant success with Velvet Revolver (for which McKagan played bass), though this band's activities are currently on hold. Slash's first, eponymous solo album appeared in 2010: he commented about it to *Guitar & Bass*, that he'd "felt sort of stifled when we did the last Velvets record...[so] it was nice to just play my guitar for once." Keeping him company on the record were guests such as Lemmy from Motörhead, Ozzy Osbourne, and Ian Astbury from The Cult. A second Slash solo CD, *Apocalyptic Love*, recorded in L.A., was issued in May 2012.

Right: The Gibson Slash Appetite Les Paul, with an "AAA" maple top, mahogany back and neck, special headstock inlays, and Alnico II Pro Slash pickups.

Favorite Gear

Slash created his trademark *Appetite For Destruction* sound not with a vintage Gibson Les Paul but with a replica instrument modeled on a '59 Les Paul Standard, and hand-made for him in Los Angeles. On Guns N' Roses records, it was tuned a semitone lower than standard pitch. It remains his "mainstay recording guitar," but he's owned and used a great many other instruments, including Gibsons, Fenders, a Fernandes, and a Gretsch Country Gentleman. In 2008, Gibson issued a "U.S. Slash Les Paul" signature model. His amplification is Marshall—a variety of heads and straight-front 4 x 12-in (30-cm) cabinets. Among his effects are a Dunlop DCR-1SR rackmounted wah, a Rocktron Hush noise-reduction unit, a dbx 166 compressor, a Yamaha SPX 900 multi-effect processor, a Boss DD-3 digital delay, an MXR 10-band graphic EQ, and a Heil Talk Box.

> *You know, what it is that I do is such a natural for me that I don't really see [it] ever changing…The thing for me is probably adding to my repertoire—which is pretty much all I can do. And when I'm 70 I just hope that I'm a much better guitar player than I am now…*
>
> Slash

Slash On His Playing Style and Its Effect

"Originally I came out playing old school rock'n'roll guitar just because that was what really turned me on. I never jumped on the whole whiz-bam Eddie Van Halen bandwagon. I did think Eddie was brilliant, but I thought that was a style all to himself. I was more into the Jimmy Page, Mick Taylor, Keith Richards, Angus Young, Joe Perry, Brad Whitford, and even Ted Nugent school of playing. You know, that sort of Chuck Berry style of guitar playing: really roots rock'n'roll guitar."

Pete Townshend

Below: Pete Townshend performing at the Ernst-Merck-Halle in Hamburg with The Who, August 1972.

Pete Townshend was born in Chiswick, West London, in 1945. His father, Cliff, was a jazz clarinettist and saxophonist, and his mother was a singer. He acquired his first, "really, really cheap guitar" at the age of 12, and recalls that "I broke a lot of strings on it and learned [some] chords [when only] the D, G, and B strings were left. I played for about six months on those three strings, [and] when I managed to get enough pocket money to buy the rest of [them], I could suddenly play." One of Townshend's school friends was John Entwistle, a brass player and pianist before he took up the bass. They formed a Dixieland duo (with Townshend on banjo), but went on to collaborate with singer Roger Daltrey in The Detours. Keith Moon became the band's drummer in 1964: by this time, they had named themselves The Who, though they were also briefly known as The High Numbers. The Who's first single, "I Can't Explain" was a U.K. Top 10 hit in 1965.

Townshend's rhythm-orientated guitar style was influenced by (among others) jazz virtuoso Wes Montgomery, country picker Chet Atkins, and bluesman Bo Diddley. Elaborate, rapid soloing was never part of his musical vocabulary: "I was very frustrated because I couldn't do all that flash stuff," he admitted. However, his aggressive playing and anthemic songwriting helped to make The Who a potent force on both sides of the Atlantic—while the group's visceral energy (captured unforgettably on 1970's *Live At Leeds*) won them a reputation as the very finest of onstage performers.

Keith Moon died, aged only 32, in 1978—shortly after the release of *Who Are You*, the last of a string of classic 1970s albums. Ex-Faces drummer Kenney Jones was brought in to replace him, but The Who broke up in the early 1980s, although there have been subsequent reunions, including an appearance at Live Aid in 1985, and later shows with Zac Starkey (Ringo Starr's son) on drums. John Entwistle died in 2002. Townshend and Daltrey continue to work together as The Who, and *Endless Wire*, the first new album bearing the band's name since 1982, came out in 2006.

Favorite Gear

Pete Townshend's guitar and amp history is complex. Among the instruments associated with him are Gibson SGs, Rickenbackers, and Fender Stratocasters, though he's also used Gibson Les Pauls, Gretsches, Schecters, a Gibson SJ-200 flat-top, and other electrics and acoustics. His amps have included models by Vox, Hiwatt, Sound City, and Mesa/Boogie, and in the mid-1960s he played a part in the development of the Marshall stack—at one stage asking the firm for a 100-W amp with a huge 8 x 12-in (30-cm) cab. "I told Pete his roadies were going to kill him. He said, 'They get paid'," commented company founder Jim Marshall.

> *Rock'n'roll is a fire that is set by young bodies, and one day you wake up and you smell your own flesh burning.*
>
> Pete Townshend

Townshend's Smashed Guitars

"One day [in September 1964], I was banging my [Rickenbacker] guitar around making noises and I [hit] it on the ceiling in this club and the neck broke off…I had no other recourse but to make it look like I'd meant to do it. So I smashed this guitar and jumped all over the bits and then picked up the 12-string and carried on as though nothing had happened. The next day the place was packed." Before long, Townshend was smashing guitars regularly, and among the instruments destroyed at The Who's gigs between 1964 and 1973 (according to information from thewho.net, quoted in *Guitar & Bass*) were five Rickenbackers, at least 35 Gibsons and 30-plus Fender Strats and Teles. In 1989, Pete broke a Rickenbacker accidentally by tripping over it: its pieces were later framed and displayed as part of the *Rock Stars, Cars & Guitars 2* exhibit at the Henry Ford Museum in Dearborn, Michigan.

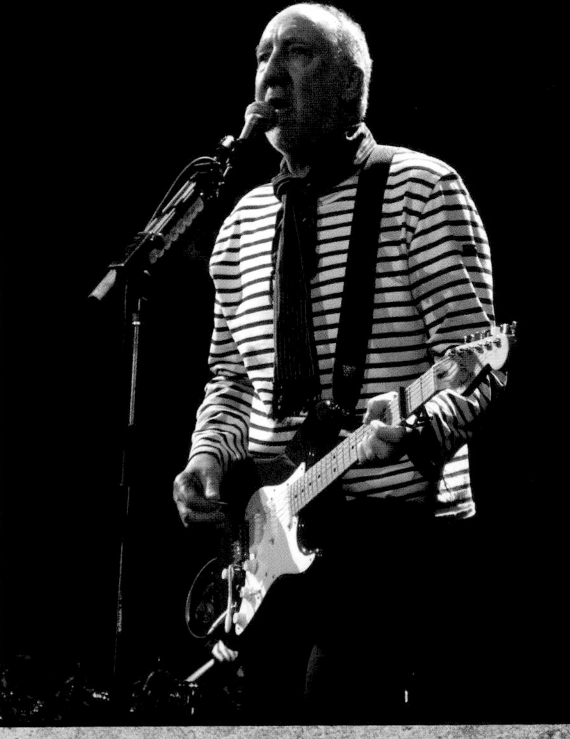

Above: *Pete Townshend contributes to a fundraising concert for the Teenage Cancer Trust at London's Royal Albert Hall in 2004.*

Right: *Performing on stage with The Who at Copps Coliseum, Hamilton, Ontario, Canada, on October 22, 2008.*

GUITAR HERO

Derek Trucks

Above: *Derek Trucks playing a Gibson ES-335 on an Allman Brothers Band gig at the Seminole Hard Rock Hotel & Casino, Florida, October 20, 2009.*

Below: *Another shot from the Allmans' Seminole show.*

Derek Trucks's surname will be familiar to any Allman Brothers fan: his uncle, Butch, was one of the band's two drummers in its late 1960s/early 1970s heyday. Derek himself was born in Jacksonville, Florida, in 1979, and his parents chose his first name as a salute to Derek and the Dominos—whose leader was, of course, Eric Clapton. Derek's been playing guitar since the age of about nine, and, as he told *Guitar & Bass* in 2006, 'Layla' and The Allman Brothers' *At Fillmore East* were the things that opened my ears when I was a kid—for a few years they were like the Bible!" He began working with The Allman Brothers Band (which continues to tour and record with a lineup that includes Gregg Allman and Butch Trucks) at the age of 11, and became a fully fledged member in 1999. His slide virtuosity quickly won him accolades from fellow -musicians as well as fans, and after witnessing the Trucks' magic at first hand, Carlos Santana referred to him as "the anointed one."

In recent years Derek has combined his work with the Allmans with other high-profile commitments. In 2006, he appeared on the J. J. Cale and Eric Clapton album, *The Road To Escondido*, and he has gone on to play live regularly with Clapton, describing the experience, in a 2009 *G&B* interview, as "certainly a trip, and quite surreal getting to [perform] all those old Derek and the Dominos songs. It's been a nice shot in the arm; I got exposed to new audiences by playing festivals in countries that I would never have visited otherwise. Eric's always been gracious that way. He knows that by taking out younger guitar players, he's giving them an opportunity."

Derek Trucks' own band, established in 1996, received a Grammy award for its *Already Free* CD (2009), and he now collaborates with his wife, blues singer/guitarist Susan Tedeschi, in the Tedeschi Trucks Band, whose *Revelator* album (2011) won the "Best Blues Album" Grammy in 2012.

Favorite Gear

Derek Trucks plays in open E tuning with a glass slide: his main solid-body guitar is a Gibson SG Standard, and he often uses a 1966 Fender Super Reverb amp. He also has a 1936 National Duolian resonator guitar that was once owned by Mississippi bluesman Bukka White (1909–77). "It's pretty special," he told *Guitar & Bass*. "I found it in Atlanta [a few] years ago, and luckily for me no one knew who Bukka White was! It's a great-sounding guitar. You can't really fret it normally because the neck's bent in a funky shape, but for slide it's amazing. It's got a real trashy thing going on, and that's the beauty of it."

> *I've been on a crazy trip recently, but all's well… It's difficult trying to juggle it all, but it seems to be falling into place…somehow!*
>
> Derek Trucks, 2006

Below: *Derek Trucks performs on stage at Shepherds Bush Empire, London, on June 29, 2011.*

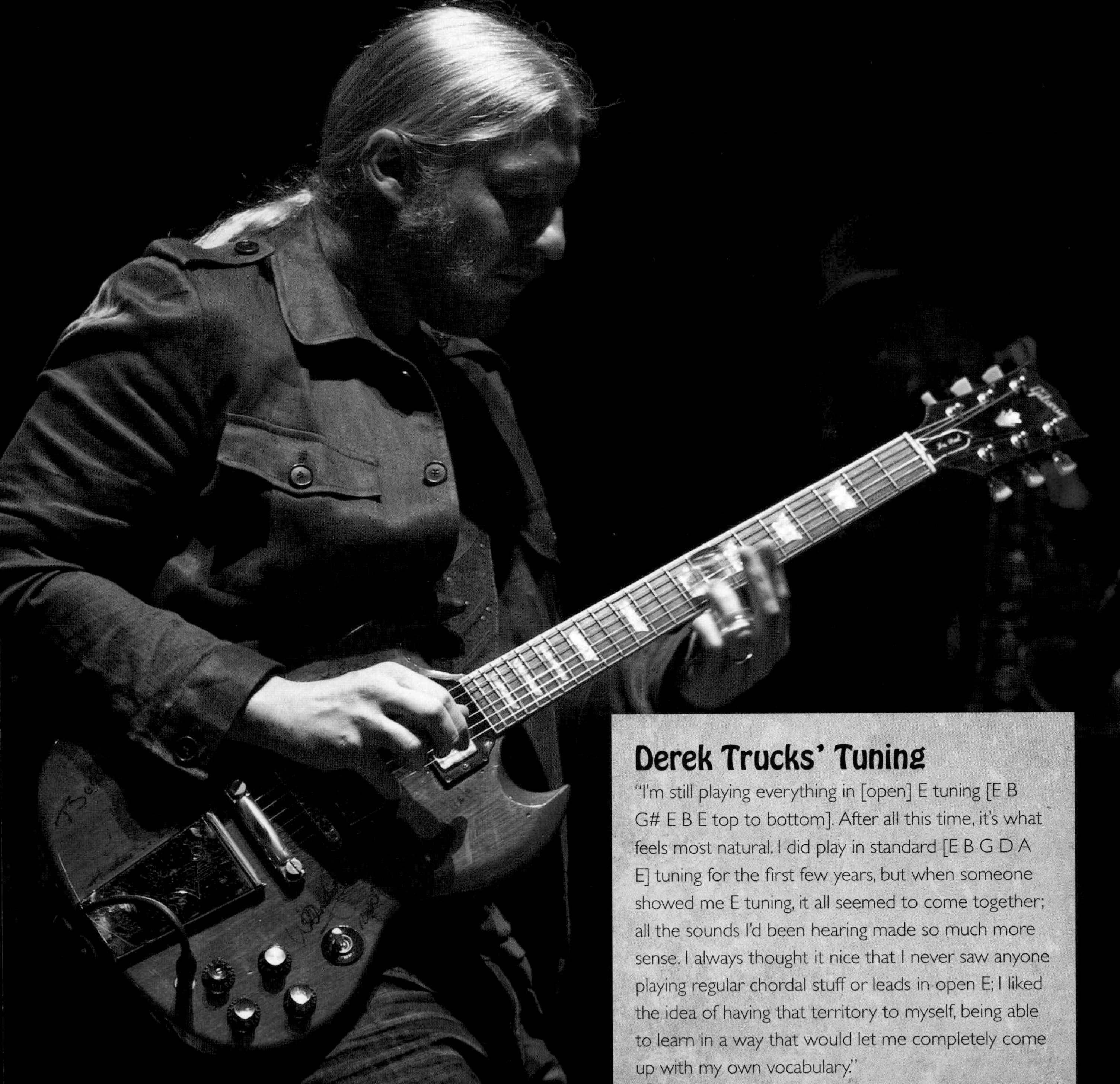

Derek Trucks' Tuning

"I'm still playing everything in [open] E tuning [E B G# E B E top to bottom]. After all this time, it's what feels most natural. I did play in standard [E B G D A E] tuning for the first few years, but when someone showed me E tuning, it all seemed to come together; all the sounds I'd been hearing made so much more sense. I always thought it nice that I never saw anyone playing regular chordal stuff or leads in open E; I liked the idea of having that territory to myself, being able to learn in a way that would let me completely come up with my own vocabulary."

Steve Vai

Above: Steve Vai. "All I do with the guitar is just try to make real what I have in my head and my heart."

Right and opposite: On September 6, 2009, Vai received an honorary Golden Stag award from the music festival of the same name in Brașov, Romania. Here he is on stage at the festival.

Steve Vai was born in Long Island, New York, in 1960. At the age of 11, he was learning the accordion—but within a few years he'd switched to guitar, and was having lessons from his friend and future collaborator Joe Satriani. Vai went on to study music at Berklee College of Music in Boston, Massachusetts, emerging with impressive aural and transcribing skills to match his fretboard prowess. This combination of talents won him a job with Frank Zappa, with whom Vai toured and recorded between 1980 and 1982.

Zappa lived in Los Angeles, and Southern California has been Vai's base ever since. His first solo disc, *Flex-Able*, recorded at his home in Sylmar, was issued in 1984. The following year saw the start of a busy period of work with mainstream rock names—Alcatrazz (replacing Yngwie Malmsteen), David Lee Roth, Whitesnake—that helped to establish Steve's credentials with audiences all over the world. However, he made a more impressively individual impact with his album *Passion and Warfare* (1990), which he summarized as "Hendrix meets Jesus Christ at a party Ben Hur threw for Mel Blanc!"

Since then, whether fronting his own bands, working with Joe Satriani on the G3 concert series, guesting with artists ranging from Motörhead to Surinder Sandhu (who plays the bowed Indian sarangi), or providing online guitar tuition in association with Berklee, Steve Vai has continued to follow his musical convictions, set out eloquently in a 2009 interview with *Guitar & Bass*: "Every step of my career, my life, and my music, I do my very best to not be swayed by ignorant trends, stifling parameters, purisms, and genre-specific things... The most vital part of my playing has been that lack of desire for conventionality." Vai's strikingly unusual CD, *Sound Theories Vol. I & II* (2007), is evidence of these aims: it features new versions of some of his famous pieces performed with an orchestra, as well as some purely orchestral compositions with no guitar parts.

Favorite Gear

Steve Vai co-designed the Ibanez JEM series of electric guitars, and has used them since their introduction in 1987. In 2009, *Guitar & Bass* reported that "Vai's main squeeze is EVO, one of four white Ibanez JEMs with gold hardware made in the early '90s. His second choice is Flo, a floral JEM painted white." He's also collaborated with the U.S.-based Carvin company on his own amps and speakers—the latest models are the Legacy 3 100-W head and 2 x 12-in (30-cm) cab. Steve's effects pedals include two Morley devices made to his specifications: the Bad Horsie wah and Little Alligator volume pedal.

"I do love playing. The guitar is a never-ending device of expression. I'll never get tired of it."

Steve Vai, 2005

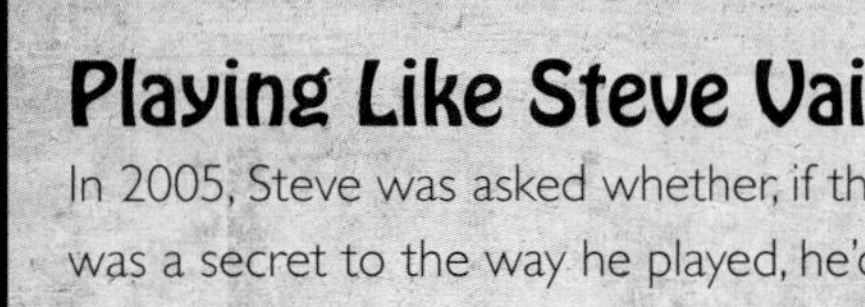

Playing Like Steve Vai

In 2005, Steve was asked whether, if there was a secret to the way he played, he'd be willing to share it with *G&B* readers.

"Of course! I don't necessarily call it 'a secret,' but I can tell you what my thoughts are…My playing is an expression of who I am. There are things that are unique about the way I play because I've made efforts since the day I picked up a guitar to do things I've never heard before. It just didn't seem right to me to copy someone. To play like me, you need to play like yourself. And I can tell you ways to do that. When you pick up your instrument, [try and] come up with something you've never done before—you'd be surprised how challenging that is. Every day you do this, you're increasing your musical vocabulary. It's a statement of what you are, because it's not who anybody else is."

Eddie Van Halen

Below: Eddie Van Halen in full flight! His stacks of EVH amps are behind him, alongside brother Alex, who's on drums.

Eddie Van Halen was born in Amsterdam in 1955, but moved to the United States with his family as a child. The Van Halens settled in Pasadena, California, where Eddie and his brother Alex (b.1953) became known for their musical skills; their father, Jan (1920–86), was a bandleader and sax/clarinet player. In 1972, the siblings formed a group initially called Mammoth but soon renamed Van Halen, with Eddie on guitar and Alex as drummer (at one time, their choice of instruments had been reversed). Its self-titled 1978 debut album won Eddie international recognition for his agile, powerful playing, whose technical secrets he sometimes tried to conceal from audiences by turning his back on them! Among the LP's highlights was "Eruption," an instrumental showcasing the "tapping" technique (where the picking hand "taps" the string against the fretboard) that he's since made famous.

Van Halen—dominated by Eddie and vocalist David Lee Roth—produced five more best-selling albums over the next six years. During this period, Eddie also contributed his celebrated guitar solo to Michael Jackson's "Beat It" (*Thriller*, 1982). Roth left Van Halen following the release of *1984* (named for its issue date); his replacement, Sammy Hagar, was to remain with the band until 1996. That year saw a short-lived, stormy reunion with Roth. In its aftermath, Gary Cherone was brought in to provide vocals, while Hagar rejoined the group for their 2004 concert dates across the United States and Canada. David Lee Roth eventually returned for Van Halen's triumphant 2007–08 North American tour, on which Eddie's son, Wolfgang, served as bassist in place of Michael Anthony.

Over the years, Eddie has faced serious health worries: he underwent hip-replacement surgery in 1999, was successfully treated for oral cancer at the start of the new century, and has also been in rehab. More recently, though, he's been keeping a higher profile: Van Halen's album *A Different Kind of Truth*—its first for 14 years—came out in February 2012, and the band (comprising Roth, the Van Halen brothers, and Wolfgang Van Halen) has been touring extensively to promote it.

Favorite Gear

Eddie Van Halen was central to the development of the "Superstrat," and has continued to seek high-performance guitar designs able to do justice to his technical prowess. In recent years, he's been associated with the "Wolfgang" electric, named for his son and initially produced by Mississippi-based manufacturer Peavey Electronics in 1996. Currently, the "EVH" range of equipment, including Wolfgang guitars and 5150 amps and cabs, is made by Fender.

> *A lot of guitarists start from me and go from there. I started from the blues and built from there upward…Whenever I play, I play from inside, which is why I don't always play the same solo night after night.*
>
> Eddie Van Halen

Below: Eddie at a dress rehearsal for a show at The Forum in Inglewood, California on February 8, 2012.

The Tribute Band Perspective

In 2003, *Guitar & Bass* asked Dan Ratcliffe, lead guitarist with top U.K.-based Van Halen tribute band 5150, to assess Eddie Van Halen's musical significance. "I think Eddie will be definitely remembered for his additions to guitar technique," Ratcliffe replied. "His approach to tapping and harmonics, yeah…but a lot of people overlook his rhythmic style, which is incredibly active. The song '5150' is a prime example. I think he laid waste to everything else from the '70s." So has Van Halen become a guitar benchmark—if you think you're good, just try playing some of his repertoire? "There's definitely that side to it. Something like 'Eruption' is daunting because as well as being incredibly fast, it's also unbelievably melodic. It's not just a lot of blazing notes…[and] because most of the solos are very tuneful, you can't get away from trying to play them as accurately as possible."

Stevie Ray Vaughan

Stevie Ray Vaughan was born in Dallas, Texas, in 1954. His older brother, Jimmie (later to be famous as one of The Fabulous Thunderbirds) was an accomplished guitarist, and though young Stevie was undoubtedly influenced by him, his earliest favorite track was probably Lonnie Mack's classic instrumental "Wham!" (1963). By the age of 10, Stevie was in a band. Soon he was becoming steeped in the blues music (Albert King, Freddie King, Muddy Waters) that was to shape his own style, and at the age of about 13 he first heard the music of Jimi Hendrix, a performer he was to idolize.

In 1971, aged 17, Stevie moved south to Austin, Texas, and it was here that he put together his band Double Trouble in 1978. The group built up a substantial local following, and found wider fame thanks to an appearance at the 1982 Montreux Jazz Festival in Switzerland, arranged through the good offices of veteran record producer Jerry Wexler. Double Trouble's performance at Montreux led to a recording contract, and David Bowie, who had been in the audience there, asked Stevie to contribute to the sessions for his *Let's Dance* album. Both the Bowie LP and Double Trouble's debut *Texas Flood* were highly acclaimed when they appeared a year later.

Success, and the hectic lifestyle that comes with it, took their toll on the brilliant young guitarist, who struggled with serious drink and drug problems that brought about an onstage collapse in 1986. However, he conquered his addictions, and the release of *In Step* in 1989 seemed to herald a healthy, optimistic future for Double Trouble: as the band's bassist Tommy Shannon commented, "After *In Step* we were clean and sober and looking forward to the next record. We had so many ideas."

Sadly, Stevie Ray Vaughan's career ended prematurely on August 27, 1990, when the helicopter flying him from a music festival in Wisconsin to Chicago crashed after taking off in darkness and fog. He and the other four people on board were all killed instantly.

***Opposite:** Stevie Ray at New Orleans' Jazz & Heritage Festival in May 1986. Over the years, he and Double Trouble played several shows at the city's Fair Grounds racecourse and at other venues there.*

Favorite Gear

Stevie Ray Vaughan was a high-profile Fender Stratocaster user, though his other instruments included a Martin acoustic and a resonator guitar made by National. His "Number One" Strat (a 1959 model with a newer neck) had heavy-gauge strings tuned a semitone below normal pitch. He was a devotee of vintage Fender amps, especially the Super Reverb, Vibroverb, and Twin Reverb, and also had a 150-W head and 4 x 12-in (30-cm) cab built by L.A.-based "boutique" amp maker Howard Dumble.

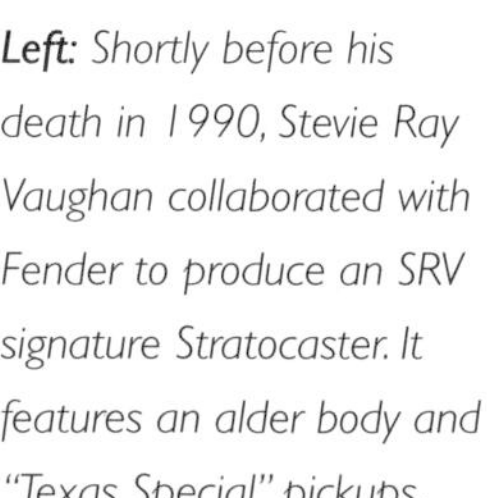

***Left:** Shortly before his death in 1990, Stevie Ray Vaughan collaborated with Fender to produce an SRV signature Stratocaster. It features an alder body and "Texas Special" pickups.*

"To me Stevie Ray was the greatest blues guitarist. For fire and passion and soulfulness, he was untouchable. He was scary to those of us who watched him. But he was so humble and gracious as a friend, and he wasn't stuck up about his playing."

Bonnie Raitt

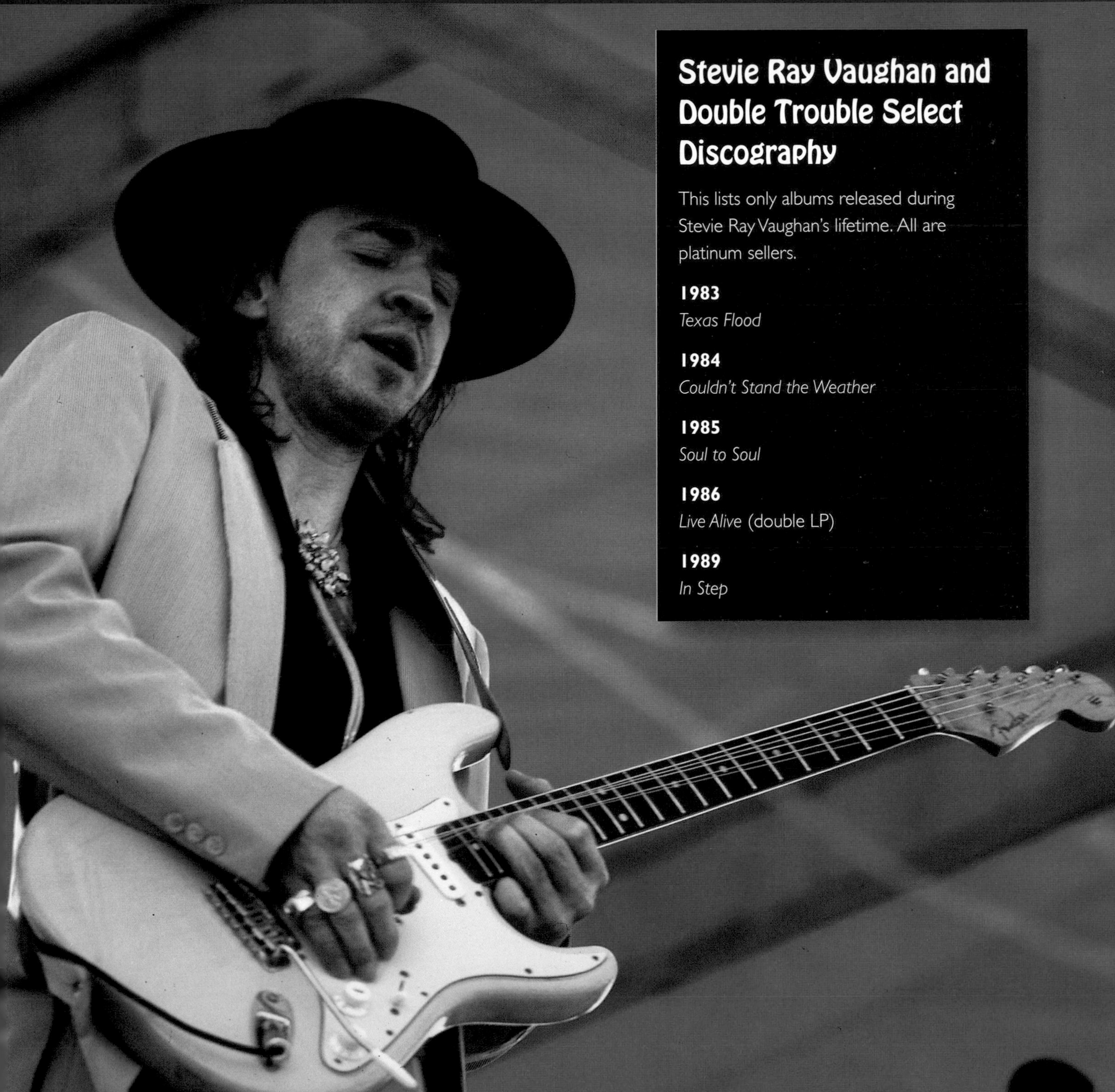

Stevie Ray Vaughan and Double Trouble Select Discography

This lists only albums released during Stevie Ray Vaughan's lifetime. All are platinum sellers.

1983
Texas Flood

1984
Couldn't Stand the Weather

1985
Soul to Soul

1986
Live Alive (double LP)

1989
In Step

Jack White

Born in Detroit, Michigan, in 1975, with the surname Gillis, Jack White started out playing drums, but switched to guitar when performing as part of a duo called The Upholsterers; he'd been an apprentice for the upholstery firm run by its other member, drummer Brian Muldoon. Gillis married Meg White in 1996: he took her surname, and formed The White Stripes with her a year later. Their subsequent divorce did not affect their musical partnership, and for some time they fooled the media into believing they were brother and sister.

The White Stripes (with Meg on drums) released their self-titled debut album in 1999, dedicating it to one of Jack's heroes, Mississippi Delta blues guitarist and singer Son House (1902–88). While rooted in Detroit-style garage rock, White's music draws on a wide range of influences, and his eclectic tastes are reflected in his production work on albums by country music star Loretta Lynn (*Van Lear Rose*, 2004) and "The Queen of Rockabilly," Wanda Jackson (*The Party Ain't Over*, 2011). The White Stripes brought Jack and Meg White international recognition: they first enjoyed major commercial success with their third CD, *White Blood Cells* (2001), featuring the hit single "Fell In Love With A Girl," while their fourth album *Elephant* (2003) won them two Grammys, and was their biggest seller. After six studio albums (the last was 2007's *Icky Thump*), The White Stripes disbanded in February 2011. In the preceding years, however, Jack White had been part of two other groups, The Raconteurs and The Dead Weather (playing drums with the latter outfit).

He's based in Nashville, Tennessee (also the home of his own record label, Third Man Records), and, in 2011, was appointed the first-ever "Music City Ambassador" by its mayor. White's been quoted as saying he won't join another band, and he released his debut solo album, *Blunderbuss*, in April 2012.

Favorite Gear

White frequently plays Gretsch guitars, but is also closely identified with the 1964 Valco Jetsons Airline solid-body he used with The White Stripes: it has a red Res-O-Glas (fiberglass) body and two single-coil pickups. Jack told *Guitar & Bass* that "you could buy them in the '60s in a department store called Montgomery Wards, but they stopped selling them in the '70s." He added, "I think it's cheating to buy brand-new guitars. They don't go out of tune and it's too easy!" He often uses Fender and Silvertone amplification, and his DigiTech Whammy pedal is another important part of his sound.

Left: *The White Stripes—Jack and his ex-wife Meg White—at the top of the bill for London's 2007 O2 Wireless festival. Jack is playing his red 1964 Valco Jetsons Airline electric.*

"I would tell anybody to not spend much money on guitars. Get as cheap a guitar as possible—It doesn't matter if it's broken. If there are only three strings on it, learn to play with three strings instead of six strings. That way you'll be truly expressing yourself, and that's what makes a good guitar player."

Jack White, quoted in *Guitar*, 2003

Jack White On Recording

Jack White has unequivocal views on the right and wrong ways to record, proclaiming that "digital equipment is evil [because] it undermines the creativity of artists. Most people are convinced that using digital equipment makes their work easier, but it's a huge misunderstanding—it makes the creative process difficult. It enables us to explore too many possibilities and overproduce as a result. Analog is definitely better. It's soulful. The worst thing is that people correct their sound with computer programs. They make rhythm faultless and the vocal pitch perfect, but I don't think that it is real music."

This page: *Jack White playing two Canadian concerts: the 2007 Bluesfest in Ottawa (above) and a gig with The Raconteurs at The Commodore Ballroom, Vancouver, 2008 (above left).*

GUITAR HERO

Angus Young

Below: A Gibson Angus Young SG Standard, with AC/DC lightning bolt fingerboard inlays.

Angus Young was born in Glasgow, Scotland, in 1955. In 1963, he emigrated, with his family, to Melbourne, Australia, where ten years later he and his older brother and fellow-guitarist Malcolm established AC/DC. In 1974, Angus first wore his soon-to-be-famous "schoolboy" uniform on stage with the band: it made a much greater impact than any of the previous costumes he'd donned for live gigs, and has recently been displayed at Melbourne Museum as part of an exhibition of items associated with the city. Vocalist Bon Scott featured alongside Angus and Malcolm on AC/DC's debut LP, *High Voltage* (1975): the other core members, drummer Phil Rudd and bassist Cliff Williams, joined in 1975 and 1977, respectively.

The group's rising international status was confirmed by the success of *Highway to Hell* (1979)—though Bon Scott's death (from alcoholic poisoning in London on February 19, 1980) occurred before the album reached its commercial zenith. His replacement by a British ex-glam-rocker, Brian Johnson, was initially a surprise. However, Scott himself had admired Johnson's singing, and the newcomer's gutsy delivery proved to be a perfect match for Angus Young's hard-riffing, wonderfully raucous guitar work.

Aside from the loss of Scott, the only other serious difficulty faced by AC/DC during its lengthy career was the dismissal of Phil Rudd in 1983, precipitated by the drummer's personal problems. Rudd's place was taken by Simon Wright and (later) Chris Slade, but he officially rejoined the band in 1994. AC/DC's status as hard-rock royalty is in no doubt. Only Michael Jackson's *Thriller* has sold more copies worldwide than *Back in Black*, AC/DC's first post-Bon Scott album, released in 1980. Their sound, though essentially unaltered for decades, is immensely powerful and instantly recognizable. The band's most recent CD is 2008's *Black Ice*: plans for a new album are under discussion, and AC/DC will celebrate its 40th anniversary in 2013.

Above: Angus Young on AC/DC's "Black Ice" Tour, Xcel Energy Center, St. Paul, Minnesota, on November 23, 2008.

Opposite: Angus performs with AC/DC at the Download Festival, Donington Park, Derby, England, on June 11, 2010.

Favorite Gear

Angus has used a 1968 Gibson SG Standard since buying it in 1970, and is a devotee of Marshall amplification. In 2009, Gibson launched three versions of its Angus Young SG: a regular production instrument, plus two limited-edition Custom Shop models. His preferred guitar string gauges are .009 to .042, and he uses heavy picks.

> *I think the vibe's been great since Phil [Rudd, AC/DC's drummer] came back. We just lock down so well together back there, and there's that "the old team's all here again" feeling in the whole band right now, and that gives out a lot of energy and makes it a lot of fun.*

Cliff Williams, AC/DC's bassist, quoted in *Guitar & Bass*, 2009

Did You Know?

In 2003, Angus Young and the other members of AC/DC were inducted into the Rock and Roll Hall of Fame in Cleveland, Ohio, by Steven Tyler of Aerosmith.

The band has a Melbourne street named after them, ACDC Lane—though it's spelt without a slash, as these aren't permitted by the city authorities. Calle de AC/DC, in Leganés, outside the Spanish capital, Madrid, doesn't have this problem!

Angus Young's onstage antics would be seriously limited by a guitar cable, and since 1977 he's taken advantage of wireless systems to send his guitar signals to his amp. His first such unit was a Schaffer-Vega diversity system, and he now uses a Lectrosonics unit.

Neil Young

Neil Young was born in Toronto, Canada, in 1945. After switching from ukulele to guitar, and moving to Winnipeg as a teenager, he started his professional career in The Squires, aged 17. The group's repertoire reflected the young musician's heroes—Hank Marvin, Link Wray, Duane Eddy, and The Ventures. Initially performing only instrumentals, it developed a folkier style, and began to feature some of Neil's own songs. Following its break-up, he played solo on Winnipeg's club circuit, and then had a brief spell in The Mynah Birds alongside singer Rick James. Plans for the band to record with Motown in Detroit didn't work out, and Neil Young moved to Los Angeles in 1966.

There, he became part of Buffalo Springfield (with Steven Stills, whom he'd previously met in Canada). The group's three albums, released between 1966 and 1968, showcased Young's distinctive guitar work, and he went on to make his first, classic solo LPs (sometimes backed by the group Crazy Horse, though its involvement with Young became more sporadic), while also performing and recording with Stills, David Crosby, and Graham Nash in the famous quartet often abbreviated as CSNY. These ventures were artistically and commercially successful, but the death from a drug overdose of Crazy Horse's Danny Whitten in 1972 led to a darker mood in Young's music. He's described *Tonight's The Night* (recorded in 1973) as being "about life, dope, and death…we got right out there on the edge where we were wide open to the mood. It was spooky." His label, too, was unsettled by the record, delaying its release for two years. Other 1970s projects included the 1978 "Rust Never Sleeps" tour, whose shows were split between acoustic sets by Young himself, and electric performances with Crazy Horse.

Neil Young's subsequently embraced a bewildering range of styles and genres—the hit single "Rockin' In The Free World" (1989), the big band feel of *This Note's for You* (1988), the grungy *Ragged Glory* (1990), and the noise and feedback of "Arc" (1991). He remains as powerful and unpredictable a musical presence as ever, and his latest offering, *Le Noise* (2010), was warmly praised by *Guitar & Bass*: "Grimy guitars meld with looping sound bites, off-the-wall effects, and Young's brittle tenor to make this one of his most assured releases to date."

Below: *Neil Young plays Toronto's Massey Hall, which seats over 2,700, in November 2007. His wife Pegi also performed at the show.*

Favorite Gear

Neil Young's favorite guitar is a 1953 Gibson Les Paul Gold Top, nicknamed Old Black. "It has a Firebird pickup on the treble side and I guess I've used it on all [my] things since 1973." Old Black is retro-fitted with a Bigsby vibrato. "I like the Bigsby because it's so expressive. The wang bars around on modern guitars aren't too expressive, they're too tight. You stay in tune, great…but you don't get the expression." For amps, Young favors a four-input tweed Fender Deluxe from 1959, which he bought in 1967, plus a custom-built device called a Whizzer that motorizes the amp's knobs to produce various preset sounds.

Below: *Neil Young launched Farm Aid, with Willie Nelson and John Mellencamp, in 1985. Here, he's pictured at the 25th anniversary concert given by the founders at Miller Park, Milwaukee, Wisconsin, on October 2, 2010.*

> *Every one of my records to me is like an autobiography. My trip is to express what's on my mind.*
>
> Neil Young, 2008

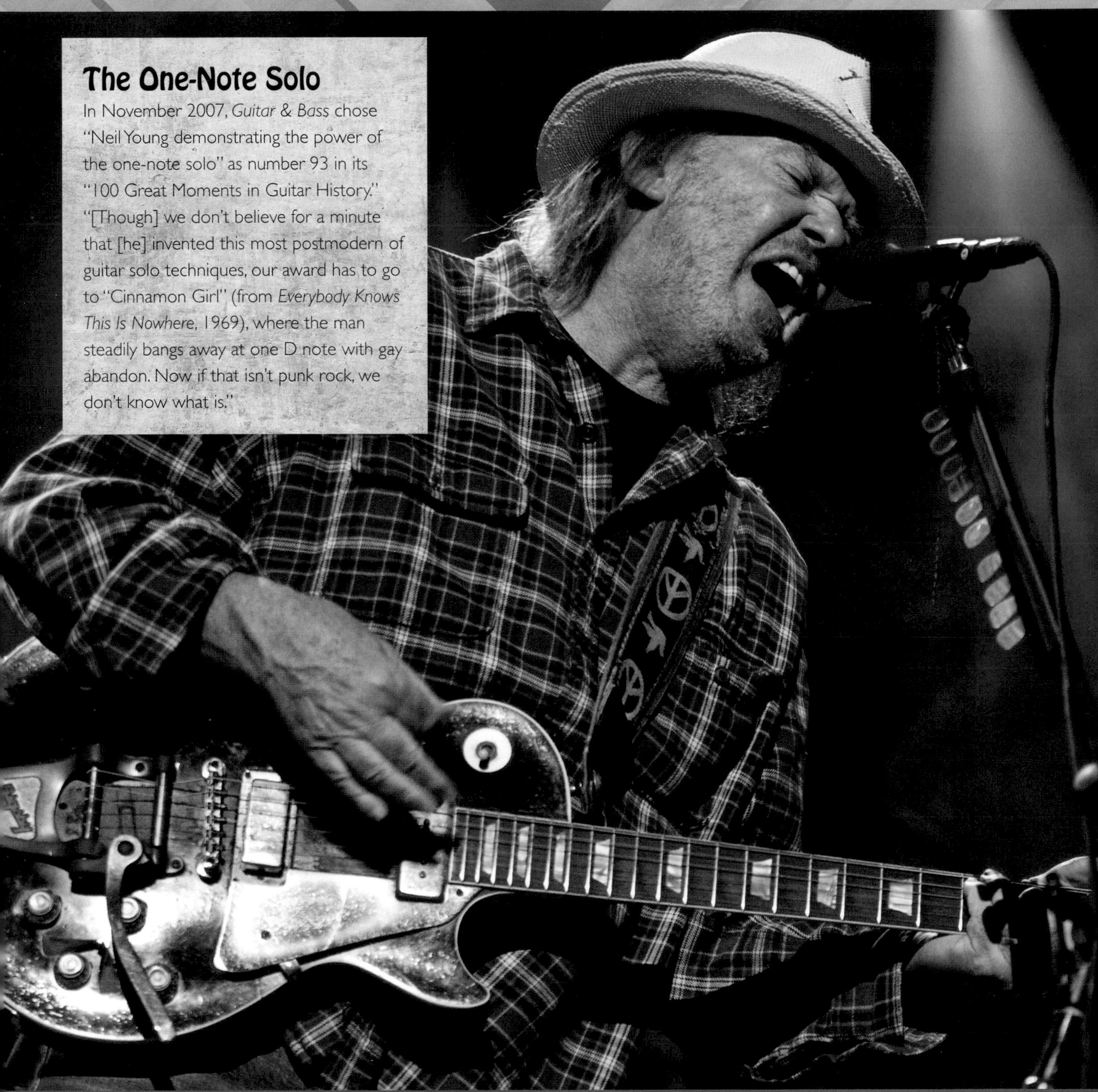

The One-Note Solo

In November 2007, *Guitar & Bass* chose "Neil Young demonstrating the power of the one-note solo" as number 93 in its "100 Great Moments in Guitar History." "[Though] we don't believe for a minute that [he] invented this most postmodern of guitar solo techniques, our award has to go to "Cinnamon Girl" (from *Everybody Knows This Is Nowhere*, 1969), where the man steadily bangs away at one D note with gay abandon. Now if that isn't punk rock, we don't know what is."

Frank Zappa

Though he was born in Baltimore, Maryland, in 1940, Frank Zappa grew up in Southern California, where he played the drums in a band he joined while at high school in San Diego. As a guitarist and musician, he was essentially self-taught, and highly eclectic in his tastes. His early (and enduring) passions were doo-wop vocal harmony records, the bluesy soloing of guitar players, such as Clarence "Gatemouth" Brown, Matt Murphy, and Johnny "Guitar" Watson, and the avant-garde compositions of Edgard Varèse (1883–1965). Among his friends and contemporaries was Captain Beefheart (Don Van Vliet, 1941–2010), whose seminal album *Trout Mask Replica* (1969) he later produced.

Zappa's own first record was *Freak Out!*, recorded with the Mothers of Invention, and released in 1966. The Mothers were to serve as his backing band until the mid-1970s, though a different set of musicians appeared on "solo" LPs such as *Lumpy Gravy* (1967) and *Hot Rats* (1969). After *Bongo Fury* (1975), the Mothers were no longer featured, and for the rest of his career Zappa had mixed feelings about the very notion of working with a band. Though he benefited from the instrumental virtuosity of many highly skilled sidemen (including, at various times, guitarists Steve Vai, Denny Walley, Adrian Belew, and Warren Cuccurullo), he was a strict musical disciplinarian who drilled his cohorts rigorously—and would sometimes abandon them in favor of the Synclavier, a hi-tech device able to reproduce his meticulously written instrumental parts with a precision that even the best human performers couldn't match.

Frank Zappa's talents and preoccupations were so multifaceted (composer, campaigner against what he regarded as censorship, satirist) that his abilities as a guitarist are sometimes overlooked...a fact that must have inspired his decision to name a boxed set of his instrumental work, released in 1981, *Shut Up 'N' Play Yer Guitar!* However, his love for what he characteristically described as "the disgusting stink of a too-loud electric" was to endure to the end of his life—and his prodigious technique has been summed up, memorably, by his guitarist son, Dweezil: "His picking was like a chicken and his fingers were like a spider, and it was an epic battle between the two."

In 1993, Zappa died of cancer in Los Angeles, aged only 52.

Above: *The Gibson SG—the choice of Frank Zappa.*

Favorite Gear

In his early days with the Mothers of Invention, Zappa used a Gibson ES-5 Switchmaster, which he later replaced with a goldtop Les Paul. Eventually, however, he graduated to the guitar with which his son Dweezil, like many of his fans, associates him most closely—the Gibson SG. "When I was little that was the [one] he would play the most." There were several features common to all Zappa's electrics: ultra-light-gauge strings, extremely low action, and built-in preamps (with parametric EQ) that supplied so much additional gain that he had no need for overdrive devices like fuzz boxes. His amps were often Marshalls, Voxes, Acoustics, and Carvins, though he was also fond of tiny Pignose practice models.

> *On a sax you can play sleaze, on a bass you can play balls, but the only instrument on which you can be truly obscene is an electric guitar…*
>
> Frank Zappa

Below: *A photo from the session that produced the cover shot for Zappa's* Shut Up 'N' Play Yer Guitar! *The sheaf of manuscript music paper behind him is probably an orchestral score.*

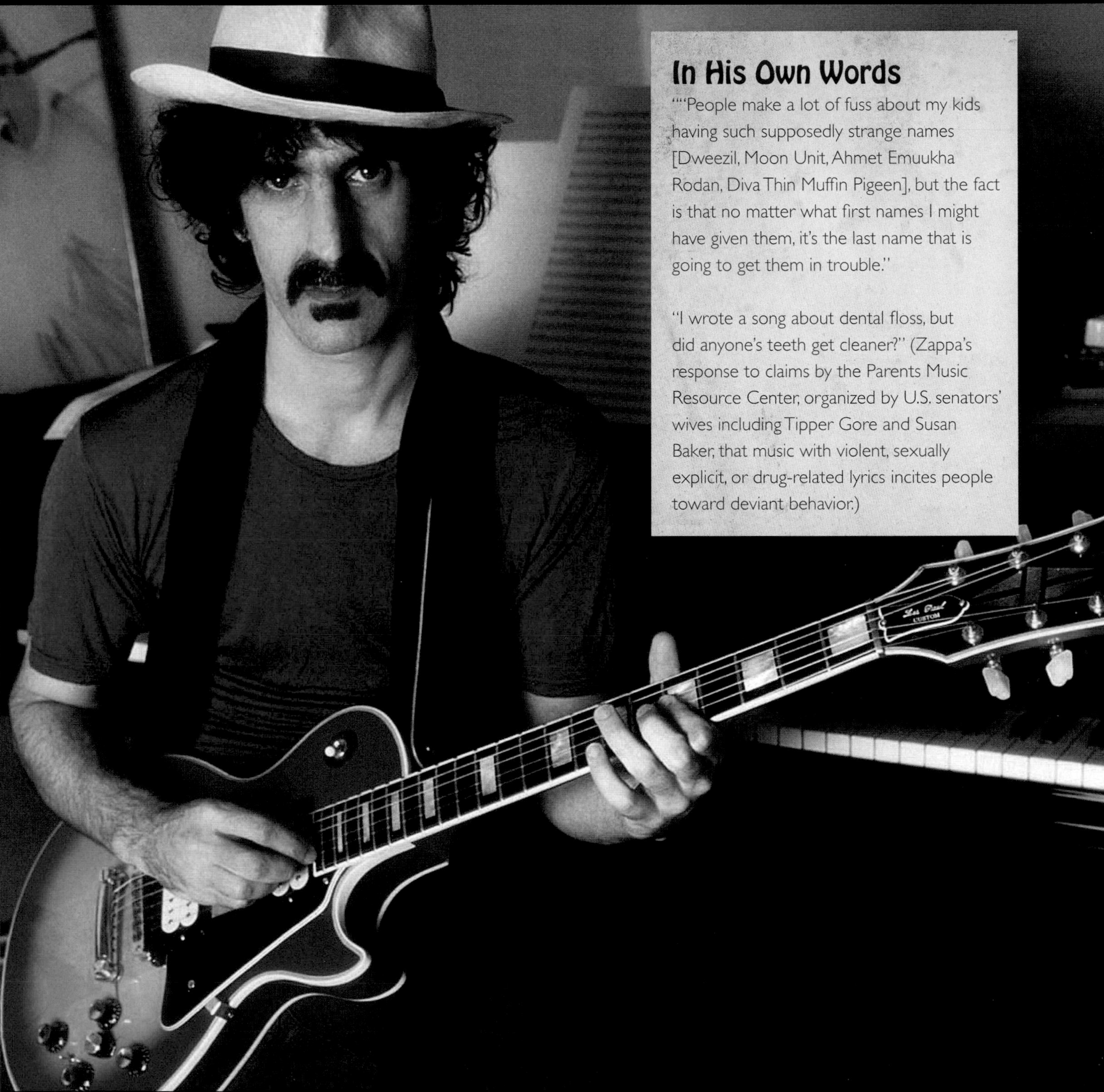

In His Own Words

""People make a lot of fuss about my kids having such supposedly strange names [Dweezil, Moon Unit, Ahmet Emuukha Rodan, Diva Thin Muffin Pigeen], but the fact is that no matter what first names I might have given them, it's the last name that is going to get them in trouble."

"I wrote a song about dental floss, but did anyone's teeth get cleaner?" (Zappa's response to claims by the Parents Music Resource Center, organized by U.S. senators' wives including Tipper Gore and Susan Baker, that music with violent, sexually explicit, or drug-related lyrics incites people toward deviant behavior.)

Upgrade your electric

A clean fingerboard and frets always make your guitar feel—and look—much better. But is it sounding out of tune higher up the neck? Are its strings buzzing or rattling against the frets? And do they seem higher or lower than they used to? These problems can sometimes be fixed by adjusting the truss rod to affect the neck's "relief" or amount of curve. With little or no relief (too shallow a dip in the neck), the string action might feel sloppy, and the strings will buzz against the frets. With too much relief (too great a dip), the action will be uncomfortably high. Place a capo at the 1st fret, press down either of the E strings at the 17th fret, and use a feeler gauge (available from a specialist guitar store) to measure the gap between the top of the 7th fret and the underside of the strings. A gap of between 0.25 mm and 0.38 mm is recommended: if you know how to adjust the truss rod to obtain it, you may find that doing so will cure any intonation and action problems. But if in doubt—or if the symptoms persist after altering the relief—take the instrument to an expert.

1 Frets and neck may need attention if your guitar's action or intonation are causing problems.

Saddling up

Fine adjustments to intonation are made via the bridge saddles. Traditional Telecaster bridges have three saddles, so intonation is always a compromise—and many Tele players choose to have six-saddle bridges fitted. The metal from which the saddles are made has a significant effect on the guitar's tone: early 1950s' Teles used brass, but Fender later switched to steel, which has a brighter, snappier quality. If you want to alter your sound, try installing new saddles before you swap pickups. Vintage-style Stratocasters have pressed steel bridge saddles, but some imported models sport zinc vibrato blocks—and for clarity, sustain, and dynamics, nothing beats a steel one. To find out whether your current block is steel, hold a magnet against it. If it doesn't stick, the block isn't steel, and once again replacing it is easier and cheaper than fitting new pickups.

2 Using a feeler gauge at the 7th fret when checking the neck relief, with a capo at the 1st fret, and the string held down at the 17th.

Other suggestions

On Gretsch electrics like the Tennessean in our photograph, getting the bar bridge reshaped or replaced so that the string heights match the fingerboard radius is another comparatively inexpensive adjustment that will improve playability. And on guitars with single-coil pickups, noise and interference can be dramatically reduced if you line the base and sides of the instrument's control cavity with adhesive copper sheets.

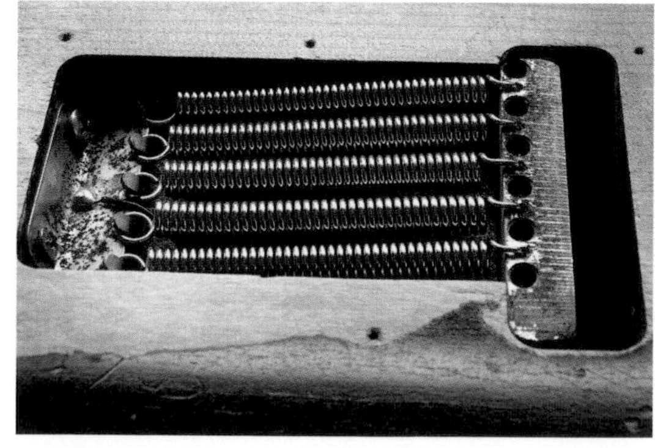

3 The rust on this Strat's vibrato block is (for once) a good thing, as it shows it's made of steel.

Top Guitar Tip

If you're shopping for new pickups, you'll find that the range of units now available is wider than ever. You can get P-90s and humbuckers for Strat and Tele slots, PAF-sized P-90s, P-90-sized PAFs…but first be sure that the quality of your guitar warrants the expense.

Below: *You won't need fire or water to transform your electric guitar into a "tone monster"—as long as you choose your upgrades carefully.*

4 New, slanted brass saddles will improve intonation, but a six-saddle unit allows more precise adjustment.

5 This Gretsch bar bridge has been bent to a 12-in (30-cm) radius to provide a better match for its 10-in (25-cm) radius fingerboard.

6 Noisy single-coil pickups? Copper shielding and conductive paint in the cavities will help.

TONE
VOLUME

Learn to Play Like. . .

PLAY LIKE Duane Allman

Above: Duane Allman, with his glass slide clearly visible.

Duane Allman was receptive to different styles of music in his formative years. "Everything influences you," he said. "As you go along, you pick up stuff. You just can't help it. It's just like how you learn to talk." All this musical input helped Allman become a talented and in-demand session musician. His greatest contributions as a sideman can be heard on Derek and the Dominos' *Layla And Other Assorted Love Songs* (1970), and he's widely credited with the creation of the opening riff for the band's signature tune, "Layla."

The six-piece Allman Brothers Band—cofounded with his brother Gregg—reflected a catholic approach to styles in its fusion of blues and jazz. "As human feelings become more complex, as the world gets a little bit more divided and intelligent, complexity is the only difference between blues and jazz," Duane mused. "It's all the portrayal of the feelings and the soul in a medium other than words."

> *For a slide, I've always used a glass Coricidin bottle, just like Duane Allman. He was the best slide player who ever lived. He had such a great touch. He was always on pitch—never sharp or flat—and that's hard to do.*
>
> Gary Rossington, Lynyrd Skynyrd

Repeated Lick

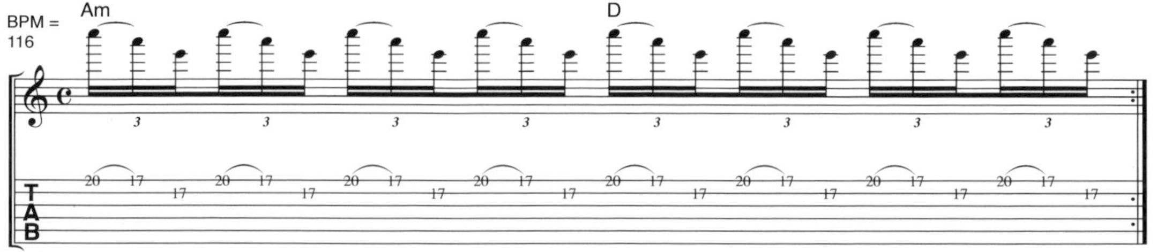

◀ *In the Dickey Betts instrumental "In Memory of Elizabeth Reed," Allman builds to a climax with a stock blues/rock lick rather like this.*

Slide Playing

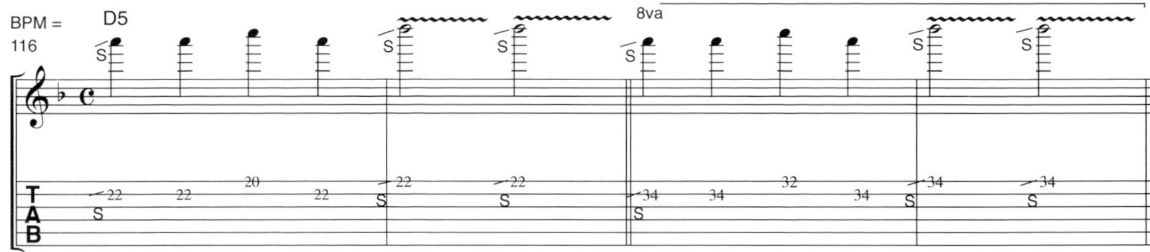

▲ *There's no need to retune your guitar for this exercise. Allman plucked the strings with his thumb, index and middle fingers, and also used his picking fingers to damp unwanted strings; in addition, his fretting hand's index and middle fingers would damp behind the slide, stopping unwanted strings from sounding. The first two bars are played near the top of the fretboard, but occasionally Allman went even farther up; bars 3 and 4 show the same phrase played one octave higher. The tab indicates the hypothetical fret numbers. Use your ear to judge the pitches, and then use visual aids on the guitar to find the notes again.*

Long Slides

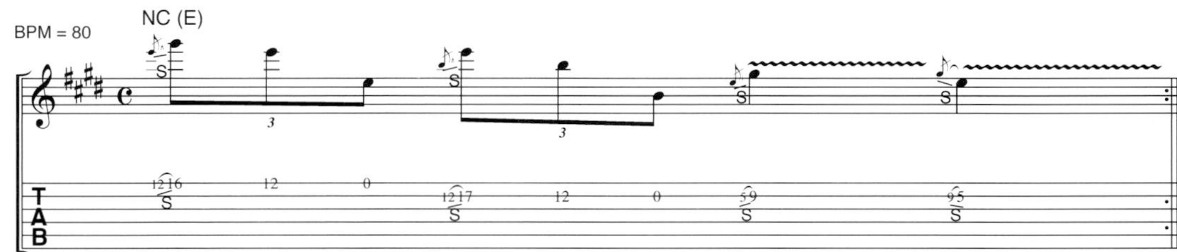

▲ *Now we're going to retune to an open E chord (E B E G# B E from bottom to top) since that's what Allman generally used when playing slide. Longer-than-normal slide maneuvers are explored here. Make sure the starting and finishing notes of the slides are accurately pitched, with a quick, smooth, pure slide between them.*

Chords with Slide

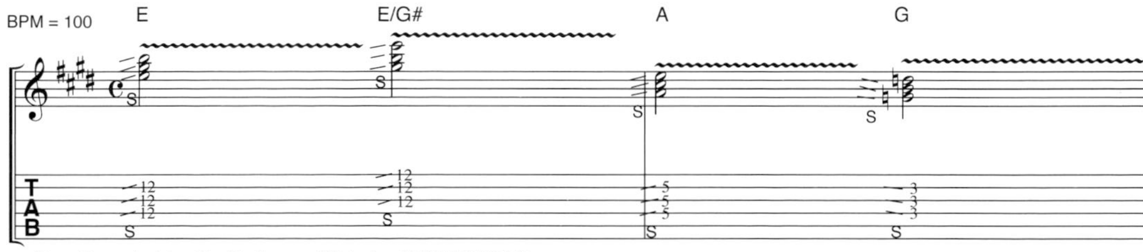

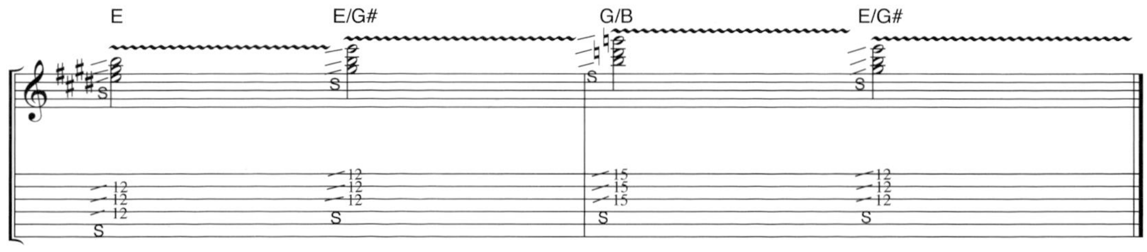

◀ *Allman occasionally fills out his single-note work on slide with chords. Slap on "Statesboro Blues" from* At Fillmore East *(originally released in 1971, reissued 1974), listen to what he does at 3'52" and 4'00"—then try this!*

PLAY LIKE Jeff Beck

Though Jeff Beck has never enjoyed as high a profile as his ex-Yardbirds cohorts Jimmy Page and Eric Clapton, he wouldn't have it any other way. "I was determined not to devote my entire life to my career," he once explained. "A good layoff makes me think a lot. It helps me get the creativity and the speed together."

Beck frequently makes use of harmonics in his playing, as on "Jeff's Boogie" (*Yardbirds*, 1966), based on Chuck Berry's "Guitar Boogie." "I'd heard Merle Travis and Chet Atkins using harmonics, which would sound great. On *Jeff Beck's Guitar Shop* (1989) I took harmonics even further on "Where Were You," and played whole phrases in harmonics with the bar."

He's used a variety of guitars during his career, but eventually settled on his signature Fender Stratocaster with its notoriously big neck. "I think if Jeff could have a tree trunk for a neck, he'd go with it…if it could be kept in tune!" says Beck's guitar tech Andy Roberts.

> *[Some of] the parts that I played, I wanted kids to be able to pick up the guitar and just ape off the first time around. Kids from age 12 could play that; it's a simple thing.*
>
> Jeff Beck on his fingerstyle riffing

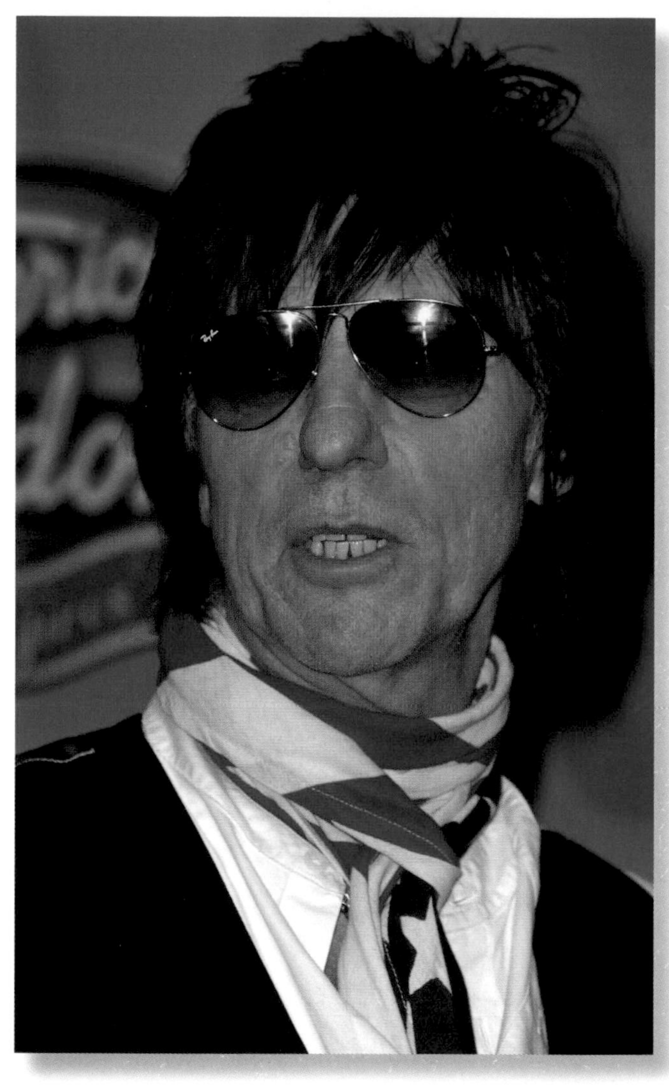

Above right: *Jeff Beck—stepping out in shades and a smart neckscarf!*

Plucking with Fingers

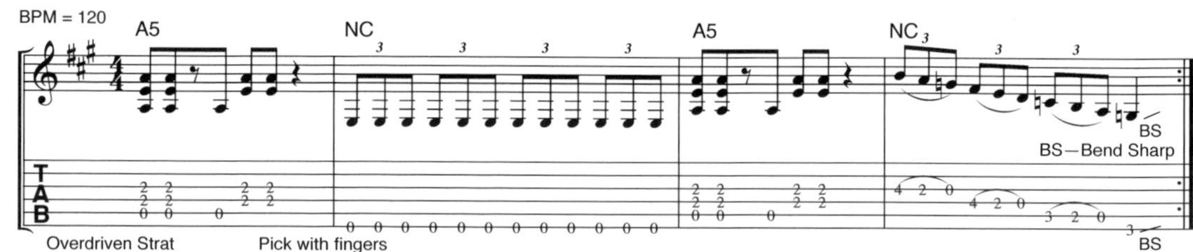

▲ *Beck is one of the very few rock guitarists who eschews a plectrum and plucks the strings with his fingers (except for the odd bit of rhythm). Use thumb and two fingers for bars 1 and 3: Beck plays similar riffs on several tracks from* Jeff Beck's Guitar Shop. *For the triplet Es in bar 2, hold the thumb and index finger together and pluck as if you're using a plectrum. For the triplet fill in bar 4, use whatever fingers feel comfortable.*

Pentatonic Minor Lick

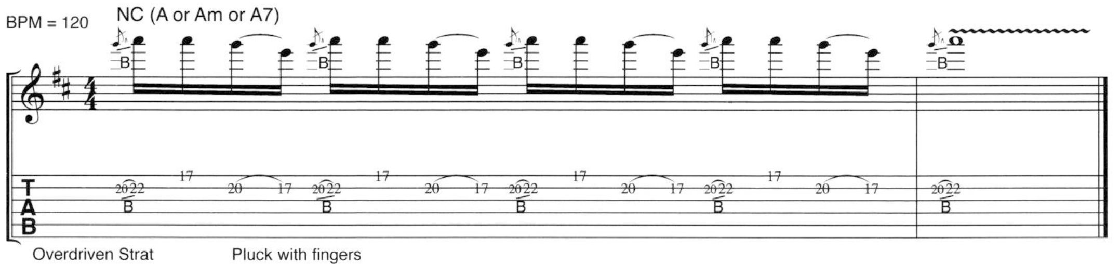

◀ *A typical Beck lick. Once again, he would play it with his fingers, but don't get bogged down over which digits to choose—just use whatever feels comfortable and fluent.*

Double Stop Bends

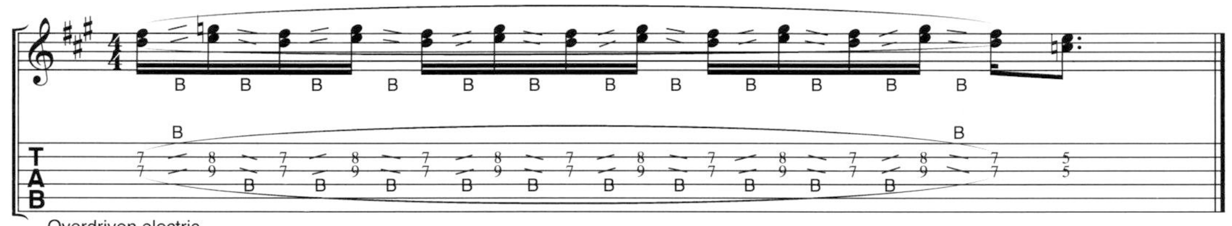

▲ *Beck likes the sound of unequal pitch bends caused by pulling two strings at the same time. Lay the third finger across strings three and two at the seventh fret, then pull the strings down toward the top string; the third string will change more in pitch than the second string, creating a dissonant effect.*

Artificial Harmonics

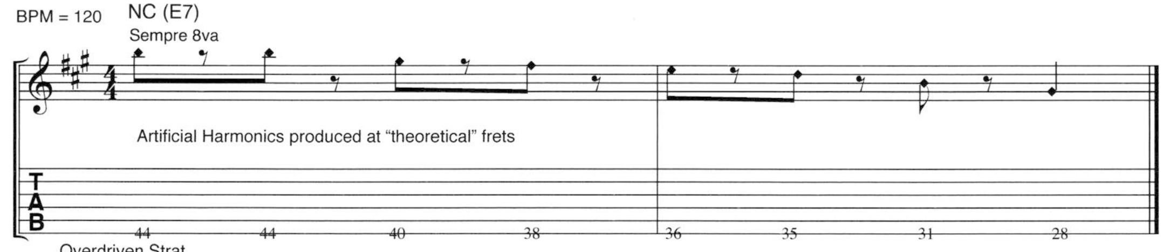

◀ *In "Savoy" (from* Guitar Shop*) Beck plays a fill employing artificial harmonics, using the notes shown in the exercise here. Touch the string at the "theoretical" fret indicated in the tab with the plucking hand's index finger, way beyond the end of the fretboard. Then pluck the string on the bridge side of the string with the thumb to produce the harmonic.*

Car Horn Effects

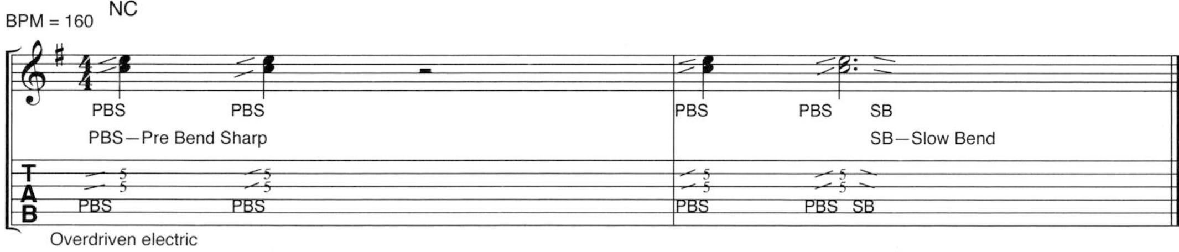

▲ *A "car horn" sound like this is featured in "Freeway Jam" on* Jeff Beck With the Jan Hammer Group Live *(1977). Fret strings three and two at the fifth fret, then bend them slightly sharp before they're plucked. In the second of the two bars, let the notes ring on after the second pluck, then slowly release the pitch to create the Doppler-like effect.*

PLAY LIKE Chuck Berry

Today, we consider Chuck Berry (born in St. Louis, Missouri, in 1926) to be a true original: the first great "crossover" artist from the Chess Records stable, and the man who married blues with teen-friendly pop lyrics. Berry himself, however, has a contrary opinion. "I still don't recognize any style of my own," he's been quoted as saying—an astonishing admission from a man rarely lacking in self-belief. "What I do is just a portion of all that I've heard before me: Carl Hogan with Louis Jordan and his Tympany Five, blues players like T-Bone Walker, Illinois Jacquet…Charlie Christian, too. 'Solo Flight'! It's so great…I got the first 16 bars down. It took me 30 years." Here, we focus on some of Berry's favorite chords, as well as examining a few of his most frequently used techniques.

Above: *Chuck Berry on stage recently: he still enjoys the limelight.*

Bb, Bb/F, A6 and A9/G Chords

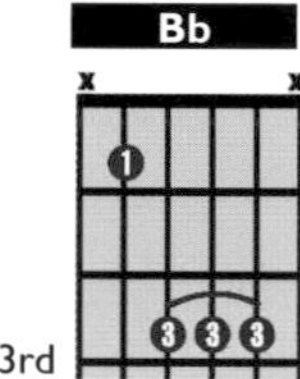

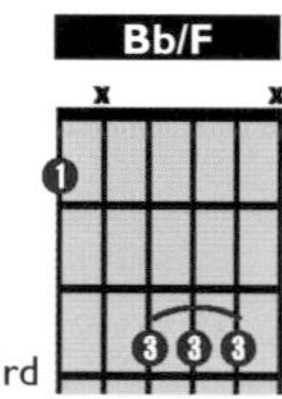

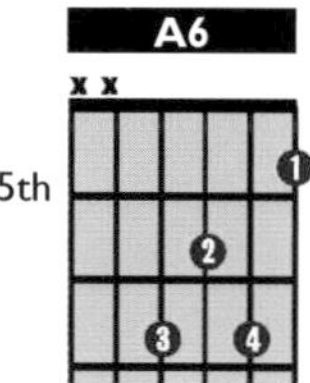

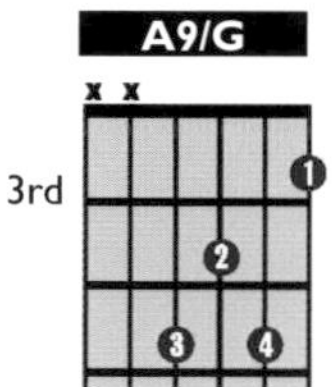

▲ *These chord shapes all appear in the "Country and Blues Influences" exercise that comes next. The Bb chords require a third finger barré across strings four, three, and two at the third fret. A6 and A9/G are the same shape, with A9/G fingered two frets lower than A6. A9/G could be called G6, but we're referring to it as A9/G because it's being used in a key of A major below.*

Country and Blues Influences

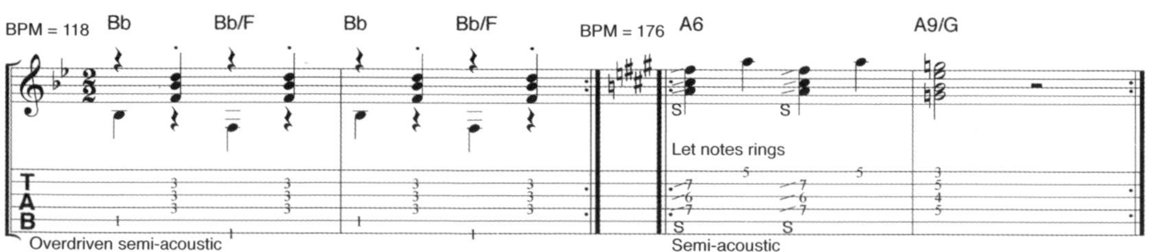

▲ *These "Berry-ish" patterns reflect the great man's musical roots: the country-style alternating bass line is used in "Maybelline," while the sliding chordal lick in bar 3 has a bluesy feel. Finger the chords using the shapes shown above.*

Three-Note Pickup

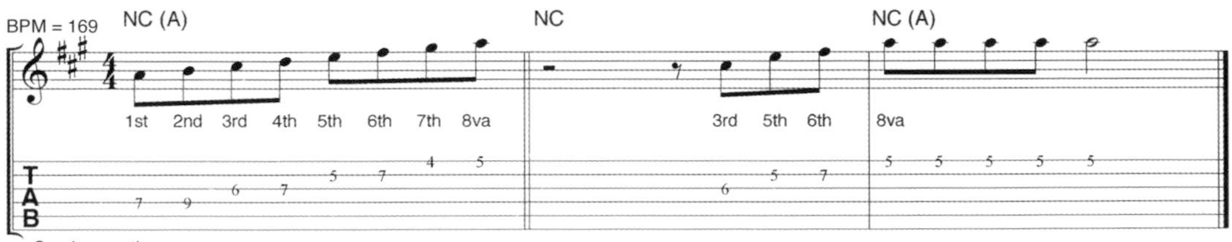

▲ *Many Chuck Berry songs begin with a three-note pickup consisting of the third, fifth, and sixth notes from the major scale. The first bar of this exercise shows an A major scale, with the notes numbered underneath. Bars 2 and 3 pick out the third, fifth and sixth notes, followed by the octave ("8va"). "Johnny B. Goode," "Roll Over Beethoven," "Carol," "Back In The U.S.A.," "Let It Rock," and "The Promised Land" all use this device.*

A5 and A6 Chords

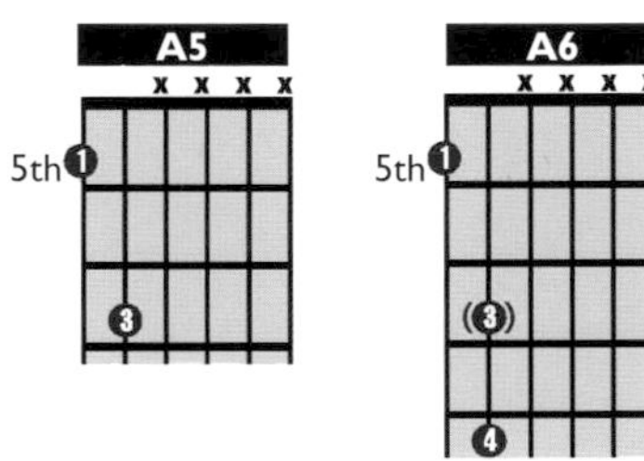

▲ *A "5" chord consists of the root and the fifth degree of the major scale; since it doesn't contain a third, it's neither major nor minor. Similarly, a "6" chord consists of the root note plus the sixth note of the scale. Both chords are staples of rock'n'roll rhythm guitar, often played in eighth note ("straight 8") patterns.*

Chuck Berry's Gear

In his early career Chuck Berry played an Epiphone archtop electric and a Gibson Les Paul Custom, but he's most closely associated with the Gibson ES-350 hollow-body and the ES-355 semi-solid. "[They're] really just about the same to me," he's commented. "One body's a bit thinner, the [355]. I haven't really paid much attention to the sound… I like [those two] Gibsons. The lighter, the better." When touring, Berry required the promoter to provide amplification, specifying "two unaltered Fender Dual Showman Reverb amplifier sets."

Right: *Berry's slimline Gibson gave him maximum freedom of movement on stage.*

▼ *Here's a selection of licks that Berry uses in various songs. The first is similar to a phrase in the "Johnny B. Goode" intro. The second resembles part of the start of "Roll Over Beethoven," with a pattern of slurred notes at frets eight, seven, and five, moved from string one to string three. Bars 3 and 4 explore the opening of "Little Queenie" with a three-note pickup.*

Other Licks

PLAY LIKE Ritchie Blackmore

Ritchie Blackmore, who made his name as one of rock's most influential guitarists in Deep Purple and Rainbow, is skilled not only in riff creation ("Smoke On The Water") but as an improviser. "Everything I do is usually spontaneous. If I get told something was good and asked to play it again, I'm not able to do it." Blackmore left the hard rock world behind when he formed the Renaissance-influenced Blackmore's Night. However, he sees similarities between "early music" and rock. "It's those parallel fourths and fifths…not unlike the 'Smoke On The Water' riff which is in fourths, and some of the harmonic structure is similar. Sometimes if you hear some of the music played for royalty [back then], it's very brash and majestic or exciting, like today's rock shows, although 500 years ago."

> *I've always played every amp I've ever had full up…rock'n'roll's supposed to be loud.*
>
> Ritchie Blackmore

Above: *Blackmore with his favorite ax—the Fender Stratocaster.*

Blues Scale with Inverted Power Chords

▲ *The main riff of "Smoke On The Water" uses the first four notes of the G blues scale (G Bb C Db) with a note a parallel fourth below. Beginners often play it on just one string, but two-note chords are far more powerful. Pluck the "diads" (pairs of notes) with the thumb and index finger, not a pick.*

Chords with Drones

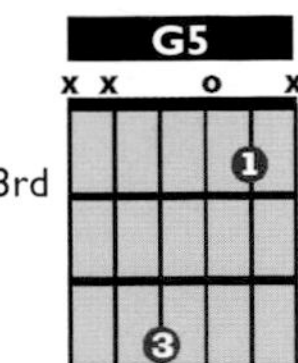

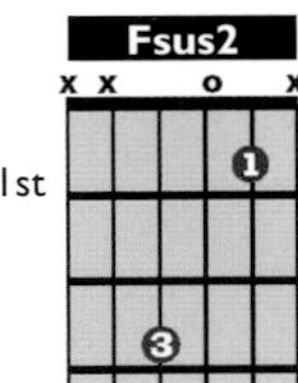

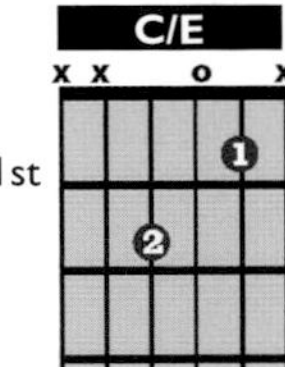

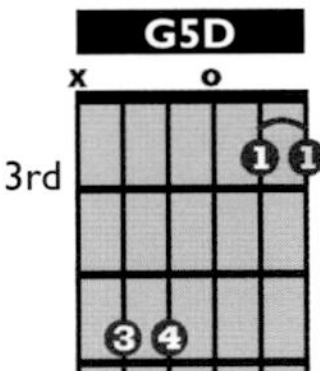

◀ *These chords all use the open third string as a drone.*

Highway Star-Style Intro

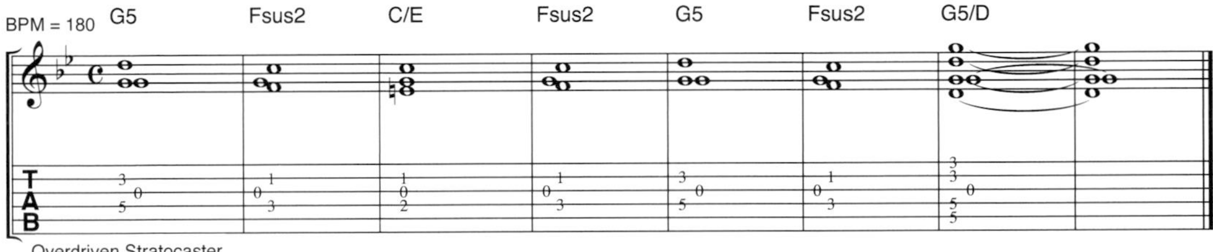

◀ *The drone chord voicings in the diagrams shown above are used at the start of the studio version of "Highway Star" from Deep Purple's* Machine Head *(1972). Note the major second clash in the Fsus2 chord between the root note on the fourth string and the open third string—play with too much overdrive and this interval sounds nasty. The notes in each chord are to be struck simultaneously—the notes in the notation are spaced so as to avoid overlapping notes, and the tab reflects this spacing.*

Highway Star-Style Chromatic Run

▲ *A chromatic scale includes every note, and the one here starts on a high A at the 17th fret of the first string. Blackmore plays a two-bar version of a similar run at 4'39" into "Highway Star" (see above), and features a longer version at 4'50". Our exercise is based on the longer run, which is played in sixteenth notes, with two chromatically descending notes (apart from the very first two notes) alternating with two open strings of top E. Blackmore occasionally uses open strings like this in his lead work—repeated "pedal" notes that let him move up or down the fretboard while the open string is sounded.*

Harmonic Minor Scale

▲ *"Black Masquerade" was recorded by Ritchie Blackmore's Rainbow as part of the 1995 album* Stranger In Us All; *this was the last reformation of the band before he founded Blackmore's Night. On the track Blackmore plays an ascending run using the A harmonic minor scale, similar to the one in the exercise above.*

PLAY LIKE Joe Bonamassa

As his colleague in Black Country Communion, Glenn Hughes, put it recently, " Joe Bonamassa is the only cat since Jimmy Page to come from blues and cross over into rock." The American guitarist's love for British music started young. As a kid, he'd try to shake his sister's TV and lamp off her bedside table in the next room by playing Free's "Mr. Big" at maximum volume! Bonamassa is currently riding high on both sides of the Atlantic, and here we look into some of the licks, scales, and chords that have helped him relight a fire under blues rock.

Right: *Joe Bonamassa and his Gibson Flying V.*

Blues Partial Chords

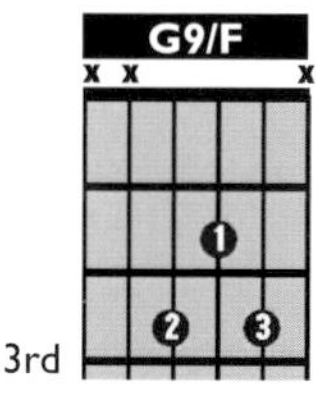

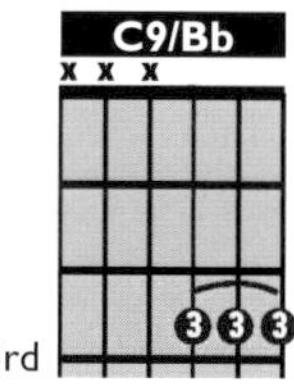

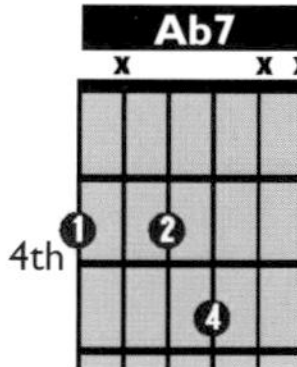

▲ *Some partial chords commonly found in blues. Fingering the third shape, Ab7, involves damping the fifth string; lightly touch the string with the first finger by angling it slightly.*

Rhythm Guitar Picking

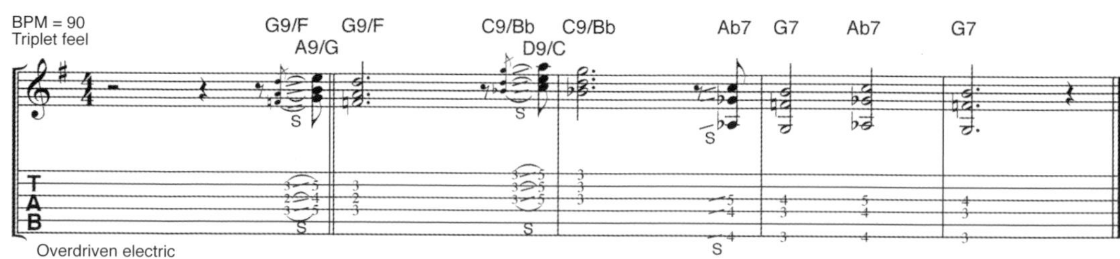

▲ *When playing rhythm guitar, Bonamassa likes to pluck the strings with his fingers for improved tone. This exercise, based on "Blues Deluxe" (2003), uses the shapes shown above, each of which is moved up or down as indicated to produce the additional chords. Try it first with the plectrum, then pluck the strings with your fingers, and listen for the difference.*

Pentatonic Minor Scales

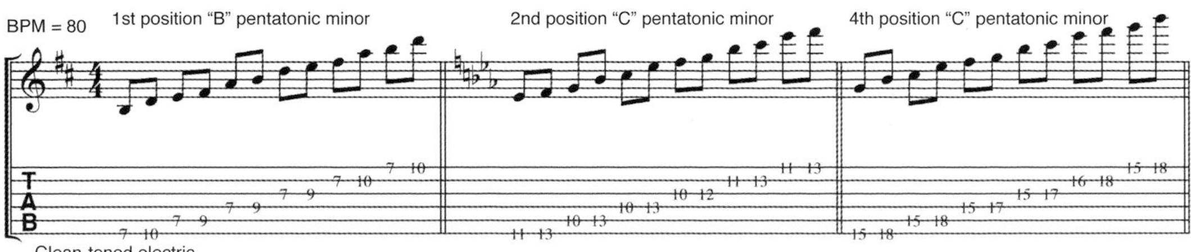

▲ *These pentatonic minor scales will be used in the next exercise. To memorize the fretboard patterns, use with one finger per fret—this way the shapes are more easily recognizable. Both the 1st position B pentatonic minor scale and the 4th position C pentatonic minor scale start with the first finger on the first note; the 2nd position C pentatonic minor scale starts with the second finger.*

Repeated Stock Licks

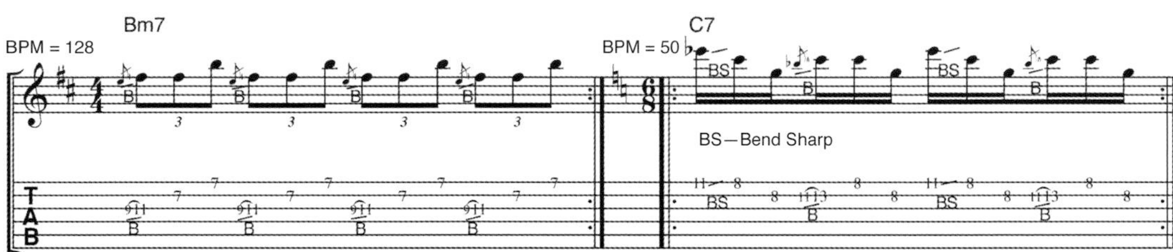

▲ *This exercise shows a couple of stock phrases that work well in many situations. The first bar is similar to a lick in "So, It's Like That" (2002). You can hear it at the start of the solo at 0'58", and it uses the 1st position B pentatonic minor scale shown above. The second bar is another stock lick similar to a phrase in "Blues Deluxe" at 4'28". It features the 1st position C pentatonic minor scale, which is simply the 1st position B pentatonic minor scale moved up one fret. "BS" ("Bend Sharp") means you should bend the note sharp by approximately a quarter tone.*

> *My heroes were…Paul Kossoff, Peter Green, Eric Clapton…Gary Moore, Rory Gallagher…Jeff Beck, Jimmy Page. There's a certain sophistication to their approach to the blues that I really like…*
>
> Joe Bonamassa talking about his influences

Fast Slurs

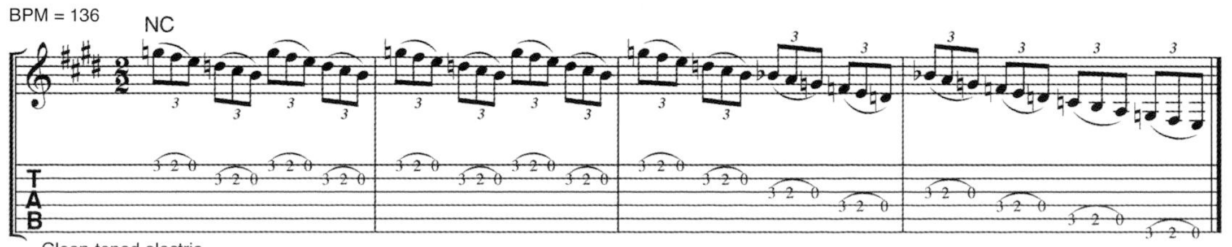

◀ *These slurred notes form a symmetrical pattern that's simply moved across the fretboard. Start practicing slowly and gradually build up speed, making sure all the notes are clearly articulated.*

PLAY LIKE Eric Clapton

Cream (1966–68) could be said to be greater than the sum of its parts. Eric Clapton, its guitarist, had just left John Mayall's Bluesbreakers, where he'd helped popularize electric blues, and created a new sound using a Gibson Les Paul through a cranked Marshall (his preference for Fender Stratocasters came later). Bassist/ singer Jack Bruce was a classically trained multi-instrumentalist who played blues and jazz, and drummer Ginger Baker was a seasoned and experienced jazz musician. Live, Cream took improvising to a new level. "It was like a jazz band playing in a rock setting," Jack Bruce commented. The brightest candles can burn the fastest, and Cream lasted for just four albums.

> *If you hand me a guitar, I'll play the blues. That's the place I automatically go.*
>
> Eric Clapton

Above: *Clapton at the 2010 Crossroads Guitar Festival in Toyota Park, Chicago.*

Badge-style Arpeggios

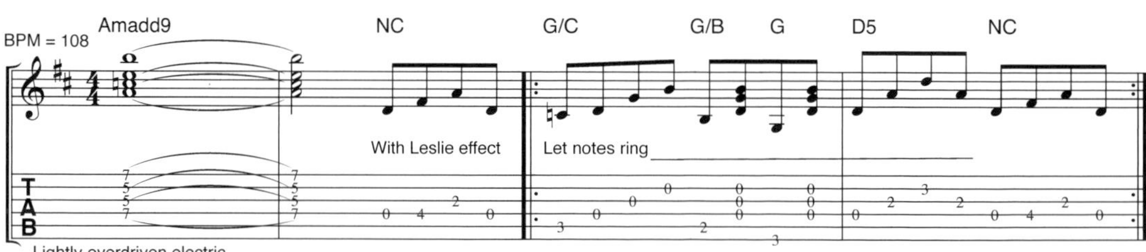

▲ *The second verse of "Badge" (Goodbye album, 1969) ends at 1'03" with a sustained Amadd9 chord, followed by a two-bar arpeggio-based pattern routed through a rotating Leslie speaker cabinet, which produces a "swirling" sound. You can get a similar effect by using a pedal intended to recreate the Leslie sound, or even a chorus or a phaser, but if you're ever lucky enough to try the real thing, you'll notice the difference. Make sure the notes are allowed to ring on.*

Chords in Sunshine Of Your Love

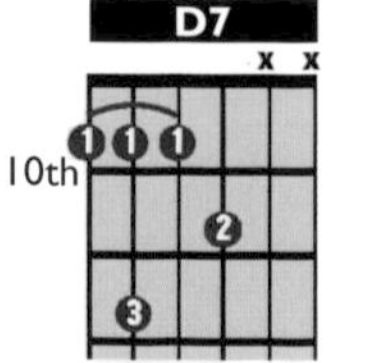

◀ *These two chord voicings from "Sunshine of Your Love" (Disraeli Gears, 1967) are produced by a basic E7 shape moved up the fretboard as indicated, but picking only the bottom four strings. Make sure the notes on the fourth string (C and Bb, respectively) sound clearly.*

Eric Clapton's Guitars in Cream

In the early days of Cream, Clapton played a variety of Les Paul Standards, mainly from 1959 and 1960. For the recording of *Disraeli Gears* (1967) he started to use a psychedelic-painted 1964 Gibson SG, also known as the "Fool Guitar."

During the band's latter period, he adopted a single pickup 1964 Gibson Firebird and a Cherry Red 1964 Gibson ES-335, while for effects he occasionally featured a Vox wah-wah.

Right: *Clapton sitting on stage with a Gibson Les Paul guitar, in front of a Marshall stack, March 1967.*

Sunshine of Your Love Chordal Harmony

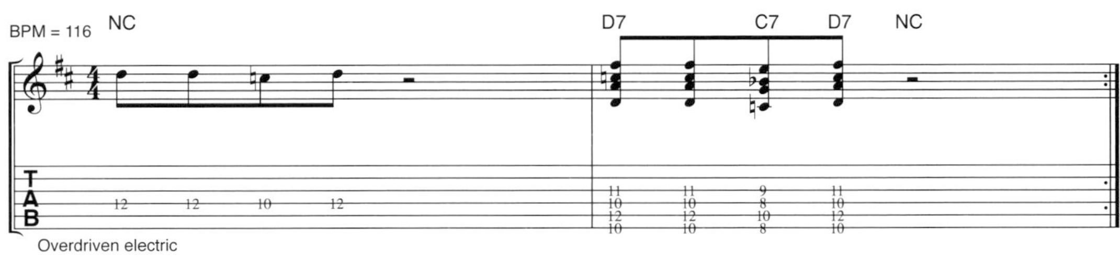

◀ *Near the start of "Sunshine of Your Love," Clapton fills out the D D C D part with the D7 and C7 chords shown left. Here's the single note motif, then its chordal equivalent—which omits the notes from bar 1.*

Pentatonic Major Scale in Crossroads

▲ *Clapton frequently uses the pentatonic major scale—as at the start of the first solo in "Crossroads" (Wheels of Fire, 1968), 1'25" into the track. This'll get you close: we begin in bar 12 of the 12-bar third verse (hence the double line section marker in the middle of the notation), and finish at the end of the solo's first bar.*

Wah-wah in White Room

▲ *This exercise, which requires a wah-wah pedal, echoes the chorus chords of "White Room" (Wheels of Fire), first heard at 0'58". Clapton employs a "fluttering" technique with the pedal, repeatedly pushing it down, then bringing it back. Once you've got a sense of his wah-wah technique, try striking the chord, then occasionally playing suitable fills later in the bar, as in bar 9 here.*

PLAY LIKE Ry Cooder

Ry Cooder has enjoyed fame as a solo artist, a writer of film soundtracks, and through his collaborations with a wide variety of musicians. Unlike many performers, whose careers naturally revolve around their own albums, Cooder says that his solo records have often "subsidize[d] me doing the things I like to do." He's especially known for his slide playing in a variety of open tunings—using a glass slide on the fourth finger of his fretting hand, leaving his first, second, and third fingers free to fret notes when required. He strikes the strings with a thumbpick and his fingers: "It's basically the nail and finger at the same time...you can really snap it with the nails, then modify that sound with the softness of the fingertips. I never bothered with a flatpick. It just doesn't come naturally to me."

Below: *Ry Cooder with a bizarre-looking electric—a four-pickup Japanese model that's usually identified as a Guyatone.*

Open Tunings

The exercises here all involve "open D" tuning (D A D F# A D bottom to top). This tuning is also known as "Vestapol" tuning—after an old parlour song that was often played with the guitar strings set to these notes. Another of Ry Cooder's favorites is "open G" (D G D G B D bottom to top), which he calls "hillbilly" tuning, and often uses for rhythm work. Both tunings involve lowering the regular pitches of some strings, which can produce unwanted buzzing. If you decide to use any alternative tuning regularly, you may want to get your instrument set up for it, and perhaps select different string gauges: talk to an experienced guitar technician for more information.

Vigilante Man-style ideas

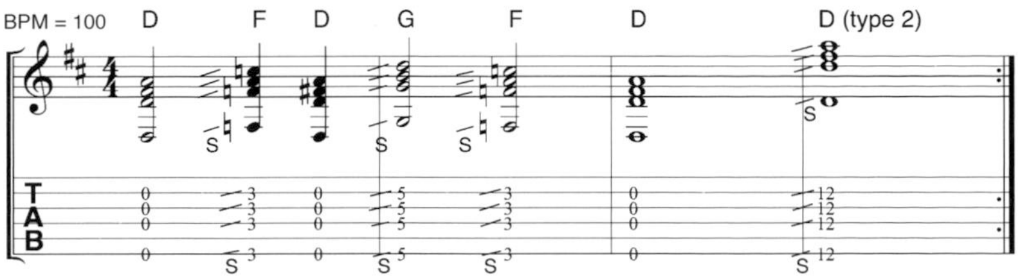

◀ *This exercise, inspired by "Vigilante Man" from Ry Cooder's* Into the Purple Valley *(1972), is played with the slide on the fourth finger, while plucking the strings with the thumb plus index, middle, and ring fingers. Where indicated, slide up to the chords: try sliding from one fret lower into F, and two frets lower into G and D (type 2).*

Chords in Open D Tuning with Common Tones

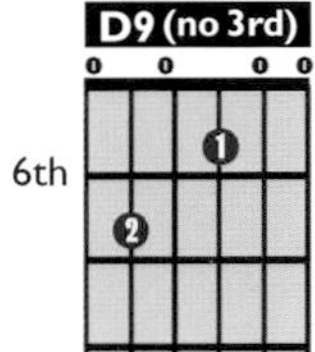

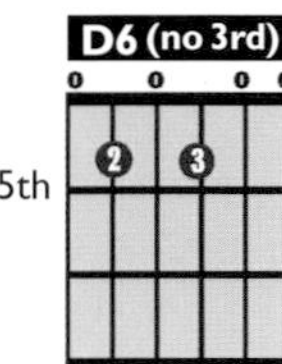

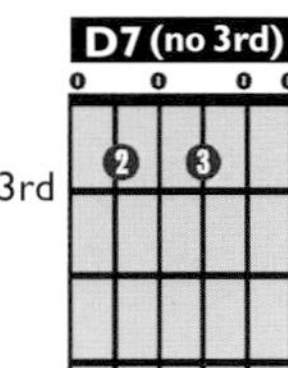

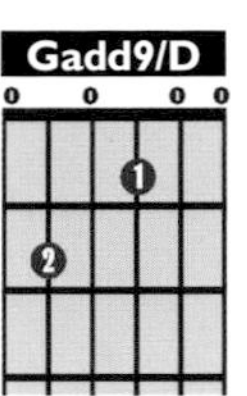

◀ *These chord shapes in open D use common tones, or drones. In each of them, the notes on strings five and three change, while strings six, four, two, and one remain open. Make sure your fingertips remain upright in order to avoid damping open strings.*

Paris, Texas-style Arpeggios

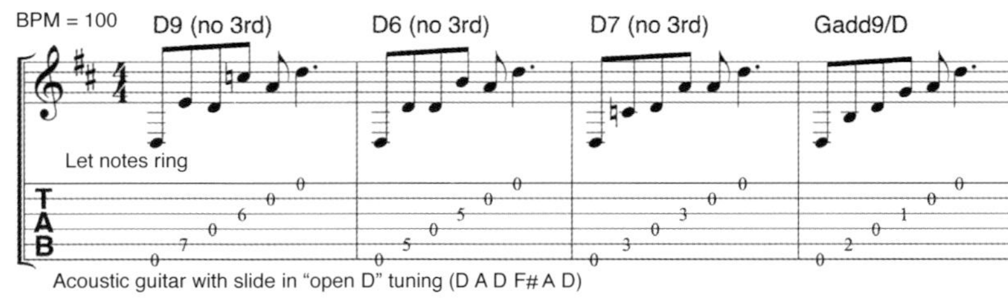

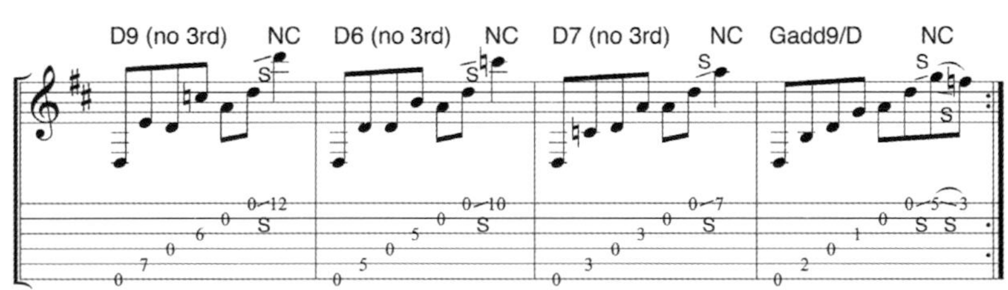

◀ *At the 1'59" point in "Paris, Texas" (*Paris, Texas *album, 1984), Ry Cooder plays a series of arpeggios using the voicings in the chord diagrams shown left. The second bar repeats the arpeggios from the first line, but with a slide up to a note added at the end of each bar, illustrating how Cooder seamlessly mixes regular fretboard work with slide work. Keep the slide on the fourth finger of the fretting hand ready to be brought into play.*

Microtones

◀ *Playing with a slide enables the pitches between the frets to be explored. This exercise features such microtones in open D tuning. Each bar starts with an open bottom D, followed by a slide to a note on the top string. The first slide is to F# at the fourth fret; the second slide is to the bluesy note between F and F#, indicated by fret 3.5 in the tab. The third slide is to F, the minor third degree of the scale, followed by a slide to the note halfway between E and F, indicated by 2.5 in the tablature. Listen closely to how Cooder uses pitches like these in his playing.*

PLAY LIKE Duane Eddy

When asked how he created his sonic "signature," Duane Eddy put it like this: "As I was playing around [in the studio], I realized that the bass strings on the guitar recorded a lot better than the high strings. And so Lee [Hazlewood, my producer] said, 'Let's go and record an instrumental just using the bass strings. Go off and write something.' I went off and I wrote 'Moovin' and Groovin',' which had a high riff and a low riff. Then we also got around to doing instrumentals where the bass strings had a melody instead of just a riff, and some hot licks to produce a real sound." These best-selling disks, released from 1958 onward, were trailblazers that influenced a generation of guitarists, and still retain their potency—even though some may consider Eddy's tone and technique a little tame by today's standards. Here, we reveal a few secrets of the "twang legend"...

Below: *Duane Eddy playing a Gretsch semi-acoustic with a personalized strap.*

Eddy and Elvis...a missed opportunity

Duane Eddy's music has featured on many movie soundtracks (among them *Forrest Gump*, *Austin Powers*, *Scream 2*, and *Feeling Minnesota*), and he's collaborated with a wide range of musicians, but one of his biggest regrets is not teaming up with Elvis Presley. "I'd met him a few years before [his death in 1977], and I was working up to calling him and saying, 'If you go back in the studio, I'd like to do something.' I think we'd have had a lot of fun with it."

The Key of F minor and Vibrato

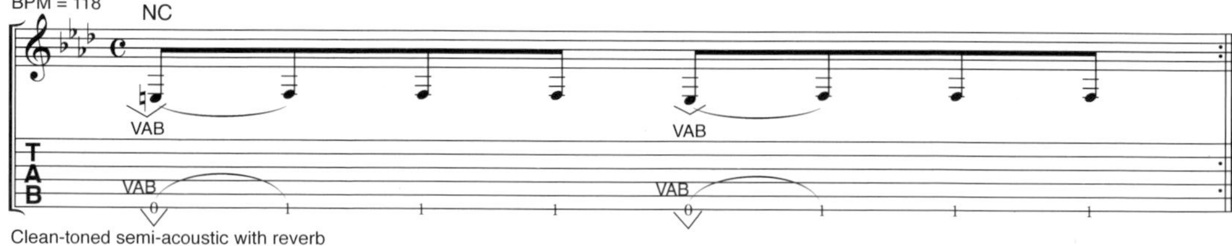

▲ *Eddy's version of Henry Mancini's "Peter Gunn" (1959 and 1986) is played in F minor, enabling him to approach the root note, F, from below (via the open bottom E string)—as we do here. The successive downward, then upward bends (or "dips") on this string are notated by the "V" sign and "VAB" ("Vibrato Arm Bend"). They indicate that you should strike the note, quickly depress the vibrato arm a little, and then immediately allow it to return to pitch.*

Dive Bomb

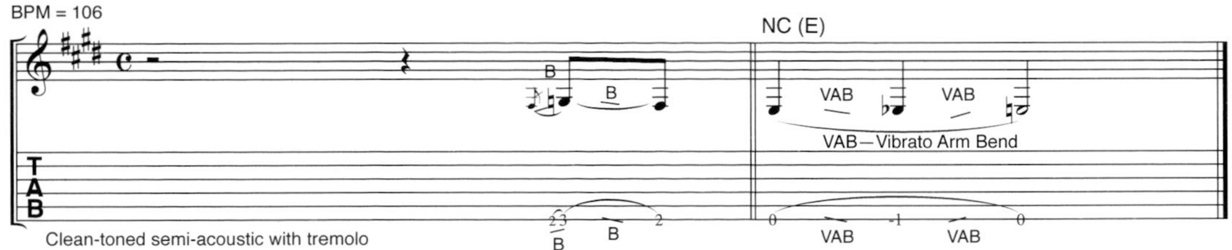

◀ *In "Rebel-Rouser" at 0'18", Eddy hits a bottom open E, then executes a "dive bomb," depressing the vibrato arm so the note drops below the natural range of the guitar before letting it return to pitch. Here, we do something similar, and the note descends to Eb, shown by "-1" in the tab.*

Clash Between Melody and Chord

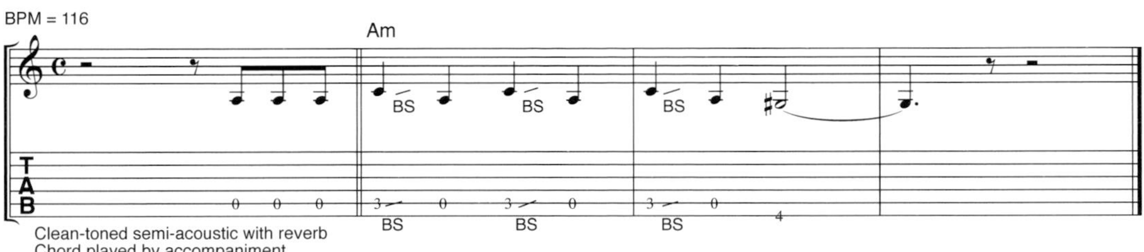

▲ *On the Duane Eddy/Ravi Shankar composition "The Trembler," used in the soundtrack to* Natural Born Killers *(1994), Eddy creates an unsettling mood by ending a bluesy riff based on the root and minor third (A and C in the key of A minor) with the leading note of the scale, G#. The accompanying chord stays on Am, so the G# creates tension against the underlying harmony.*

Slurred Triplets Lick

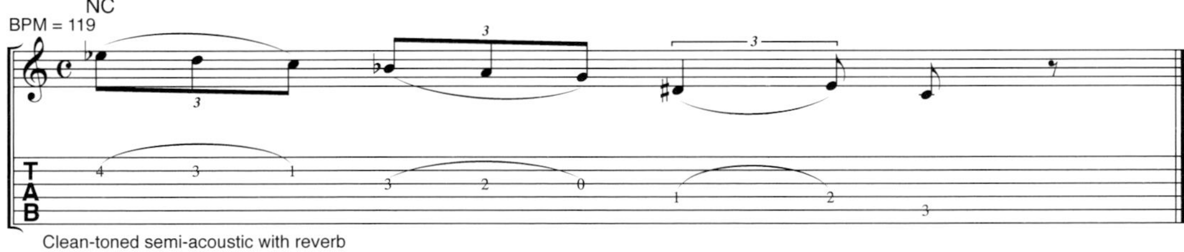

◀ *Eddy's version of Chet Atkins's "Trambone"* (Down Home, *1962) is played at a slower tempo than the original, and the licks are slightly simplified. Here we pay tribute to a move at 0'13", which ends with a stock blues/jazz lick of the augmented second (D#) hammered-on to the major third (E), and followed by C, the root.*

Chords with Vibrato Arm

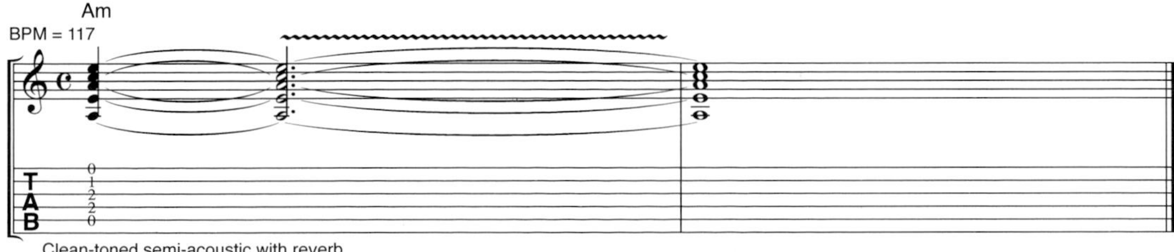

▲ *For our last glimpse into the uniquely twangy world of Duane Eddy, we'll revisit the Eddy/Shankar tune "The Trembler." Dig out that movie soundtrack and listen to how Eddy colors the basic open Am chord with the vibrato arm. His vibrato is fast and shallow; aim to emulate the same speed and depth. Different effects can be created by using different speeds and depths of vibrato.*

PLAY LIKE Noel Gallagher

"I try not to challenge myself in any aspect of my life," claims Noel Gallagher, with his tongue (to some degree) in his cheek. "Why do that? Why make it hard on yourself?…Get your comfort zone—stay in it! That's what it's there for…" Despite this seemingly easygoing attitude, however, Gallagher's achievements as a guitarist, songwriter, and singer haven't come about without dedication and practice. Here we'll be focusing on some of the stylistic trademarks he made his own while he and his brother Liam were dominating Britpop with Oasis.

Noel Gallagher's gear

Noel Gallagher's most immediately recognizable instrument is probably his Epiphone Sheraton, which sports a Union Jack paint job. In 1995, Epiphone introduced its Supernova model, inspired by Noel's guitar and produced in both "Manchester City blue" and "Union Jack" finishes. Over the years, Noel's favored several other Epiphones, as well as Gibsons and Fenders. Among his favorite amps are Vox AC30s, a Marshall Bluesbreaker, and an Orange Overdrive 120 with Orange 4 x 12-in (30-cm) cabs. Effects have included a Roland RE-201 Space Echo, a ProCo Rat, and numerous Boss pedals—DD-5, DD-6, and DD-9 digital delays, a PH-3 phaser, and a PN-2 tremolo.

Above: *Noel on stage with a Cherry Red Gibson ES-355.*

Riff in dropped D

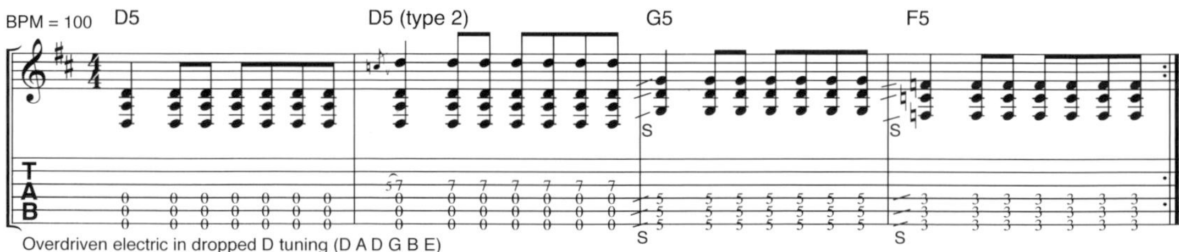

▲ *This slightly altered tuning—in which the sixth string is lowered from E to D—was a favorite with Noel Gallagher on Oasis' later albums. The riff shown here has a similar feel and sound to the intro of "Bag It Up" (from* Dig Out Your Soul*, 2008). The second bar uses a third-string hammer-on: place your first finger on the third string at the fifth fret, and strike the note, along with the bottom three strings. Then immediately hammer-on to the third string, seventh fret with the third finger. The grace note at the third string, fifth fret is played very quickly, with as small a time value as possible.*

Chords in G/Em

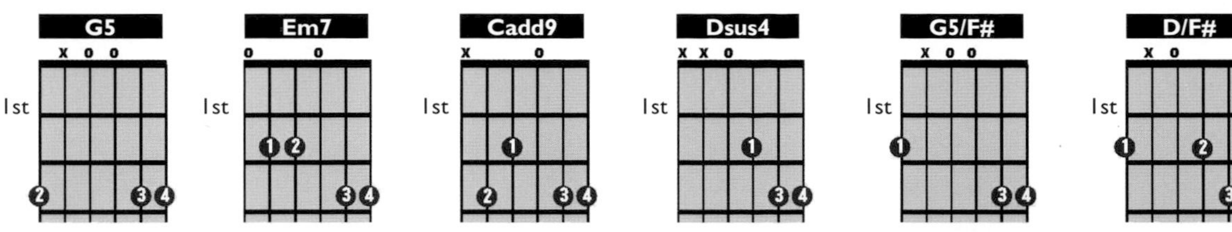

▲ *Two of Oasis' favorite keys are G major and its relative minor, E minor. Since these are related keys, they share several chords. The first four chords here all have the same two top notes—G on the first string, third fret and D on the second string, third fret. G5 is a strong rock chord since it lacks the third degree of the scale. G5/F# is simply a G5 with F# as its lowest note, implying an imminent "walk" down to E minor. Similarly, D/F# consists of a D chord on the upper strings with an F#—the third of the scale—in the bass.*

Right: *The boys in the band: Andy Bell, Liam Gallagher, Noel Gallagher, and Gem Archer.*

Progression with Common Tones

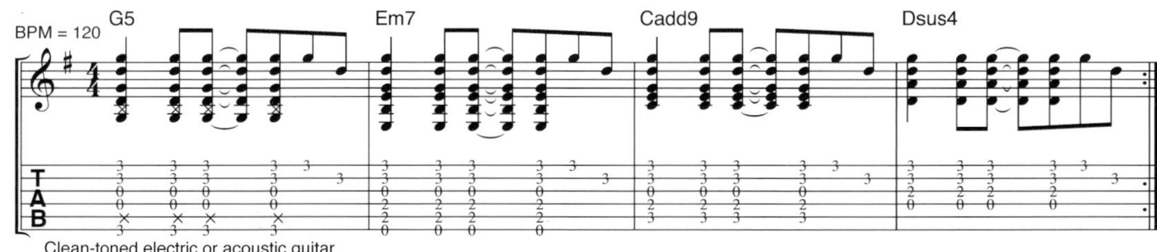

◀ *This exercise uses the first four chords from our diagrams to illustrate the use of common tones. The same rhythmical pattern—strumming followed by plucking the common tones individually—is used in each bar. When changing between these chords, leave fingers three and four in place on the top two strings; don't lift them. A similar progression to this can be heard in "(Probably) All In The Mind" from* Heathen Chemistry *(2002).*

Passing Chords

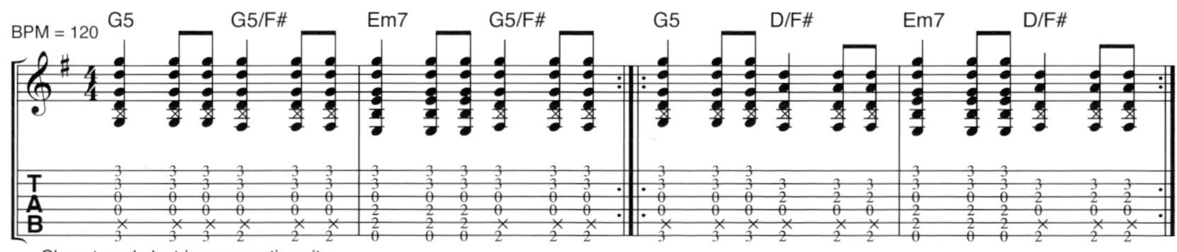

▲ *A passing chord smooths the change from one chord to another, both musically and physically, since it involves shared notes and shared fingering. A common route to take from G5 to Em is via G5/F#, as shown in the first two bars. There's a good example in Liam Gallagher's "Songbird" (from* Heathen Chemistry*). G5/F# has to be treated carefully since it's rather dissonant. By changing the open G third string to A at the second fret and omitting the top string, it can be converted into the less dissonant D/F#, which also serves to link G and Em, as shown in bars 3 and 4. You'll find it in "I'm Outta Time" from* Dig Out Your Soul.

David Gilmour

Drafted into Pink Floyd to deputize for an increasingly erratic Syd Barrett, David Gilmour quickly became an integral part of the band. He briefly played alongside Barrett, then replaced him one fateful night when the band decided not to pick up Syd for a gig. As Floyd drummer Nick Mason observed: "After Syd, Dave was the difference between light and dark. He was into form and shape, and he introduced that into the wilder numbers we'd created." Gilmour commented: "My role was to try to make it a bit more musical, help create a balance between formlessness and structure, disharmony and harmony." Many of Gilmour's formative years were spent listening to blues. "I had a lot of blues records when I was young…[and] my last [studio] album *On An Island* is a blues album—my sort of blues…I don't want to restrict myself to a 12-bar form or anything like that."

Right: *David Gilmour in his rehearsal room.*

▶ *Here we look at three stock pentatonic minor scale Gilmour licks. The first is inspired by "Shine On You Crazy Diamond" at 5'33". The second is similar to the start of the solo from "Another Brick in the Wall Part 2" at 2'08". It's in the key of D minor, with the first finger at the tenth fret. Notice how at the end of the phrase the last note is sustained before vibrato is applied—one of Gilmour's trademarks. The phrasing in the final lick looks complicated, but that's mainly due to the slow tempo. It's similar to the start of the epic second solo in "Comfortably Numb" at 5'00"; this time he's in B minor pentatonic, with the first finger at the seventh fret. The first note is a pinched harmonic, which creates an ear-catching start to the solo.*

Stock Blues Licks

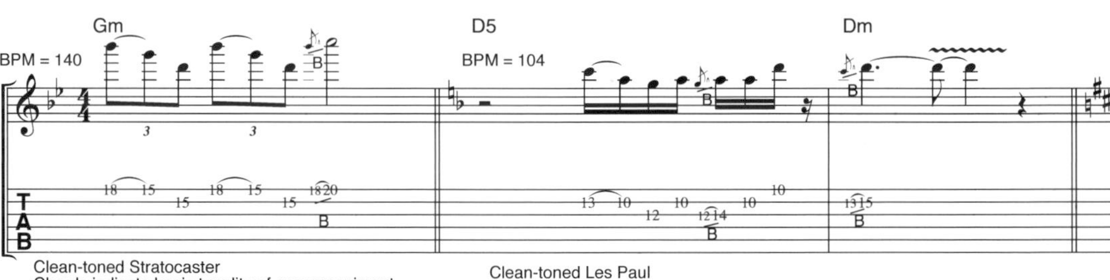

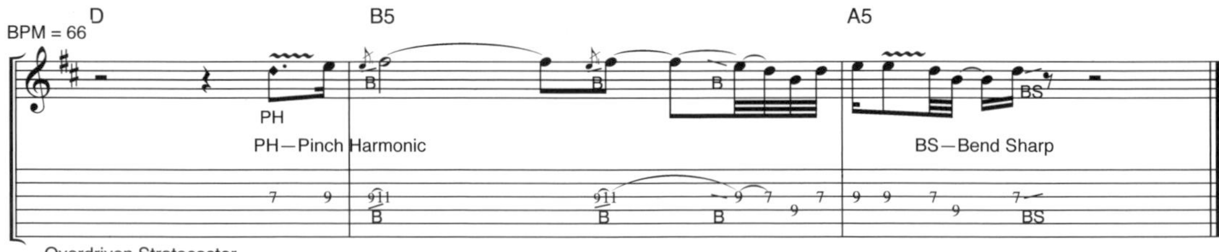

Compound Bends

▶ *On "Another Brick in the Wall Part 2," Gilmour uses multiple compound bends on the second string at 2'29", and this exercise illustrates his approach. The initial bend is a regular-sounding one, from the flattened seventh note of the D pentatonic minor scale up to the root note on the second string—but after that it all changes. The bend is released back to the initial C pitch, then, without re-striking, the string is pushed up two frets to E at the 17th fret, where it's sustained for two beats before being pushed up a further fret to F, so the overall bend is from C to F, a perfect fourth. The bend is finally released back down to C, then bent up to the D root note. It's a challenge to sustain the string throughout all this bending and releasing with only one pluck.*

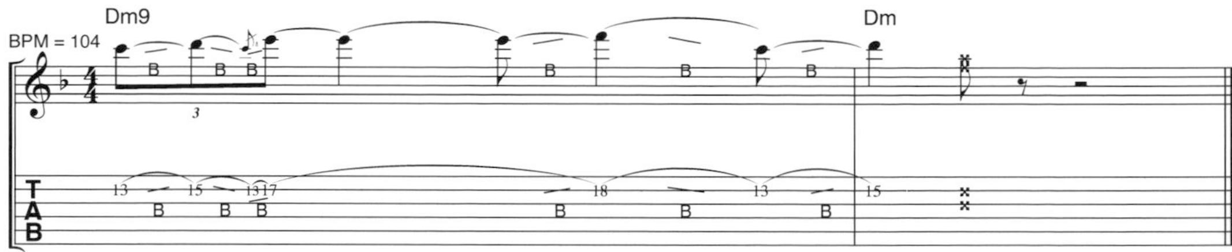

Chords E, E7b5b9 and Emaj7

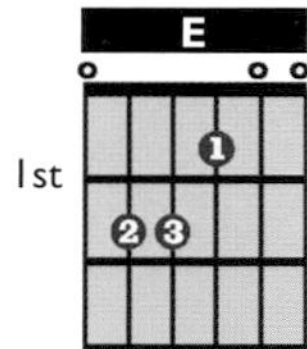

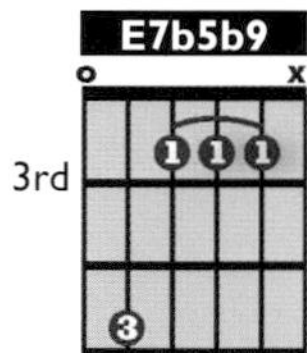

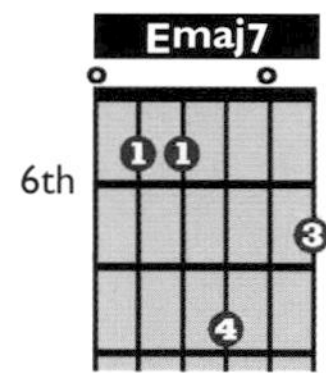

▲ *Here we have the basic open E chord plus two rather more unusual voicings. The E7b5b9 shape could also be thought of as a Bb/D chord on the middle four strings, all played over open bottom E. On the right is a voicing of Emaj7 with an unusual octave gap between the top two notes—both Bs.*

Above: *David Gilmour on stage with his famous black Strat.*

Arpeggios in the Key of E

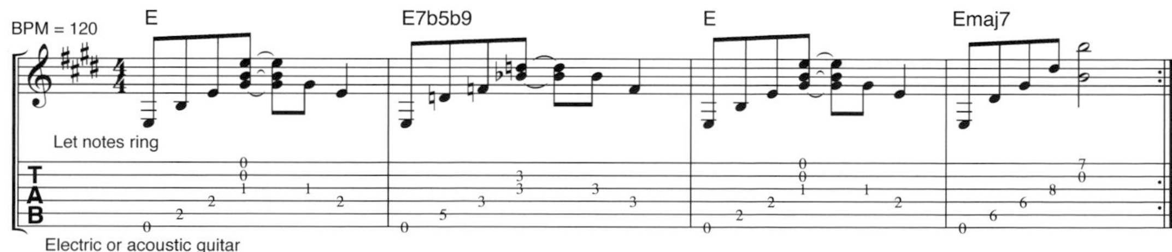

▲ *If you were slightly puzzled by the last two chords, don't worry: both are used by Gilmour in E major songs from his solo album* On An Island *(2006), and this exercise shows how they can be deployed in conjunction with their key chord. E7b5b9 features in "Take A Breath;" Emaj7 in "The Blue," where it's essentially the only chord for the first eight bars, setting the song's mood and feel.*

PLAY LIKE Kirk Hammett

Above: *Kirk Hammett often wears protective tape around his right hand.*

The guitar tuition Metallica's Kirk Hammett received from Joe Satriani in the early 1980s provided him with a valuable musical grounding, as he told *Guitar & Bass* in 1996, shortly after the release of the band's album *Load*. "Joe showed me how to use modes, and he showed me a lot of theory—like what chords to play over what scales, and vice versa…In fact, I think I was probably his last student." Much of Hammett's soloing on *Load* was based around the E blues scale at the 12th fret, often using double-stop bends on strings two and three. In fact, without the key of E minor, there really would be no Metallica, and many of these exercises are in it. They're all marked to be played at a tempo of BPM = 120—but try them at a variety of speeds.

Hammett's string gauges

For a while, Hammett used .011" top E strings, but he found that they didn't suit his technique, and caused him tendon problems. "I had trigger finger on my left-hand ring finger, which isn't a good condition for a guitar player to have!" His finger recovered, and now he's gone back to using .010" first strings.

Double Stops

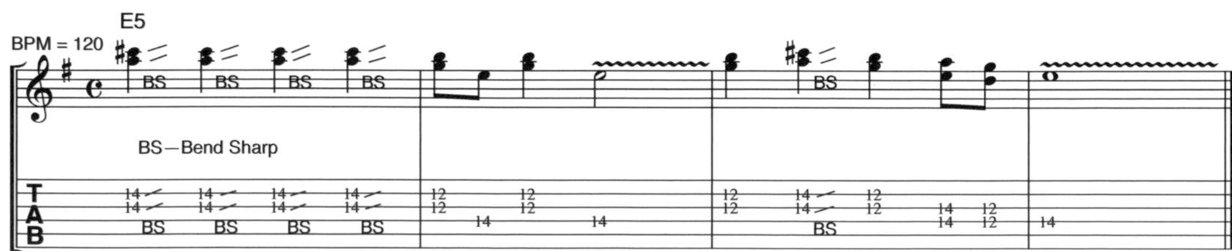

▲ *Hammett frequently starts his solos with a double stop consisting of the fourth and major sixth degrees of the scale—A and C# in the key of E minor. This is fingered by laying the third finger flat across strings three and two at the same fret, in this case the 14th. The double stop is often treated with a "bend sharp"—a downward pull raising the notes by approximately a quarter tone. The third string rises slightly further, creating an effective dissonant effect.*

Double Stop with Bends

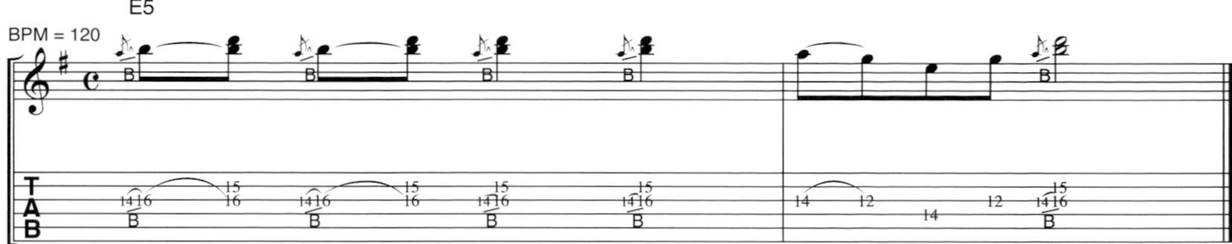

Distorted electric Chord indicates basic tonality of accompaniment

▲ *Another common Hammett blues/rock device consists of a third string bend from the fourth degree of the scale to the fifth, combined with the flattened seventh on the second string. Hammett can be heard using licks like this one in many places—"Enter Sandman" at 3'08" (based on the F# pentatonic minor scale) and "2 X 4" from* Load *at 3'21" in the key of E minor.*

Stock Repeated Licks with Slurs

Distorted electric Chord indicates basic tonality of accompaniment

◀ *In "Through the Never" from* Metallica *(1991) at 2'34", Hammett plays a lick similar to the one in our first bar, using a hammer-on and a pull-off on the second string alternated with a plucked note on the third string. Our second bar shows this lick on the first and second strings. Make sure all notes sound equally in volume.*

Classic Stock Repeated Licks with Bends and Slurs

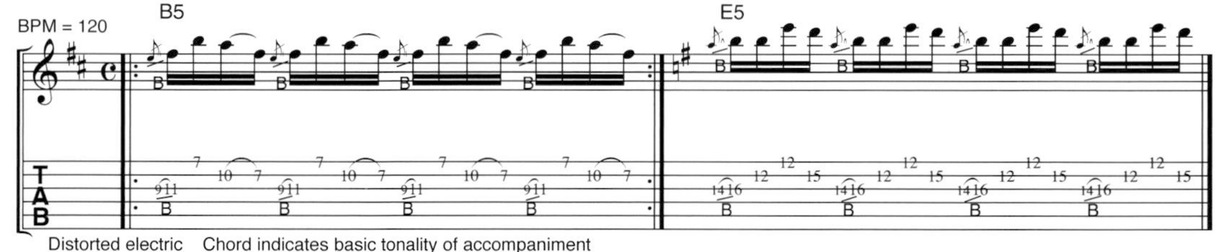

Distorted electric Chord indicates basic tonality of accompaniment

▲ *In "Hit the Lights" from* Kill 'Em All *(1993), Hammett articulates a classic stock lick in the key of B minor. This takes the form of a bend on the third string from the fourth to the fifth, then the octave on the top string followed by a pull-off on the second string from the flattened seventh to the fifth, as illustrated in the first bar of this exercise. In "Dyer's Eve" from* And Justice for All *(1988), Hammett plays another classic blues/rock lick in the key of E minor, consisting of a bend on the third string from the fourth to the fifth, followed by the fifth on the second string, the octave on the top strings and, finally the flattened seventh on the second string.*

Pull-offs to Open Strings

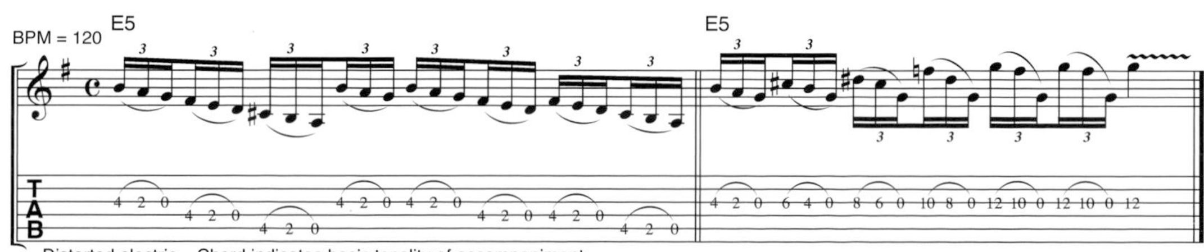

Distorted electric Chord indicates basic tonality of accompaniment

◀ *Kirk enjoys pull-offs to open strings. The first bar is in E Dorian mode (E F# G A B C# D E), while the second bar uses notes from the G whole tone scale—G A B C# D# F G.*

Setting up whammy bars

There are several different types of spring-loaded guitar unit that can produce vibrato. (They're often called "tremolos," but this is incorrect, as *vibrato* is the musical term for fluctuations in pitch, while *tremolo* refers to variations in amplitude.) However, they all function similarly, and involve two forces working against each other: the tension of the strings and the counteracting tension of the springs. If these are both set correctly, the vibrato will be balanced and the guitar will stay in tune. Here you can learn how to keep three different kinds of vibrato working at their best.

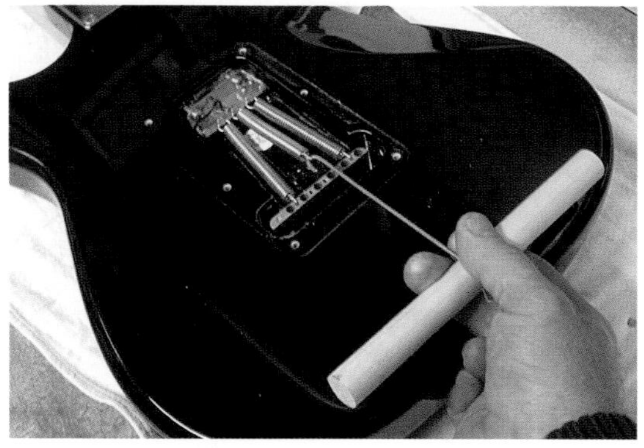

1 This special spring remover is designed to avoid causing scratches when working on your Strat.

Fender Stratocaster

The first type we'll look at is the commonest: Stratocaster-type vibratos. These aren't really made for dropping the pitch much more than a semitone, but are fine for lighter, warbling effects. To adjust a Strat's vibrato, take the strings off the guitar, then remove the cover plate from the back of the body to allow access to the springs. The tool being used to take off the springs in the photograph is a special, homemade one that hooks over their ends; a pair of pliers could slip off and scratch the instrument. With the springs removed, turn the guitar over and examine the screws on which the bridge pivots. Leo Fender's original design featured six of these, while some newer Strats have just two (see illustrations). The screws should be level and just making contact with the surface of the baseplate. If the vibrato isn't sitting flat on the body of the guitar, it means that at least one of them is too tight. Loosen each one, screw it down until you can just feel it pushing the plate up at the back, and then wind it out an eighth of a turn; this will allow the vibrato to work freely and return to the correct position.

2 A modern, two-screw Stratocaster bridge: other strats, old and recent, are fitted with six screws.

When you're happy with the height of the screws holding down the plate, check to see if they are in line. Hold the vibrato and try rocking it across its width while it's flat on the body. If it rocks at all, then the screws—or the holes in the bridge plate—aren't in line. This can be due to a number of things: incorrect original installation; "uneven wear;" or problems with the holes in the baseplate. Fixing such problems can be tricky, so it's best to seek expert advice. When you're done, refit the vibrato springs, and restring the guitar. Remember, two and a half turns of string around the tuners is sufficient: more than this will add to tuning problems. Bring the strings up to pitch, and then stretch them a little to help them stay in tune.

3 Backing one of the pivoting screws off by an eighth turn on a older-style six-screw bridge.

Top Guitar Tip

The whammy bar evolved rapidly in the hands of guitarists like Jimi Hendrix and Jeff Beck, and has enabled guitarists to mimic everything from dive bombers to horses. To hear it being used to imitate talking, listen to Steve Vai's "The Audience Is Listening" from *Passion & Warfare* (1990).

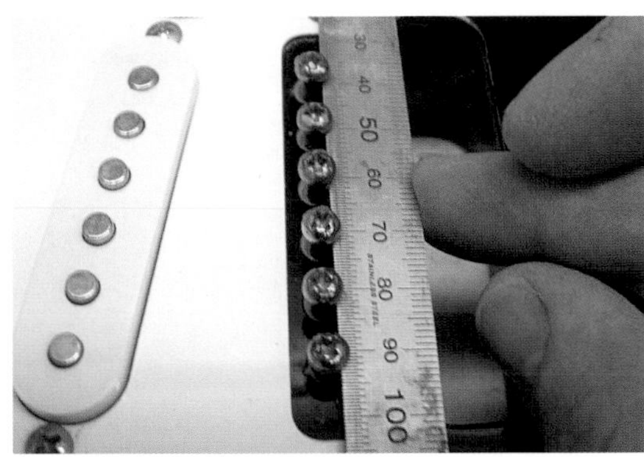

4 If these six screws (seen here without the bridge's cover plate) aren't in a straight line, the bridge will rock.

5 Two and half turns of the string on the machine head are all that's needed.

Below: *Each of the three electric guitars shown here has a different type of vibrato. The Stratocaster in the center has had its whammy bar unscrewed.*

6 Stretching the strings can help them settle—but be gentle with them.

7 Locking tuners like the ones on this Strat can help a string to retain its correct pitch.

Setting up whammy bars

Now have a look at the back of the baseplate where the vibrato unit meets the body. The optimum gap here is about 2.5 mm (1/10 in), which will stop you pulling the vibrato too far back. If it's any wider, then the springs need more tension on them to counteract the strings' tension; if it's less, they will need less. To bring the back of the vibrato down, tighten the screws that hold the anchor plate for the springs, being sure to use a screwdriver that fits properly. One turn on the screws at a time is all that is needed—and remember, each time you adjust the springs, you'll have to retune the guitar. Once the springs are adjusted, we can have a look at the nut end. If the string slots are too tight or not smooth, the strings can stick in the slots, and won't return to their correct tension. To cure this, the slots should all be cleaned out and, if necessary, filed using the correct size nut file. A little pencil lead or graphite in the bottom of the slots will also help the strings to move around freely.

8 Mind the gap! The vibrato springs should keep this height at 2.5 mm (1/10 in).

Floyd Rose

Floyd Rose-type vibratos work on two pivots, and the plate of the vibrato doesn't touch the body at all. They also incorporate locking nuts that prevent any tuning problems over the nut and decrease the length of string, so there's less of it to stretch and go out of tune. However, the springs on these vibratos work in exactly the same way as on the Strat type, and just as on a Strat, the plate should be adjusted so that it lies at a slight upward angle to the body, not parallel to it. It needs to pull slightly one way so that there's a positive position for it to return to—one where it has an equal amount of tension on it each way. If set at the correct angle, Floyd Roses are generally pretty trouble-free. The only real problem is with wear on the pivots or on the edge of the baseplate that rocks on them…and in either case a replacement will be necessary.

9 If necessary, the string slots in the nut may be widened with a special file. Proceed with caution!

Bigsby

Last of all, a quick look at maintaining and adjusting a Bigsby. This design is fairly foolproof, and all that's generally needed is a little lubrication around all the pivoting points. The springs rarely need replacing, although they can lose their tension, allowing the arm to come out too far. All that's required in this case is a healthy replacement spring.

10 Graphite, supplied here from the tip of a pencil, will help the string move more freely in its slot.

Top Guitar Tip

When any changes are made to the vibrato's positioning, then the intonation will need to be re-adjusted. On Floyd Rose units, where the bridge saddles are locked in place, you must slacken off each string in turn and unlock the saddle to move it.

Below: *This handsome green solid is fitted with a Bigsby-type vibrato. This is a simple, reliable design that requires little maintenance and has been popular for decades.*

11 Unlocking a Floyd Rose bridge saddle to adjust the intonation, with the string slackened (see tip above.)

12 A Floyd Rose's locking nut; like the bridge saddles, its locks are adjusted with a hex key.

13 Lubricating a Bigsby vibrato: a touch of WD-40 keeps everything working smoothly.

PLAY LIKE John Paul Jones

Although he will always be primarily thought of as Led Zeppelin's bass player, John Paul Jones is also a multi-instrumentalist, and a skilled composer and arranger. Here we're focusing on the first three Zeppelin albums where, arguably, his bass work shines the brightest. When you listen to him, try to bear in mind the accepted and limited palette that rock bass players today are supposed to draw from, and compare how different Jones's approach was. Sure, he's happy to play driving eighth notes when required, but his highly funky and improvisational approach on classics like "The Lemon Song" (from *LZ II, 1969*) tend to make you wonder exactly who is soloing. There's soul and blues and no small degree of experimentation in there, but it's his feel that is truly awesome.

Above right: *In this photo, Jones is holding a Hugh Manson bass mandolin.*

Incommunicado

▲ *Many of the ensuing examples show Jones' penchant for funky sixteenth-note phrasing, but he was always prepared to take the eighth-note option when required. "Communication Breakdown"* (Led Zeppelin, *1969), which our first example is loosely based on, is as close to thrashy hard rock as Zeppelin ever came. This one is all about attitude: your groove should be solid and not pushy, and the accents in the second bar (denoted by the sideways "v") need just a little more weight than normal for the right effect.*

Rambling Melody

▲ *Jones was certainly no one-trick pony...whether it be straight eighths, funky sixteenths, or the pseudo-folk of songs like "Gallows Pole" (LZ III), he was always armed and ready to deliver. This example pays tribute to the sweet pentatonic melody from the verse sections of "Ramble On" (LZ II), where the bass part descends from the high-voiced major third of each chord to the root note, with a tasty lick at the end of bar 2 for good measure.*

AMP or DI?

Bass players, especially when they work in studios, often debate over whether they should DI (direct inject) their instruments to the control desk, or use an amp with a mic in front of it. John Paul Jones told *Guitar & Bass* in 2007 that he chooses the best of both worlds. "I mix. I prefer the sound of the amplifier, but I'll put just a bit of the direct signal in to balance it up a bit. Of course it depends on the song, but I've never liked direct on its own."

Riff-Meister

◀ *Here we've chosen to get you close to the riffing vibe on a Zeppelin classic from LZ II, "Heartbreaker." Take note of the tab, as using the open D and G strings makes this particular riff much easier to play.*

Tangy Turnaround

◀ *"The Lemon Song" (LZ II) is a classic piece of bass improvisation. Right from the start, and especially during the verses immediately preceding the final double-time section, Jones's playing is a tour de force of tasteful, effortlessly grooving variation. With this example we've tried to echo the ideas that Jones plays in unison with Page at the end of each half-time chorus in the first half of the song.*

A Heavy Night

▲ *This is based on "Out On The Tiles" from LZ III—an album considered by many to be a much less aggressive offering with more of a folky mood. Think again! As if the rapid-fire arpeggio in bar 1 isn't enough, you've then got to deal with the fierce descending riff that Jones and Page play in seamless unison. The open D string is a lifesaver here.*

PLAY LIKE Mark King

Level 42 issued its self-titled debut album in 1981, and had its first U.K. hit single, "Love Games," the same year. The group comprised slap bass maestro Mark King, who was born on the Isle of Wight in 1958, brothers Phil and Boon Gould on drums and guitar, and keyboardist Mike Lindup. They quickly found themselves at the forefront of early 1980s Brit funk. Because he was also the lead vocalist, King's profile was especially high, and his exciting, virtuosic style of playing inspired many new bass players. The year 1987, which saw the release of *Running In The Family*, an LP featuring no fewer than five successful singles, proved to be Level 42's commercial zenith. Subsequently, the original lineup broke up, but there have been various remodeled versions, and the band's current incarnation—which undertook a thirtieth anniversary tour in 2010—includes two of its founder members, Mark King and Mike Lindup.

Above: *Mark King's virtuoso right-hand technique in action.*

▶ *Those unfamiliar with the diversity of Level 42's output should check out Mark King's funky, innovative fingerstyle lines. Listen to "Kansas City Milkman" and "True Believers" (both from 1984's* True Colours *LP): the first is a sleazy, hypnotic riff; the second is bubbling finger-funk at its best. The two bars here might remind you of "Starchild" (featured on 2006's* The Definitive Collection, *like all the tracks that have inspired our examples). They may look simple, but the need for tight note length control and staccato phrasing will test your chops.*

Funky Star

A Family Affair

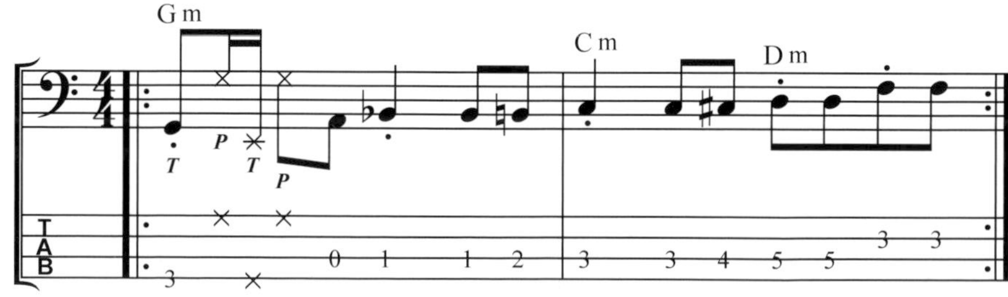

▲ *It's a tribute to King's single-mindedness as a player that while Level 42's songs became dominated by layered synthesizers and the melodies more pop-oriented, he never lost sight of the way he wanted to play. This example is the first using the slap technique, and should get you close to the main groove from "Running In The Family" (1987). King inserts the dead-note lick more or less every second time, and while it may look a little awkward, the dead-note "pitch" merely serves to indicate which string to damp for the necessary "click."*

Sun Up, Groove Down

Below: King's Status Graphite bass has LED fingerboard markers.

▲ Bass players tend to forget about using simple scale ideas for grooves because they mistakenly feel the need to be more creative with melodic lines. This ascending scale gives you an idea of King's approach in "The Sun Goes Down (Living It Up)" (1983), this time using A minor pentatonic. It requires seriously staccato phrasing; for the right burpy tone, place your playing hand close to the bridge.

> *I know I didn't invent slap playing, but the point is, I did it a slightly different way.*
>
> Mark King, 2005

Lessons in Slap

Played with thumb

◀ For Level 42's poppier material, King had to think more in terms of catchy hooks than blistering percussion. On "Lessons In Love" (1986) he reclaims the "galloping horse" groove from heavy metal, and uses the arpeggio of each chord to create a simple but effective bass melody.

Method in Oriental Madness

▲ It's difficult not to listen to King's more kinetic fingerstyle lines without recognizing the huge influence of Jaco Pastorius (Weather Report, Joni Mitchell). King's tone, while not as rich as Jaco's, is replete with the same high-mid bias that comes from playing way back over the bridge pickup. Our example should put you in mind of "The Chinese Way" (1982, single 1983), and you'll find it's almost a homage to Pastorius's finger-funk. It's also tricky to execute cleanly so, once again, start at a slow tempo and make sure you can hear every note.

PLAY LIKE

Mark Knopfler

Mark Knopfler is a left-hander who plays guitar right-handed—and for picking the strings, he prefers bare fingers to a plectrum. "When I was learning the guitar I used to play with a pick a lot…[but] when flatpicking and fingerpicking were fusing together for me, I realized [that] doing things with my fingers that I used to do with a pick was more comfortable and more rhythmic." As Knopfler's style developed, he was influenced by country player Chet Atkins, and while he readily concedes that his picking technique isn't as advanced as Chet's, he has adopted some aspects of it. "Like Chet, I tried to make the thumb sound like a pianist's left hand in order to be more creative with the rhythm, and I also play all six strings with my fingers and thumb. That's really how my solo style started to develop."

Left: *Mark Knopfler with a "Hot Rod Red" Stratocaster.*

▶ *In the outro section of Dire Straits' "Sultans Of Swing" (1978), Knopfler plays a series of fast sixteenth note-based arpeggios starting at 5'18". Here's our take on this kind of technique. In order to attain Mark's fluency, use your thumb, index, and middle fingers to pluck the strings: so, for each group of four sixteenth notes, you pluck the top string with the middle finger, then pull off; then pluck the second string with the thumb, then pluck the top string with the index finger, and repeat for the other sixteenth note-based passages. This avoids playing a string with the same finger twice in a row, which is awkward at fast tempos.*

Fast Picking

Diads Lick

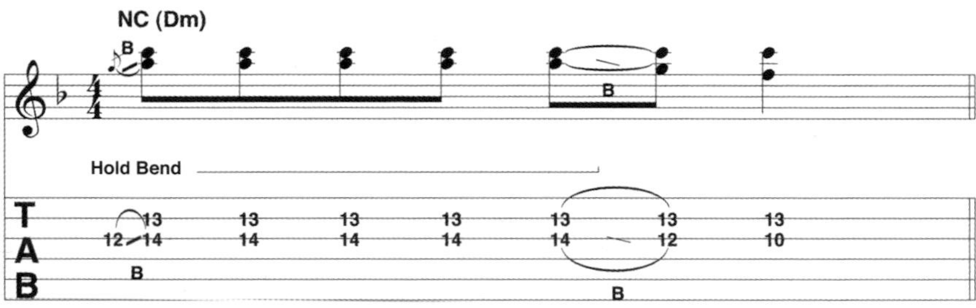

Fingerstyle

◀ Knopfler often uses diads (two-note chords) in his lead playing. The notes in this exercise are from the D pentatonic minor scale (D F G A C D) and the phrase involves bending the fourth degree of the scale up to the fifth on the third string while sounding the minor seventh on the second string. Try picking it with index and middle, then thumb and index; Knopfler isn't averse to using his thumb to pluck the upper strings.

Above: Knopfler plays a Gibson Les Paul with a capo.

Chords Dm/A, C/G, Bb/F and F/A

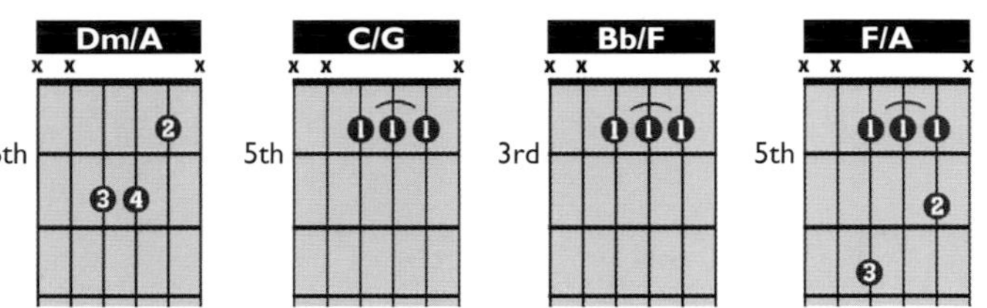

▲ These chords are all three-note voicings or triads—three-note chords consisting of root, third, and fifth. Dm/A signifies that the A (fifth) is at the bottom of the triad; its presence there makes this chord a second inversion. C/G and Bb/F are also second inversions, while F/A is a first inversion.

> "All my songs tend to be written on sofas with acoustic guitars."
>
> Mark Knopfler

Fill with Triads

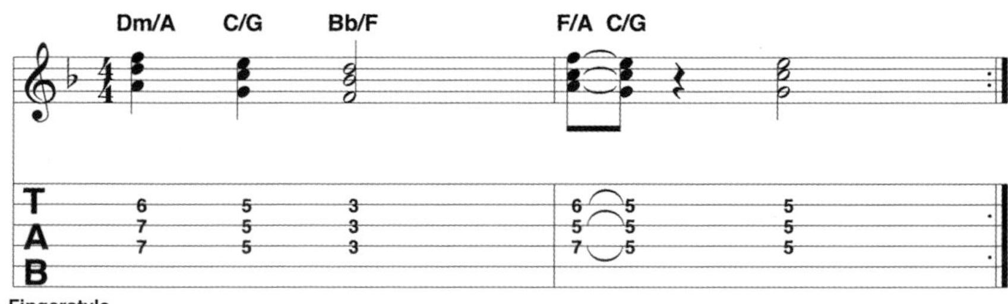

Fingerstyle

◀ The triads whose fingerings are shown above lend themselves nicely to being plucked with the thumb, index, and middle fingers. Knopfler plays a similar fill to this one in "Sultans Of Swing" at 1'15". Notice that with these F/A and C/G voicings, the chords lie very close together (in fact, they share a common note: C on the third string, fifth fret). By fingering the F/A chord with a barré, as shown in the diagram, it is possible to pull off from F/A to C/G, as in the second bar of this exercise.

PLAY LIKE Paul Kossoff

Paul Kossoff's guitar style was from the school of "less is more." "He was a man who didn't use very many notes," recalled British bluesman Alexis Korner. "He was a much sparser player. One of the things that impressed me most was that he knew when not to play. It made him exciting." Kossoff started his musical studies with six years of classical training, but was left uninspired. His interest in the guitar was rekindled when he heard Eric Clapton playing with John Mayall; suddenly, he realized that while his classical studies had helped his finger dexterity, they had little relevance to playing blues. He went on to develop his own style, featuring a distinctive approach to chords. As he explained, "I use a lot of open strings, and the chords are neither major nor minor. I don't like to play a major chord unless it's necessary. I prefer to use a chord that rings, having neither major nor minor dominance." We'll be exploring some of these chords here.

Right: *Understated power: Paul Kossoff with Free.*

Kossoff's chord voicings—G5/D, C5/G, D5/G, F5/G, and A5 chords

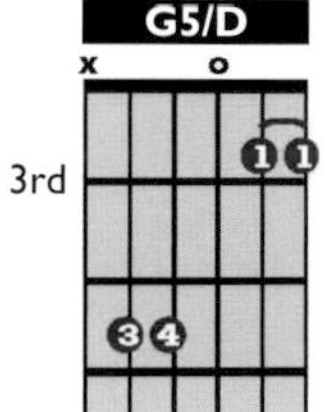

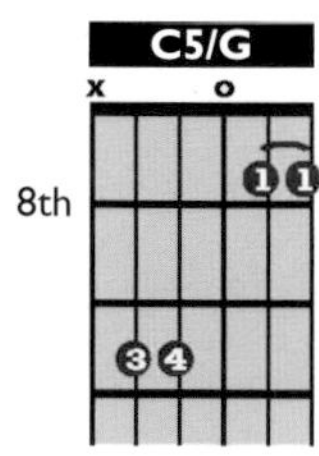

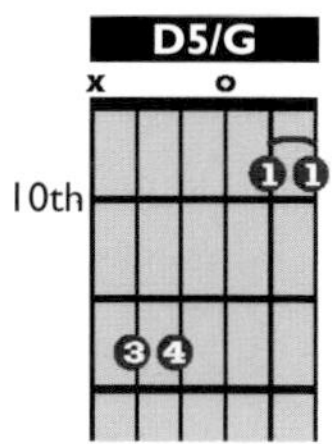

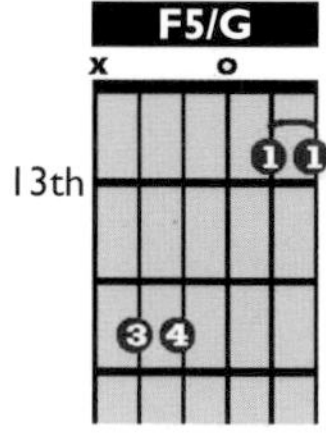

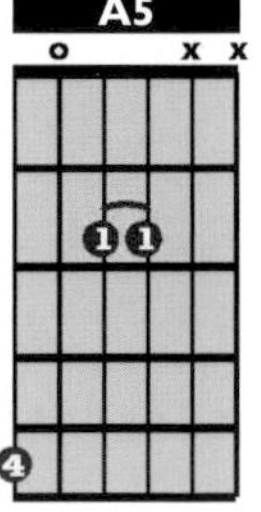

▲ *The first four of these voicings are based on the same chord shape, shifted up the fretboard. Each of them contains an open G string, but when the shape moves, the harmonic relationship of the open G to the chord changes. For example, in G5 the open G note doubles the root note of the chord; in C5, the open G note doubles the fifth. As the shape is moved up the fretboard, the static open G becomes an increasingly lower note in the chord, and in both D5/G and F5/G it's the lowest one. When fingering the fifth (A5) shape, make sure your fourth finger (on the bottom string, fifth fret) is kept upright in order to allow the open fifth string to ring on; by doing this, the bass note is doubled, creating a strengthened lower register.*

Progression using Kossoff's chord voicings

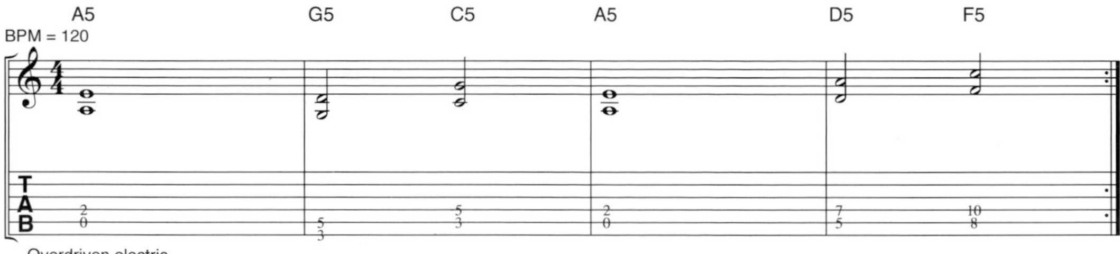

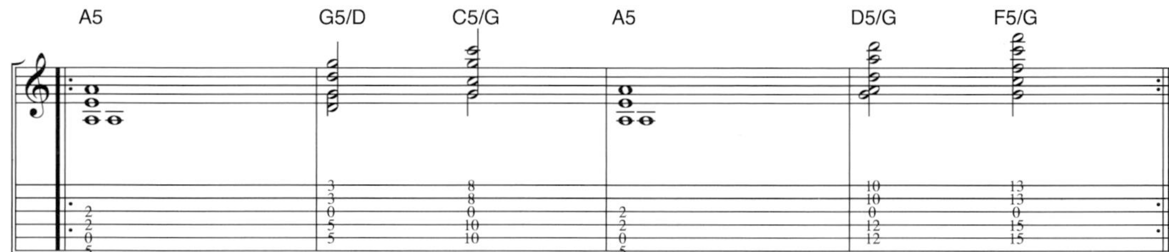

▲ *The first line of the exercise shows a fairly stock rock chord progression using standard root/fifth power chords—no chord diagrams needed here!—whereas the second line shows the equivalent progression using Kossoff's voicings as given above. Listen carefully to the difference…*

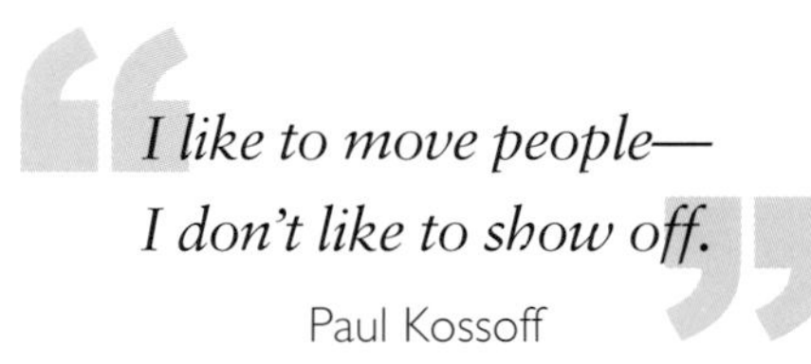

"All Right Now" chords—A5 (type 2), D/A,Dadd4add9/F#

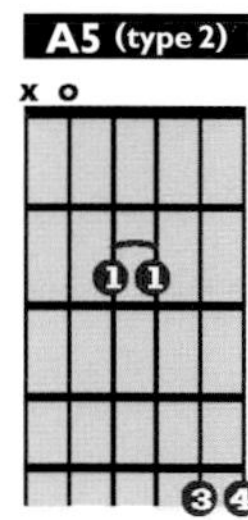

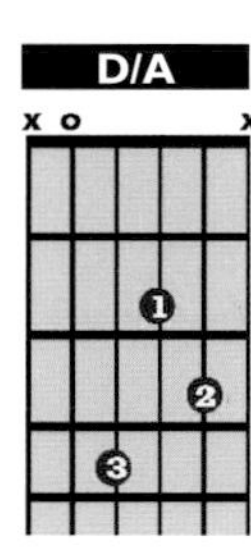

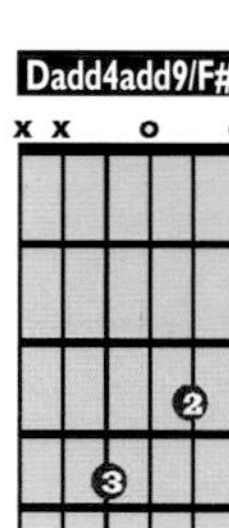

◀ *A5 (type 2) here uses five notes, as opposed to the more common two-note voicing of A5. This voicing is spread over two octaves, creating a bigger sound. D/A means a D chord over an A bass note. Dadd4add9/F# uses open third and open top strings.*

"All Right Now"-style riff

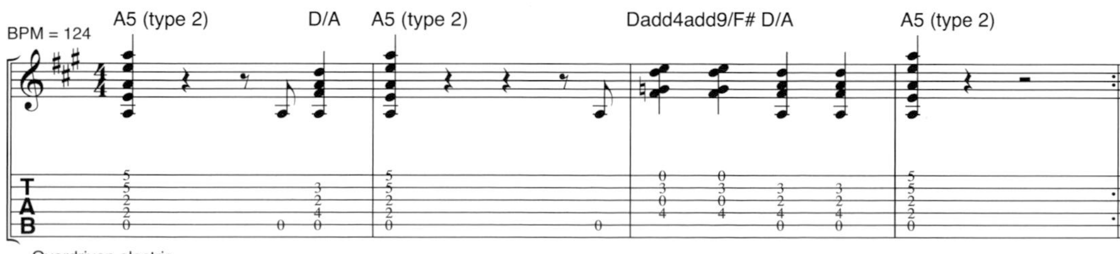

▲ *This exercise, similar to the main riff of "All Right Now," features the chords whose fingerings you've just learned. Play it with an overdriven tone, but be careful not to use too much distortion, otherwise the close intervals in the Dadd4add9/F# chord will sound particularly ugly.*

PLAY LIKE Lemmy

One man has been a constant presence throughout Motörhead's long decades of aural assault: Lemmy, the Lord of the Rickenbacker. He achieves his inimitable, biting timbre by soloing the neck pickup on his bass, maxing its tone and volume controls, and running it through his Marshall amp with its bass and treble settings backed right off, and its mid-range fully boosted. He often uses power chords (generally root and fifth) to fill out Motörhead's trio sound, and invariably assaults his bass with a pick. If the results are too loud for you, then—to quote another veteran hard rocker, Ted Nugent—"you're too old!"

> *I sound like a gorilla on valium.*
>
> Lemmy

Left: *Lemmy's microphone placement wouldn't suit many other singers!*

Reaped by the Reaper

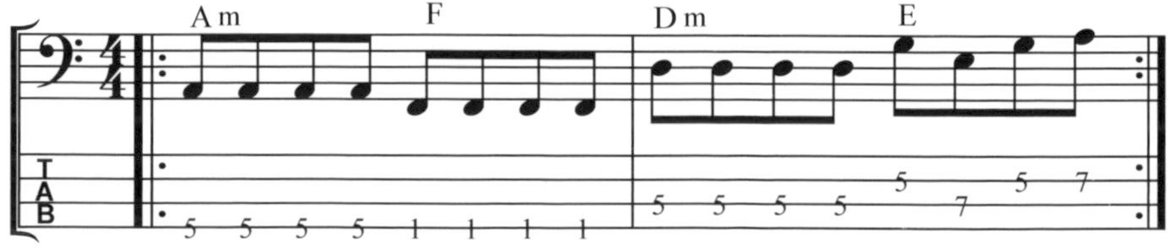

◀ *Although you could never accuse Lemmy and the boys of playing ballads, they have plenty of songs in the mid-tempo spectrum. Our first exercise is based on the grinding rocker "Killed By Death." We've halved the time on each chord to fit in the full sequence, and approximated Lemmy's neat fill in bar 2.*

Expired for Eternity

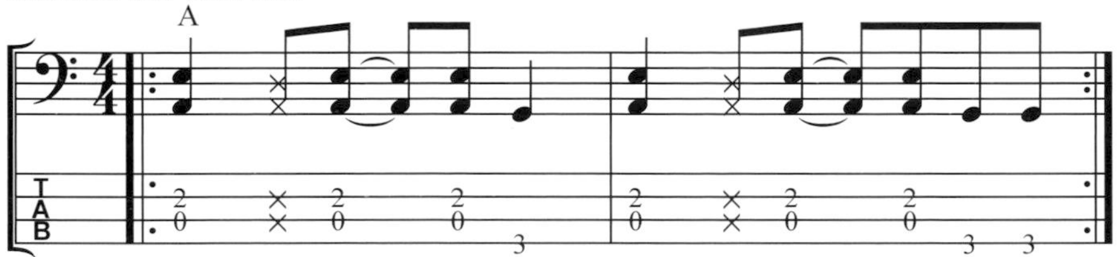

◀ *Lemmy's penchant for power chords or double-stops—like Paul McCartney's—is drawn from his rhythm guitar days, though Lemmy bases whole lines on the technique, and plays a lot louder than McCartney ever did, or wanted to. Inspired by "Stone Dead Forever," our example looks easy until you add a tempo of around 140 bpm into the equation, and imagine banging it out for four minutes…*

Tempted Behind Bars

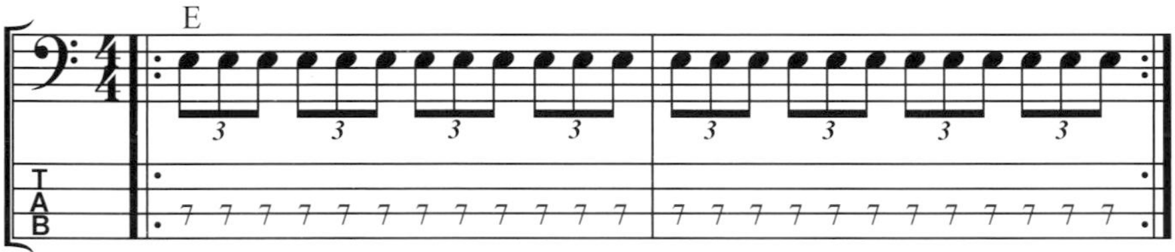

▲ *Due to the sheer level of tempo involved and the force he uses on his Rickenbacker, many of Lemmy's basslines are a grueling exercise in stamina. Relax a bit, juice up the tone, and have a go at this exercise, designed to bring to mind the essence of "Jailbait."*

Slamming Home the Groove

▲ *Lemmy often supplies an idea that catches your ear and adds a little extra. The chord thrash-up on "Stone Dead Forever" is one example, but the rhythmic variation on the breakdown in the seminal "Overkill" is another excellent one. Check out our exercise and remember that you have to keep the rhythm cleanly phrased at a seriously challenging tempo, as well as keeping something in reserve for the rest of the song.*

Above: *A heavy plectrum is essential if you play like Mr Kilminster...*

An Ace Up Your Sleeve

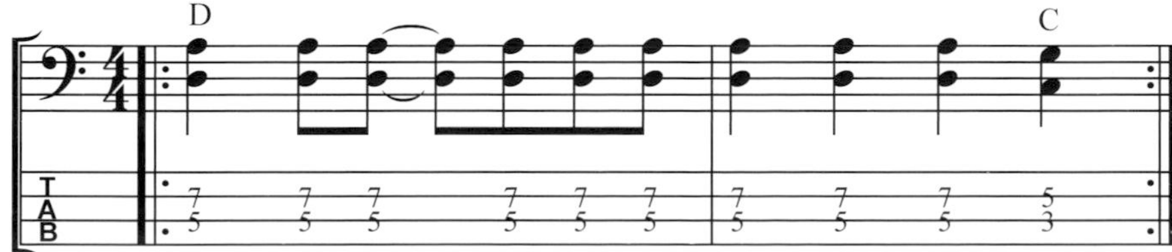

▲ *Our final example is a homage to the glory that is "Ace Of Spades." Lemmy's monstrous bass intro is delivered at a killing tempo, but the most impressive thing about his chordal vibe is how consistent he is with both phrasing and sound. You can reduce any of these lines to root notes, but that simply kills the fun—stone dead, forever.*

PLAY LIKE Brian May

One of the many unique things about Queen was its four members' individual songwriting abilities. While Freddie Mercury penned the operatic bombast of "Bohemian Rhapsody," bassist John Deacon banged out the groove-heavy "Another One Bites The Dust," and drummer Roger Taylor wrote "Radio Ga Ga" (a No.1 in 19 different countries), Brian May was responsible for some of the band's rockier songs—including one of its heaviest numbers, "Hammer To Fall." But as well as generating the powerful riffs that dominate that track, May's also famous for his harmony guitar work. He recalls "listening a hundred times" to records by the Everly Brothers and the Crickets "to make sure I knew where [their vocal harmonies] were going and why it sounded so amazing." These insights enabled him to create his own ingeniously structured guitar parts. Here we'll be exploring how he did it.

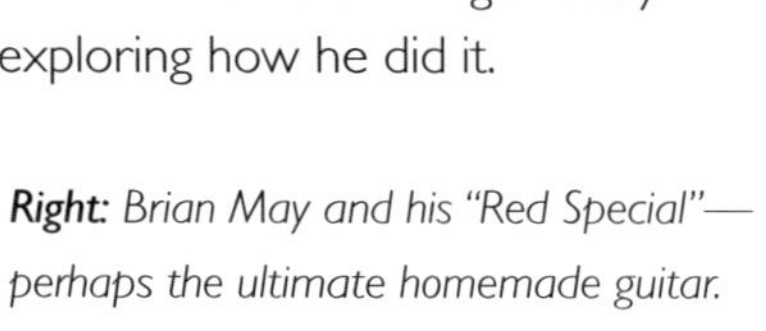

Right: *Brian May and his "Red Special"—perhaps the ultimate homemade guitar.*

► *"Hammer To Fall" (1984) starts with A and D/A chords like those in the first two bars of this exercise. Brian May moves the fretted notes in these chords an octave higher to produce the A (type 2) and D/A (type 2) chords that first appear in our third bar. Note the double pull-off from D/A (type 2) to A (type 2) in the second half of bar 3—May can be heard using pull-offs like this in "A Kind of Magic" (1986) at 2'05".*

Riff with A, D/A, A (type 2), and D/A (type 2)

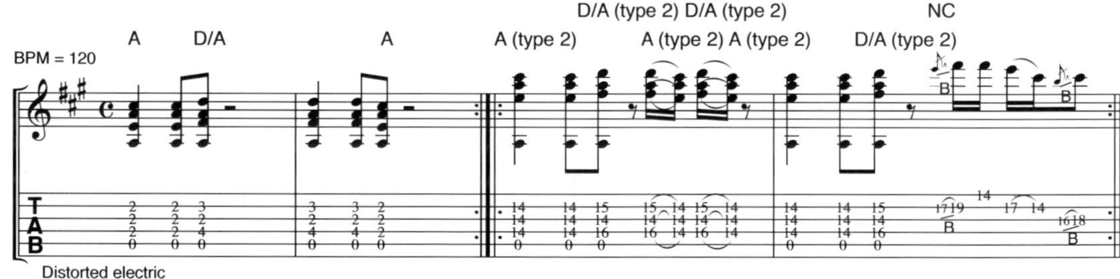

Lead Melody

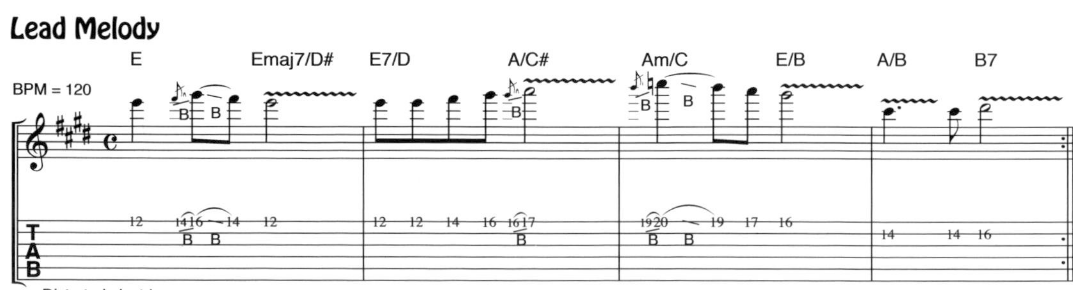

▲ *This Brian May-type lead line, accompanied by the indicated chords with their chromatically descending bass notes, can be combined (using multitrack recording) with the "bell" harmonies that appear next. Notice how the bend up to C at the start of bar 3 highlights the chord change from A to A minor.*

"Bell" Harmonies

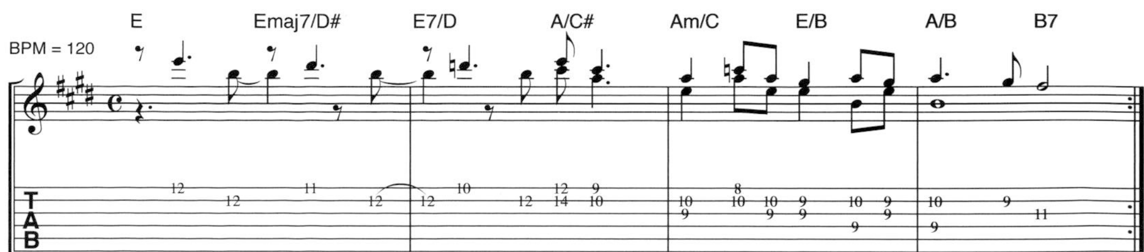

Two distorted electrics Chords played by rhythm guitar

▲ *This is intended to be played as two separate guitar parts, using overdubbing. While it's physically possible to play all these notes on one guitar, doing so won't give you the same feel and expression. The upper part is written with upward-pointing stems in the music notation, and is always played on the higher string in the tab; the lower part is written with downward-pointing stems, and is always played on the lower string in the tab. Combining the "lead melody," its chords, and the harmonies will require a total of four tracks on your recording device.*

Three-part Harmony

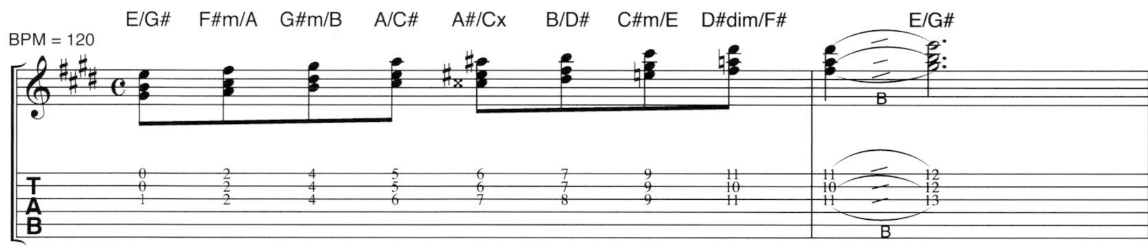

Three distorted electrics

▲ *May sometimes uses overdubbed guitars playing in parallel harmony, as on "Keep Yourself Alive" (1973) at 3'03". In the tab each voice is given its own string. Note the A#/Cx chromatic passing chord in the first bar. A#/Cx means an A# chord with C double sharp in the bass as the lowest note. C double sharp is the enharmonic equivalent of D—the same note on the fretboard but with a different name.*

Delay

Overdriven electric

Overdriven electric: delay = 500ms

▲ *Brian May occasionally deploys an electronic delay to create a harmony guitar part—a technique we've illustrated in our first two bars. Bar 1 shows the first five notes of the D major scale in quavers or eighth notes, marked to be played at a tempo of 120 beats per minute (bpm). The second bar shows what would happen if bar 1 was played through a delay set to 500ms (half a second), with its "feedback" level set to produce one note ("feedback" in this context means the number of repeats). Using these settings and tempo, each struck note would be repeated exactly one beat after the first one, as indicated. Bars 3 and 4 show a phrase similar to one played by May in "Seven Seas Of Rhye" (1974) at 1'29". Again, it's played at a speed of bpm = 120 and with a delay time of 500ms, so the notes will repeat a beat after they're originally struck.*

PLAY LIKE Randy Rhoads

Randy Rhoads's virtuosity earned him high praise during his short career, and he also made use of some ingenious methods to optimize his sound. According to producer Max Norman, when Rhoads was recording his contributions to Ozzy Osbourne's 1980 *Blizzard of Ozz* album, his amp was sometimes driven at a much lower voltage than normal, in order to "smoke up the distortion—give it a creamy edge." (Special equipment was required to do this, and no one should try it without expert knowledge, as its potential dangers are obvious.) Elsewhere on the record, the engineers took advantage of the "unreal high-frequency response" provided by Randy's Karl Sandoval "Flying-V"-style guitar, while for a "thicker, chunkier" timbre, the instrument of choice was his cream-colored Gibson Les Paul Custom. Ultimately, however, all these techniques were secondary to Rhoads's own playing skills—and though they can never entirely be recreated, the exercises below will provide some helpful guidelines for anyone who wants to emulate his musical achievements.

An enduring influence

Among Randy Rhoads's many admirers is Tom Morello from Rage Against the Machine, who named his son Rhoads, and has described the guitarist as "the greatest hard rock player of all time."

Above right: *Randy Rhoads on stage with the Ozzy Osbourne band.*

Power Chord Pedal Point Riff

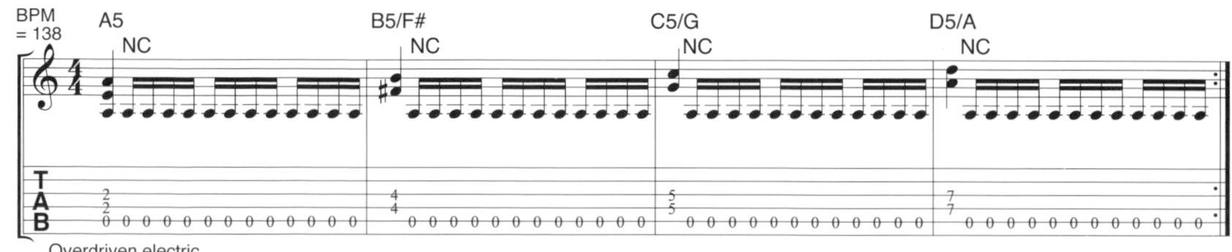

▲ *"I Don't Know" from* Blizzard of Ozz *starts with a riff based around a pedal point of open A. Over it, Rhoads sounds an inverted power chord on strings four and three, using a first finger barré; this gradually moves up the fretboard, played against the static, repeated, pedal open A.*

Chords A, E/G#, D/F#, and A (type 2)

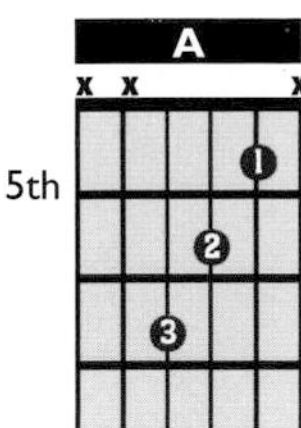

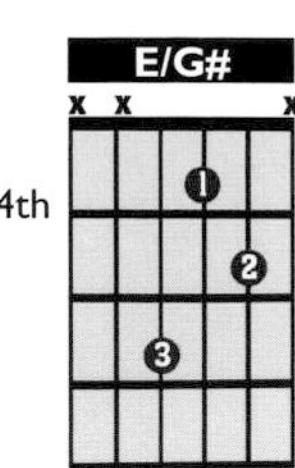

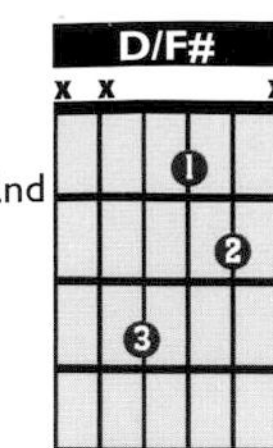

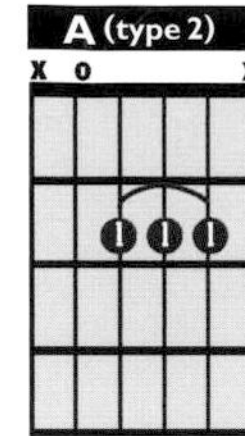

◀ *Here we begin with three triads. These are three-note chords consisting of root, third, and fifth. The first chord shown, A, comprises the three notes in that order; the next two, E/G# and D/F#, are made up with the third, fifth, and root, going from lowest note to highest. The final chord shown is a basic open A chord, fingered with a barré.*

Pedal Point with Triads

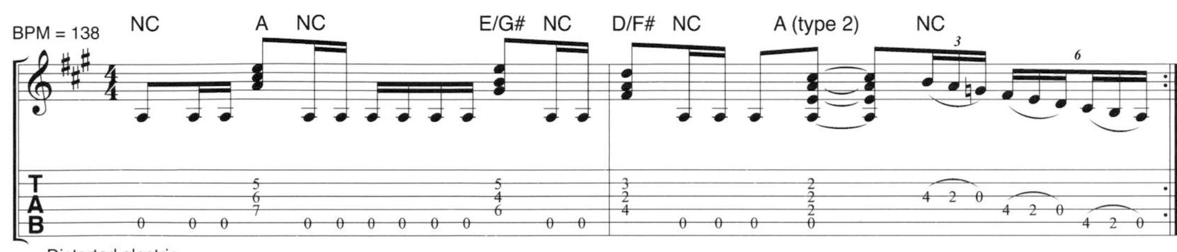

▲ *The intro riff from "Crazy Train" (from Blizzard of Ozz) at 0'18" is in the key of F# minor, based around a pedal note of F# on the bottom string, second fret. For the first verse, the song changes to the relative major key, A major. This exercise is similar to the "Crazy Train" verse riff at 0'32". Like our "I Don't Know"-style riff, it uses a pedal note of open A—but now combined with the chords from our preceding diagrams on strings four, three, and two. Note the slurred fill at the end of the riff; Rhoads uses a symmetrical pattern similar to this in "Crazy Train" at 0'38".*

Repeated Licks with Bends

◀ *Rhoads starts the first solo in "Mr Crowley" (from Blizzard of Ozz) at 0'28" with a pentatonic minor lick similar to the one in bars 2 and 3 here. Rhoads gives the lick forward momentum by starting it at the end of the previous beat. To maximize this feel, make the bend as quickly as possible, then hold onto it for a fraction.*

Repeated Licks with Pull-offs

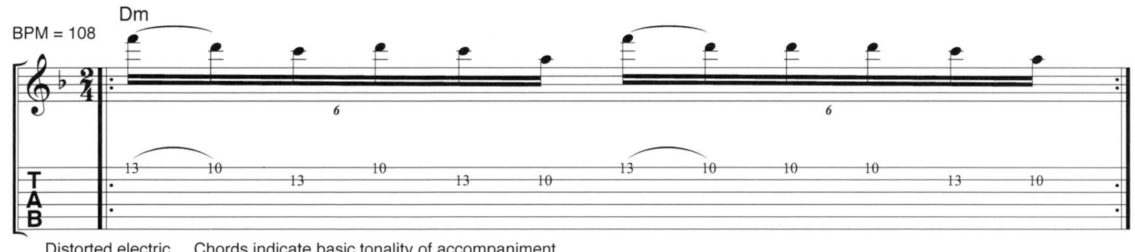

▲ *Rhoads starts the second half of the first solo in "Mr Crowley" at 2'26" with another blistering stock pentatonic minor lick, similar to this one. It's a repeated two-beat phrase, but there's only one different note between the first beat and the second beat. It's probably best to practice each beat on its own, over and over, before alternating between them as in the exercise.*

Build your own pedalboard

A custom-built pedalboard is a convenient and tidy way to set up your collection of stompboxes. Here we outline a design for one: to make it, you'll need some DIY skills. To determine the size of your pedalboard, decide on a suitable layout for your pedals, and take measurements. To save space, organize them in a "front and back row" arrangement. Units you switch on and off regularly, and effects like delays with tap tempo controls, should be at the front. Wah-wahs obviously need to be accessible, too. On the other hand, a digital tuner pedal can be tucked out of the way, along with other effects that may be left permanently switched on, like compressors. The board on which the pedals will rest (the "footboard") should be made from 12-mm (1/2-in) plywood, and battens and side panels should be used when joining a second piece of ply (a "backboard") securely to it. Having a sloping footboard will make the back row of pedals reasonably accessible. Choose the angle carefully, especially if you're using a wah-wah, and bear in mind that a four-way power block with plugs and/or wall warts will need to be mounted underneath, requiring a reasonable amount of clearance. Drill a matrix of holes across the footboard; these must be wide enough for the pedals' cables to pass through, popping up where they're needed.

Velcro strips are an effective method of securing stompboxes to effects boards. You could simply stick the hooked side to the effects pedals and the fuzzy side to the sloping wooden surface, but, alternatively, carpet tiles glued to the footboard (as in our photographs) will provide a strong bond for the Velcroed pedal bases. Thread the pedals' power cables through the holes in the footboard; use a screwdriver to poke through its carpet covering, and remember that you'll need straight connectors, as angled ones won't fit! Fix a four-way outlet power board to the underside of the footboard, and attach its ground, live, and neutral connections to a power inlet so that the pedal board will have a single power connection. Get help if you aren't sure how to do this: safety is paramount, and no live wires must ever be exposed. See the "top guitar tip" opposite for more about making the audio connections between the pedals—and when deciding the order in which they should be connected up, consult the guidelines provided earlier in this book.

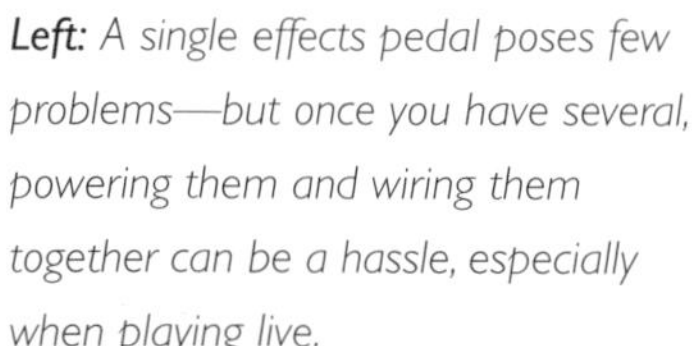

Left: *A single effects pedal poses few problems—but once you have several, powering them and wiring them together can be a hassle, especially when playing live.*

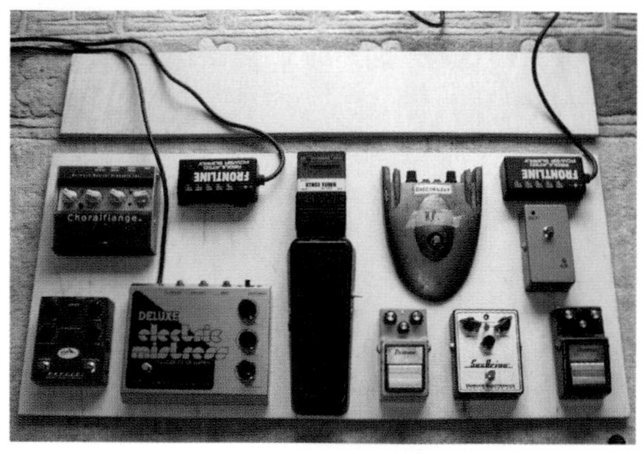

1 Positioning pedals on an uncut piece of board is the best way to determine the size you need.

2 Footboard, backboard, battens, and side panel—use screws and glue for maximum rigidity.

3 The footboard has been covered in carpet, and the entire unit has been painted; both steps are optional.

Top Guitar Tip

Some of our pedals draw power from the Frontline units seen in the photographs, whose wiring has been tucked away below the footboard. The pedals' audio cabling has also been installed very neatly, with specially made patch cords. As an alternative, regular jack leads can be used between them.

Below: *This guitarist is using an impressively large pedalboard—though it isn't as compact or as tidily wired as ours!*

4 A power cable emerges through the carpet, providing a tidy solution to a tricky wiring problem.

5 The pedals have Velcro strips ("hooked" side) attached to their bases, which grip the carpet.

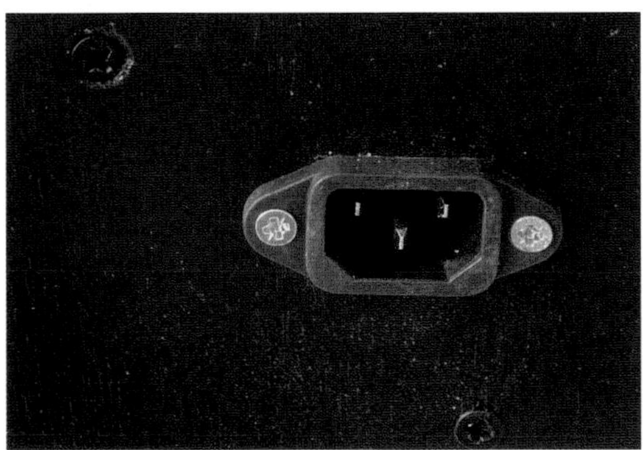

6 This power inlet provides a single connection to the line. Make sure it's installed safely.

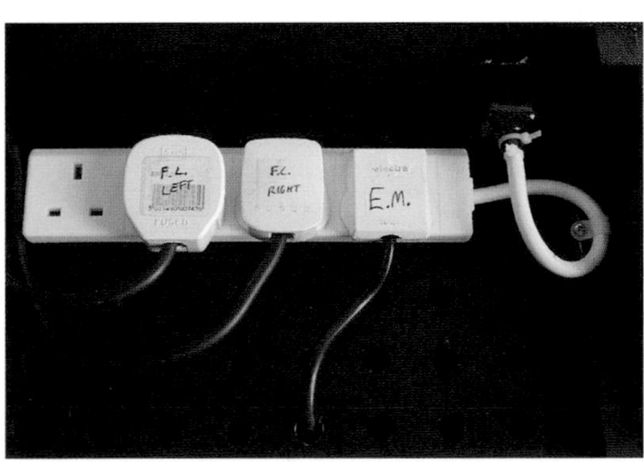

7 The four-way outlet board supplies power to the pedal units, and is connected to the power inlet.

PLAY LIKE Slash

Though *Appetite for Destruction*, Guns N' Roses' 1987 debut album, coincided with the rise of shred, Slash's influences were mainly from 1960s and 1970s blues/rock. "The Who, Zeppelin, and Mick Taylor—the most underrated player—and Rory Gallagher," he told *Guitar & Bass* in 1995. "The aggression side, though, that comes mostly from Aerosmith. I learned some of Brad Whitford's solos, and from Joe Perry I think I just picked up slam-bam dynamics." Slash is modest about his abilities. "You hear me, and it's pentatonic forever—and maybe some minor stuff, because I don't know what I'm doing," he grins. A little too modest, we think...

Right: *Slash—his appearance is as distinctive as his guitar sound!*

▶ *Slash loves double stops on strings three and two. He'd probably play this A pentatonic minor lick (plus F#, the major sixth) by placing his third finger across strings three and two at the seventh fret, and fretting the double stop in bar 3 at the fifth fret with the first finger. Note the dissonant slow bend sharp (SBS), which can be heard on "Nightrain" at 1'57", "Out To Get Me" at 2'17", and "Paradise City" at 3'20", 5'07" and 5'41" (all from* Appetite for Destruction*).*

Double Stop Lead Licks

Double Stop Rhythm Guitar

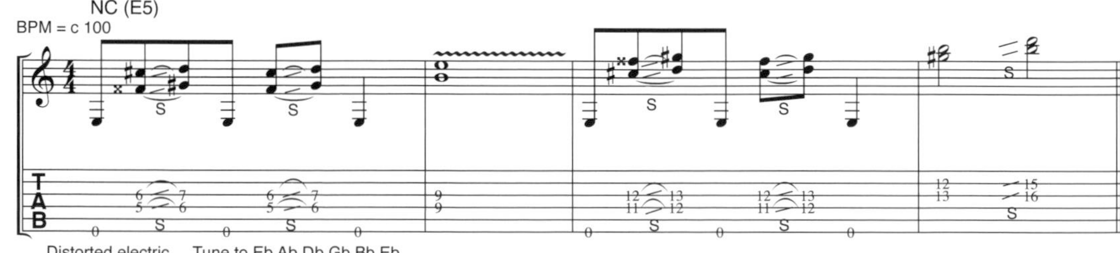

▲ *Slash also uses double stops when playing rhythm guitar. This exercise is based on the ones in "Welcome To The Jungle"* (Appetite for Destruction) *at 1'34" and 2'39". Those in bars 1 and 3 are diminished fifth/augmented fourth intervals, slid up a fret.*

Pedal Steel-type Pentatonic Lick

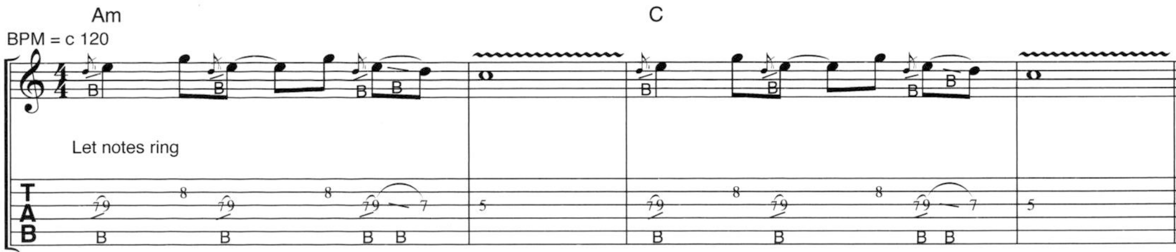

▲ *Slash often uses a pedal steel-type lick where a note on the third string is bent while a note on the second string is sustained. Here, we're in A minor, and the fourth of the scale is bent up to the fifth on the third string. The bend is held while the minor seventh (fingered as G at the eighth fret) is struck on the second string.*

> *I don't like to over-think. If something comes into my head, I want to be able to play it instantly. That's what improvising is all about, and that's why I go and jam a lot.*
>
> Slash

Chromatic Pentatonic Major Lick

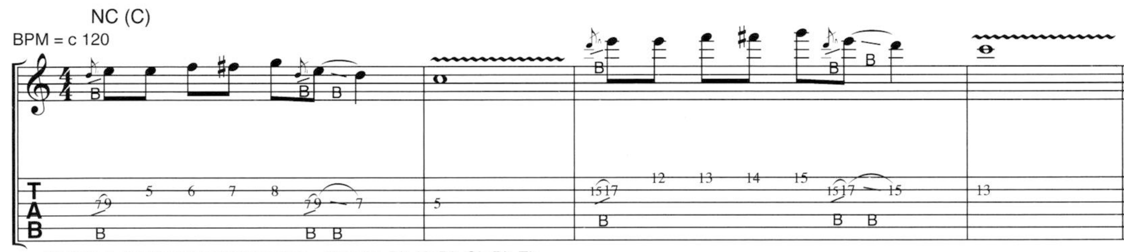

▲ *Occasionally, Slash adds the fourth and augmented fourth to the pentatonic major scale to create chromatic linking notes between the major third and fifth degrees of the scale; in the key of C, this would make the scale C D E F F# G A C. Here, we have a phrase using this scale on strings three and two, then the same phrase repeated an octave higher on strings two and one. Listen to "Paradise City" from* Appetite for Destruction *at 5'46", "Patience" from* G N'R Lies *(1988) at 0'24", and "Coma" from* Use Your Illusion I *at 7'03".*

Dorian Mode

▲ *While Slash most commonly uses the pentatonic minor and pentatonic major scales, he occasionally wanders off into the Dorian mode, which could be thought of as the pentatonic minor plus the major second and major sixth degrees of the scale. The A Dorian mode, for instance, is A B C D E F# G A. Our example contains a phrase based on this scale. Slash can be heard getting stuck into the Dorian mode during the single-note intro at the start of "Nightrain" from* Appetite for Destruction.

PLAY LIKE Sting

Sting (Gordon Sumner) was born in Wallsend, a suburb of the northern English city of Newcastle upon Tyne, in 1951. His songwriting and singing—whether with The Police (from 1977 through to its final reunion in 2007–8) or as a soloist—have earned him well-deserved plaudits, but it's his bass playing that has been a particular source of delight to many fans during his long career. His instruments of choice have ranged from a weighty Aria to (occasionally) an upright double bass, but he's most frequently seen and heard with a Fender Precision. He's said to have two favorite models: a 1957 and 1955; and in 2001, Fender produced a special Sting Precision bass, bearing his signature inlaid at its 12th fret. His amplification has varied over the years, but he currently uses Ampeg equipment.

Right: *Sting playing a Fender Jazz Bass at the Gorge Amphitheater in George, Washington, D.C., in August 1991.*

Sting's recent projects

In 2011, Sting was busy with his "Back To Bass" tour: it began in North America in the fall, and there were concerts throughout Europe and in South Africa during 2012. His most recent studio album is *Symphonicities* (2010), on which he performs a range of songs (including "Roxanne" and "Every Little Things She Does Is Magic") with orchestral accompaniment.

Jamming On The Moon

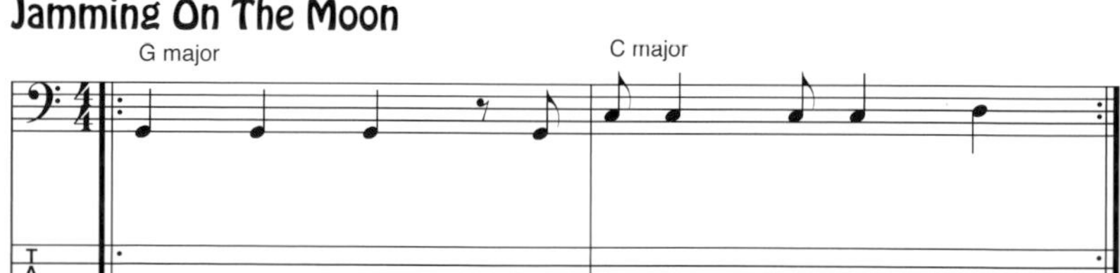

▲ *It's interesting how artists' influences often manifest themselves through what they write. Sting, in "Walking On The Moon"* (Reggatta de Blanc, *1979), was certainly tipping his hat toward Bob Marley. Our first example also contains hints of Marley's "Jamming" (from* Exodus, *1977): the first bar is mainly straight quarter-notes, with the second providing the necessary swing. You need to be solid and relaxed with this one.*

Left: *Sting, pictured here with a double bass.*

Offbeat the Retreat

Below: Sting on The Police's North American Reunion Tour, in Sacramento, California, July 17, 2008.

▲ *Pseudo-reggae verses, invariably leading to a rocking chorus, were among the defining elements of early Police singles. Check out "So Lonely," "Can't Stand Losing You," and "Roxanne" (which our example is very loosely based upon); all of these can be found on the Police's debut album* Outlandos d'Amour *(1978). We've written this one in double time, so if you wind your drum machine down to 60 bpm you'll be getting the right feel. Strict control of the space between the notes is definitely just as crucial as the notes themselves.*

Every Eighth Note You Play

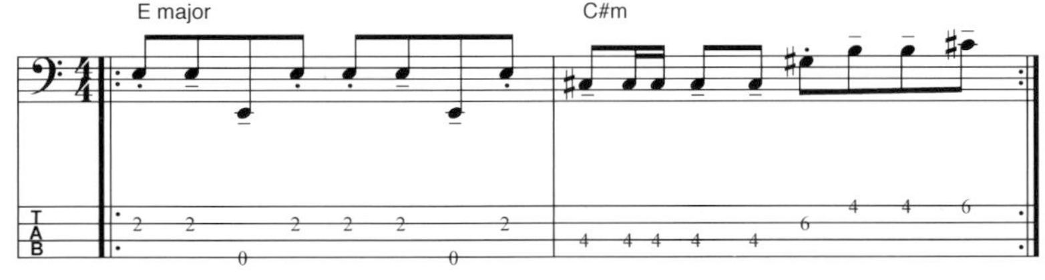

◀ *"Every Breath You Take"* (Ghost In The Machine, *1981) was virtually a study in eighth-note control, with selective clipping of note lengths to create and release tension. Our example has echoes of Sting's bassline from its middle eight and verses. The dots below some of the notes mean "play them half their written length," and the short lines below others indicate when the note should be given its full value.*

Faith in the Pocket

◀ *"If I Ever Lose My Faith In You" opens Sting's excellent* Ten Summoner's Tales *set (1993), and our example cops a similar groove.*

Odd Time and Space

◀ Ten Summoner's Tales *also features the use of odd-time signatures. This example is based on the 7/4 verse sections from "Love Is Stronger Than Justice." Counting it is easy—just go from one to seven and start again—but feeling it as you play is a bit harder!*

PLAY LIKE Pete Townshend

Pete Townshend sees himself as more of a songwriter than a guitarist. As he's explained, "The joy I would get from expressing myself through a solo would never be as fulfilling as the joy I get from expressing myself through a song." He adds that The Who's unique sound derived in part from a kind of musical role reversal. "[Bassist] John [Entwistle] was the lead guitar player, and although I'm not the bass player he did produce a hell of a lot of the lead work." Furthermore, Keith Moon was a far from conventional drummer, and his manic contributions have been likened to those of a keyboardist! Our exercises tackle various aspects of Townshend's playing technique.

Right: *Pete Townshend poses with a Gibson EDS-1275 in the 1970s. The double-neck was also favored by John McLaughlin and Jimmy Page.*

Fingerings for advanced power chords

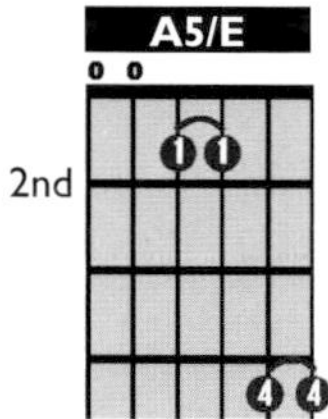

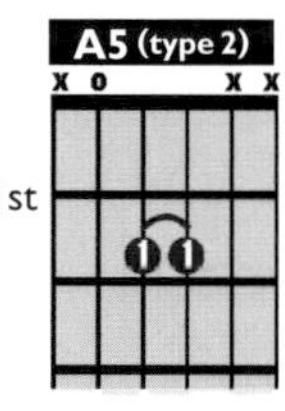

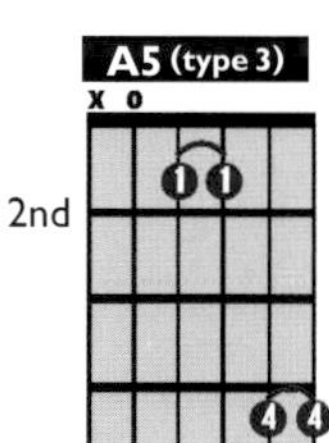

◀ *Shown here are fingerings for three of the power chords Pete Townshend's made his own. "I always leave out the third in a chord," he says. "On an A major, I'll only play the A and the E—no C#. When you [play A chords without a C# on] electric guitar, the C# [can be heard] as a harmonic because of the distortion, but it's clean distortion. If you actually play the C# it clashes and you get into modulation distortion, which throws up other notes you don't want."*

Advanced Power Chords

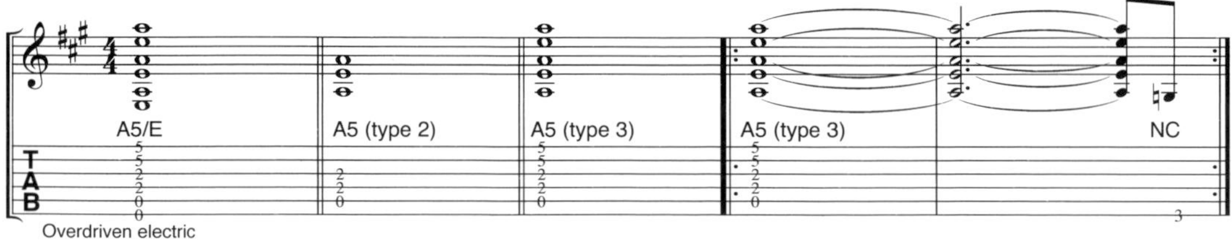

▲ *Here are notation and tablature for these three chords. The A5/E (a second inversion, as it has the fifth as its bass) can be heard at the start of "Won't Get Fooled Again." A5 (type 2) is a truncated, root position version of the chord. A5 (type 3) is a five-string variant, and the last two bars contain a repeated riff similar to one in "Won't Get Fooled Again."*

The Art of the Drone

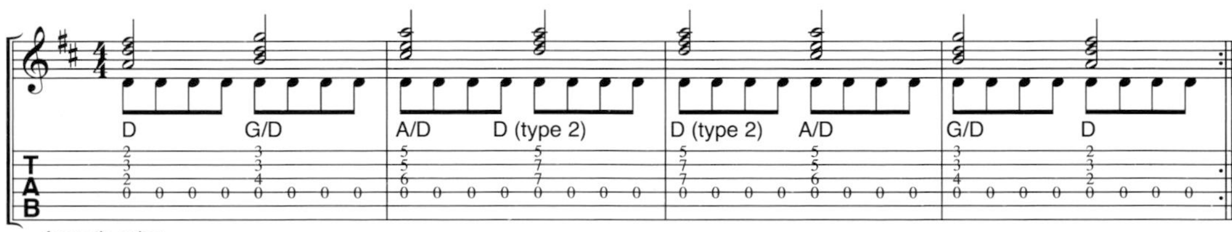

▲ *"From 'Substitute" (1966) onward I became very interested in the drone," says Townshend. "Indian music influenced me, and country has a drone going through it as well." The start of "Substitute" uses chords on the top three strings played over a static open D note—D, G/D, A/D, and D (type 2). Our version, which has the chords going up, then down, is inspired by what's on the record.*

Townshend's other gear

In addition to the gear mentioned earlier, Townshend's also used a 1958 Gibson Flying V. It was given to him by The Eagles' Joe Walsh, and featured on *The Who by Numbers* (1975). He also uses Takamine electroacoustics and (briefly) a Roland GR-300 guitar synthesizer. You'd be well advised to avoid his famous "windmilling" chord strums, which have led to serious hand lacerations, and the excessive volume settings that have caused him permanent hearing damage.

Classical Harmony

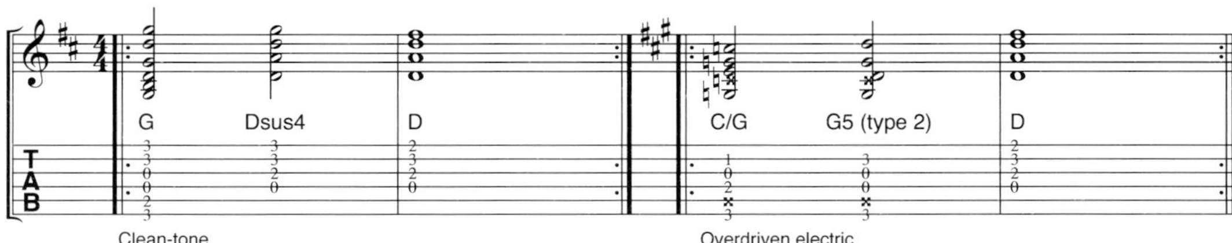

▲ *Classical-style harmony can often be heard in Pete Townshend's music, once you've learned how to spot it. It involves* preparation, suspension, *and* resolution*—as in our first two bars, which contain G, Dsus4 (a D chord with a suspended fourth—G—as its highest note), and D chords. Another classical-type progression appears in the last two bars, where a second inversion major chord (C/G) resolves onto a chord of G (with no fifth) and is followed by D.*

Lead Work

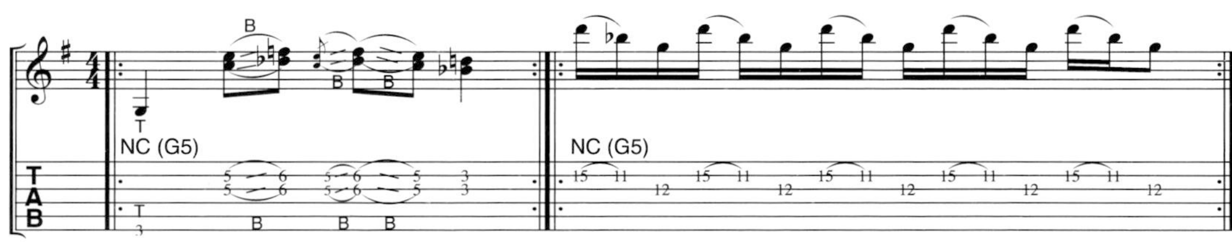

▲ *In between John Entwistle's "lead bass" solo phrases in "My Generation" (1965), Townshend plays a blues/rock lick similar to that in bar 1, using a double stop on strings three and two. Fret the first note on the bottom string with the thumb of the fretting hand. For the double stops, put your third finger flat across strings three and two. For the bends, pull the third finger toward the top string, causing both strings to rise in pitch. Our second bar shows a flashy Townshend-style lick, inspired by what he plays in the John Entwistle song "Heaven And Hell" (1970). It outlines a G minor chord, and uses a pull-off between the top two notes, which adds a touch of* legato *(smoothness).*

PLAY LIKE Stevie Ray Vaughan

The blues rhythm guitar technique shown here is similar to the one in "Pride And Joy" from Stevie Ray Vaughan's *Texas Flood* (1983). It consists of a walking bass part on the lower strings, punctuated by short stabs on the top two open strings. All the exercises should be played in a shuffle rhythm, so that instead of keeping the eighth notes even, the first eighth note of each beat is lengthened and the second eighth note correspondingly shortened—roughly equivalent to a three-eighth-note triplet with its first two notes tied together. A shuffle can vary from barely perceptible, through to a lazy feel or a sharp, clipped style, depending on the desired effect.

Left: *Stevie Ray Vaughan—wearing one of the very distinctive hats specially made for him by Texas Hatters of Lockhart, Texas.*

Correct Plectrum Technique

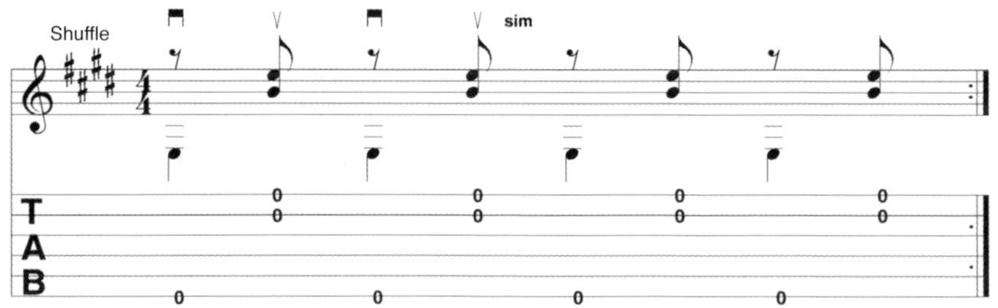

▲ *Here we use open strings, enabling you to concentrate on your plectrum work. The bass note is played on the beat with a downstroke (⊓ in the notation), and the top two strings are struck on the upbeat with an upstroke (indicated with a* **V***). "Sim" is short for simile (i.e. continue, in a similar manner, with the alternate strumming pattern). When the second, third, and fourth bass notes are played, the top two strings are to be stopped dead at the same time, by sticking the palm of the plectrum hand onto the strings. This requires a slightly different hand position from normal—closer to the bridge, so that the palm can deaden the top two strings without touching the bottom three strings.*

Combining the Exercises

To assemble a 12-bar cycle using the patterns shown here, play Walking Bass Pattern twice, IV Chord Riffs once, Walking Bass Pattern once more, and then Blues, bars 9–12. Disregard the repeat signs when doing this.

Walking Bass Pattern

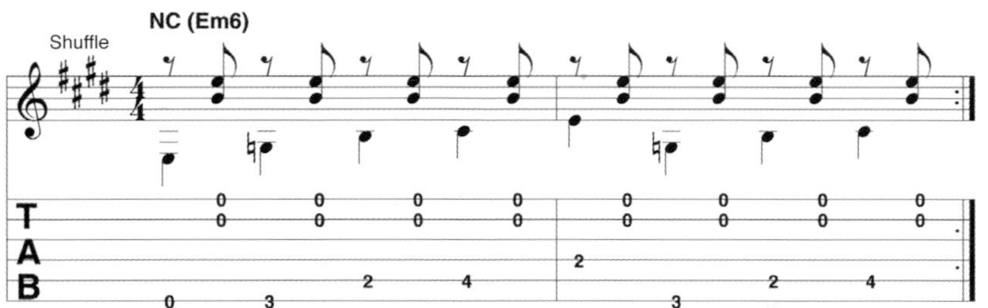

◀ *Let's apply this picking technique to a two-bar walking bass pattern in the key of E. First, play the bass part on its own. Then add the chordal stabs on the top two strings. Make sure each bass note lasts for a full beat in order to produce the "walking" effect with maximum clarity. The walking bass line implies an Em6 chord, hence the bracketed "Em6."*

IV Chord Riffs

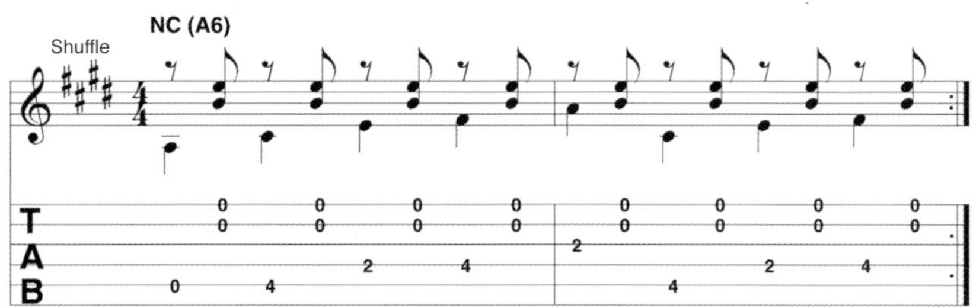

▲ *These riffs are played over what would be chord IV (A) in a 12-bar E major blues, though our walking bass line implies an A6 chord. When the bass part moves onto the third string at the beginning of the second bar, you need to stop the top two strings while striking the third string, so precise positioning of the strumming hand is required.*

Blues, Bars 9-12

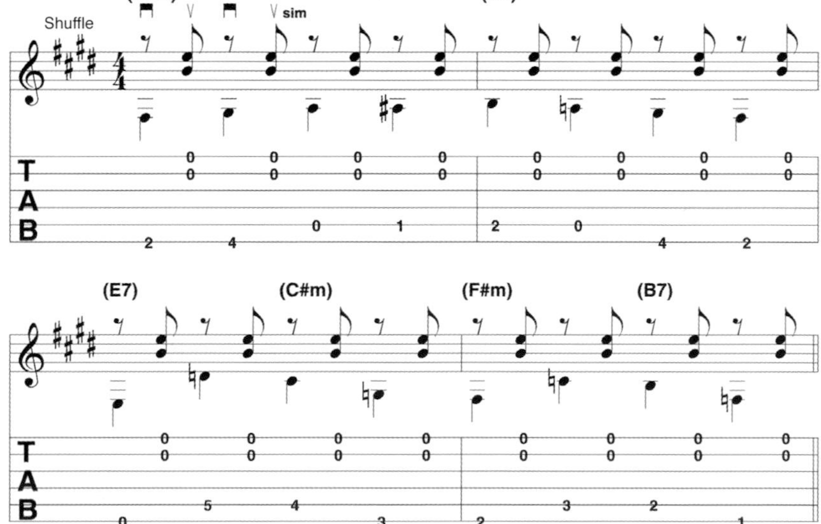

▲ *This four-bar excerpt forms the last four bars of a 12-bar blues. See the panel opposite for an explanation of how to combine all the exercises as a complete blues cycle.*

Above: Stevie Ray strikes a pensive pose for a record company publicity photo.

> *Stevie's ideas were limitless. He flowed.*
>
> B. B. King

Jack White

Jack White of The White Stripes and The Raconteurs is not a man to make things easy for himself. A big fan of blues, he nevertheless has little truck with 12-bar shuffles in E and the pentatonic minor scale. "I want more of a challenge," he says. "I want to play non-typical blues within the rules of blues and its codes. I'm hugely influenced by blues, as for me [it's] synonymous with truth, and a lot of my heroes are bluesmen. I don't want to copy or imitate them, but I can sympathize with their attitude." A largely unschooled guitarist, his technique gradually evolved by chance. "In my teens, when I first started, I didn't use plectrums at all and played with fingers all the time. Now I switch from plectrum to fingers in the middle of songs. I play with my thumb, index finger, and ring finger, while holding the plectrum…[against] my middle finger."

Right: *Jack's Gretsch Jupiter Thunderbird is modeled on one of Bo Diddley's guitars.*

Left: *The White Stripes in 2003.*

Jack White and the POG

Jack White is an outspoken critic of technology, but ironically, The White Stripes' "Blue Orchid" (from *Get Behind Me Satan*, 2005) was inspired by a piece of hi-tech gear: the Electro-Harmonix POG (Polyphonic Octave Generator), which adds a blend of upper and lower octaves to a guitar signal. "[The song's riff was] the first one I got when I tried it," he recalls. "The whole thing just came out automatically."

"Aluminum"-style Blues Riff

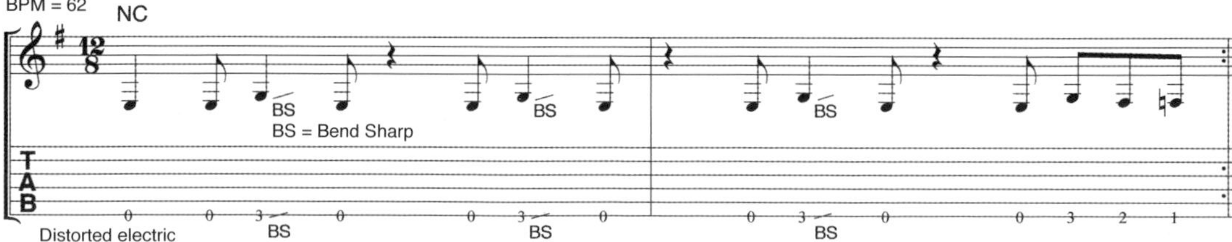

▲ *"Aluminum" (from The White Stripes'* White Blood Cells, *2001) is based on a couple of classic blues riff traits—a movement from the root to the minor third, with the minor third given a quarter-tone bend (indicated by BS, or Bend Sharp), and a lilting 12/8 feel. These are illustrated in the first bar and a half of our exercise—rounded off, like the original, with a three-note descending chromatic run on the last beat of the second bar, which leads back into the riff.*

"Ball and Biscuit"-style Blues Licks

◀ *"Ball and Biscuit," on The White Stripes' fourth album* Elephant *(2003), also uses some traditional-style blues licks, played with a rather less traditional overdriven tone and percussive deadened strings. Our exercise, inspired by the song, can be played with plectrum, or thumb and fingers, or a combination of plectrum and fingers. The next example looks more closely at White's picking technique.*

Thumb and Fingers

▲ *White often keeps his plectrum in his plucking hand by holding it with his middle finger; he then uses the thumb to pluck the lower strings, and the index and ring fingers to pluck the upper strings. The top two open strings, struck at the start of this exercise, can either be deadened with the fingers, or allowed to ring on; try both ways to create different effects.*

"Seven Nation Army"-style Riff

◀ *Our riff is similar to the one in "Seven Nation Army" (on* Elephant*). Although the song's in open A (E A E A C# E, bottom to top), the riff uses just the fifth (A) string, so it can be played in standard tuning. At the start of "Seven Nation Army," White uses a DigiTech Whammy pedal to drop the guitar's pitch by an octave, emulating a bass.*

"Salute Your Solution" Riff

▲ *In the bridge of The Raconteurs' "Salute Your Solution" (from* Consolers of the Lonely*, 2008), White plays an ascending, then descending riff similar to this. It's based on the E pentatonic minor scale (E G A B D E), with the addition of the stock blues/jazz hammer-on from a minor to a major third (G to G#). White makes good use of rests between the component parts of the riff in order to give definition and momentum to the part.*

PLAY LIKE Neil Young

While not a technically accomplished guitarist, Neil Young plays with great feel, imagination, and personality. Throughout his career, he's immersed himself in many diverse musical styles and genres, often surprising, delighting, and even alienating fans and critics. His songwriting frequently reflects his physical or emotional state: for example, his LP *Harvest* (1972) was made after he'd slipped two disks in his back, making it impossible to hold an electric. "I recorded most of it in a neck brace, which is why it's such a mellow album." Two decades later, he created the acoustic-based *Harvest Moon* (1992) after incurring hearing damage following his work on two much noisier discs, *Ragged Glory* (1990) and *Weld* (1991). When speaking about one of his more extreme-sounding records, he's said that it was "meant to appeal to people on the ****ing edge." Young's guitar playing has always been central to his musical expression—and here we examine some of the characteristic elements of his style.

Left: *Neil Young and his Bigsby-equipped Gibson Les Paul.*

Embellished Accompaniment Patterns

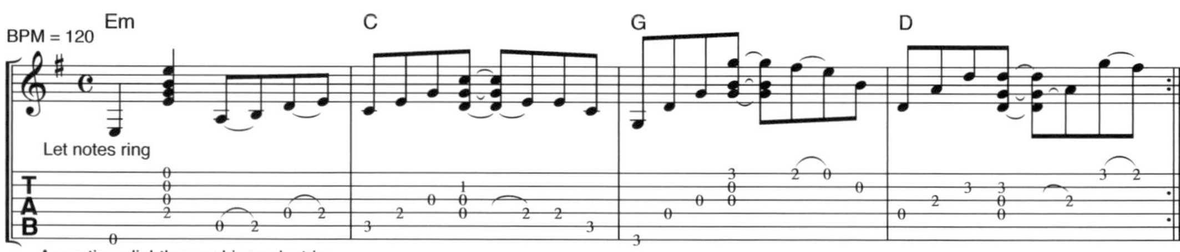

▲ *This exercise is based around a chord progression using the basic open voicings of Em, C, G, and D, but with Neil Young-style hammer-ons and/or pull-offs to make the accompaniment more interesting. In all cases, let the notes ring on for as long as possible. Young uses such progressions on both acoustic and electric guitars.*

Golden Heart

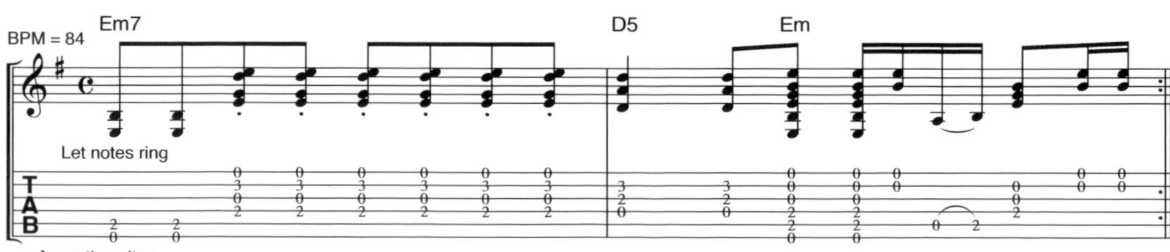

▲ *Here we pay tribute to the classic strummed part at the start of Young's "Heart Of Gold" (from Harvest). The first bar is based entirely on an Em7 voicing. The staccato chords on its last three beats (staccato is indicated by dots below the notes) add character to the part—use downstrokes for the eighth notes in order to give them a consistent tone, volume, and feel. Notice how, once again, the basic open voicing of Em in bar 2, beat three is embellished with hammer-ons.*

Take a Look at Your Life

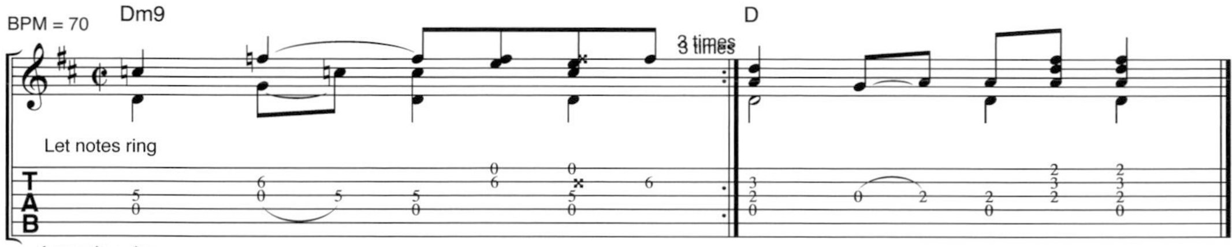

▲ *Neil Young's use of a Dm9 chord at the start of his song "Old Man" (from* Harvest*) is a masterpiece of minimalism, and our approximation shows just how far you can go with a single chord, by picking selective combinations of notes and, in this case, by using a hammer-on from an open string. Young uses a pick and plays downstrokes on the downbeat and upstrokes on the upbeat.*

"Sugar Mountain"

At the age of 19, Neil Young wrote "Sugar Mountain"—a paean to lost youth, about a place where "you can't be twenty." After hearing it, his Canadian contemporary and friend Joni Mitchell composed "The Circle Game," a song with a more positive outlook about growing a little older.

Right: *Young plays a Gretsch White Falcon.*

Spice of Life

◀ *This exercise is inspired by the start of "Cinnamon Girl," originally released in 1969. To play it, we retune to "double dropped D," where the first and sixth strings are lowered from E to D, but the others aren't altered. The chords in bar 1 are fingered with a barré; you could use a barré or separate fingers for the bare fifths in bar 2.*

One Note Guitar Solo

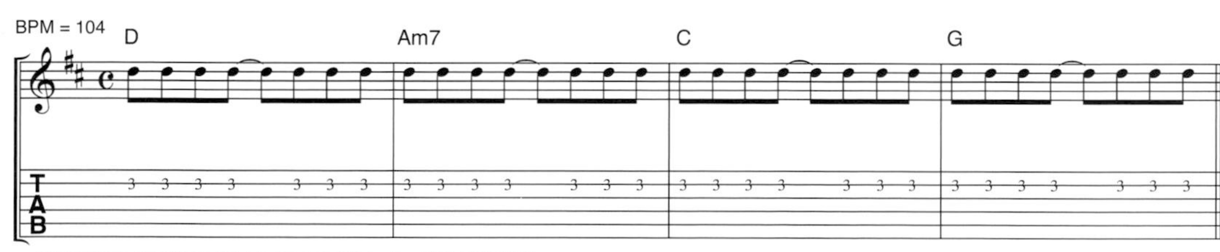

▲ *Here we pay tribute to the so-called "one note guitar solo" in "Cinnamon Girl." Although the song's in double dropped D, there's actually no need to retune in order to play the exercise, since it only uses D on the second string, third fret. Note the repetitive rhythm, with a tie across the middle of the bar from beat two and a half to beat three, which gives the phrase a sense of rhythmic propulsion.*

Having the right tools

Having the right equipment at a concert may save the show, your reputation, or prevent personal injury, and the items described here can prove invaluable on stage or backstage. Some are inexpensive utility products; others are more specialized pieces of gear designed to solve specific problems that arise when guitars and electronics are used in live situations. The recommendations come from seasoned guitar tech, Adrian Vines.

A small, powerful torch, such as a Maglite, is widely used by technicians and others who work on darkened stages. Its beam is bright and focusable, and if you remove the body of the torch from the cap and stand it upright, it will serve as a kind of electric candle.

When nail varnish dries, it is useful stuff, and cheaper than professional "threadlock," which performs the same function. When applied to loose or rattling parts—bridge saddle screws and springs are common culprits—nail varnish will seize them up in a (breakable) grip and remove buzzes.

A small drop of Teflon-based lubricant, such as Tri-Flow, on a guitar's nut slots, saddles, and string trees will prevent strings sticking and may help to avoid breakages. Handle with care, as any more than the tiniest amount will dull the vibration of the strings.

Use a little switch cleaner on noisy guitar pickup selector switches and volume and tone controls.

A pedal power supply like the Voodoo Lab unit is expensive, but has eight individually isolated power outlets, capable of supplying pedals with a range of electrical power requirements.

A multimeter is a professional electronic/electrical engineer's tool. Its functions include the ability to measure voltage, current, and resistance.

Hum created by grounding loops is a frequent nuisance on stage, and there are various—often unsafe—methods of trying to deal with it. A properly specified hum suppressor unit is a sensible solution.

Adrian Vines considers the Boss LS-2 Line Selector "possibly the most useful thing I possess. To describe it as a variation of the traditional A/B box doesn't do justice to its versatility: it's an all-in-one solution to virtually any signal routing problem."

The Boss NS-2 Noise Suppressor is another invaluable, inexpensive show-saver. It can reduce the amount of unwanted noise heard from guitar rigs when they're used in proximity to strip lights, walkie-talkies, stage lighting, and other potential generators of buzzes, clicks, and other bugbears.

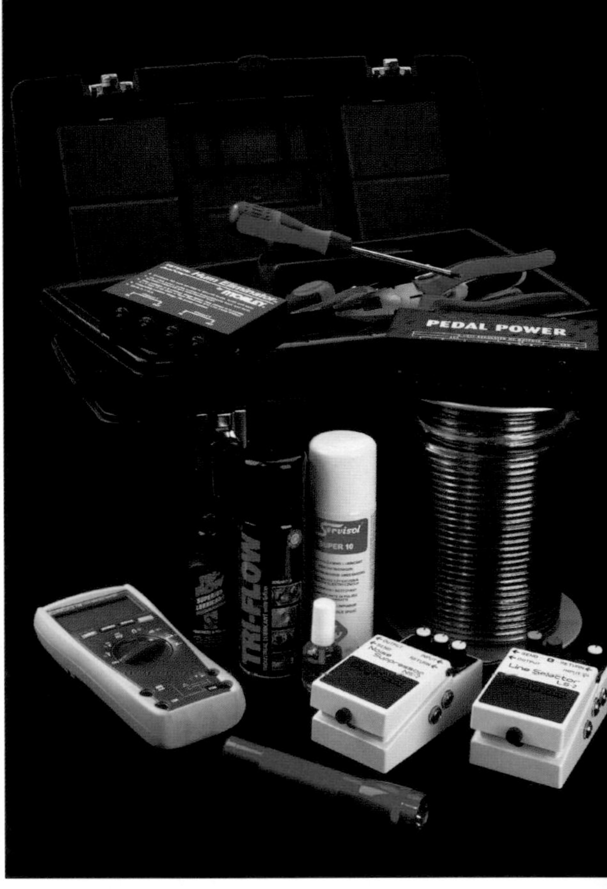

Above: *Some of the items in guitar tech Adrian Vines's toolkit, including several of those described opposite.*

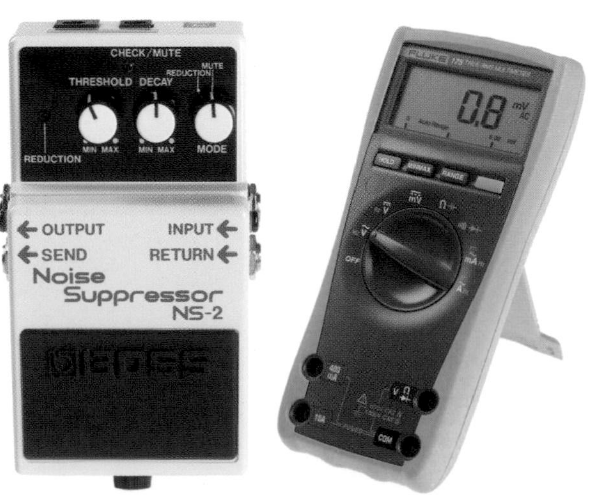

Right: *To quote Adrian Vines, "if a nasty [electrical] noise happens every time someone boils the kettle in the dressing room, then this Boss unit could save the day, [though] its threshold and decay controls are pretty crude." He also swears by his multimeter.*

Top Guitar Tip

Some of the gear shown here is intended for more elaborate stage setups… but even if you're playing the smallest gig, there are a few items that are essential. They include a set of spare guitar strings, extra plectrums, and replacement batteries for your pedals, if they aren't line powered.

Below *Being prepared to handle all the possible snags that can affect a performance makes good sense. Musicians can then concentrate on blowing away the audience!*

PLAY LIKE "Unplugged" Rockers

It's impossible to imagine rock music without the electric guitar…but almost all its leading exponents have switched back to the humble, more homely acoustic at some point. This is probably because it's been central to their musical roots. Many of them formed their first chords on inexpensive flat-tops, had their sensibilities shaped by the Delta blues greats and the Everly Brothers, and went on—like Eric Clapton and Jimmy Page—to make acoustic playing integral to their own styles. Other British stars who emerged in the 1960s, including George Harrison and John Lennon, also made prominent use of acoustic guitars. Even Keith Richards can be heard in action with one on "Wild Horses" from *Sticky Fingers* (1971) and "Angie" from *Goats Head Soup* (1973).

More recently, developments in technology have made amplifying acoustic instruments on stage less haphazard and feedback-prone, while MTV's *Unplugged* concerts, launched in 1989, have proved so successful that some of those featured (Nirvana, Clapton) have released material from the show as albums. Here are three exercises based on the acoustic activities of famous rockers.

Left: *Hendrix is famous for his electric work—but also had a distinctive way with an acoustic.*

Jimi's Blues

◀ *This exercise is based on the introduction to Hendrix's "Hear My Train A Coming" (featured on his 1994* Blues *compilation), which he played on a borrowed acoustic 12-string. It outlines a progression of D7, G/B, A 8va (basically, two A notes an octave apart), and A7 with no third. This leads into a descending phrase using the A pentatonic minor scale (A C D E G A). The "x"s in the A 8va and A7 no third chords mean you should damp the note on the second string by lightly touching it with the fretting hand's first finger—the one that's holding down the note on the third string. Notice the descending phrase that runs from bar 6 to bar 7—it's similar to the introduction to "Hey Joe."*

Escalator to Heaven

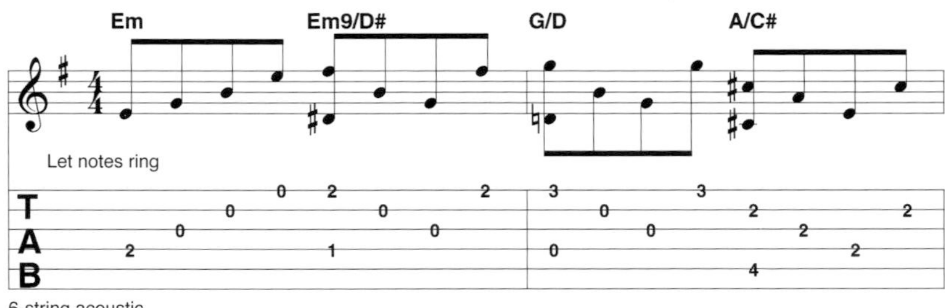

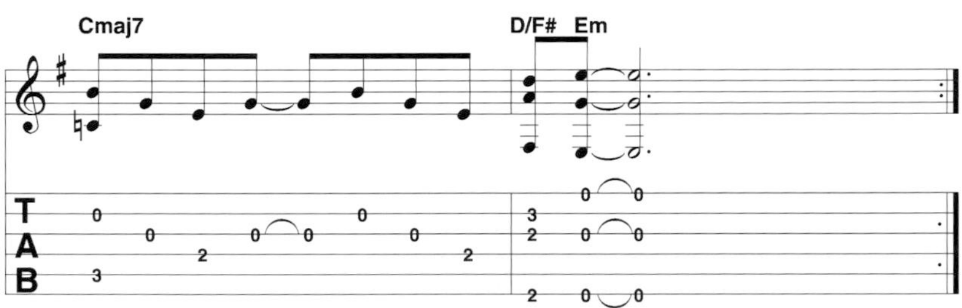

Above: Jimmy Page with a contact mic taped to his acoustic, 1975.

◀ Here we demonstrate the playing and harmonic techniques Jimmy Page uses in the intro to "Stairway To Heaven" (1971). Since the piece involves plucking a bass note and an upper note simultaneously at the beginning of each chord change, it's best played either with fingers or with pick and fingers. Page prefers the latter. Harmonically, the intro is a series of chords played as arpeggios. It's written as a series of eighth notes, and the indication "let notes ring" has a significant effect on the way the part is heard.

The "Unplugged" Effect

In July 2003, *Guitar* (as *Guitar & Bass* was then known) quoted the words of MTV *Unplugged* producer Alex Coletti, originally speaking to *Guitar World Acoustic*: "I think we've shown a larger audience that acoustic music can rock. Just because you don't plug in doesn't mean you can't have balls. The popularity of the format [has also] had a knock-on effect on instrument manufacturers… We're told that acoustic guitar sales are up 50 percent, and that *Unplugged* is one of the big reasons."

Roots of Clapton

Above: Eric Clapton playing a Martin on stage in Germany in 2010.

◀ This fingerstyle piece has a vibe that's close to Clapton's version of Big Bill Broonzy's "Hey Hey" (Unplugged, 1992). It's got a constant low E bass note and a simple, bluesy melody on top. The tune is based on a two-note chord—G on the second string, D on the third string—but notice how the phrase lifts in bars 2 and 4 by ending on a C#, the major sixth note of the E Dorian mode. The "BS" indication means "bend sharp"—in other words, bend the relevant notes sharp by about a quarter tone for a bluesy effect.

Index

AC/DC 57, 168, 182, 183
Acoustic amplifiers 134, 186
acoustic guitar, setting up an inexpensive model 78–79
Adler, Steven 168
Aerosmith 183, 234
Alcatrazz 136, 174
Alembic guitars 124
Allman Brothers Band, The 82, 172, 192
Allman, Duane 82–83, 192–193
Allman, Gregg 82, 83, 91, 172, 192
Alnico II Pro Slash pickup 168
Alnico V transducer 40, 48
Altec 417-8H loudspeakers 158
Alvarez-Yairi guitars 88
Ampeg 236
  Baby Bass 132
  SVT-VR amplifier 132
amplifier, choosing an 108–109
AMS (Advanced Music Systems) 102
Analog Man compressor 132
Anderson, Jon 122
Anthony, Michael 166, 176
Archer, Gem 209
archtop Gibson guitars, 16, 17, 19
Aria bass guitar 236
"Arm the Homeless" guitar 150
Armstrong, Billie Joe 54
Arnold, Eddy 58
Art Of Noise, The 100, 101
Ashman, Matthew 105
Asia 122
Astbury, Ian 168
Atkins, Chet 58, 59, 60, 126, 127, 170, 194, 207, 222
Audioslave 150, 151
Augustine, Albert 13

Bad Cat amplifiers 156
Baker, Ginger 94, 118, 146, 202
Baldwin Music Company 60
Ball, Ernie 91
Barrett, Aston 44
Barrett, Syd 110, 210
Bassman amplifier 42
Bauer, Billy 166
BBM 146
BC Rich Mockingbird 134
Beard, Frank 106
Beatles, The 30, 36, 64, 70, 72, 118, 119
Bechtel, Perry 15
Beck, Jeff 84–85, 116, 120, 121, 152, 153, 194–195, 201, 215
Belew, Adrian 186
Bell, Andy 209
Bell, Eric 134, 135
Bellamy, Matt 86–87
Berry, Chuck 50, 160, 169, 194, 196–197
Best, Pete 118
Betts, Dickey 82, 83, 192
Bhatt, V. M. 98, 99
Bigsby, Paul 20, 21, 24, 25
Bigsby vibrato 25, 100, 184, 216, 217, 244
Black, Bill 148
Black Crowes, The 29
Black Country Communion 90, 200
Black Label Society 69
Black Sabbath 57
Blackmore, Ritchie 88–89, 136, 166, 198–199
Blackmore's Night 88, 89, 198, 199
Bogle, Bob 45
Bonamassa, Joe 90–91, 200–201
Bonham, Jason 90, 152
Bonham, John 152
Bono 102
Boss LS-2 Line Selector 246
Boss NS-2 Noise Suppressor 246
Boss pedals 138, 150, 154, 156, 166, 168, 208
Bowie, David 178
Bozeman, Montana 28
Bramlett, Delaney and Bonnie 94
Brian Moore guitars 31
Broonzy, Big Bill 249
Brown, Clarence "Gatemouth" 186
Brown, Zac 77
Browne, Jackson 156
Bruce, Jack 94, 120, 146, 202
Bruford, Bill 122, 132
Bryant, Jimmy 122
Buchanan, Roy 35, 92–93
Buck, Peter 71
Buffalo Springfield 184
Bulsara, Farrokh see Mercury, Freddie
Bundrick, John 128
Burton, James 101
Butler, Bernard 50
Butts, Ray 60, 148
Buzzcocks, The 138

Cale, J. J. 172
Campbell, Phil 109, 130
Cantanese, Nick 69
Captain Beefheart 186
Carlton, Larry 50
Carter, Maybelle 16
Carter, Walter 52
Carvin amplifiers 174, 186
Cash, Johnny 65, 107
Chandler, Chas 120, 134
Channing, Chad 96, 97
Chapman, Emmett 132, 133
Chapman Stick 132, 133
Charvel, Wayne 74, 75
Cherone, Gary 176
Chickenfoot 166
Christian, Charlie 19, 196
Clapton, Eric 15, 36, 50, 52, 57, 82, 83, 84, 94–95, 112, 118, 120, 128, 145, 162, 163, 172, 194, 201, 203–203, 224, 248, 249
Clarke, Stanley 124
classical guitar 12, 13
Clarke, "Fast" Eddie 130
Clayton, Adam 102, 103
Cobain, Kurt 45, 96–97, 114
Cobham, Billy 144
Coletti, Alex 249
Collen, Phil 75
Collins, Albert 90, 147
Collins, Phil 118
Colosseum II 146, 147
Coltrane, John 82, 116, 144, 145
Commerford, Tim 150
Cooder, Joachim 98
Cooder, Ry 76, 98–99, 101, 160, 204–205
CoolTube unit 76
Cooper, Alice 132, 168
Cornell, Chris 150
Corona, California 28, 29
Costello, Elvis 45
Cotton, James 90
Cox, Billy 120
Cray, Robert 95
Crazy Horse 184
Cream 57, 94, 95, 120, 128, 202, 203
Cribs, The 138
Cropper, Steve 35, 101
Crosby, David 184
Crosby, Stills, Nash & Young 184
Crover, Dale 97
Crudup, Arthur 148

Daltrey, Roger 170
Dan Armstrong equipment
  Orange Squeezer 98
  Plexiglas bass 134
Danelectro guitars 100
Davis, Dale 64
Davis, Jeremy 42
Davis, Jesse Ed 82
Davis, Miles 144
Davis, Reverend Gary 157
Day, Paul 31
de la Rocha, Zack 150
De Lucía, Paco 144
Deacon, John 142

Dead Weather, The 180
Dee, Mikkey 130
Deep Purple 88, 116, 136, 166, 198, 199
Def Leppard 75
Demeter Tremulator 98
Derek and the Dominos 82, 83, 94, 172, 192
Derringer, Rick 91
DI (direct inject) technique 219
Di Meola, Al 144
Dickson, Lee 94
Diddley, Bo 61, 170, 242
Diezel VH4 amplifier 86
DigiTech pedals 166
 Whammy 150, 180
Dio, Ronnie James 89
Dire Straits 126, 127, 222, 223
Dobro guitars 18, 94
Dopyera, John 18
Double Trouble 178
Downey, Brian 134
Dream Theater 154, 155
Duffy, Billy 60
Dumble amplifiers 178
Dunlop effects 158
 Crybaby wah-wah 116, 150
 DCR-1SR 168
Dunn, Donald 42
Dylan, Bob 92, 94, 118, 126, 156
Dynacord amplifiers 134

Eagles, The 76, 239
EBS Octabass 132
Echoplex delays 142
EchoSonic amplifiers 148
Eddy, Duane 100–101, 131, 184, 206–207
Edge, The 102–103, 153
effects pedals 140–141
Einziger, Mike 140
electric amplification 18–19
electric guitar, upgrading 188–189
Electro 70
Electro-Harmonix
 Big Muff 132
 POG 242
Electronic 138
EMG pickup 69, 150
Eno, Brian 102
Entwhistle, John 42, 72, 100, 124, 130, 170, 238, 239
Epiphone guitars 16, 17, 20, 25, 26, 197
 Casino 102
 Emperor archtop 16, 17
 Sheraton 208
 Supernova 208
equipment, useful when gigging 246–247
Ernie Ball/Music Man guitars 154
ESP guitars
 KH signature model 116
 KH-2 Ouija 116
Estes, Sleepy John 98
Evans, Bill 144
Evans, David Howell see Edge, The
Evans, Richard (Dik) 102

Eventide effects 154
Everly Brothers, The 46, 124, 228, 248
EVH amplifiers 176
Ezrin, Bob 103, 132

Fabulous Thunderbirds, The 162, 178
Fatboy Guitars 41
Fender amplifiers 84, 114, 116, 152, 180
 Bandmaster 112
 Bassman 166
 Champ 160
 Deluxe 184
 Dula Showman Reverb 197
 EVH 5150
 Hotrod DeVille 410 86
 Princeton 108
 Super Reverb 92, 172, 178
 Twin 94, 160
 Twin Reverb 138, 178
 Vibrolux 92
 Vibroverb 178
Fender Custom Shop 28
Fender, Leo 20, 22–23, 26, 28, 34, 35, 36, 42, 44, 214
Fender guitars 20, 22–23, 26, 28, 29
 1000 pedal steel 110
 Aloha Stratocaster 86
 Artist Series Stratocaster 23
 Bass V 124
 "Black Strat" Stratocaster 110, 210
 "Blackie" Stratocaster 94
 Bonnie Raitt Stratocaster 156
 Broadcaster 22, 34
 Buddy Guy Signature Stratocaster 23
 Eric Johnson Signature Stratocaster 23
 EVH Wolfgang 176
 Jag-Stang 96
 Jaguar 45, 96, 105, 138
 Jazz Bass 44, 124
 Jazzmaster 23, 45, 105
 "Jurassic Strat" 126
 "Malcolm" 160
 "Micawber" 160
 Mustang 96, 144
 Precision (P-Bass) 42–43, 124, 134, 236
 SRV signature Stratocaster 178
 Sting Precision 236
 Stratocaster 23, 28, 36–37, 38–41, 74, 84, 88, 94, 102, 104, 105, 112, 116, 120, 126, 136, 150, 156, 178, 188, 194, 198, 202, 214, 215, 222
 Telecaster 4–5, 22, 23, 34–35, 52, 92, 105, 107, 110, 118, 150, 152, 160, 188
 Telecaster Deluxe 34, 35
Fernandes guitars 168
Filter'Tron pickups 58, 59, 60, 148
Firebird pickup 184
Fishman Aura system 67
Fishman pickup 166
Fitzpatrick, Jim 135
flat-top Martin guitars 14–15
Flea 104
Fleetwood Mac 112, 113
Fleetwood, Mick 112, 147

Floyd Rose vibrato 23, 74, 75, 216, 217
Fontana, D. J. 148
Foo Fighters 114, 115
Ford, Mary 52, 56
Frame, Roddy 66
Frampton, Peter 68
"Frankenstrat" 74
Franklin, Aretha 156
Fraser, Andy 128
Fraser, Dan 87
Free 128, 129, 224
Frey, Glenn 76
Fripp, Robert 132
Fritz, Roger 92
Frusciante, John 45, 104–105
Fuller, Walter 19
Fullerton, California 22, 23, 28
Fullerton, George 23, 36
Fulltone
 DejáVibe 166
 Ultimate Octave 166
"Funk Fingers" 132
Fuzz Face 120

G & L 22, 23
G3 concert tours 166, 174
Gabriel, Peter 132, 133
Gadd, Steve 132, 133
Galás, Diamanda 124
Gallagher, Liam 208, 209
Gallagher, Noel 208–209
Gallagher, Rory 38, 39, 41, 91, 201, 234
Garcia, Jerry 76
Garland, Hank 58
George Tripps Custom Crybaby 90
Gibbons, Billy 27, 106–107
Gibson amplifiers
 GA-20 98
Gibson guitars 12, 16–17, 19, 24–25, 26, 28
 Angus Young SG Standard 182
 Byrdland 29
 Chet Atkins Country Gentleman 148, 149
 Custom Shop Flametop Les Paul 29
 DG-335 114, 115
 Dove 29
 EB-2 50
 EDS-1275 152, 153, 238
 EH-150 19
 ES-5 48, 186
 ES-150 19, 20
 ES-175 47, 122
 ES-175D 122
 ES-250 19
 ES-295 49, 148
 ES-330 118
 ES-335 24, 29, 50–51, 88, 89, 114, 118, 146, 172, 208
 ES-345 144
 ES-350 152, 197
 ES-355 50, 138, 197, 203
 ES-1275 144
 ES-Artist 123
 Everly Brothers 152

Explorer 102, 146, 150
Firebird 25, 90, 147, 203
Flying V 25, 29, 90, 120, 200, 239
Gary Moore signature Les Paul 146
Howard Roberts 112
J-160E 118
J-200 46
Johnny Smith 144
Joe Bonamassa Les Paul Studio 90
Jumbo 46
L-0 46
L-00 46
L-1 46
L-5 and L-5CES 16, 17, 48, 49, 148
L-7 20
L-200 29
Les Paul models 20, 29, 52–55, 56, 82, 83, 84, 86, 90, 100, 102, 106, 112, 116, 120, 126, 128, 129, 146, 150, 151, 152, 168, 170, 184, 186, 202, 203, 223, 244
Melody Maker 106
Old Black, Les Paul Gold Top 184
"Pearly Gates" Les Paul Standard 106
Premiere models 17
Randy Rhoads Les Paul Custom 158, 230
SG 29, 55, 56–57, 83, 105, 146, 170, 172, 182, 186, 203
SG-X 86
SJ-200 29, 46, 102, 144, 152, 170
Slash Appetite Les Paul 168
Super 400 and Super 400CES 17, 48, 148
Trini Lopez Standard 114, 115
"VOS" 152
Gibson, Orville 16
Gillan, Ian 88
Gillet, Charlie 126
Gilmour, David 36, 110–11, 141, 210–211
Glover, Roger 88
Godin LGXT 144
Goodman, Benny 19
Gorham, Scott 134, 135
Gould, Boon 220
Gould, Phil 220
Graham, Larry 44
Grand Ole Opry 76
Grateful Dead 76
Green Day 54, 103
Green, Peter 90, 112–113, 146, 147, 201
Gretsch III, Fred 60
Gretsch Jr., Fred 58, 60
Gretsch Sr., Fred 58
Gretsch guitars 25, 30, 170, 180, 206
6120 100
6120 Chet Atkins 58
6121 61
6128 Duo-Jet 118
Bo Diddley 61
Country Club 61
Country Gentleman 58, 59, 118, 168
G6120DE Duane Eddy 100
Jupiter Thunderbird 242
Monkees Rock'n'Roll 58, 59
Solid Body 58
Super Chet 59
Synchromatic 200 58
Tennessean 58, 119, 188, 189
White Falcon 60, 105, 245
Grohl, Dave 50, 96, 97, 114–115, 124
Gruhn, George 30, 35
guitar, choosing a 62–63
guitar, cleaning of 164–165
guitar, history of 12–31
Guns N' Roses 168, 234
Guthrie, Woody 150
Guy, Buddy 23
Guyatone guitars 98, 204

Hagar, Sammy 166, 176
Hagstrom eight-string bass 120
Hall, F. C. 20, 70
Hammer, Jan 85, 144
Hammett, Kirk 116–117, 166, 212–213
Hampton, Lionel 42
Hancock, Herbie 162
Harmony guitars 15, 152
Harris, Emmylou 29, 46, 127
Harris, Jet 124
Harris, Phil 43, 55, 61, 65
Harrison, George 58, 70, 94, 101, 118–119, 248
Harvey, P. J. 45
Hawkwind 130
Hayward, Justin 29
Hazlewood, Lee 100, 206
Healers, The 138
Heil Talk Box 168
Hendrix, Jimi 36, 74, 82, 96, 106, 120–121, 128, 130, 136, 141, 145, 154, 159, 166, 178, 215, 248
Henry, Joe 156
Hetfield, James 117
Hewson, Paul *see* Bono
Hi-Gain pickup 71
Hill, Dusty 106
Hill, Lauryn 162
Hirade Mass K. 76
Hiseman, Jon 146
Hiwatt amplifiers 110, 170
Hoffs, Susanna 71
Höfner guitars 30
500/1 Violin Bass 64, 72
V2 126
Hogan, Carl 196
Holdsworth, Allan 158
Holly, Buddy 36
Hollywood Rose 168
Homme, Josh 114, 124
Hooker, John Lee 156, 157, 163
House, Son 157, 180
Howard, Dominic 86
Howe, Dylan 122
Howe, Steve 47, 122–123
Howe, Virgil 122
Hudson, Saul *see* Slash
Hugh Manson guitars 86, 87, 218
John Paul Jones signature bass 124, 125
Hughes, Glenn 90, 200
humbucking pickup 35, 47, 48, 50, 52, 60, 61, 68, 69, 74, 75, 77, 189
Hurt, Mississippi John 157

Ibanez guitars
Destroyer 86
Galvador 150
JEM series 174
JS series 166
JSA 166
RG 2570EX 74
Roadster 134
Ibanez Tube Screamer 90, 116, 146
Illsley, John 126
Incubus 140
Iommi, Tony 57
Iron Maiden 155
Ives, Burl 58

Jackson guitars 75
Rhoads V 158
SL2HT Soloist 75
SL4 thru-neck Soloist 75
Jackson, Michael 168, 176, 182
Jackson, Wanda 180
Jacquet, Illinois 196
Jagger, Mick 160, 166
Jamerson, James 42
James, Ricky 184
James, Skip 65
Jansch, Bert 138
Jean, Wyclef 162
Jeff Beck Group, The 84
Jerry Jones double-neck 152
Jim Dunlop Rotovibe 166
Jiminez, Flaco 98
Johanson, Jai Johanny 83
Johansson, Patrick 136
John, Elton 156
John Mayall's Bluesbreakers 94, 112, 202
Johnson, Blind Willie 99
Johnson, Brian 182
Johnson, Eric 23, 50, 166
Johnson, Roy 42
Jones, Booker T. 162
Jones, John Paul 114, 124–125, 152, 218–219
Jones, Kenney 170
Jones, Mick 54
Jones, Tom 124
Jordan, Louis 196
Jordan, Steve 95
Joyce, Mike 138
Judas Priest 136
Juszkiewicz, Henry 28, 103

Kalamazoo, Michigan 16, 21, 25, 28
Kauffmann, "Doc" 22
Kaye, Tony 122
Kessel, Barney 93
Kiedis, Anthony 104
Kilmister, Ian Fraser *see* Lemmy
King, Albert 147, 178
King, B. B. 47, 50, 90, 91, 94, 126, 147
King, Ben E. 124

King, Bobby 98
King, Freddie 52, 178
King, Mark 124, 220–221
King Crimson 132
Kirke, Simon 128
Kirwan, Danny 112
Klein, Matthew 106
Klinghoffer, Josh 104
Knopfler, David 126
Knopfler, Mark 126–127, 222–223
Knowles, Anthony 31
Korg delay effects 102
Korner, Alexis 49, 66, 67, 128, 224
Kossoff, Paul 128–129, 201, 224–225
Kottke, Leo 77
Kramer 75

Lady Gaga 142
Ladysmith Black Mambazo 156
Lakewood guitars 88
Lang, Eddie 16
Lanois, Daniel 102
Lea, Jim 134
Leckie, John 87
Lectrosonics wireless system 183
Led Zeppelin 124, 125, 152, 153, 218, 219, 234
Lee, Albert 128
Lee, Alvin 50
Lee, Geddy 72
Lehle ABC switch 90
Lemmy 72, 73, 100, 109, 130–131, 168, 226–227
Lennon, John 70, 92, 118, 248
Les Paul guitars *see* Gibson
Leslie speakers 202
Level 42 220, 221
Levene, Keith 105
Levin, Tony 132–133
Lifeson, Alex 23, 50
Lifetime 144
Lindley, David 76
Lindup, Mike 220
Line 6 amplifiers 122
  Echo Pro 86
Line 6 Variax guitars 122
Liquid Tension Experiment 154
Little Richard 120
Lloyd Webber, Andrew 147
Lloyd Webber, Julian 147
Loar, Lloyd 16, 48
Locking Tremelo 74
Log, the 52
Longworth, Mike 14
Lord, Jon 88
Lover, Seth 35, 50
Lovetone Meatball 116
Lowe, Mundell 58
"Lucille" guitar 50
Lynn, Loretta 180
Lynne, Jeff 101, 118
Lynott, Phil 134–135, 146
Lynyrd Skynrd 192
Lyon & Healy 15
Lyon, George Washburn 15

McCartney, Paul 64, 72, 73, 101, 114, 118, 120, 130, 227
McCarty, Ted 20, 21, 24–25, 26, 47, 50, 52
McDowell, Mississippi Fred 156
McGhee, Brownie 65, 157
McGuinn, Roger 70
McClaren, John C. 28
McClaren, Johnny 23
McIver, Joel 159
McKagan, Duff 168
McLaughlin, John 85, 144–145, 162, 163, 238
McVie, John 112
Mack, Lonnie 178
Maglite torch 246
Magnatone amplifiers 98, 100
Mahavishnu Orchestra 144
Maher, John *see* Marr, Johnny
Majesty 154
Malmsteen, Yngwie 136–137, 159, 174
Mandela, Nelson 142, 143
Mangini, Mike 154
Manson, Hugh 86, 124
Mare, Don 92
Marley, Bob 236
Marr, Johnny 45, 71, 138–139
  signature model Jaguar 45
Marshall amplifiers 52, 83, 84, 88, 90, 92, 94, 105, 109, 116, 120, 128, 134, 136, 152, 158, 168, 170, 182, 186, 203
  1992LEM 130, 166
  2205 150
  Bluesbreaker 208
  JCM 2000 DSL 100 86
  Plexi head 136
  Super Bass 100 MkII 130
Marshall, Jim 88, 170
Martin I, Christian Frederick 14, 65
Martin IV, Chris 65
Martin, George 84, 118
Martin guitars 12, 14–15, 26, 105, 178, 249
  00 models 66, 67
  00-28 98
  00C-16DBRE 67
  000 models 14, 15, 66, 94
  000-18 98, 122
  Auditorium 66
  B40E 67
  D12-28 65
  D-18 110, 152
  D-28 65, 92, 152
  D-35 92, 110
  D-41 66, 67
  D-45 66
  Dreadnought 46, 65, 66
  electroacoustics 67
  Grand Concert 66
  Hawaiian models 14
  JC-16RE Aura 67
  MC-28 122
  MC-38 Steve Howe Special 122
  OM (Orchestra Model) 14, 65, 66
  Style 41 66

Martyn, John 128
Marvin, Hank 36, 184
Mascis, J 45
Mason, Nick 110, 210
Matchless amplifiers 116
  DC-30 86
Matlock, Glen 42
Maton Guitars 31
Matthews, Dave 77
May, Brian 142–143, 228–229
Mayall, John 94, 112, 224
Mayer, John 23
Meehan, Tony 124
Meek, Joe 88
Mellencamp, John 185
Mercury, Freddie 142, 228
Mesa amplifiers 114
Mesa/Boogie amplifiers 116, 154, 162, 166, 170
  Mesa/Boogie preamp 96
Metallica 116, 117, 212, 213
Metheny, Pat 47
Miles, Buddy 120, 162
Mitchell, Joni 221, 245
Mitchell, Mitch 120
Modest Mouse 138, 139
Monkees, The 58, 59
Montgomery, "Monk" 42
Montgomery, Wes 47, 122, 170
Moody Blues, The 29
Moon, Keith 152, 170, 238
Moore, Gary 36, 112, 134, 146–147, 158
Moore, Scotty 48, 60, 148–149, 160
Morello, Tom 121, 150–151, 230
Morley pedals
  Bad Horsie wah 174
  Little Alligator pedal 174
Morrison, Sterling 105
Morrissey, Steven Patrick 138
Mothers of Invention, The 57, 186
Motörhead 72, 73, 109, 168, 174, 226
MTV *Unplugged* 248, 249
Muldoon, Brian 180
Mullen, Larry 102
Mumford, Spencer 40
Murphy, Matt 186
Muscle Shoals studio 82, 83
Muse 86, 87
Music Man 22, 31, 94
  Stingray bass 132
Mustaine, Dave 116
MXR products 142, 158, 168
  Phase 90 86
Myung, John 154

Nashville, Tennessee 28
National guitars 18, 94, 178
  Duolian 172
Nazareth, Pennsylvania 14, 65
Neal, Bob 148
Ned Steinberger basses
  Cello 132
  Electric Upright 132
Nelson, Carl and Julius 15

Nelson, Rick 46
Nelson, Willie 185
Night, Candice 88
Nightwatchman, The 150
Nirvana 96, 114, 248
Nitzsche, Jack 160
Nord Lead synthesizer 132
Norlin Industries 26
Norman, Max 158, 230
Notting Hillbillies, The 126, 127
Novoselic, Krist 96, 114
Nugent, Ted 29, 68, 169, 226
nylon strings 13

Oakley, Berry 44, 83
Oasis 208, 209
Onkyo company 28
Orange amplifiers 152
  Overdrive 120 208
  Rockerverb 146
Orbison, Roy 50, 118
Osbourne, Ozzy 158, 159, 168, 230
Owens, Tim "Ripper" 136

P-90 pickup 47, 48, 52, 54, 55, 189
Page, Jimmy 35, 65, 103, 124, 152–153, 169, 194, 201, 219, 238, 248, 249
Paice, Ian 88
Paramore 42
Parker, "Colonel" Tom 148
Parker Fly 86
Parsons, Gram 46
Pass, Joe 47
Pastorius, Jaco 44, 221
Patton, Charley 91
Paul, Les 20, 24, 52, 56 84, 88, 122
  see also Gibson Les Pauls
Peavey amplifiers 150, 166
  Classic 92
Peavey guitars
  EVH Wolfgang 86, 176
  Wolfgang Special QT 74
pedal effects 140–141, 232, 233
pedalboard, building a 232–233
Pensa, Rudy 126
Pensa-Suhr guitars 126
Perkins, Carl 52, 148, 149
Perry, Joe 169, 234
Petrucci, John 154–155
Petty, Tom 118
Phillips, Sam 149
Pickett, Wilson 82
Pignose amplifiers 186
Pink Floyd 110, 111, 210
Plant, Robert 152
Police, The 236, 237
Ponty, Jean-Luc 144
Portnoy, Mike 154
Powell, Cozy 112
Presley, Elvis 46, 106, 148, 153, 160, 206
Presley, Gladys 148
Price, Huw 38, 39, 41
Prince 77

ProCo Rat 208
PRS 7 pickup 68
PRS (Paul Reed Smith) guitars 31, 152, 162
  electric bass 69
  McCarty models 25
  Mira 68
  Nick Cantanese 69
  SE range 69
  SE Torero 69
  Singlecut 68

Queen 43, 142, 143, 228
Quiet Riot 158, 159

Raconteurs, The 180, 181, 242
Radio Shack loudspeakers 96
Rafferty, Gerry 156
Rage Against The Machine 150, 230
Rainbow 88, 198, 199
Raitt, Bonnie 156–157, 179
Randall, Don 36
Ratcliffe, Dan 177
Red Hot Chili Peppers 104, 107
"Red Special" guitar (Brian May) 142, 143, 228
Redding, Noel 120
Reed, Jimmy 106
Reed, Lou 105
Regal 42
Reinhardt, Bob 126
resonator cones 18
Retrospec compressor 132
Rey, Alvino 16
Rhoads, Randy 158–159, 230–231
Rice, Tony 65
Richards, Keith 148, 160–161, 169, 248
Rickenbacker, Adolph 19, 20, 70
Rickenbacker guitars 20, 30, 34, 42, 134, 170, 226, 227
  250 El Dorado 71
  300 series 70
  325S/1966 71
  330 138
  360/12 70, 71
  360/F12 71
  370/12 118
  4000 model 72
  4001 and 4001S 72, 73
  4003 72, 130
  4003S/8 73
  4004 72
  4004LK 72, 130
  4005 semi-acoustic 73
  Capri 70
  Combo 70
  Paul McCartney model 73
  Silver Hawaiian 19
Rising Force 136
Rivera amplifiers 100
Ro-Pat-In 18, 20, 70
  Frying Pan 18
Road Crew 168
Roberts, Andy 194
Robertson, Brian 134, 146

Robertson, Robbie 92, 128
Robinson, Rich 29
Rocktron Hush unit 168
Rodgers, Paul 128, 142
Roger Mayer Octavia octave doubler 120
Roland amplifiers
  JC120 92
Roland distortion pedal 96
Roland GR-300 guitar synthesizer 239
Roland RE-201 Space Echo 158, 208
Roland VG-8 processor 116
Rolling Stones, The 92, 124, 160, 161
Root, Jim 23
Rose, Axl 168
Rose, Floyd 74
Rossington, Gary 192
Rossmeisl, Roger 70
Roth, David Lee 174, 176
Rourke, Andy 138
Rubin, Rick 107, 117
Rudd, Phil 182, 183
Rudess, Jordan 154
Rush 23
Rzeznik, John 77

Sandhu, Surinder 174
Sandoval, Karl 158, 230
Sands, Rena 155
Santana 162
Santana, Carlos 68, 69, 144, 162–163, 172
Satriani, Joe 116, 121, 136, 147, 154, 163, 166–167, 174, 212
Schaffer-Vega wireless system 183
Schecter, David 126
Schecter guitars 170
Schenker, Michael 158
Schenker, Rudolf 29
Schoenberg, Eric 66
Schultz, Bill 28
Schultz, Wilhelm 15
Scorpions 29
Scorsese, Martin 160
Scott, Bon 182
Scott, Keith 60
Segovia, Andrés 13, 97
Selmer amplifiers 110
Setzer, Brian 60, 100
Seymour Duncan pickup 75. 106
Shakespeare, Robbie 64
Shakti 144
Shankar, Ravi 119, 207
Shannon, Del 156
Shannon, Tommy 178
Shed pickups 40, 41
Sherininian, Derek 90
Shiels, Brendan 134
Silvertone amplifiers 180
Simon, Paul 132, 133
Skid Row 134, 146
Slade 134
Slade, Chris 182
Slash 114, 168–169, 234–235
Slipknot 23

Slovak, Hillel 104
Smith, Chad 104, 166
Smith, Dan 28
Smith, Dennis 86
Smith, Paul Reed 25, 68
Smith, Randall 162
Smiths, The 138, 139
Soldano Decatone amplifier 86, 166
Sound City amplifiers 170
Spector, Phil 118
Spencer, Jeremy 112
Sperzel machine heads 40
Splinter Group 112, 113
Springsteen, Bruce 76, 150
Squier guitars 28
  Affinity Strat 38, 39, 40, 41
  Fat Strat 28, 29
  Masters Series Chambered Tele 29
Squire, Chris 72, 122
Standel amplifiers
  25L 98
Starkey, Zac 138, 170
Starr, Ringo 118
Status Graphite bass guitar 221
Stauber, Philipp 17
Stauffer, Johann 14, 65
steel strings 12, 14
Stevens, Guy 129
Stevensville, Maryland 68
Stewart, Rod 84, 85
Stills, Stephen 60, 184
Sting 236–237
Stone Sour 23
Stradlin, Izzy 168
Stratocaster *see* Fender guitars
  ageing a Stratocaster 38–41
Stratocaster vibrato 214, 215, 216
Stromberg guitars 16, 17
  Master 400 17
Sullivan, Big Jim 88, 152
Sullivan, Ed 119
Sumlin, Hubert 52
Sumner, Bernard 138
Sumner, Gordon *see* Sting
Sunn amplifiers 120
Superstrats 74–75, 176
Supro amplifiers 152
Sutcliffe, Stuart 118
SWR amplifiers 124

Takamine guitars 98
  EAN 10C 76
  EF360SBG Bluegrass 76
  EGMINI-BK Travel 76
  GOO80TH 76
  PT-007S 76
Tavares, Freddie 45
Taylor, Bob 77
Taylor guitars
  214 Grand Auditorium 77
  900 series 77
  Presentation series 77
  T5 Standard 77
Taylor, Mick 169, 234
Taylor, Phil "Philthy Animal" 130
Taylor, Roger 142, 228
TC Electronic 102, 154
Tedeschi, Susan 172
Tedeschi Trucks Band 172, 173
Teisco guitars 98
Terry, Sonny 157
Them Crooked Vultures 114, 124
Thin Lizzy 134, 135, 146
Thunders, Johnny 54
Thompson, Richard 138
Tokai guitars 26, 27
  Silver Star 26, 27
  Springy Sound 26
  ST55 Goldstar Sound 27
Touré, Ali Farka 98, 99
Townshend, Pete 46, 57, 71, 94, 120, 121, 170–171, 238–239
Traveling Wilburys, The 118, 119
Travis, Merle 20, 21, 25, 194
Travis-Bigsby guitar 20, 21, 22
Traynor amplifiers 108
Tri-Flow lubricant 246
Tristano, Lenny 166
Trucks, Butch 83, 172
Trucks, Derek 95, 172–173
Tune-O-Matic bridge 24
Turner, Ike 37, 120
Turner, Tina 120
Tyler, Steven 183

U2 102, 103
Uni-Vibe tremolo/vibrato 120, 141
Urban, Keith 54

Vai, Steve 136, 147, 166, 174–175, 186, 215
Valco guitars
  Jetsons Airline 180
Van Halen 75, 176, 177
Van Halen, Alex 176
Van Halen, Eddie 74, 158, 163, 169, 176–177
Van Halen, Wolfgang 176
Van Vliet, Don 186
Van Weelden amplifiers 90
Varèse, Edgard 186
Vaughan, Jimmie 178
Vaughan, Stevie Ray 36, 178–179, 240–241
Vega 15
Velvet Revolver 168
Ventures, The 184
Verlaine, Tom 45
Vexter Wah Probe 86
vibrato, setting up 214–217
Vines, Adrian 246
von Keller, Friedrich 12
Voodoo Lab power supply 246
Vox amplifiers 116, 170, 186
  AC30 30, 118, 142, 208
  AC30TB 102
Vox wah-wah pedal 120, 128, 203
Wainwright III, Loudon 156
Walker, T-Bone 196
Waller, Micky 85
Walley, Denny 186
Wallscourt, Elizabeth, Lady 12
Walsh, Joe 27, 37, 239
Wannenwetsch, Bernd 17
Washburn X40 74
Waterman, Dick 157
Waters, Muddy 106, 178
Waters, Roger 110
Watson, Johnny "Guitar" 186
Way Huge Pork Loin overdrive 90
Weather Report 221
Webster, Jimmie 58, 60
Wechter, Abraham 144
West, Leslie 55, 91, 158
Wexler, Jerry 178
whammy bar, setting up 214–217
Wheeler, Tom 56
Whirlwind Phaser 90
White, Bukka 172
White, Jack 103, 152, 180–181, 242–243
White, Josh 98
White, Meg 180
White Stripes, The 180, 242, 243
Whitesnake 174
Whitford, Brad 169, 234
Whitley, Ray 46
Whitten, Danny 184
Who, The 57, 170, 171, 234, 238, 239
Wilk, Brad 150
Williams, Cliff 182, 183
Williams, Tony 144
Wilson, Carl 45
Withers, Pick 126
Wolstenhome, Chris 86
Wood, Chris 64
Wood, Ronnie 36, 84, 85, 148
Wray, Link 184
Wright, Rick 110
Wright, Simon 182
Wrixon, Eric 134
Wylde, Zakk 69, 159

Yamaha guitars
  Pacifica 86
  SG2000 162
Yamaha SPX 900 processor 168
Yamauchi, Tetsu 128
Yardbirds, The 84, 94, 112, 152, 194
Yes, 122, 132
Young, Angus 57, 169, 182–183
Young, Malcolm 60, 182
Young, Neil 58, 60, 65, 184–185, 244–245
Young, Pegi 184

Zappa, Dweezil, 186, 187
Zappa, Frank 57, 174, 186–187
Zvex Fuzz Factory 86
ZZ Top 106, 107

Picture credits

l = left, r = right, a = above,
b = below, c = center.

Wikipedia Commons (Creative Commons-licensed content): 94 (l), 96 (l), 100, 102 (l), 110 (l), 118; 3rdparty! 184; Alterna2 http://www.alterna2.com 136; Arnoldius 20 (l); Massimo Barbieri 23 (al), 23 (ac), 92; Matt Becker 182 (r); Bodoklecksel 60 (l); Oli Gill 64 (r); Alex Harden 15 (b); Int21Int21 15 (a); Jeffturner 125 (al), Ilias Katsouras 110 (r), 211; Phyllis Keating 171 (r); Raphael Kirchner 18 (c); Heinrich Klaffs 170; Kreepin Deth 116 (r); Kris Krug 181 (l); Mr. Littlehand 28 (bl), 29 (bc); livepict.com 147 (bl) 147 (ar), 166 (r), 167; Majvdl 94 (r), 249 (b); Museum of Making Music at en.wikipedia 18 (ar); Sarah N 181 (r); Bengt Nyman 91 (r); Scott Penner 242 (ar); phillyist 42 (r); Piso17 24 (bl); Harry Potts (background) 135; Rama 131 (l); PH1 Gary Rice, USN 65 (ac); Nick Soveiko 88; Stoned59 244; Fabio Venni 180, xrayspx 102 (r).

Wikipedia Commons/Public Domain:
12 (a), 12 (b), 14 (a), 21 (ar), 75 (l), 116 (l), 120, 122 (l), 124 178 (r); George D. Beauchamp 18 (al); Fender Media Center 45 (r); Gibson Corporate Press Kit 16 (a); William P. Gottlieb 52 (ar); OhWeh 17 (a).

Flickr.com (Creative Commons-licensed content):
Joe Cereghino 196; Clownhouse III 245; egvvnd 212; flimsical 115 (al); Roger Jones 76 (ar); Carl Lender 172 (a), 172 (b); Man Alive! 139 (l), 139 (r); ocad123 122 (ar), 123 (bl); PedalFreak 95 (main), 202; Scott Penner 150; Razvan Orendovici 115 (r), 115 (bl); Lindsey Turner 156, twak 57 (ar); Paul Williams 6–7, 142, 143 (l), 143 (r), 228.

© Shutterstock.com: 3 song photography 140 (b); Silvia Antunes 126; Ryan Rodrick Beiler 103 (main); Dean Bertoncelj 3, 18 (b), 217 (r); bioraven 165 (r); Andre Blais 63 (b); Bomshtein 2; Franck Boston 13(al); caesart (background) 55, 127, 167, 181; chris87 95 (b), 127, 222, 223; criben 132 (r), 133; Phil Date 79 (r); Dewitt 10-11; Laszlo Dobos 232 (bl); Dooley Productions 72 (r); Eky Studio (background) 83, 99, 151, 177, 185; Featureflash 194; Gustavo Miguel Fernandes 87 (r); David Fowler 134, 135, 147 (background); gcluskey 234; Harmony Gerber 208; Andreas Gradin 13 (br), 247; haak78 117, 130, 226; Mat Hayward 109 (a), 227; Philip Hunton 80–81; mike.irwin 32–33; Doug James 29 (r); kps1664 13 (ar); Aija Lehtonen 54 (a); LHF Graphics 12–31 (guitar graphic); Ken MacDougall 190–191; Mark III Photonics 86, 87 (l), 146, 174 (al); Ralf Maassen (DTEurope) 9; Girish Menon 166 (al); Olga Miltsova 1; Randy Miramontez 237; Dana Nalbandian 84 (r), 162 (r), 163 (l), 236 (ar); Northfoto 87 (main); Iurii Osadchi 233 (br); Narcis Parfenti 75 (c);
Poleze 140 (a); Ra Studio 189 (r); Julian Rovagnati 63 (ar); Shaun Sadler 220, 221; Stokkete 13 (bl); Ronald Sumners 250–251; Ferenc Szelepcsenyi 90 (r), 91 (l), 163 (r); Ana-Maria Tanasescu 174 (r), 175; TDC Photography 23 (r), 50 (l), 106 (r) 107 (l), 107 (r), 131 (r), 151, 154, 155 (l), 155 (r); Valeria73 103 (ar); vipflash 160; VolkOFF-ZS-BP 109 (b); Faiz Zaki 169 (l).

© Getty Images: 22 (a), 101, 105, 119 (al), 153 (main), 159, 161, 171 (l), 177, 185, 224; Redferns 19 (a), 21 (b), 85, 89, 93 (main), 97, 99, 111, 121 (ar), 129, 137, 145, 149, 158 (r), 173, 179, 183, 203, 230, 249 (a); Michael Ochs Archives 21 (al); 82–83 (c), 192; Future Publishing 123 (r), 125 (main); Roger Viollet 248.

© Gibson.com/Epiphone.com (Press pictures):
17 (c), 24 (c); 24 (r), 25 (l), 28 (ar), 82 (l), 84 (l), 90 (l), 106 (l), 112 (r), 114, 128, 152, 158, 168, 169 (r), 182 (l), 186.

Anthem Publishing Ltd (Press pictures)
93 (b), 119 (r), 144, 148, 153 (br), 157, 162 (al) 178 (al), 187, 197, 198, 206, 209, 210, 236 (bl), 238, 240, 241, 242 (bl); Matt Bruck 176: James Cumpsty 112 (al), 113 (main), 113 (ar), 138, 218; Experience Hendrix 121 (bl); Karen Miller 204; Roger Philips 132 (ar); Bob Thacker 200.

The author and publishers have made every reasonable effort to credit all copyright holders. Any errors or omissions that may have occurred are inadvertent and anyone who for any reason has not been credited is invited to write to the publishers so that a full acknowledgment may be made in subsequent editions of this work.